The Scottish Criminal Courts in Action

The Scottish Criminal Courts in Action

Alastair L Stewart BA, LLB, Advocate
Sheriff of Tayside, Central and Fife at Dundee

Edinburgh
Butterworths
1990

Butterworths

United Kingdom	Butterworth & Co (Publishers) Ltd, 88 Kingsway, LONDON WC2B 6AB and 4 Hill Street, EDINBURGH EH2 3JZ
Australia	Butterworths Pty Ltd, SYDNEY, MELBOURNE, BRISBANE, ADELAIDE, PERTH, CANBERRA and HOBART
Canada	Butterworths Canada Ltd, TORONTO and VANCOUVER
Ireland	Butterworths (Ireland) Ltd, DUBLIN
Malaysia	Malayan Law Journal Sdn Bhd, KUALA LUMPUR
New Zealand	Butterworths of New Zealand Ltd, WELLINGTON and AUCKLAND
Puerto Rico	Equity de Puerto Rico, Inc, HATO REY
Singapore	Butterworth & Co (Asia) Pte Ltd, SINGAPORE
USA	Butterworth Legal Publishers, ST PAUL, Minnesota, SEATTLE, Washington, BOSTON, Massachusetts, AUSTIN, Texas and D & S Publishers, CLEARWATER, Florida

A CIP Catalogue record for this book is available from the British Library.

ISBN 0 406 17990 5

Typeset by Phoenix Photosetting, Chatham
Printed and bound by Thomson Litho Ltd, East Kilbride

Preface

It was David Fletcher, Scottish Director of Butterworths, who suggested that I might produce a Scottish version of their successful English textbook *The Criminal Court in Action* by David Barnard (3rd edn, 1988). I read Mr Barnard's book with great interest, and I also had the privilege of meeting the author and discussing the project with him. I had little difficulty in reaching the conclusion that a Scottish version of the book would be a useful addition to the Scottish legal catalogue, and with some trepidation I undertook the task of writing it.

Barnard is aimed primarily at those studying for or in practice at the English Bar, and its emphasis is on the procedure in what we in Scotland call courts of solemn jurisdiction. By contrast this book is intended to be of assistance to future and present members of both branches of the legal profession in Scotland. It recognises that solicitors as well as members of the Faculty of Advocates practise advocacy in the Scottish courts, including pleading before juries. It also deals in perhaps greater depth than does *Barnard* with summary procedure. Its wider scope is intended to be reflected in the use of the plural 'courts' in the title.

Barnard starts with an account of a fictional case which proceeds to trial in the Crown Court. I have adopted a similar approach, but with two cases, one solemn and one summary, rather than only one. I hope that readers will enjoy following the fortunes of Messrs David Balfour and Nicol Jarvie. It may be objected that these cases are not true to life in respect that both would probably have resulted in negotiated pleas rather than in going to trial. I can plead only the defence of literary licence and the necessity of illustrating as many points of procedure as possible without the undue suspension of disbelief. In any event, have we not all from time to time sat through trials, which in a perfect world should never have proceeded to the bitter end, but which somehow did so?

This book is not intended to be a comprehensive guide to criminal procedure. Such already exists in the form of Renton and Brown's *Criminal Procedure according to the Law of Scotland* (5th edn, 1983), and no one writing on criminal procedure can fail to acknowledge a very great debt to Sheriff Gordon's masterly edition of this work. What I have sought to write is a textbook directed primarily at students in the Diploma in Legal Practice in the five faculties of law of the Scottish universities. I hope, however, that it will also prove useful to practitioners in the criminal courts at all levels, especially to those at the earlier stages of their careers. To this end I have endeavoured not only to state the most important procedural rules and practices, supported by appropriate authority both statutory and case law, but also to include some practical advice on the conduct of a case in court. So far as possible I have referred to recent decisions of the courts rather than to older ones. My citation of authority has made no attempt to be exhaustive.

A book such as this is not written without assistance from a large number of people. The staff of Butterworths have been unfailingly helpful. The writing of the book took place while I was a sheriff in Aberdeen. To my colleagues on the Bench, to court practitioners, both prosecuting and defending, and to the sheriff clerk's staff there I am grateful for discussing matters and answering my queries. In particular I have to thank Mr Brian K Crookshanks, Procurator Fiscal Depute, for reading the first two chapters of the book in draft and offering many helpful comments as well as providing the forms from the prosecution side. Mr John Hamilton of Grampian Region Social Work Department, court liaison social worker at Aberdeen Sheriff Court, has produced a wonderfully realistic social enquiry report for David Balfour. My special thanks go to Mr Michael E Monro, solicitor and tutor in criminal advocacy in the Diploma in Legal Practice at Aberdeen University. He read the whole text of the book in draft and made innumerable helpful suggestions and comments, the great bulk of which I have been very happy to follow. He has also produced the defence forms. To him especially I owe a very deep debt of gratitude.

While acknowledging my debt to these friends and colleagues, I must of course emphasise that all errors and omissions are mine alone.

The names of all persons (with the exception of that of the present Lord Advocate, who will, I trust, take no offence) and places used in the two fictional cases are imaginary, and, that exception apart, have no relation to any person, living or dead.

I have attempted to state the law as it was at the end of March 1990 with a few later additions. At the time of writing this preface the Law Reform (Miscellaneous Provisions) (Scotland) Bill 1990 is making its somewhat uncertain way through Parliament. It is to be hoped that at least that part of it will become law which provides (what most people thought to be the law already) that a means enquiry court has power to give a further opportunity to pay while at the same time imposing imprisonment in the event of future default.

Alastair L Stewart
Sheriffs' Chambers
Sheriff Court House
Dundee

August 1990

Abbreviations

Statutes

1967 Act	Criminal Justice Act 1967 (c80)
1975 Act	Criminal Procedure (Scotland) Act 1975 (c21)
1978 Act	Community Service by Offenders (Scotland) Act 1978 (c49)
1980 Act	Criminal Justice (Scotland) Act 1980 (c62)

Statutory instrument

AA(C) 1988	Act of Adjournal (Consolidation) 1988

Law reports

Adam	Adam's Justiciary Reports 1894–1919
All ER	All England Law Reports 1936–
Arkley	Arkley's Justiciary Reports 1846–48
Couper	Couper's Justiciary Reports 1868–85
Crim App Rep	Criminal Appeal Reports (England) 1908–
Crim LR	Criminal Law Review (England) 1954–
Irv	Irvine's Justiciary Reports 1851–68
JC	Justiciary Cases 1917–
QB	Law Reports, Queen's Bench Division (England) 1891–1901, 1952– (year precedes)
RTR	Road Traffic Reports 1970–
SCCR	Scottish Criminal Case Reports 1981
SCCR Supp	Scottish Criminal Case Reports Supplement 1950–80
SC(J)	Justiciary Cases in Session Cases 1907–16
SLT	Scots Law Times 1893–
White	White's Justiciary Reports 1885–93
WLR	Weekly Law Reports (England) 1953–

Books

Alison *Principles*	Archibald Alison *Principles of the Criminal Law of Scotland* (1832) (reprinted 1989)
Alison *Practice*	Archibald Alison *Practice of the Criminal Law of Scotland* (1833) (reprinted 1989)
Gane and Stoddart	CHW Gane and CN Stoddart *Criminal Procedure in Scotland: Cases and Materials* (1983)
Gordon	GH Gordon *The Criminal Law of Scotland* (2nd edn, 1978) (Supplement 1984)

Hume   David Hume *Commentaries on the Law of Scotland,
                    Respecting the Description and Punishment of Crimes* (2 vols,
                    1797) (reprinted 1986)
Macdonald   JHA Macdonald *The Criminal Law of Scotland* (5th edn,
                    1948) (reprinted 1986)
Nicholson   GB Nicholson *The Law and Practice of Sentencing in Scotland*
                    (1981, with Supplement 1985)
Renton and Brown RW Renton and HH Brown *Criminal Procedure according to
                    the Law of Scotland* (5th edn, 1983 by GH Gordon)

Contents

Table of Statutes

(**Note** – statutory references are to the statutes as amended)

Table of Orders, Rules and Regulations

Table of Cases

Chapter 1

The Case of David Balfour

HM ADVOCATE v DAVID BALFOUR: DETENTION, ARREST, JUDICIAL EXAMINATION AND COMMITTAL

At two o'clock in the morning of Saturday, 29 April 1989, John Henry Starr was in St Mary's Street, Duncairn outside the Flamingo Night Club when he was stabbed twice in the right arm. The precise circumstances of how this came about were to be the subject of considerable dispute at a later date. An ambulance was called and Mr Starr was taken to hospital, where his injuries were treated and he was interviewed by the police. As the wounds were quite deep the doctor wished him to remain in hospital for at least the rest of the night, but Mr Starr was unwilling to do so and discharged himself.

The police made immediate investigations in the area of St Mary's Street, and about 2.20 am PC McIntyre detained a slightly built young man called David Balfour. David was aged nineteen. He had been in trouble with the law before but not for anything terribly serious. When he was seventeen he had been fined £25 in the sheriff court for possessing an offensive weapon (a piece of wood which he had picked up in the course of a skirmish between two groups of youths). Then, a year later, he had been fined £15 in the district court for breach of the peace. Only six weeks ago he had again appeared in the district court on a charge of breach of the peace. He had pleaded guilty, but the youth who was charged with him had pleaded not guilty. Trial had been fixed for the co-accused and sentence had been deferred on David until the trial date. He had been released on bail.

PC McIntyre told David that he was being detained under s 2 of the Criminal Justice (Scotland) Act 1980 on suspicion of having assaulted John Starr by stabbing him a short time previously in St Mary's Street, and that he was not obliged to say anything other than to give his name and address. At that stage David said 'It was him or me'. He was then taken the short distance to Divisional Police Headquarters in John Street. There the appropriate forms (see pp 2, 3) were completed. David was told of his right to have a solicitor or any other named person informed of his detention, but said that he did not want to. This was not a very sensible thing for David to do, but he was not particularly bright and did not yet realise what a serious position he was in. He was then searched and his fingerprints were taken. In his left jacket pocket was found a penknife the blade of which bore reddish brown stains.

David was placed in a cell for about two hours and then two CID officers, DC Black and DC White, came to see him. They introduced themselves to him and told him that they were inquiring into the stabbing of John Starr

(b) "   " Division   (c) Ref. No.
                                              P.F. Ref. No.

A

CRIMINAL JUSTICE (SCOTLAND) ACT, 1980

STATEMENT TO BE COMPLETED BY OFFICER DETAINING SUSPECT UNDER SECTION 2

In terms of the Criminal Justice (Scotland) Act 1980, Section 2,

I ..... ANDREW McINTYRE ..... Pc E 7592 ..... (designation of detaining officer)

detained ..... DAVID BALFOUR ..... (name of suspect)

of ..... 19 GAIRN STREET, DUNCAIRN ..... (address of suspect)

at (d) ..... 0220 ..... (time) on (e) ..... 29 April 1989 ..... (date) at (f) ..... George Street

..... Duncairn ..... (place detention commenced).

At the time the above named was so detained I informed him/her that I was detaining him/her under Section 2 of the Criminal Justice (Scotland) Act 1980; that because *(Here state circumstances giving rise to suspicion)* ..... he answered description of man sought .... m. walking nearby a short time previously .....

.....

I suspected that he/she had committed an offence punishable by imprisonment, namely *(Here state general nature of offence) (g)* ..... answer by stabbing .....

.....; that the reason for his/her detention was to enable further investigations to be carried out and that he/she was under no obligation to answer any question other than to give his/her name and address. When detained the above named ~~declined to comment~~/stated ..... "It was him or me" .....

.....

(If statement lengthy, use separate sheet(s); each sheet to be signed by detainee and officers concerned). I thereafter took the above named to ..... Div. H.Q. John Street ..... (police station or other premises) and timed his/her arrival there at (h) ..... 0229 ..... (time).

Signature of Detaining Officer ..... A. McIntyre ..... Pc E 7592 .....

Signature of Corroborating Officer ..... George Smith ..... Sgt. .....

PROCEDURE ON DETENTION UNDER SECTION 2

Detention accepted/rejected by station or other officer (i)   Time (j) ..... 0230 .....

(Note: If detention is accepted complete form as appropriate. If detention is rejected proceed either to release or arrest suspect and complete form on page B or C).

STATEMENT TO DETAINEE BY STATION OR OTHER OFFICER

It has been reported to me that you have been detained under Section 2 of the Criminal Justice (Scotland) Act 1980. I must inform you that you are under no obligation to answer any question other than to give your name and address.
                                              Time (k) ..... 0231 .....

What is your name? ..... DAVID BALFOUR .....

What is your address? ..... 19 GAIRN STREET, DUNCAIRN .....

What is your date of birth? (l) ..... 23-11-69 .....

The above named declined to comment/~~stated~~ .....

.....

(If statement lengthy, use separate sheet(s); each sheet to be signed by detainee and officers concerned).

Signature of Station or other Officer ..... George Smith Sgt. .....

Signature of Detaining/Corroborating Officer ..... A. McIntyre E7592 .....

DETAINEE NOT UNDER 16 YEARS OF AGE (ADULT)

Name of detainee .... DAVID   BALFOUR ....

B

INTIMATION TO SOLICITOR AND NAMED PERSON

You are entitled to have intimation of your detention and of the place where you are being detained sent to a solicitor and to one other person reasonably named by you:

Do you wish to have such intimation sent to a solicitor? *(m)* YES/NO Time *(n)* .... 0236 ......

If YES, name and address of named/duty solicitor (If solicitor not named, intimation to duty solicitor to be offered) ....

....

Rank, number and name
of person giving intimation .... Time *(p)* ....

If contact not made with solicitor, note reason ....

....

**Do you wish to have such intimation sent to
one other person (i.e. other than a solicitor)?**   *(q)* YES/NO Time *(r)* .... 0236 .....

If YES, name and address of person named ....

....

Rank, number and name
of person giving intimation .... Time *(s)* ....

If contact not made with such person note reason ....

....

(If some delay in sending intimation to solicitor or other person is necessary in the interest of the investigation, the prevention of crime or the apprehension of offenders, specify the reason for such delay)

(t) ....

....

....

(COMPLETE IF APPLICABLE)

You may now be taken elsewhere and may be questioned and searched and your fingerprints and other impressions may be taken.

Time *(u)* .. 0240 ....

Signature of Station or other Officer .... *George Smith* Sgt.

Signature of Detaining/Corroborating Officer ...... *A. McIntyre* E7592

---

* RELEASE FROM DETENTION

**You are being released from detention
and are now free to leave these premises.**   Time *(v)* ....

Reason for release   *(w)* * Grounds for detention no longer exist.
* Detainee has been detained for a period of six hours.

Departure from premises   Time *(x)* ....

* ARREST

Up to now you have been detained under Section 2 of the Criminal Justice (Scotland) Act, 1980.

You are now under arrest.   Time *(y)* .. 0518 ....

Signature of Station or other Officer .... *George Smith* Sgt.

Signature of Detaining/Corroborating Officer ...... *A. McIntyre* E7592

*Delete inapplicable

about which he had been detained. They then asked David if he was willing to be interviewed 'on tape'. David said that he was, and the three of them went to one of the rooms which contained equipment for tape-recording interviews with suspects.

The tape of the interview was later transcribed, and it ran as follows:

Time injection 5.05 am

DC BLACK: The time is 5.07 am on Saturday 29 April 1989. I am DC Angus Black and this other detective officer present is DC Tom White, both of the CID, Grampian Police. At this time we are in interview room no 2 within the Divisional Police HQ, John Street, Duncairn. What is your full name?

ACCUSED: David Balfour.

DC BLACK: What is your date of birth?

ACCUSED: 23 November 1969.

DC BLACK: So that means you're nineteen, David?

ACCUSED: Yes.

DC BLACK: What's your occupation?

ACCUSED: Unemployed.

DC BLACK: And your address?

ACCUSED: 19 Gairn Street.

DC BLACK: And that's in Duncairn?

ACCUSED: Yes.

DC BLACK: Now, David, we're going to ask you some questions about an assault which happened outside the Flamingo in St Mary's Street about two o'clock this morning. You're not bound to answer any question, but if you do your answers will be tape-recorded and noted and may be used in evidence. Do you understand?

ACCUSED: Yes.

DC BLACK: Now, David, when you were detained by the uniformed officer, he says that you said 'It was him or me'. Do you agree with that?

ACCUSED: Yes.

DC BLACK: And when you were searched you had in your pocket a knife with what looked like blood on the blade. What do you have to say about that?

ACCUSED: This guy came at me so I used the knife in self defence.

DC BLACK: Just a minute. Who's 'this guy'?

ACCUSED: I dinna ken his name except that his mates call him Starry.

DC BLACK: OK, so what happened?

ACCUSED: I was just walking along the street when he came at me with his hand up. I thought he was going to hit me. I minded I had the knife in my pocket, so I took it out. I only meant to frighten him, but he kept coming, so I hit him with it. I didn't mean to hurt him.

DC BLACK: What happened then?

ACCUSED: I ran off. The polis got me just a few minutes later.

DC BLACK: OK David, I'm now going to charge you, but before I do so I must caution you that you don't need to say anything in answer to the charge, but anything you do say will be noted and may be used in evidence. Do you understand that?

ACCUSED: Yes.

DC BLACK: All right then. The charge against you is that on 29 April 1989 in St Mary's Street, Duncairn outside the premises known as the Flamingo Night Club, you did assault John Henry Starr, unemployed, c/o Grampian

Police, St John's Street, Duncairn, and stab him repeatedly on the arm with a knife or similar instrument to his severe injury. Do you understand the charge?

ACCUSED: Yes, I do.

DC BLACK: Have you anything to say?

ACCUSED: It was self defence.

DC BLACK: OK. This is DC Black. I'm terminating the interview with David Balfour at 5.17 am on Saturday 29 April 1989.

Time injection: 5.15 am

DC Black then told David that he was now being arrested for the crime with which he had just been charged. Another form was completed (see p 6). David was again given the opportunity to have information about his arrest given to a solicitor or any other named person, but again, foolishly, he declined. He was then locked up in a cell until Tuesday morning. Normally he would have appeared in Court on Monday, but, unfortunately for him, that was the May Day holiday, and there was no court sitting.

On Tuesday he was taken to the sheriff court along with other persons who had been arrested during the weekend. While in the cells at the court he received a copy of a petition containing two charges against him together with a paper containing statements alleged to have been made by him to or in the presence of police officers (see pp 7–9). He was told that he was entitled to see the duty solicitor. By this time David had at last realised that he was in a serious position, and he decided that he did want to see a solicitor. Thus it came about that he met Margaret McKenzie, who was an associate with one of the bigger legal firms in Duncairn and who had considerable experience of criminal cases in both the sheriff and district courts.

David had an interview with Miss McKenzie which lasted about fifteen minutes. During that time he explained to her what had happened in the early hours of Saturday morning. She said that, if what he had told her was true, he should plead not guilty to the charges against him, and David agreed that he would do so. Miss McKenzie explained that, as he was on petition and not on a summary charge, he would not actually make any plea when he first appeared in court that day. What would happen was that he would be taken before a sheriff for 'judicial examination'. There he would be asked questions by the procurator fiscal. She advised him to answer the questions as fully as possible. She explained self defence in simple terms and emphasised how important it was that he gave an account of what Starr had done, and how afraid he had been that Starr was going to attack him.

David asked if he would be able to get out on bail, and Miss McKenzie said that she would apply for bail on his behalf, but that there might be difficulties as he was on bail already. Miss McKenzie obtained some details from David about his personal background and his previous criminal record. She asked him if he had a solicitor who would act for him at his trial. David said that he did not have any other solicitor, and would she please be his lawyer? Miss McKenzie agreed and said that she assumed that David would want to apply for legal aid. She produced a legal aid form and filled it in on the basis of the information given to her by David who then signed it (see pp 10, 11).

About half an hour later David, now handcuffed to a policeman, was taken into a small room which seemed to be very crowded. There was a big table on which lay a tape recorder. At the far end of the table sat the sheriff. On his left was a woman wearing a gown (the sheriff clerk depute, Miss Grant), and on

ARREST — RIGHTS OF ACCUSED

Date ..29. April 1989

Ref. No. ....

(NOTE: Parts A and B are to be completed for ALL arrests.
Part C is to be completed for accused NOT UNDER 16 years only (adult).
Part D is to be completed for accused UNDER 16 years only (child).

A. Name ......DAVID BALFOUR.......................................

Date of birth ..23-11-69....

B. Informed of right to have solicitor informed   Time ....0520.....

Solicitor requested?   YES/NO

If YES, name & address of solicitor requested ....

....

Informed by (rank, no. & name) .... Time ....

If contact not made, note reason ....

If solicitor attends, time of arrival .... time of departure ....

C. Informed of right to have reasonably named person informed   Time ....0521.....

Reasonably named person requested?   YES/NO

If YES, name & address of person requested ....

....

Informed by (rank, no. & name) .... Time ....

If contact not made, note reason ....

If some delay in sending intimation is necessary in the interest of the investigation, the prevention of crime or the apprehension of offenders, note reason for such delay.

....

D. Informed re police duty to inform parent/guardian   Time ....

Name & address where likely to be found ....

....

Informed by (rank, no. & name) .... Time ....

If contact not made, note reason ....

If parent/guardian attends, time of arrival .... time of departure ....

Name, if different from above ....

(A parent/guardian MUST be permitted access to accused unless there is reasonable cause to suspect he/she has been involved in the same alleged offence, in which case, he/she MAY be permitted access. The nature and extent of any access is subject to any restriction essential for furtherance of the investigation or well-being of the child).

Duration of access   From .... To ....

Nature & extent of access (if restricted note reason) ....

....

Note any request made by parent/guardian ....

....

Signature of Station Officer .... George Smith Sgt. ....

Signature of Corroborating Officer .... A. McIngre E7592 ....

F. 10

PF Ref . . . .

UNTO THE HONOURABLE THE SHERIFF OF   GRAMPIAN, HIGHLAND & ISLANDS
AT DUNCAIRN

. . . . . . 2 May . . . . 19 .89. .

THE PETITION OF   GEORGE WILLIAM BROWN

PROCURATOR FISCAL of Court for the Public Interest:

HUMBLY SHEWETH,

That from information received by the Petitioner, it appears, and he/she accordingly charges, that

DAVID BALFOUR (23.11.69)
Unemployed
19 Gairn Street
Duncairn

(1)   On 29 April 1989 at about 2am, in St Mary's Street, Duncairn, outside the premises known as the Flamingo Night Club, DID ASSAULT John Henry Starr, c/o Divisional Police Office, John Street, Duncairn, and strike him repeatedly with a knife or similar instrument to his severe injury.

(2)   Being an accused person and having been granted bail on 17 March 1989, at Duncairn District Court in terms of the Criminal Procedure (Scotland) 1975 and the Bail Etc (Scotland) Act 1980 and being subject to the condition inter alia that he would not commit an offence while on bail, DID on the date and at the place libelled in charge (1) FAIL without reasonable excuse to comply with the said condition in respect that he committed the offence libelled in charge (1): CONTRARY to the Bail Etc (Scotland) Act 1980.

In order, therefore, that the said Accused may be dealt with according to Law,

MAY it please your Lordship to grant Warrant to Officers of Law to search for and apprehend the said Accused

DAVID BALFOUR

and meantime, if necessary, to detain him/her in a police station house or other convenient place and to bring him/her for examination in respect of the above charge(s); thereafter grant Warrant to imprison him/her within the Prison of   DUNCAIRN   therein to be detained for further examination or until liberated in due course of Law: Further, to grant Warrant to search the person, repositories, and domicile of the said Accused, and the house or premises in which he/she may be found, and to secure, for the purpose of precognition and evidence, all writs, evidents, and articles found therein tending to establish guilt or participation in the crime(s) foresaid, and for that purpose to make patent all shut and lockfast places; and also to grant Warrant to cite Witnesses for precognition and to make production for the purposes foresaid of such writs, evidents, and articles pertinent to the case as are in their possession: Further, to recommend to the Judges of other Counties and Jurisdictions to grant the Warrant of Concurrence necessary for enforcing that of your Lordship within their respective territories; or to do further or otherwise as to your Lordship may seem meet.

According to Justice, &c.

Jack Fraser

Procurator-Fiscal   Depute

Duncairn,   2 May   19 89.—The Sheriff having considered the foregoing Petition, grants Warrant to Officers of Law to search for, apprehend, and bring for examination
the said Accused

and meantime, if necessary, to detain   him   in a police station or other convenient place, as
also to search, secure, and cite for precognition and to open shut and lockfast places, all as craved:
Further, recommends Judges of other Counties and Jurisdictions to grant any Warrant of Concurrence necessary for enforcing this Warrant within their respective territories.

Walter Scott
                                                        Sheriff

For further   19 .—The Sheriff having again considered this
Examination
                         Petition, and the said Accused
No Declaration

having intimated that   do   not desire to emit a Declaration, on the motion of the Procurator
Fiscal, grants Warrant to imprison the said Accused in the Prison of
                              , therein to be detained for further examination.

For further   19   .—The Sheriff having again considered this
Examination
                         Petition and the Declaration of the Accused

Declaration

on the motion of the Procurator Fiscal, grants Warrant to imprison the said Accused in the Prison
of   , therein to be detained for further
examination.

Bail   19   .—The Sheriff, on the motion of the Agent
                         of the said Accused

and of consent of the Procurator Fiscal, admits the said Accused to bail, and grants Warrant for
                 liberation from Prison on   finding Caution for   appearance for
further examination or trial in common form, under the penalty of £   sterling.

For Trial   19   .—The Sheriff having again considered this
                         Petition, on the motion of the Procurator Fiscal grants Warrant to imprison the said Accused

in Prison of   , therein to be detained until liberated
in due course of Law.

For Trial   19   .—The Sheriff having again considered this
Letter under   Petition and letter in terms of Section 102 of the Criminal Procedure (Scotland) Act, 1975, granted
Section 102   by the Agent of the said Accused

No Declaration

and the said Accused having intimated that   do   not desire to emit a Declaration, on the
motion of the Procurator Fiscal grants Warrant to imprison the said Accused in the Prison of
                              , therein to be detained until liberated
in due course of Law.

For Trial   19   .—The Sheriff having again considered this
Letter under
Section 102   Petition, Declaration of the said Accused

Declaration

and letter in terms of Section 102 of the Criminal Procedure (Scotland) Act, 1975, granted by the
Agent of the said Accused, on the motion of the Procurator Fiscal grants Warrant to imprison the
said Accused in the Prison of   , therein to be detained until liberated
in due course of law.

PETITION AGAINST   DAVID BALFOUR

Dd 8037106 10M 7/87 22314 (16107) 244

CRIMINAL JUSTICE (SCOTLAND) ACT 1980, SECTION 6

Extrajudicial statement allegedly made by:

(Name) .... (Age) ....20 years..
        DAVID BALFOUR

(Address) ....
        19 Gairn Street

        Duncairn
....

to or in the hearing of Officers of Police, namely

the Officers undermentioned

Date(s), Time(s) and Place(s) made	At 2.20am, on 29 April 1989, in George Street, Duncairn, when detained by PC McIntyre, he said:

"It was him or me"

At Divisional Police Headquarters, in Duncairn, at about 5.10am, on 29 April 1989, when being interviewed by DC Black and DC White, he said:

"This guy came at me so I used the knife in self defence".

"I was just walking along the street when he came at me with his hand up. I thought he was going to hit me. I minded I had the knife in my pocket, so I took it out. I only meant to frighten him, but he kept coming so I hit him with it. I didn't mean to hurt him".

Jack Forbes

Procurator Fiscal Depute

**APPLICATION TO THE COURT FOR CRIMINAL LEGAL AID
IN SOLEMN PROCEEDINGS AND IN TERMS OF
SECTION 23 1 (b) AND 30 (1) OF THE LEGAL AID (SCOTLAND) ACT 1986**

Note: Part I and Page 2 to be completed by the Applicant in Block Letters or Typing

Forms incomplete or illegible will be returned

PART I:

David Balfour	Full Name
19 Gairn Street,	and
Duncairn.	Home Address

Court Case No.

I 59/89.

FOR OFFICIAL USE

LOCATION OF COURT: DUNCAIRN

DATE OF RECEIPT BY COURT: 2|5| 89 .

Age: 19   Occupation: Unemployed   If in detention, place of custody: Sh..Ct..Cells,..Duncairn

Brief description of charge(s): Assault to severe injury: Bail etc (S) Act 1980 3(1)(b)

Date of first Court appearance on above charge: 2.5.89

Date of next Court appearance:

Name(s) of Co-accused (if any): None

I intend to plead Not Guilty/Guilty/I have not yet decided how to plead (delete as appropriate)

	YES	NO	
I have previously applied to the Court for Legal Aid in this case:		✓	(tick
I have obtained Advice and Assistance for this case under the Advice and Assistance (Scotland) Regulations 1987, or under the Legal Advice and Assistance (Scotland) Regulations 1973:		✓	appropriate box)
I have been granted Legal Aid on another Charge which has not yet been disposed of:		✓	

My nominated Solicitor in that Case is:

I hereby apply for Legal Aid. In the event of my being granted Legal Aid, I wish to nominate the undermentioned Solicitor:

Name of Solicitor: Margaret McKenzie

Name of Firm: Messrs D Russell & Co,

Address of Firm: 4 Exchequer Street,
                   Duncairn

PLEASE INSERT SOLICITOR'S LEGAL AID CODE NUMBER:

59631

DECLARATION OVERLEAF TO BE COMPLETED.

PART II: DECISION OF SHERIFF

Legal Aid Granted for Solemn Proceedings	✓	W.S. Date of Decision: 2|5| 89.
Legal Aid Granted under Section 23 (1) (b)		
Legal Aid Granted under Section 30 (1)		
Legal Aid Refused		Clerk of Court: Mary Grant .

NOTE: It is the responsibility of the person granted Legal Aid to communicate with the Solicitor nominated to act for him.

SCLA 2

DECLARATION OF MEANS BY APPLICANT

Are you: Single / Married / Divorced / Widowed / Living Apart. (Delete as necessary)

Note: If living apart from your spouse, disregard references to income and capital of Husband and Wife.

What persons do you support: (e.g. Wife and three children aged 4, 7 and 9)

Income	£	p.
Average Net Weekly Wages or Salary, including Overtime and Bonuses (Less Income Tax, National Insurance, etc.)		
State any Income of Wife/Husband		
Family Allowances		
Retirement/Disability/Other Pensions		
Social Security/Labour Exchange	29	40
Other Sources (Specify) (e.g. own business)		
Total Weekly Income	29	40

Weekly Expenditure	£	p.
Rent and Rates or Board payable by you or your Wife/Husband	10	00
If you or your Wife/Husband own the house you live in:		
(a) What is its Capital Value? £		
(b) Weekly outgoings on Rates, Loan interest, etc.	5	00
Other special commitments — H.P. etc.		
Aliment for wife and children		
Total	15	00

	£	p.
If you or your Wife/Husband possess any savings, capital or house property (excluding the house in which you live), state their total gross value		
What money or other assets could be used for obtaining Legal Aid at your own expense?		
Total	NIL	

Have you any rights or other facilities available to you for payment of your defence? (e.g. under Insurance Policy or member of Motoring Organisation) or Member of a Trade Union?   YES ☐   NO ☑

Give any additional information affecting your own financial circumstances or those of your Wife/Husband or of any dependant which you think may assist the Court in deciding whether you are unable without undue hardship to yourself or your dependants to meet the expenses of your defence.

Date: ....2.5.89................................   Applicant's Signature: *David Balfour.*

NOTE: APPLICATION TO BE FORWARDED TO THE CLERK OF COURT IMMEDIATELY IT IS SIGNED.

her left sat Miss McKenzie also wearing a gown. Opposite Miss McKenzie was a woman with a shorthand notebook open in front of her (Mrs Simpson from the procurator fiscal's office), and between her and the sheriff was a youngish man, also wearing a gown (Jack Forbes, procurator fiscal depute). David was asked by Miss Grant if he was David Balfour and, having said that he was, he was told by the sheriff to sit down. He sat at the end of the table between Miss McKenzie and Mrs Simpson.

Miss McKenzie told the sheriff that she appeared for David, and that he 'made no plea or declaration'. Mr Forbes said that he wished to have David judicially examined. The sheriff then told Mrs Simpson to stand up and asked her if she declared that she would faithfully discharge the duty of shorthand-writer to the court. Mrs Simpson said that she would. Miss Grant pressed the button to start the tape recorder running, and what now follows is the transcript of the proceedings at the judicial examination:

SHERIFF CLERK: Judicial examination of David Balfour in the presence of Sheriff Walter Scott at Duncairn Sheriff Court on 2 May 1989 commencing at 11.45 am.

SHERIFF: Mr Balfour, you are here for what is called a judicial examination, the purpose of which is to give you an opportunity to say anything which you may wish about the charges against you. Have you received a copy of a petition containing two charges?

ACCUSED: Yes, sir.

SHERIFF: Do you understand the charges?

ACCUSED: Yes.

SHERIFF: Have you also received a piece of paper which gives details of statements alleged to have been made by you to police officers?

ACCUSED: Yes.

SHERIFF: Have you had an opportunity of discussing all these matters with your solicitor?

ACCUSED: Yes.

SHERIFF: You are now going to be asked some questions by Mr Forbes, this gentleman sitting here, who is a procurator fiscal depute. You are not obliged to answer any of the questions, and you may consult with Miss McKenzie before deciding whether or not to answer any question. If you do answer a question, your answer will be recorded on the tape recorder which you see on the table in front of you and will also be taken down in shorthand by the lady sitting on your left. Evidence of your answers may be given at your trial. If you decide not to answer any question and, at your trial, you say anything which you could have said today in answer to that question but chose not to, then that may be commented on at your trial and may go against you. Do you understand?

ACCUSED: Yes, sir.

SHERIFF: Yes, Mr Forbes.

PFD (PROCURATOR FISCAL DEPUTE): Obliged to your lordship. Is your full name David Balfour?

ACCUSED: Yes.

PFD: Is your date of birth 23 November 1969?

ACCUSED: Yes.

PFD: Are you employed?

ACCUSED: No.

PFD: Is your home address 19 Gairn Street, Duncairn?

ACCUSED: Yes.

PFD: Now, you have received a copy of a petition containing two charges. The first states that on 29 April 1989 at about 2 am in St Mary's Street, Duncairn outside the premises known as the Flamingo Night Club, you did assault John Henry Starr, c/o Divisional Police Office, John Street, Duncairn, and did stab him repeatedly on the arm with a knife or similar instrument to his severe injury. Do you understand the charge?

ACCUSED: Yes, sir.

PFD: Do you deny that charge?

ACCUSED: Well, I did hit him with the knife, but it wasn't repeatedly, and I only did it because he was coming at me.

PFD: How many times did you strike him with the knife?

ACCUSED: Twice at the most.

PFD: You said that he was coming at you. Did he have anything in his hand?

ACCUSED: I thought he did, but I wasn't sure. I couldn't see very clearly as it was dark.

PFD: Do you have any further explanation or comment to make with regard to the matters in that charge?

ACCUSED: I thought he was going to attack me. I was scared. I was defending myself.

PFD: The second charge states that, being an accused person and having been granted bail on 17 March 1989 at Duncairn District Court in terms of the Criminal Procedure (Scotland) Act 1975 and the Bail Etc (Scotland) Act 1980 and being subject to the condition inter alia that you would not commit an offence while on bail, you did on the date and at the place libelled in charge (1) fail without reasonable excuse to comply with the said condition in respect that you committed the offence libelled in charge (1). Do you deny being granted bail on 17 March 1989 at Duncairn District Court?

ACCUSED: No, sir.

PFD: Please now turn to the paper with the statements allegedly made by you. The first statement is said to have been made by you at 2.20 am in George Street, Duncairn when you were detained by PC McIntyre. Do you deny then saying: 'It was him or me'?

ACCUSED: I said that. It was true.

PFD: The second statement is alleged to have been made by you at Divisional Police Headquarters in Duncairn at about 5.10 am on the same day when you were being interviewed by DC Black and DC White. It is alleged that you said: 'This guy came at me so I used the knife in self defence.' Do you deny saying that?

ACCUSED: No. I admit it.

PFD: It is alleged that you then said: 'I was just walking along the street when he came at me with his hand up. I thought he was going to hit me. I minded I had the knife in my pocket, so I took it out. I only meant to frighten him, but he kept coming, so I hit him with it. I didn't mean to hurt him.' Do you deny saying that?

ACCUSED: I'm not sure of the exact words, but I said something like that.

PFD: Do you have any comment which you wish to make about the circumstances in which you made these statements?

ACCUSED: What do you mean?

PFD: Well, do you want for instance to suggest that there was anything unfair about the way in which you came to make these statements?

ACCUSED: Oh, no.

PFD: Thank you, my lord. I have no further questions.

SHERIFF: Miss McKenzie, do you have any questions?

SOLICITOR: No thank you, my lord.

SHERIFF: That concludes this judicial examination.

SHERIFF CLERK: This judicial examination is concluded at 12.01 pm, Mary Grant, clerk of court.

Miss Grant then switched off the tape recorder, and the following exchange took place:

PFD: My lord, I move for full committal.

SOLICITOR: My lord, I would ask that my client be released on bail.

PFD: Bail is opposed, my lord.

SHERIFF: I suggest, Miss McKenzie, that I hear the Crown's reasons for opposing bail and then I'll hear what you have to say. Mr Forbes.

PFD: Bail is opposed for two reasons. Firstly, the accused is on bail already. Secondly, he has a conviction in July 1987 for an analogous offence, a contravention of the Prevention of Crime Act 1953, s 1.

SHERIFF: That is being in possession of an offensive weapon?

PFD: Yes, my lord.

SHERIFF: Have you any information as to what the weapon was? And what sentence was imposed?

PFD: I am sorry, my lord, but I don't know what the weapon was. The sentence was a fine of £25.

SHERIFF: That suggests that the court did not take a terribly serious view of the offence, doesn't it?

PFD: Perhaps, my lord. In any event, there remains the fact that he is on bail already – bail granted only some six weeks ago.

SHERIFF: In the district court?

PFD: Yes. I have nothing further to add.

SOLICITOR: My lord, my client lives with his parents. He is unemployed at present but has recently worked in the fish trade and would hope to obtain a similar job in the near future. I cannot deny that my client is on bail at present, but I would suggest that your lordship should take into account that he has no previous convictions for a contravention of the Bail Act, and that the bail order concerned is from the district court. I understand that my client pleaded guilty to a breach of the peace charge there and sentence was deferred for the trial of a co-accused. It is perhaps rather surprising that he was not simply ordained to appear. So far as the offensive weapon charge is concerned, that was a bit of a tree branch which my client picked up in the course of a fracas involving two lots of youths. As your lordship has pointed out, the court did not apparently take a very serious view of it and there was no order for forfeiture of the weapon. In my submission there would be no prejudice to the public if your lordship were to grant bail.

SHERIFF: Mr Forbes, is there anything further that you wish to say?

PFD: No, my lord.

SHERIFF: In my opinion this is a case where I would not be justified in refusing bail. Stand up please, Mr Balfour. You will be committed for trial and will be released on bail on the following conditions. Firstly, you must attend court on any date when you are told to attend. Secondly, you must not commit any offence while on bail. Thirdly, you must not interfere with witnesses or in any way obstruct the course of justice. Do you understand these conditions?

ACCUSED: Yes, sir.

SHERIFF: Do you accept them?

ACCUSED: Yes.

SOLICITOR: My lord, I have a legal aid application which I would ask your lordship to consider now.

SHERIFF: (*Having looked at form*) Yes, Miss McKenzie, in view of the fact that your client is unemployed, he is certainly entitled to legal aid. I shall grant your application.

David was then taken back to the court cell and, a short time later, was released, having been served with a full copy of the petition and with his bail order (see p 16). Before he left the court building he again saw Miss McKenzie, who told him that he would in due course receive a copy of the transcript of the judicial examination and, later, would be served with an indictment. She asked him to contact her when he received the transcript.

Some ten days later both David and Miss McKenzie received the copy of the transcript. David telephoned Miss McKenzie and made an appointment to see her. What happened at their meeting will be described below.

HM ADVOCATE v DAVID BALFOUR: PREPARATION BY CROWN, INDICTMENT, PREPARATION BY DEFENCE, MOTION TO POSTPONE TRIAL

Because David had been allowed bail, there was no immediate urgency about proceeding with preparation of the prosecution case against him, as there would have been had he been remanded in custody. In the latter event strict time limits would have applied, as is described in chapter 4.

At this stage the procurator fiscal's office did not have full witness statements but only a summary of the evidence made by the police. It seemed highly probable that the case was going to be fought. The police were therefore instructed by Mr Forbes to obtain full statements from the witnesses, and this they did. When the full statements had been sent to the fiscal's office Mr Forbes read through them. He was satisfied that there was a good case, and instructed that precognitions of the witnesses should be obtained. A precognition officer in the fiscal's office then interviewed each witness and produced a full precognition of the case. This, with a copy of the petition, was then sent to the Crown Office in Edinburgh, with a request for instructions from Crown Counsel.

In the Crown Office the precognition was read by one of the advocates-depute. He considered that this was a case which should be prosecuted. Although a knife had been used and the injuries inflicted were not trivial, the advocate-depute did not consider that the crime was likely to attract a sentence of more than three years' imprisonment. He accordingly marked the papers 'Pro sheriff and jury', rather than instructing indictment in the High Court.

These instructions were returned to the fiscal's office in Duncairn on 5 September 1989, where they again landed on the desk of Jack Forbes. Mr Forbes prepared an indictment containing two charges, virtually the same as

F103

Case No *I59/89*

**UNDER THE CRIMINAL PROCEDURE (SCOTLAND) ACT 1975 AND
THE BAIL ETC (SCOTLAND) ACT 1980**

Bail
Order

SHERIFF COURT   *DUNCAIRN*

ON   *2 MAY*   19 *89*

ACCUSED *DAVID BALFOUR*   Date of Birth *23/11/69*

ADDRESS *19 GAIRN STREET
DUNCAIRN*

which is the address to which any citation to appear at any diet relating to the offence charged
and any other document or intimation may be sent.

OFFENCE

1   ASSAULT TO SEVERE INJURY

*2   CONTRAVENTION OF BAIL ETC. (SCOTLAND)
ACT 1980 SEC. 3(1)(b)*

The Court granted bail and imposed the following conditions namely:—

(a)   That the Accused appears at the appointed time at every diet, including every continuation
of a diet, relating to the offence charged or which due notice is given.

(b)   That the Accused does not commit an offence while on bail.

(c)   That the Accused does not interfere with witnesses or otherwise obstruct the course of justice
in relation to himself/herself or any other person.

(d)   That the Accused makes himself/herself available for the purposes of enabling inquiries or
a report to be made to assist the Court in dealing with him/her for the offence charged.

[1] Insert any
Additional
Conditions

(e)[1]

[2] Where appropriate
add- "on the
pre-release
condition(s)
being met".

The above conditions having been accepted, the Court authorised the Accused's release.[2]

Mary Grant

CLERK OF COURT

Certificate that copy has been given to Accused.

I hereby certify that a copy of the foregoing Bail Order was given to the said accused by me on
this date.

Signature *William Blair*   Date *2/5/89*

Designation *P C   87145   Court Officer*

RECEIVED BY   David Balfour.

HMSO Dd8130698 C100 12/89 (53791)

those in the petiton. The indictment had appended to it a list of productions, the documentary ones being referred to as 'productions' and the others being called 'labels'. There was also appended to the indictment a list of witnesses. Mr Forbes checked with his office that the case could be put down for the jury sitting at Duncairn Sheriff Court beginning on Monday 6 November and gave instructions for a copy of the indictment and its accompanying lists together with a schedule showing David's previous convictions to be served on David in good time for that sitting.

On 15 September 1989 a policeman called at David's house. David was at home – he had unfortunately not managed to obtain a job yet – and the officer handed him the service copy of the indictment, the annexed lists and the notice of previous convictions, together with a notice calling on him to appear at the sheriff court on 6 November 1989 at 10 am. (See pp 18–22 for copies of the papers which David received and p 23 for a copy of the execution of service and citation.)

David had already appeared again in the district court for his deferred sentence. The justice had taken a lenient view of the breach of the peace and had fined David £25, payable at £5 per fortnight.

As mentioned above, David had also already had a meeting with Miss MacKenzie. At that meeting she took a full statement from him about himself and about the events of 29 April. She asked him if there were any witnesses who might be able to give evidence to help him, and David gave her the name of his friend Alan Stewart, who had been with him that night. David did not know Alan's address, so Miss McKenzie told him to see Alan and get him to arrange an appointment with her. She told David that, after the indictment had been served, she would get statements from the prosecution witnesses and would then see him again. On the basis of the statement which David had given to her Miss McKenzie prepared a precognition. This is it:

Precognition of David Balfour

My full name is David Balfour. I am unemployed. I live with my parents at 19 Gairn Street, Duncairn. I am nineteen years old (dob 23/11/69).

I have one conviction for possessing an offensive weapon. I was fined £25. I have two district court convictions for breach of the peace. I was fined £15 in 1988, and this year I had sentence deferred for the trial of a co-accused and I was then fined £25.

I left school when I was sixteen. I was unemployed for about six months and then got a job in the fish. I was made redundant at the end of last year. I have not had a job since then. My only income is social security benefit.

I don't go out much – only at weekends.

On Friday 28 April 1989 I went out for the evening. I was alone. I went to the Red House pub about 9 pm and there I met Alan Stewart, a friend of mine I know from playing in the same football team a couple of years ago. I don't know Alan's address. In the Red House I had about three pints of lager. Alan had the same. We stayed there till closing time at 11 pm and then went to Sandy's Night Club in High Street. We stayed there till about 1.50 am. I had another three pints to drink there. I was not drunk, just happy. I had more to drink than usual that night. I usually can't afford to drink very much, but my dad had given me some money from a win he had had on the pools. Alan had more to drink than me. I should say he was drunk.

We left Sandy's at 1.50 am and started to walk to St Mary's Street where there is a taxi rank. As we approached the Flamingo two men came out. I knew one as 'Starry'. I had met him a few times in pubs. I didn't like him much. He is very loud mouthed and has a reputation as a hard man. I didn't know the other man. Starry saw me and started running towards me. He was shouting. It was

Diet:
6 November 1989
at **10 am**

DAVID BALFOUR, (23.11.69), whose domicile of citation has been specified as 19 Gairn Street, Duncairn, You are Indicted at the instance of THE RIGHT HONOURABLE, THE LORD FRASER OF CARMYLLIE, HER MAJESTY'S ADVOCATE and the charges against you are that:

(1)　On 29 April 1989, in St Mary's Street, Duncairn, District of Duncairn, <u>YOU DID ASSAULT</u> John Henry Starr, c/o Grampian Police Divisional Headquarters, John Street, Duncairn, and did stab him repeatedly in the arm with a knife or similar instrument to his severe injury.

(2)　Being an accused person and having been granted bail on 17 March 1989, at Duncairn District Court in terms of the Criminal Procedure (Scotland) Act 1975 and the Bail Etc (Scotland) Act 1980 and being subject to the condition <u>inter alia</u> that you did not commit any offence while on bail, <u>YOU DID</u> at the date and place libelled in charge (1), fail without reasonable excuse to comply with the said condition in respect that you committed the offence libelled in charge (1):

CONTRARY to the Bail Etc (Scotland) Act 1980, Section 3(1)(b).

BY AUTHORITY OF HER MAJESTY'S ADVOCATE

Jack Forbes

PROCURATOR FISCAL DEPUTE AT DUNCAIRN

LIST OF PRODUCTIONS

Production Number   1   Transcript of Proceedings at Judicial Examination and Executions of Service

                                  2   Transcript of interview at Police Office, Duncairn on 29 April 1989

                                  3   Hospital records

                                  4   Joint Report by Kenneth Duff and Fiona McDougall, dated 24 May 1989

                                  5   Bail Order

Label Number   1   Knife

                                2/3 Blood Samples

                                4   Tape

                                5   Tape Recorder

Jack Forbes

PROCURATOR FISCAL DEPUTE AT DUNCAIRN

LIST OF WITNESSES

1. JOHN HENRY STARR, Unemployed, c/o Grampian Police, Divisional Headquarters, John Street, Duncairn.

2. WILLIAM BROWN, Labourer, 3 North Street, Duncairn.

3. JOHN WATSON, MB, ChB, c/o Royal Infirmary, Duncairn.

4. ANDREW McINTYRE, Constable E7592, Grampian Police.

5. ANGUS BLACK, Detective Constable, Grampian Police.

6. THOMAS JAMES WHITE, Detective Constable, Grampian Police.

7. KENNETH DUFF, Forensic Scientist, Grampian Police.

8. FIONA McDOUGALL, Forensic Scientist, Grampian Police.

Jack Forbes,

PROCURATOR FISCAL DEPUTE AT DUNCAIRN

F.14

Diet: **6 November 1989 at 10.00 am**

DAVID BALFOUR within designed ....TAKE NOTICE that in the event of your being convicted under the indictment to which this notice is attached, it is intended to place before the Court the undernoted previous conviction applying to you.

	Date	Place of Trial	Court	Offence	Sentence
1.	11 February 1987	Duncairn	Sheriff	Con: Prevention of Crime Act 1953 Section 1	Fined £25
2.	8 March 1988	Duncairn	District	Breach of the Peace	Fined £15
3.	17 March 1989	Duncairn	District	Breach of the Peace	Sentence Deferred until 15 May 1989

Date.........*11 September 1989*.........   ....*John Forbes*.........Procurator Fiscal
                                                                                    Depute

Dd. 8357820 3/82 M. & I. Ltd.

F37/3

NOTICE TO ACCUSED TO APPEAR

Under the Criminal Procedure (Scotland) Act 1975

NOTICE TO ACCUSED IN TERMS OF SECTION 75

To: MR DAVID BALFOUR

19 Gairn Street, Duncairn.

TAKE NOTICE THAT YOU MUST APPEAR at the H̶X̶X̶X̶X̶X̶X̶

SHERIFF COURT,   DUNCAIRN

on   6 November 1989   at 10.00 am

for a diet of trial at which you will be required to answer to the indictment to which this Notice is attached.

Served on the   *15 ot*   day of   *September*

19 *89*

(Name & designation)   by me   *DONALD WILLIAMS*

(Method of service)   by   *handing it to him*

personally

Donald Williams
(Signature of Officer of Law effecting service)
PC E 8156

John Davidson *PC E 7912.*
(Signature of witness to service)

Dd 8693857   300 pads   1/84   L.P.Ltd. 240

F37/3

EXECUTION OF SERVICE OF INDICTMENT AND OF CITATION OF ACCUSED

(To be returned to the Procurator Fiscal)

Under the Criminal Procedure (Scotland) Act 1975

(Name & designation of person serving)

I, *DONALD WILLIAMS*

(Date of Service)   on *15/9/89* duly served on

(Name & address of accused)

DAVID BALFOUR

19 Gairn Street

Duncairn

the indictment against him, with a notice of compearance thereto attached for the said diet in the ~~XXXXXX~~ Sheriff Court

DUNCAIRN

at 10.00 am on 6 November 1989

(Method of service)   This I did by *handing it to him personally*

Donald Williams
(Signature of Officer of Law effecting service)

PC E 8156

John Davidson PCE 7912.

(Signature of witness to service)

something like: 'I'll get you, you wee bastard.' I don't know why he would want to attack me. I hardly know him. He had his right hand up in the air as if he was going to strike me. I don't know if he had anything in his hand. I was scared. I didn't think of running away. He was too close. I remembered that I had a knife in my pocket. It was just a penknife. I always carry a penknife. It's just a habit. I pulled out the knife and opened it. I just meant to scare him. He kept coming at me and I struck out with the knife at his arm. I think I hit him twice. He fell down. I ran away. I don't know what happened to Alan.

I didn't know what to do. I still had the knife. I sort of wiped it and put it back in my pocket. I walked about for a bit. I saw the police. One of them yelled at me. I tried to run away but he caught me. I said to the police 'It was him or me.' I was taken to the police station where they found the knife in my pocket. I was interviewed by two detectives and I told them that I had stabbed Starry but that it had been in self defence.

After the indictment had been served on David, Miss McKenzie instructed the inquiry agents whom she used as precognoscers to obtain precognitions from the Crown witnesses. Some three weeks later she received the precognitions. The one which concerned her most was, of course, that of Mr Starr. It was in the following terms:

Precognition of John Henry Starr

My full name is John Henry Starr. I am unemployed. I live at 76 Riverside Terrace, Duncairn. I am 26 years old. I have a criminal record. I have sixteen previous convictions including some for assault. I am not prepared to give you details.

On 28 April 1989 I went to the Flamingo Night Club about 11 pm. I had previously been drinking in several different pubs. I had had about eight pints. In the Flamingo I had another couple of drinks. I can't remember what I had to drink. I met up with Bill Brown (witness). At about 2 am we decided to go home. We went out of the door of the Flamingo into the street. I saw two youths coming towards us. I knew one of them by sight, but I do not know his name (accused). I waved at him. I was being friendly. Suddenly, for no reason, he rushed at me, and I saw that he had a knife in his hand. I put my arm up to protect my face and he stabbed me in the arm. He stabbed me twice. I did not realise I had been stabbed until I saw the blood. I fell to the ground. An ambulance took me to hospital. My injuries were cleaned and stitched. The doctor wanted me to stay in hospital, but I refused and got a taxi home. I have had a bit of trouble with my arm since then. It is stiff and it aches at times. I have difficulty moving my fingers.

I don't know why the accused should attack me. I have nothing against him. I would recognise him again.

Note. *This witness is a heavily built man. He was not inclined to be co-operative. I would describe his attitude as truculent.*

The precognition from William Brown gave a similar account of events. The note appended to it indicated that he also had not been a willing witness. He too admitted to having a criminal record but was coy about disclosing details.

The precognition from the doctor at the hospital indicated that the two stab wounds to Starr's arm had been deep, penetrating the muscle. He had lost a substantial quantity of blood, but there had been no reason to think that complications would be likely. Starr had not returned to the hospital since the incident. The doctor's opinion was that a good deal of force would have been required to make such deep wounds with a small knife. The injury could equally well have been caused by the knife being lunged at the arm, or by the arm being brought down onto the knife. The doctor also said that Starr had been fairly heavily under the influence of alcohol when admitted to hospital. A blood sample had been taken which had shown a blood/alcohol level of 240 mgs of alcohol per 100 mls of blood (ie three times the legal limit for driving). His blood group was O MN Rh+.

The precognition from PC McIntyre told how he had received a description of Starr's alleged attacker over his personal radio, had seen a man answering that description (the accused) about a quarter of a mile from the locus at about 2.20 am, had given chase and had detained the accused, who had said: 'It was him or me.'

The precognitions from DC Black and DC White gave an account of their interview with David as contained in the transcript reproduced at pages 4, 5.

The two forensic scientists had not been precognosced, but Miss McKenzie obtained a copy of their report which stated that bloodstains had been found on David's knife and that the blood was of the same group as that of Starr.

Miss McKenzie arranged a further appointment with David. She told him what the precognitions of the Crown witnesses said and asked him some searching questions about his own statement. David stuck to his story. Miss McKenzie had heard nothing from David about his witness, Alan Stewart, and she asked David if he had seen him. David said he had not yet been able to find him. Miss McKenzie emphasised the importance of continuing the search. 'You see, David, even although you, as the accused, don't need corroboration, it always helps if you have someone to support your evidence.'

Miss McKenzie then went on to talk about another very important matter. 'As you know, David, I'm a solicitor. Now, I would be perfectly entitled to appear for you at your trial, as solicitors are allowed to take jury trials in the sheriff court. But your case is a serious one, and I was thinking that we might be better to bring counsel in.' 'You mean a QC?' 'Well, not actually a QC, who is a senior member of the Bar. I was thinking of a junior advocate. I think you would get legal aid approval for counsel all right. What do you say?' David agreed that counsel should be brought in.

Miss McKenzie applied to the Scottish Legal Aid Board for permission to employ junior counsel, using the appropriate form (see p 26) and enclosing a copy of the indictment. Her application was granted, and she immediately telephoned Edinburgh and spoke to Mr McTaggart, the advocates' clerk of whose 'stable' Robert MacGregor was a member. Mr MacGregor, who had been a member of the Faculty of Advocates for six years, was free to come to Duncairn for the trial on 6 November. He was going to be in Duncairn on other business about two weeks earlier, so Miss McKenzie arranged for him to have a consultation with David then. She then prepared a full set of instructions for Mr MacGregor and sent it off to him in Parliament House, Edinburgh. The instructions consisted of: the indictment with its attached lists; the schedule of previous convictions; the precognitions of the Crown witnesses and David's own precognition; and a copy of the forensic scientists' report. The covering letter confirmed the arrangements for the consultation and attendance at the trial. It also stated that the case was on legal aid.

A few days before the date of the consultation Miss McKenzie saw Alan Stewart, David's witness with whom he had at last succeeded in making contact. Miss McKenzie produced a precognition from his statement. It supported David's evidence in all essentials. However, there was one diffi-

This form should be completed in duplicate by the Nominated Solicitor and forwarded to the Board for certification in all cases involving the employment of Counsel. Duplicates may not be issued.

Part I   TO BE COMPLETED BY NOMINATED SOLICITOR

1. Name and Address of Solicitor

Margaret McKenzie,
Messrs D Russell & Co,   2. Legal Aid Ref No. <u>83/13/654321/ED</u>
4 Exchequer Street,
DUNCAIRN   3. Name of Accused   David Balfour

                              4. Solicitor's Legal <u>59631</u>
                                  Aid Code No.

PART II   TO BE COMPLETED BY SOLICITOR WHEN APPLYING FOR AUTHORITY TO
              SANCTION COUNSEL

I hereby apply for sanction to employ Junior
(state whether applications is for ~~Senior~~/Junior, both or two
Junior) for the following reasons (a) Accused on very serious charge
(b) Complicated special defence of self defence plus also intention
by accused to attach character of complainer (c) Although
accused has no record as such if convicted he may well receive a
lengthy custodial sentence (d) due to complicated matters of law it is
submitted that the defence should be represented by an experienced
(continue overleaf, if necessary; state reasons as fully as   advocate.
possible and forward copy of indictment or complaint)
                                        Margaret McKenzie

PART III   TO BE COMPLETED BY THE BOARD WHERE SANCTION IS REQUIRED

I certify that the Nominated Solicitor may employ Senior/Junior
Counsel/2 Junior Counsel and that the information in Part I
Nos 1 - 4 is correct.

                    .... for The Board

PART IV   TO BE COMPLETED BY THE BOARD WHERE SANCTION HAS NOT
              SPECIFICALLY BEEN REQUESTED

I certify that the information contained in Part I
Nos 1 - 4 is correct.

                    .... for The Board

PART V   TO BE COMPLETED BY COUNSEL WHEN PAYMENT IS REQUESTED PRIOR TO
              SUBMISSION OF SOLICITOR'S ACCOUNT

              I certify

1)   that I was only/leading Counsel in the above case,
2)   that the case proceeded in the High Court (delete if inapplicable)
              and sanction for Counsel was not required,
3)   that the case is concluded,
4)   that the accompanying fee notes are all the fee notes held by
              Faculty Services Limited relative to this case and that I have
              instructed the Company to pass copies of these to the
              Nominated Solicitor.

                    Signature of Counsel ....

CR/33

culty about Alan being a witness. He had arranged to go to California on holiday on 30 October and was not due back until 13 November. The holiday was a once in a lifetime opportunity for a young man like Alan who was unemployed. His uncle lived in Los Angeles and was paying for the trip. The flights were all booked, and the dates could not be changed.

The problem was discussed at the consultation which took place on 20 October in Miss McKenzie's office. Mr MacGregor considered that, as Alan Stewart's evidence was so important, an attempt should be made to have the trial diet postponed. Miss McKenzie said that she would try to have this done. Mr MacGregor went through David's account of events with him and questioned him closely about it. David stuck to his story. Mr MacGregor was particularly anxious to find out whether David could make any suggestion about why Starr should attack him. Eventually David conceded that, the last time he had seen Starr in a pub, he had had a bit of an altercation with him – and he had given Starr some cheek. Starr had been very annoyed with him, but had taken no action at that time, just saying that he would get him later. This would have been about two weeks before 29 April.

Before the end of the consultation Mr MacGregor instructed Miss McKenzie to lodge a special defence of self defence on David's behalf and also a notice that the defence intended to attack Starr's character.

After the consultation was over Miss McKenzie took steps to have the trial postponed. She decided that the appropriate way of doing this was to make an application to the sheriff under s 77A of the Criminal Procedure (Scotland) Act 1975. She accordingly prepared and lodged the appropriate minute. She also lodged with the sheriff clerk a notice of special defence, a notice of intention to attack character, and a list of defence witnesses (see pp 28, 29). She sent copies of these documents to the procurator fiscal. Two days later she was informed by the sheriff clerk that the sheriff had ordered that the hearing on her motion to postpone the trial should take place on 26 October.

On that date Miss McKenzie appeared before the sheriff along with David. (It would have been possible for counsel to appear at this hearing, but Mr MacGregor had agreed with Miss McKenzie that she should do it herself.) The Crown was represented by Mr Forbes. The hearing proceeded as follows:

SOLICITOR: My lord, I appear for the accused, and my motion is that your lordship postpone the trial diet fixed for 6 November until a later date, some time after 13 November. The reason is that a witness who is considered by counsel and myself to be essential to a proper presentation of the defence case, will be out of the country until 13 November.
SHERIFF: For what purpose will the witness be abroad?
SOLICITOR: It is only for a holiday, but the circumstances are rather exceptional. The witness concerned is an unemployed teenager, and this is the chance of a lifetime for him. He has an uncle who lives in Los Angeles, who is paying for him to travel there. All the travelling is booked and dates cannot be changed.
SHERIFF: Mr Forbes, what is the Crown's attitude to this motion?
PFD: The Crown would be in a position to proceed on 6 November, my lord, but I have no desire to deprive the defence of the attendance of an essential witness. The Crown's attitude is thus one of neutrality.
SHERIFF: Miss McKenzie, as the Crown is not opposing your motion, I am, with some hesitation, prepared to grant it. I shall postpone the trial until 14 November.

SHERIFFDOM OF GRAMPIAN HIGHLAND AND ISLANDS AT DUNCAIRN

NOTICE ON BEHALF OF DAVID BALFOUR

in causa

HER MAJESTY'S ADVOCATE

against

DAVID BALFOUR

McKENZIE for the Panel David Balfour states that the panel pleads not guilty to the charges and specially and without prejudice to said plea intimates that evidence may be led by or on behalf of the Panel or by any Crown witness to attack the character of the complainer, John Henry Starr.

IN RESPECT WHEREOF

Margaret McKenzie

Margaret McKenzie,
Solicitor,
4 Exchequer Street,
Duncairn.
Panel's Agent

SHERIFFDOM OF GRAMPIAN HIGHLAND AND ISLANDS AT DUNCAIRN

SPECIAL DEFENCE

in causa

HER MAJESTY'S ADVOCATE

against

DAVID BALFOUR

McKENZIE for the Panel, David Balfour, states that the Panel pleads Not Guilty and specially and without prejudice to said plea with regard to charge 1 states he was acting in self defence, he having been first assaulted or threatened by John Henry Starr.

IN RESPECT WHEREOF

Margaret McKenzie

Margaret McKenzie
Solicitor,
4 Exchequer Street,
Duncairn,
Panel's Agent.

SHERIFFDOM OF GRAMPIAN HIGHLAND AND ISLANDS AT DUNCAIRN

LIST OF DEFENCE WITNESSES

in causa

HER MAJESTY'S ADVOCATE

against

DAVID BALFOUR

1. Alan Stewart, 67e Glebe Street, Duncairn.

As soon as she returned to the office Miss McKenzie telephoned Mr MacGregor's clerk and told him of the new date for the trial. She asked whether Mr MacGregor would be free then, and Mr McTaggart said, 'You're lucky, a sheriff court proof he had down for that day has just settled. I'll put the trial in his diary.'

Miss McKenzie then instructed a sheriff officer to cite Alan Stewart to attend as a defence witness on 14 November. She also wrote to the procurator fiscal asking if she could be informed of the criminal record of John Starr. Mr Forbes sent Miss McKenzie a copy of Starr's record. He also sent a draft joint minute (see p 31) agreeing the evidence of the two forensic scientists to the effect that the blood on the knife was O MN Rh+ (ie the same as that of Starr), and the fact that David was on bail with the condition of not offending. Miss McKenzie returned the draft joint minute with a letter saying that she agreed to its terms.

On 30 October Miss McKenzie had a final consultation with David.

HM ADVOCATE v DAVID BALFOUR: TRIAL

David's trial began at 10 am on 14 November 1989. Before the sheriff came into court Miss Grant, the sheriff clerk depute who was clerking the trial, spoke briefly with the members of the public who had been cited to attend for jury service and who were sitting in the public benches of the courtroom. She explained to them that fifteen of them would be selected to sit on the jury. She also explained that both the Crown and the defence had the right to object to three jurors without giving any reason, and that, if they were objected to, they should not feel offended. The potential jurors had in fact all received along with their jury citations a leaflet which explained what would happen in court, but Miss Grant assumed, probably correctly, that some of them had not read the leaflet very carefully. When the sheriff came on the bench the first thing which he did was to administer the oath *de fideli administratione* to the shorthand writer.

The following is the transcript of the shorthand notes of the trial:

BEFORE SHERIFF LAWSON AND A JURY
FOR THE CROWN: Mr Forbes, Procurator Fiscal Depute, Duncairn
FOR THE ACCUSED: Mr MacGregor, Advocate, instructed by Miss McKenzie, Solicitor, Duncairn
CLERK OF COURT: Miss Mary Grant

CLERK: Call the diet, Her Majesty's Advocate against David Balfour. Are you David Balfour? – Yes.
COUNSEL: My lord, I appear for Mr Balfour. He pleads not guilty, and he has lodged a special defence to which he adheres.
SHERIFF: Thank you. Miss Grant, please empanel a jury.
CLERK: Will the ladies and gentlemen whose names I call please come forward and take their seats in the jury box?

On the clerk's table was a glass jar containing slips of paper, on each of which were written the name and jury list number of a member of the jury panel. Earlier both the prosecution and the defence had been provided with a list of assize (as the list of jurors is called) giving the names, addresses and occupations of those summoned for jury service.

Under the Criminal Procedure (Scotland) Act 1975

JOINT MINUTE

in causa

HER MAJESTY'S ADVOCATE

against

DAVID BALFOUR

FORBES for the Prosecutor and MCKENZIE for the Panel concur in admitting to the Court without the necessity of proof:

(1)   that the findings contained in the Joint Report by Kenneth Duff and Fiona McDougall (Crown Production Number 4) are true and accurate to the effect that the blood on the knife (Crown Label Number 1) and the blood sample from the Complainer (Crown Label Number 3) are both of blood groups O MN Rh+; and

(2)   that on 17 March 1989, at Duncairn District Court the Panel was admitted to bail on standard conditions in terms of the Criminal Procedure (Scotland) Act 1975 and the Bail Etc (Scotland) Act 1980 and that on 29 April 1989, the Bail Order made on 17 March 1989 was still of full force and effect.

IN RESPECT WHEREOF

Jack Forbes

For the Prosecutor

Margaret McKenzie

For the Panel

Miss Grant began to empanel the jury by picking out a slip of paper at random and calling out the name and number written on it. Each juror took a seat in the jury box as his or her name was called out. When the name of one man was called out Mr MacGregor quietly said 'He needn't come,' and Miss Grant told him to resume his seat. Another member of the jury panel (a woman) was then called in his place. The reason for Mr MacGregor's objection was that the man's address was in the same street as that of John Starr, and Mr MacGregor was concerned that this might make the juror favourably disposed to Starr. There were no other objections. When all fifteen jurors (nine women and six men) had been balloted Miss Grant asked them to stand up as she called their names. She then called the name of each juror in turn, beginning with the fifteenth to be empanelled and ending with the first. All were then standing.

CLERK: Ladies and gentlemen, the accused is indicted at the instance of Her Majesty's Advocate, and the charges against him are (*she then read out the charges in the indictment substituting 'he' for 'you' wherever it occurred*). Will you please take the oath? Raise your right hands. Do you swear by Almighty God that you will well and truly try the accused and give a true verdict according to the evidence?

THE JURY: I do.

CLERK: Please be seated. The accused has lodged a special defence which is in the following terms (*she read out the special defence*).

SHERIFF: Ladies and gentlemen who have been selected to sit on this jury, and the other ladies and gentlemen who have not been selected, for technical reasons which I need not go into I cannot allow those of you who have not been selected to leave until after the first witness has taken the oath. I am therefore going to ask the prosecutor to call his first witness, who will be sworn. We shall then have a brief adjournment, before which I shall be able to allow those of you who have not been empanelled to leave if you wish. Mr Forbes.

PFD: My lord, my first witness is number one on the Crown list, Mr John Starr.

JOHN HENRY STARR (SWORN)

SHERIFF: Sit down please, Mr Starr. Those ladies and gentlemen, who have been summoned here today for jury service, but have not been selected to serve on this jury, are now free to go, if you wish. I must thank you for your attendance here today in performance of the very important public duty of making yourselves available for jury service. As there are no other cases still to be tried at this sitting, your services will not be required again at present. If you have any expenses to claim arising out of your attendance here, please go to the sheriff clerk's office, where your claims will be attended to. (*Turning to the jury*) Ladies and gentlemen we shall now have a short adjournment so that you may take off your coats and make yourselves comfortable.

The court adjourned for approximately 15 mintues. On its resumption without, at this stage, Mr Starr in the witness box –

SHERIFF: Ladies and gentlemen, before we start the trial I should like to say a few words to explain the procedure to you, as it may be that it will be strange to some of you. The first advice which I would give give you is to forget anything of criminal trials which you may have seen on television. These would probably have been English or American, and our procedure is quite different. In any event real life is rather unlike what is portrayed on television. In Scotland we do not have any opening speeches; we just go straight into the evidence. Evidence for the prosecution will be presented to you by Mr Forbes, the gentleman sitting on my right, who is a procurator fiscal depute. Each witness in turn will be asked questions by Mr Forbes and may then be asked further questions by Mr MacGregor. He is the gentleman in the wig sitting on my left, and he is appearing as counsel for the accused, Mr Balfour. After Mr MacGregor has asked a witness questions Mr Forbes has a limited right to ask further questions. This process of examination by Mr Forbes, cross-examination by Mr MacGregor and re-examination by Mr Forbes goes on with each witness until all the evidence for the Crown has been led. There may then be evidence led for the defence. That is a matter for the defence to decide. If defence evidence *is* led, the same process takes place except that this time it is Mr MacGregor who starts off and Mr Forbes who cross-examines. When all the evidence has been completed Mr Forbes will address you on behalf of the Crown, and Mr MacGregor will address you on behalf of Mr Balfour. I shall then charge you, that is to say I shall give you such directions in law as I consider appropriate in this case. You will then retire to consider your verdict. That may sound rather complicated, ladies and gentlemen, but I think that you will find that it all falls into place. I would remind you that you have taken an oath to decide the case according to the evidence. Please now listen carefully to the evidence as it is presented before you.

John Starr was then brought back into Court, and the sheriff reminded him that he was on oath.

JOHN HENRY STARR EXAMINED BY THE PROCURATOR FIS-
CAL DEPUTE: Is your full name John Henry Starr? Do you live at 76 Riverside Terrace, Duncairn and are you presently unemployed?—Yes.

How old are you?—26.

Now, Mr Starr, I want to take you back to the early hours of the morning of Saturday 29 April this year. I think that something happened to you then?—Yes. I got stabbed in the arm.

Whereabouts did this happen?—Outside the Flamingo in St Mary's Street.

Just tell us what happened.—Well, it was about two o'clock. We'd just come out of the Flamingo – me and Bill Brown – when I saw this guy I kind of knew. I gave him a wave – just to say hi! to him. The next thing I knew he ran at me and I saw that he had a knife in his hand. I put my hand up to protect my face, and he stabbed me in the arm. I fell down.

Would you recognise this man again?—Yes. That's him sitting there (indicating accused).

What happened then?—I'm not sure. I think I may have passed out. The next thing I remember is an ambulance coming and taking me to DRI (*Duncairn Royal Infirmary*). I saw a doctor there who stitched up my cuts. He wanted me to stay in hospital, but I didn't want to stay, so I got a taxi home.

How many times were you stabbed?—Twice.

Do you have any problems with your arm now?—It's a bit stiff and sore, and I can't move my fingers very well.

Was there any reason why the accused should attack you?—No. I didn't do anything to him.

It is now the turn of counsel to cross-examine the witness. In doing so he will challenge the witness's version of events and put to him David's version. He will also seek to attack the witness's credibility and suggest that he is a man of bad character and, in particular, of violence. The attack on character raises a risk for David as we shall see later. Counsel starts, however, by trying to show that the witness had had a lot to drink.

CROSS EXAMINED BY MR MacGREGOR: How much had you had to drink that night, Mr Starr?—A few pints. I don't remember how many.

Hadn't you had at least ten pints? Eight before you went to the Flamingo and another two while you were there?—It's possible, but I wasn't drunk.

Were you aware that the blood sample which they took from you in the hospital showed a level of alcohol in your body three times the legal amount for driving?—I can hold my drink.

Why did you discharge yourself from hospital?—I don't like hospitals.

Did you go to your own doctor about your injuries?—No.

Isn't it the case that there's nothing wrong with your arm now?—I've told you. It's sore and stiff and I can't move my fingers properly.

Why didn't you go to your doctor then?—I don't like doctors, in hospital or anywhere else.

Do you remember meeting my client in a pub, the Green Man, about the middle of April?—I could have done. I've seen him a few times.

Didn't he give you a bit of cheek and weren't you very annoyed?—He was cheeky, but I wasn't worried. I just told him to go away.

Didn't you say that you would get him for it?—I don't think so.

And isn't that exactly what happened outside the Flamingo on the 29th? Didn't you run at him with your hand raised, shouting that you were going to get him?—I've already told you. Nothing like that happened. It was him who came at me.

You've got a record for violence, haven't you?—What if I have?

How many convictions for assault do you have?—Do I have to answer that?

BY THE COURT: I'm afraid that you must.—Well, I've been done three times for assault.

CROSS EXAMINATION CONTINUED BY MR MacGREGOR: What sentences did you get for your assault convictions?—I got fined twice, and the last time I got 60 days.

So, it would be fair to describe you as a man of violence?—I don't agree.

Well, that will be something that the jury may have to decide. Would you say that you were an honest man?—I've got convictions for theft if that's what you're getting at. But that doesn't mean I'm telling lies here.

Isn't the truth of the matter that you went for my client, and he had no option but to defend himself?—That's rubbish.

Why should he attack you?—I don't know.

He's much smaller than you, isn't he?—You can see that, but he had a knife.

Counsel decides to leave it at that. He has not shaken the witness in his account of the actual events – he had not really expected to do so – but he has obtained an admission of a large amount of drink having been taken, and he has sown in the jury's minds the idea that the witness is a violent man. Mr Starr will certainly not appear lily-white in the eyes of the jury.

JOHN WATSON (SWORN)

EXAMINED BY THE PROCURATOR FISCAL DEPUTE: Is your name John Watson, and are you a medical practitioner with the qualifications MB ChB?—Yes.

What is your age?—25.

What is your present post?—I am a casualty officer in the Accident and Emergency Department of Duncairn Royal Infirmary.

Did you hold that post at the end of April this year?—Yes.

Please have before you Production No 3. (*The court officer handed Mr Starr's hospital records to the witness.*) Are these the records relating to a patient who was admitted by you in the early hours of Saturday 29 April?—Yes.

Do you recollect the case?—Vaguely.

Please refresh your memory from the records. The patient's name was John Starr?—Yes.

What was his condition when you first saw him?—He was bleeding profusely from two incised wounds in his right forearm – the anterior aspect. He was conscious. I thought he was drunk.

By the anterior aspect do you mean the front of the arm?—Yes.

What position would the arm have been in when he was struck if his assailant had been in front of him?—In that event I think that his arm must have been raised.

As if to defend himself? (OBJECTION BY MacGREGOR on the ground that the question is leading. Question withdrawn.)

What did you consider had caused his injuries?—A sharp object with a point. Something like a small knife.

Please look at Label No 1. (*The court officer handed him the knife.*) Could that have caused the injuries?—Yes, certainly.

How deep were the wounds?—It is difficult to be precise, but they appeared to be quite deep. They had certainly penetrated the muscle.

Are you able to say how much force would have been required to inflict these wounds if the knife you have before you was the weapon used?—Quite a lot of force, I think, given the depth of the wounds and the relatively small size of the knife.

What treatment did you give Mr Starr?—His wounds were cleaned and sutured. I wanted to detain him as he appeared to have lost a lot of blood, but he discharged himself from hospital against medical advice.

Do you consider it likely that his injuries will have left him with any permanent ill effects?—I don't think so, but I can't be sure as I saw him for such a short time.

How would you describe the injuries – serious, trivial or what?—Well, they certainly weren't trivial, but they were not life-threatening.

CROSS-EXAMINED BY MR MacGREGOR: Could his arm have been raised as if to strike a blow when he received the injuries?—That is possible. All I can say is that, if he were struck from the front, then I think that his arm must have been raised in such a way as to present the front of it to his assailant.

You concluded that a fair amount of force must have been used, to judge from the depth of the wounds. At least part of the force, if indeed not all, could have consisted in Mr Starr bringing his arm down to strike at my client, couldn't it?—Yes, that is quite possible.

I know that doctors are reluctant to categorise the gravity of injuries, but I wonder if you could help me a little. You say the injury was not trivial. You wouldn't say that it was severe, would you?—Well, severity is not really a term that we use very much. We are more concerned as to whether life is endangered.

You formed the impression that Mr Starr was drunk. On what basis?—He smelt strongly of alcohol. His speech was slurred. He was unsteady on his feet. He was unco-operative. Subsequent analysis of his blood showed a high concentration of alcohol.

How high?—240 milligrammes of alcohol per 100 millilitres of blood. That is three times the legal amount for driving.

You say he was unco-operative. In what way?—He was truculent. He swore at me and the nurse and wouldn't keep still when I was examining his injuries.

RE-EXAMINED: Apart from the alcohol reading, the other things about which you have told us could have been caused by shock? (OBJECTION BY MR MacGREGOR on the ground that the question is leading.)

BY THE COURT: Yes, Mr Forbes, you really must remember that leading questions are just as impermissible in re-examination as in examination in chief. I shall sustain the objection.

RE-EXAMINATION CONTINUED BY THE PROCURATOR FISCAL DEPUTE: You say that part of the force required to cause the wounds could have been Mr Starr bringing his arm down. What if his arm had been held still?—In that event all the force must have come from the strength of the blows.

WILLIAM BROWN (SWORN)

EXAMINED BY THE PROCURATOR FISCAL DEPUTE: Is your full name William Brown, and do you live at 3 North Street, Duncairn?—Yes.

How old are you?—25.

Are you a friend of John Starr?—Yes.

Were you and he together during the early hours of Saturday, 29 April this year?—Yes.

Where were you?—We were in the Flamingo. I met Starry there.

What time did you leave?—About two o'clock.

Did something happen when you got outside?—Yes.

Just tell us about it in your own words—Well, we came out into the street, and I saw these two geezers walking along the road. Starry like waved at them, and then the wee guy just ran at him and stuck this dirty great knife into his arm. I couldn't believe what was happening.

Do you see in court the person you've described as 'the wee guy'?—Yes, that's him there (indicating the accused).

What happened then?—I was sort of confused, but I think that Starry fell down and the wee guy ran away. I went back into the Flamingo and got one of the bouncers to phone for an ambulance. I could see that Starry was bleeding badly.

Did Mr Starr say or do anything, so far as you could see, that might have caused the accused to attack him?—No, not at all. He just gave him a friendly wave.

CROSS-EXAMINED BY MR MacGREGOR: Mr Brown, are you a good friend of Mr Starr?—Well, I've known him since we were at school.

How often do you usually see him?—Most weekends.

So you'll have seen him quite often since the end of April?—Aye.

Tell me, have you spoken at all about what happened that night?—Oh no, I know you mustn't talk about a case that's coming to court.

Of course, you have quite a lot of experience of courts, don't you?—Well, I've been in them a few times.

Have you ever been in the dock?—Yes.

Mr MacGregor has no specific information about Brown's criminal record, and therefore decides to take this line of cross-examination no further.

How much had you had to drink that night?—Just a few pints.

How many is 'just a few'?—Maybe about seven or eight. I can't remember.

Were you drunk?—Oh no, just happy.

Isn't the truth of the matter that you were very drunk indeed?—That's not true at all.

Were you able to give the police a description of what had happened?—Yes, and I told them what like the guy was that did the stabbing.

You've described the weapon used as 'a dirty great knife'. Look at Label No 1, please. Would you describe that as a 'dirty great knife'?—No. The knife I saw was much bigger than that.

So that couldn't be the knife that was used to stab your friend?—I don't think so. I suppose it could have been. The light wasn't that good.

So you're not so sure now about the knife. Could you perhaps be mistaken too about who started the trouble?—Oh no. There's no mistake about that.

Isn't it the case that it was Starry who ran at my client as if he was going to attack him?—No, I don't think it happened like that.

You don't *think* it happened like that. Are you not sure?—Now you're getting me confused. It happened like I told you.

And you're still asking us to believe that you and Mr Starr have never discussed the case together?—Yes.

Even although you've been seeing each other every weekend since? Do you really think that's credible?

BY THE COURT: Surely that's a matter for the jury, Mr MacGregor?

MR MacGREGOR: I apologise, my lord. Of course it is. I'm afraid I got carried away. I have no more questions of this witness.

ANDREW McINTYRE (SWORN)

EXAMINED BY THE PROCURATOR FISCAL DEPUTE: Is your full name Andrew McIntyre, and are you a constable of Grampian Police stationed at Duncairn?—Yes.

How old are you and how many years' police service do you have?—I am 33 years old and I have fourteen years' service.

In the early hours of 29 April this year were you on duty on mobile patrol in Duncairn, and did you receive a message about an incident in St Mary's Street?—Yes.

What time was this?—Just after 2 am.

What did you do?—The message gave a description of the man who was suspected of committing an assault outside the Flamingo, so I decided to tour the streets and see if there was anyone about answering that description.

Did you see anyone who did answer the description?—Yes, in George Street I saw a young man walking along the street. When he saw me he ran away, but I chased after him and I caught him.

Do you see that young man in court?—Yes, there in the dock. (Pointing at the accused).

What happened then?—I informed him that I was detaining him under s 2 of the Criminal Justice (Scotland) Act on suspicion of assault and that he didn't need to say anything.

What do you mean by s 2 of the Criminal Justice (Scotland) Act?—That allows me to detain someone if I have reason to suspect he has committed a crime.

Did he say anything?—He said 'It was him or me'.

What happened then?— I took him to the police office. When I got him there I searched him, and in his pocket I found a knife, which appeared to be bloodstained.

Please look at Label No 1. Is that the knife?—Yes.

CROSS-EXAMINED BY MR MacGREGOR: What state was the accused in when you came across him?—He was out of breath, as if he had been running. And he seemed frightened. He had been drinking, but I did not think that he was very drunk.

Apart from running away when he first saw you, did he make any attempt to obstruct you?—Oh no. In fact he was thoroughly co-operative.

ANGUS BLACK (SWORN)

EXAMINED BY THE PROCURATOR FISCAL DEPUTE: Is your full name Angus Black, and are you a detective constable in the Grampian Police, stationed at Duncairn?—Yes.

How old are you and how many years' police service do you have?—I am 40 years old and I have 21 years' police service.

In the early hours of 29 April this year did you interview a man called David Balfour in interview room no 2 at Divisional Headquarters in Duncairn? And was that in connection with an alleged assault which had taken place some time earlier?—Yes.

Do you see in court the man who you interviewed?—Yes, that's him there. (Pointing at the accused).

Please have before you Label No 2 and Production No 2. Is the Label a tape recording of your interview, and is the Production a transcript of that interview?—Yes.

If my learned friend, Mr MacGregor, has no objection, I would ask you to read out the transcript. *(Mr MacGregor indicated that he had no objection, and the witness then read out the transcript reproduced at pp 4, 5.)*

NO CROSS-EXAMINATION

PROCURATOR FISCAL DEPUTE: My lord, that is the last witness I intend to lead. There are, however, certain matters on which my learned friend and I are agreed, and they have been incorporated into a joint minute, which I would ask your lordship's clerk to read out. I would also ask her to read out the transcript of the judicial examination.

(Miss Gibb then read out the terms of the joint minute (see p 31) and the transcript of the judicial examination (see pp 12–16)

PROCURATOR FISCAL DEPUTE: My lord, that is the case for the Crown.

MR MacGREGOR: My lord, I intend to call my client and one other witness. I now call Mr Balfour.

DAVID BALFOUR (SWORN)
EXAMINED BY MR MacGREGOR: Is your full name David Balfour, do you live at 19 Gairn Street, Duncairn, and are you nineteen years old?—Yes.

Do you have a job?—No, I'm unemployed at present, but I hope to get a job soon.

Do you know John Starr?—I don't know him well, but I've met him a few times in pubs. I call him Starry.

Did you ever see him in the Green Man?—Yes, I've seen him there several times.

Is there any particular time that you remember?—Yes. About a fortnight before he was stabbed I saw him in the pub, and he got angry with me. He said that he would get me.

Was there any particular reason for that?—Well, I suppose that I was a bit cheeky to him, but I didn't mean any harm.

Let me now come to the evening of 28 April this year. What did you do then?—I went to the Red House. That's a pub. I met Alan Stewart there. He's a friend of mine. We stayed till closing time, and then we went to Sandy's Night Club.

How long did you stay there?—Until about ten to two.

What happened then?—We went out into the street and walked towards the taxi rank in St Mary's Street. Outside the Flamingo I saw Starry and another man. Starry came at me, shouting he was going to get me. I was scared.

What did you do?—I remembered that I had a knife in my pocket, so I pulled it out. He kept coming so I held out the knife. I just meant to frighten him, but when he didn't stop I stuck the knife into his arm.

How was he holding his arm?—It was up above his head. I thought he had something in his hand, but I wasn't sure. When I cut him he fell down.

What happened then?—I ran away, and the polis caught me.

Please look at Label No 1. Do you agree that that is your knife and that it was stained with Starr's blood?—Yes.

I think that you don't dispute any of the evidence given by the police as to what you said when you were caught or in the police station?—That's right.

Why didn't you run away when Starr came at you?—He was too close, and I thought he could run faster than me as he's much bigger.

CROSS-EXAMINED BY THE PROCURATOR FISCAL DEPUTE:
How much had you had to drink that night?—About six pints.

Were you drunk?—No. I maybe wasn't completely sober, but I wasn't really drunk.

You say that you did not have time to run away?—That's right.

Can you explain then how you had time to open the knife?—I don't know. I just did.

Isn't it the case that you had time to open the knife because it wasn't Mr Starr who came at you but you who went for him?—That's not true. I wouldn't go for him. He's much bigger than me, and he's got an evil reputation.

PROCURATOR FISCAL DEPUTE: My lord, at this stage I have a motion to make which it would be appropriate to deal with outwith the presence of the jury.

SHERIFF: Ladies and gentlemen, Mr Forbes wishes to address me on a point of law, so I must ask you to withdraw. (*The jury left the jury box*.) Yes Mr Forbes.

PROCURATOR FISCAL DEPUTE: My lord, I move you to allow me to cross-examine the accused as to his criminal record and character in view of the attack which he has made on the character of the complainer, John Starr. I refer your lordship to the terms of s 14(1) of the Criminal Procedure (Scotland) Act 1975.

SHERIFF: Mr MacGregor, do you oppose that motion?

MR MacGREGOR: Yes my lord, indeed I do. I am, of course, familiar with the terms of the section to which my friend has referred your lordship, but I would remind your lordship that it was clearly laid down in the very recent Seven Judge case of *Leggate v HM Advocate* that your lordship has a very wide discretion in the matter and that the fundamental test is fairness. The case is reported in 1988 SCCR at page 391. I refer my lord to the rubric at the foot of page 391 and the top of page 392: 'Held . . . (2) that a trial judge has a wide discretion to refuse to allow an accused to be cross-examined on his character, that the fundamental test in exercising that discretion is one of fairness having regard both to the position of the accused and the public interest in bringing wrongdoers to justice, and that a significant factor in the exercise of the discretion is whether the questions asked of the Crown witnesses were integral and necessary to the defence or were a deliberate attack on the character of the witness.' I submit, my lord, that the questions which I asked of Mr Starr, although they may have been an attack on character, were also necessary to the defence. I submit also that it would be very unfair to the accused to allow his character to be put in issue. He has a very trivial criminal record. It is such that I should have no concern about your lordship's having knowledge of it, but I should be afraid that a jury might be unduly prejudiced if they were to get to learn about it.

SHERIFF: Mr MacGregor, if you are unconcerned about my knowing your client's record, perhaps you would tell me what it is.

MR MacGREGOR: Certainly, my lord. In 1987 he was convicted of being in possession of an offensive weapon, which sounds relatively serious. However, the weapon concerned was only a piece of wood, and the court clearly took a not very serious view of the offence as it imposed a fine of only £25. Last year he was fined £15 for a breach of the peace, and in March this year he pleaded guilty in the District Court to another breach of the peace, for which he was eventually fined £25. I submit, my lord, that the prejudicial effect of allowing this record to go before the jury would far outweigh the very necessary task of the defence to show that the complainer is a man of violent disposition. I therefore ask your lordship to refuse my friend's motion.

SHERIFF: Mr Forbes, what do you say?

PROCURATOR FISCAL DEPUTE: My lord, in my submission what the defence did here was not essential for the presentation of their case, but was quite simply an attack on the character of the complainer. As far as fairness is concerned, I am sure that your lordship would give sufficient directions to the jury to ensure that they would not be unduly prejudiced by the disclosure of the accused's criminal record. I have nothing further to add.

SHERIFF: In my opinion, it would be unfair to allow the jury to hear details of the accused's criminal record. He has not been convicted of any crime implying dishonesty, so his creditworthiness would not be impugned by allowing reference to his record. He might, however, be shown, in the eyes of some members of the jury, to be a violent person because of the offensive weapon charge, and I consider that that might give a misleading impression and could be very prejudicial to the defence. Accordingly I shall refuse the Crown motion. Please bring the jury back into court.

(The jury was brought back into court.)

CROSS-EXAMINATION BY THE PROCURATOR FISCAL DEPUTE CONTINUED: If you thought that you had done nothing wrong, why did you run away?—I was scared about what I had done. I thought that they wouldn't believe me.

But you are now asking the ladies and gentlemen of the jury to believe you?—Yes, because I am telling the truth.

You knew perfectly well that Starr didn't have any weapon in his hand, didn't you?— I wasn't sure then, but I think now that he probably hadn't.

RE-EXAMINED BY MR MacGREGOR: Is what you have told us today in any way different from what you told the police or what you said at judicial examination?—No, sir.

ALAN STEWART (SWORN)
EXAMINED BY MR MacGREGOR: Is your full name Alan Stewart, do you live at 67A Glebe Street, Duncairn, and are you nineteen years old?— Yes, Sir.

Are you employed?—No.

Are you friendly with David Balfour, who is sitting there in the dock?—Yes. I've known him for a few years.

Were you with Mr Balfour in the late evening of Friday, 28 April, and the early hours of Saturday, 29 April, this year?—Yes. We met in the Red House. I had got there before him. He came in about nine o'clock.

How much had you had to drink before Mr Balfour arrived?—Probably a couple of pints.

How much did you have to drink after he came?—I think three or four pints and a couple of nips.

What time did you leave the Red House?—I'm not sure, but I think it must have been after eleven. We went on to Sandy's.

Did you have some more to drink there?—Yes, I think I had another couple of drinks.

How would you describe your state by this time?—I was pretty well on, but I wasn't falling about.

Did you leave the night club with Mr Balfour?—Yes.

What happened when you got outside?—Well, I saw these two men coming and one ran at David. David defended himself and the man fell.

Let's take this a bit more slowly. First of all. Where did this happen?— Near the taxi rank.

Is that in St Mary's Street?—Yes.

Did you know the man who came at David?—I knew him as Starry. I'd seen him around.

Now, tell us slowly and clearly what happened?—Like I told you, he ran at David. He had his arm up. I thought he had something in his hand. He was shouting something about getting David.

What did David do?—He backed off a bit and then took something out of his pocket. I thought it was a nail file or something like that. And he stuck it into Starry's arm. That's all I saw, because I ran away then.

Why didn't David run away?—I don't know. I think that it happened too fast.

CROSS-EXAMINED BY THE PROCURATOR FISCAL DEPUTE: Mr Stewart, if I've understood your evidence correctly, you must have had about ten pints to drink during the evening. Is that right?—I wasn't just drinking pints.

Were the shorts you drank singles or doubles?—Probably doubles. That's what I usually have.

So you must have had the equivalent of at least ten pints?—I suppose so.

Do you think that your recollection is really clear?—I reckon so. I got such a fright when I saw what was happening that I sobered up.

You say you don't know why David didn't run away. He could easily have done so, if he'd wanted, couldn't he?—I don't know. I was scared. I guess he was scared too.

In fact are you really certain that it was the man who ran at David? Wasn't it the other way round, that David ran at the man?—No, I'm quite sure about that.

Have you talked about this case to the accused at all?—No. I've hardly seen him since April.

MR MacGREGOR: My lord, that is the case for the defence.

SHERIFF: Ladies and gentlemen, that is all the evidence in the case now. It is just after one o'clock, so we'll now adjourn for lunch, which will be provided for you in the jury room. I suggest that you avoid discussing the case, if possible. You have heard all the evidence, but you have not heard speeches or my charge, so it is too early to be making up your minds in any way yet. The court will sit again at 2.15.

AFTER THE ADJOURNMENT

PROCURATOR FISCAL DEPUTE: May it please your lordship. Ladies and gentlemen of the jury, it is now my privilege to address you on behalf of the Crown. In what I have to say to you I may deal a little with the law which you will have to apply to the case, but anything I say about the law is subject to correction by his lordship, and you must accept what he says about the law.

I accept that the burden of proof is on the prosecution and that the standard of proof which the prosecution must reach is proof beyond reasonable doubt, which is a very high standard of proof. I submit, however, ladies and gentlemen, that the Crown has achieved that standard of proof in this case and that you should therefore find the accused guilty of the crimes with which he is charged.

He is charged with assault, which needs no definition by me. As I understand the line the defence has taken, the accused is not denying that he struck Mr Starr with a knife. He is saying that he was *entitled* to do it because he was acting in self defence. Now, ladies and gentlemen, subject as always to correction by his lordship, I understand the law to be that a person may use violence to defend himself only in certain special circumstances. Firstly, he must have a reasonable fear that he is being attacked.

Secondly, he must have no other means of escape, and, thirdly, the retaliation he uses must not be excessive.

In the present case, even if you accept the defence version of what happened – and I shall, at the end of the day, be inviting you to reject it – you could not, in my submission, hold that the accused had been acting in self defence. I say this for two reasons. Firstly, he could have run away. Secondly, the retaliation which he used was grossly excessive. So far as running away is concerned, he had time to take the knife from his pocket and to open it. Surely he could better have spent that time by taking to his heels. He retaliated with a knife. There is not a shred of evidence that Mr Starr had a weapon at all. Therefore, for the accused to use a weapon was far in excess of anything that may have been required to protect himself. I urge you, ladies and gentlemen, to reject self defence.

But I suggest that you should never even get to the stage of considering self defence, because you should not accept the basic premise on which it depends, namely that it was Mr Starr who attacked the accused. I submit to you that you should accept the evidence of Mr Starr and Mr Brown and find it proved that what happened here was an unprovoked attack by the accused on Mr Starr. You may ask what motive the accused would have had for such an attack, but, as I am sure his lordship will direct you, the Crown does not have to prove motive. I would remind you that the accused had had a lot to drink. Perhaps his passions were simply inflamed by liquor. It is true that Mr Starr also had had a good deal to drink, but he is an older man and, you as men and women of the world may think, might therefore be able to hold his drink better than the accused.

The second charge on the indictment follows on from the first, and I don't think that it is disputed that, if you find the accused guilty of charge 1, you must also find him guilty of charge 2.

Ladies and gentlemen, I do not think that I need detain you any longer. I submit that, whatever view you may take of the facts, your clear duty here is to find the charges proved. I therefore confidently ask you to return a verdict of guilty as libelled on both charges.

SHERIFF: Thank you, Mr Forbes. Mr MacGregor.

MR MacGREGOR: Thank you, my lord. Ladies and gentlemen, it is now for me to address you on behalf of David Balfour, the accused in this case. I would begin by reminding you of a cardinal principle of our law: every person is presumed innocent until proved guilty. So you must not say to yourselves, as I am sure you *will* not, that, just because my client is in the dock, he must be guilty. As my friend has already reminded you, the burden of proof is on the prosecution. And I would add that that is still so even although the accused is putting forward a special defence of self defence, as I am sure his lordship will direct you.

My friend has asked you to accept the evidence of Mr Starr and Mr Brown in this case. I ask you to reject their evidence as being unworthy of any credit at all. I would remind you that both have criminal records, including, in Starr's case a conviction for violence which attracted a prison sentence. It is clear from the evidence that both were considerably under the influence of alcohol. Look at the respective sizes of Starr and of my client, and ask yourselves whether it is likely that my client would deliberately attack Starr. I suggest to you that you should be satisfied that the initial attack came from Starr. The only question which you have to ask yourselves therefore is whether anything my client did was done in self defence.

I agree in general terms with my friend's statement of the criteria which are essential for self defence, but I disagree with him in his suggestion that these have not been established.

If you accept my client's version of events, he was attacked by a much bigger man who had threatened him on a previous occasion. He therefore had every reason to fear for his own safety. What was he to do? The learned procurator fiscal depute suggests that he should have run away. Perhaps in an ideal world he would have done so, but, ladies and gentlemen, we are dealing here with real life where decisions have to be taken in the heat of the moment. You must not weigh things too finely. Should Mr Balfour have taken the risk of being pursued by a bigger and more powerful man? The fiscal criticised him for having time to take out and open his knife. But ladies and gentlemen, you probably all know how easy it is to open a penknife – it doesn't take a moment. I submit to you that that criticism by the fiscal is quite unjustified. And again my friend suggested that there was no evidence that Starr was armed. I put it to you that my client had every reason to suspect that he *was*. Mr Balfour told you himself that he *thought* he might be. The fact that he did not say that he was *sure* demonstrates his honesty to you, in my submission. Mr Stewart also raised the possibility of Mr Starr having a weapon. The question is not, ladies and gentlemen, whether he *did* have a weapon, but whether my client was reasonably justified in *thinking* that he did. I suggest to you that he had every reason for thinking that. In that event, to use a knife himself was in no way excessive retaliation. It was a perfectly reasonable thing to do.

Ladies and gentlemen, my friend did not detain you long. Nor shall I. I submit to you that this is a clear case of a frightened young man acting legitimately in defence of his own skin against an attack by a larger and older drunken lout. I confidently ask you to find my client not guilty.

SHERIFF: Thank you, Mr MacGregor.

Ladies and gentlemen , we now come to the final stages of this case. As I explained at the beginning, I must now charge you.

The first thing which I must tell you is about our respective functions. It is for me to deal with the law, and you must accept whatever I may say about the law. Your province is the facts. You and you alone are the masters of the facts. The facts have nothing to do with me, and, if, in the course of anything I say to you, I give any indication of a view I may have formed on the facts (which I hope I will not) you should ignore it, because the facts are no business of mine. It follows from that, that it is your recollection of the evidence which counts, not mine or Mr Forbes' or Mr MacGregor's. If anything any of us says about the evidence differs from your recollection, it is yours that counts and not ours.

What I have to say next is merely intended to assist you with how you may care to approach the facts in this case. If you do not agree with any suggestion I may make, please feel perfectly free not to follow it.

Credibility is clearly an important issue in this case. That is entirely for you. It is for you to decide which witnesses to believe and which witnesses to disbelieve. It is perfectly possible for you to accept part of a witness's evidence and to reject part; or you may accept it all or reject it all. Remember, though, that, if you reject a witness's evidence on any matter, you are not entitled to assume that the opposite of what he said is in fact what happened.

How you decide questions of credibility is really a matter of applying your common sense to the evidence, but there are certain factors which you may find it helpful to consider. What, for instance, was the witness's demeanour when he was giving his evidence? Did he appear comfortable or did he seem evasive? You should, of course, make allowances for the fact that a witness may feel nervous and overawed by being in court. What does a witness have to gain by not telling the truth? You may think that a witness would be unlikely to tell lies without a good reason for doing so. Well, what might be the reason? Was the witness's evidence consistent with other evidence in the case? Was it internally consistent? In other words was each part of his evidence consistent with the other parts? These, ladies and gentlemen are all pointers which you may or may not find helpful in assessing credibility.

Another factor which you should bear in mind when assessing a witness's evidence is reliability. You see, a witness may be doing his very best to tell the truth, but he may simply not remember things very well. This may be because a long time has passed since the events which he is describing, or it may be because his vision at the time was blurred because he was drunk or because he simply did not have a very good view. So, ladies and gentlemen, you should consider carefully the credibility and reliability of all the witnesses.

I now turn to the directions in law which I must give you, and I remind you that you *must* accept the law from me. It may be that some of what I say about the law has already been said to you by either Mr Forbes or Mr MacGregor, and, if that is so, I apologise for repeating it, but I must do so as it is I who must direct you in the law.

The first direction is about the burden of proof. In a criminal trial such as this, the burden of proof rests fairly and squarely on the prosecution. It is not for an accused person to prove anything. In this case the accused has lodged what is called a special defence, but that does not mean that he has to prove anything. All it means is that he is founding on a defence of a sort that he must give notice of to the Crown. That is the only special thing about the defence. Put another way, an accused person is presumed innocent until proved guilty. This is a fundamental principle of our law, and you must always have it in mind.

The next direction which I must give you is about the standard of proof which the Crown must satisfy. It is a very high standard: proof beyond reasonable doubt. What that means is that, if, after considering all the evidence, you are left with a reasonable doubt about the guilt of the accused, the benefit of that doubt must go to the accused, and you will acquit him. What is meant by a reasonable doubt? Well, it is not some airy-fairy, speculative doubt. Nor, on the other hand, does the law require that the Crown proves its case to a mathematical certainty. Human frailty being what it is, that would be impossible. Reasonable doubt is a doubt which is the result of your exercising your reasoning faculties on the evidence. You might care to look at it this way. Supposing that you had an important decision to make in your own life, either at home or at work. You would weigh all the factors both for and against the line of action which you might take. If, having done that as carefully as you could, you still were unable to reach a decision on the matter, you would have, I suggest, a reasonable doubt. If you have that sort of doubt about the guilt of the accused, you must, as I have said, give the benefit of that doubt to him and acquit.

Now I must tell you about what is called corroboration, although it is not, I think, a very controversial issue in this case. According to the law of Scotland, no person can be convicted of a crime such as those we are dealing with here on the evidence of only one witness, no matter how credible or reliable you may think that witness is. There must be evidence from at least two separate sources pointing at the guilt of the accused. In other words, in respect of each charge the Crown must prove every essential fact by the evidence of more than one witness. In this case there are really only two essential facts: was the crime committed; was it the accused who committed it. What I have said applies only to the Crown case. The accused does not require to be corroborated. I don't think that, in the context of the present case, I need to say anything further about corroboration.

I now pass from general directions, such as you would get in any criminal trial, to deal with this specific case.

There are two charges on the indictment. You must consider the evidence on each charge separately, although, in the present case, that is rather academic as the accused has admitted he was on bail and that it was a condition of bail that he did not commit any offence. Accordingly, if you were to convict him of the first charge, you would be bound to convict him of the second charge also. I shall therefore concentrate mainly on the first charge.

It is a charge of assault. An assault is a deliberate attack on the person of another. Sometimes an attack which would otherwise be an assault is excusable, and the attack does not amount to an assault. That is the situation where a person acts in self defence. In the present case the accused does not deny attacking Mr Starr, but he says that the attack was justified because he was defending himself. Remember, as I have said, it is not for the accused to prove anything. The proper way to look at it is that, the possibility of self defence having been introduced by the defence, the onus is on the Crown to negative it.

Now I must tell you what is meant by self defence. There are three requirements if what would otherwise be an assault is to be justified. Firstly, the accused must reasonably be afraid that he is in immediate danger of being seriously injured. It is not necessary that the basis for his fear be factually well founded, provided that it is reasonable. Thus, in the present case, you should consider whether or not there was any reasonable basis for the accused's saying (if you believe him) that Starr had a weapon. Secondly, there must be no other reasonable means of escape. If a person can avoid an attack by running away, he must do so. He must not remain and resist by force. Thirdly, the retaliation used must not be cruelly excessive. It should not be more than is necessary for his own safety. Now you must not weigh any of these factors in too fine a scale. You must make due allowance for the heat of the moment and the state of fear which the accused may be in.

I now turn to deal very briefly with the evidence in the case. I do not intend to rehearse it to you as it will be very fresh in your minds, and, in any event, it is not the function of a Scottish judge in a jury trial to go through all the evidence. First of all, a general point: you will give just as careful attention to the evidence for the defence as to that for the Crown. Turning to the more specific: if you believed the evidence of Mr Starr and Mr Brown (and therefore rejected the evidence of the accused and Mr

Stewart), it is difficult to see how you could do anything other than find that the accused was guilty of assault, because these witnesses spoke of an attack for no reason at all. As Mr Forbes said, it is the law that the Crown does not have to prove motive.

If you believed the accused's evidence, you would have to consider whether he was acting in self defence, using the test I've just told you about. If you concluded that he *was* acting in self defence, you would acquit. If the accused's evidence raised a reasonable doubt in your mind, equally you would acquit, as you would not then be satisfied of his guilt beyond reasonable doubt. You will note that I have referred only to the accused's evidence, and that is because, as I have told you, the accused does not require to be corroborated. Mr Stewart did, however, also give evidence for the defence, and you will consider his evidence as well.

If you came to the conclusion that the accused was not acting in self defence (and whether or not you do is for you alone to decide), you might consider whether there had been any provocation. The difference between self defence and provocation is that self defence is a complete answer to the charge, while provocation is consistent with guilt, but might be reflected in sentence. I emphasise that you would consider provocation only if you were going to return a verdict of guilty of assault.

There is one other minor matter which I should mention before I tell you about the verdicts which you may return. It is this. The charge alleges that Mr Starr was assaulted 'to his severe injury'. Has the Crown proved that the injury was severe? That is entirely a matter for you. You will take account of the medical evidence and of what Mr Starr himself said in reaching your conclusion. You would also be entitled to take account of the fact that Mr Starr did not seek any further medical attention for his injury after his discharge from hospital. One way of looking at it might be: supposing that you yourself suffered an injury like this, would you be inclined to call it severe?

As you probably know, there are three verdicts open to a jury in Scotland. These are: guilty, not guilty, and not proven. If your verdict were to be guilty, you would have to decide whether the injury had been proved to be severe, and you might consider the question of provocation. The other two verdicts are both verdicts of acquittal, and both have exactly the same effect in law. They both mean that the accused is for evermore free from the charges against him.

You may reach your verdict either unanimously or by a majority. There is just one proviso to that. There must be at least eight of you in favour of a verdict of guilty before you could return that verdict. You see, there are fifteen of you in the jury. You might be split, for example, seven for guilty, five for not guilty, and three for not proven. In that event, the largest number among you would be in favour of a verdict of guilty, but that would be a minority of the jury as a whole. In such an event you would have a majority for acquittal, and it would be for you to decide which of the two possible verdicts your acquittal verdict would be.

I suggest that the first thing you do when you go to the jury room is to elect one of your number as foreman. He or she will have two functions. One will be to act as chairman while you are discussing the case, and the other will be to tell my clerk what your verdict is when you return to court. When you come back my clerk will ask your foreman to stand up and will ask if you have reached a verdict. You will then be asked what your verdict is on the first charge, and whether it is unanimous or by a majority. You will then be asked the same questions in relation to the second charge.

Ladies and gentlemen, will you please now retire and consider your verdict.

The jury retired at 3.30 pm.

Upon their return at 4.45 pm:

CLERK OF COURT: Ladies and gentlemen, have you reached a verdict?

FOREMAN OF THE JURY: We have.

CLERK OF COURT: What is your verdict in respect of charge 1?

FOREMAN OF THE JURY: Guilty of assault but not to severe injury, and we find that the accused was provoked.

CLERK OF COURT: Is that unanimous or by a majority?

FOREMAN OF THE JURY: Majority.

SHERIFF: May I ask how many of you were in favour of a verdict of guilty?

FOREMAN OF THE JURY: Eight, my lord.

CLERK OF COURT: And what is your verdict in respect of charge 2?

FOREMAN OF THE JURY: Guilty.

CLERK OF COURT: Is that unanimous or by a majority?

FOREMAN OF THE JURY: By a majority.

CLERK OF COURT: Ladies and gentlemen, your verdict will now be recorded.

SHERIFF: Ladies and gentlemen, my clerk will now write down your verdict and will read it back to you for you to confirm that it is correct.

CLERK OF COURT: Ladies and gentlemen, is this a true record of your verdict? The jury by a majority finds the accused guilty of charge 1 under deletion of the word 'severe' and under provocation, and by a majority finds the accused guilty as libelled of charge 2.

FOREMAN OF THE JURY: Yes.

PROCURATOR FISCAL DEPUTE: My lord, I move for sentence. I produce a schedule of previous convictions to which no exception has been taken. The accused was arrested on 29 April, as your lordship has heard, and he appeared in court from custody on 2 May when he was released on bail. I move for forfeiture of the knife, which is Label No 1.

SHERIFF: Thank you Mr Forbes. Mr MacGregor, your client is under 21. I think before we can go any further I shall have to have reports.

MR MacGREGOR: I am in your lordship's hands. Might I with respect submit that your lordship should ask for a community service assessment as well as a social enquiry report? And I move that my client's bail be continued. I should say that my client has no objection to forfeiture of the knife.

SHERIFF: Very well, I shall order forfeiture of the knife, and I shall ask for the two reports which you have suggested. I am prepared to continue bail. Stand up, Mr Balfour. You will continue to be on bail with the additional condition that you will make yourself available to the social workers who will wish to see you in order to compile the reports I have asked for. Do you understand that additional condition, and do you accept it?

ACCUSED: Yes, sir.

CLERK OF COURT: Sentence deferred for social enquiry and community service reports until 10 am on 5 December 1989. Bail continued.

SHERIFF: Ladies and gentlemen, I have to thank you for your services on this jury and for the careful consideration which you have given to this case. I should explain that, because the accused here is under 21, I really have to obtain reports before I can decide what is the appropriate sentence. This is why I have not been able to sentence him today in your presence as I might otherwise have done. As this is the only case in the sitting, your services will not be required any more at present. If you have any expenses to claim arising out of your attendance here today, my clerk will advise you what to do. May I now wish you good day?

HM ADVOCATE v DAVID BALFOUR: SENTENCE

On 8 December David appeared in court again. In the meantime he had been interviewed by two social workers, one of whom was a member of the community service team, and a social enquiry report had been prepared (see pp 50–52). Miss McKenzie and David had had a brief meeting at the end of the previous week at Miss McKenzie's office in order to bring Miss McKenzie up to date with David's personal details. Before the court started Miss McKenzie went through the report with David, and confirmed that there was no factual statement in it with which he disagreed. Miss McKenzie was going to make the plea in mitigation on David's behalf herself, as Mr MacGregor was not available. She had sat through the trial and knew as much about the case as Mr MacGregor would have done. When the case called in court the proceedings took the following form:

CLERK OF COURT: Call the indictment, HM Advocate against David Balfour. Are you David Balfour?
ACCUSED: Yes.
MISS McKENZIE: My lord, I appear for the accused. I take it that your lordship has had an opportunity to read the report?
SHERIFF: Yes, Miss McKenzie.
MISS McKENZIE: I submit that the report is reasonably favourable. My client's personal circumstances are fully detailed in it. So far as the previous convictions are concerned, your lordship will see from the social enquiry report that the accused was ultimately fined £25 in respect of the breach of the peace for which sentence was deferred in the district court. The fine has been paid in full. Unless your lordship wishes any further information, I do not wish to add anything to what is said in the report with the exception of one very recent development. He has been fortunate enough to obtain a job starting next week if he is at liberty to do so. I have myself been in contact with his prospective employers and have confirmed that the offer of a job is genuine and definite. The employers are aware of the circumstances of this case, as my client has made no attempt to conceal his unfortunate situation. He will be employed as a fish filleter at a weekly wage of approximately £85 net. From that he will pay to his parents board of £25 per week, and the only other regular commitments which he will have are a club payment of £5 per week and the community charge of about £6 per week.

So far as the facts of the case are concerned, your lordship of course heard all the evidence. I submit that the assault of which my client was convicted is not nearly as serious as it appeared at first sight. The jury deleted the

AO 1

GRAMPIAN REGIONAL COUNCIL - SOCIAL WORK DEPARTMENT

SOCIAL ENQUIRY REPORT FOR COURT

Case No. ......6031983............................ Date of Typing ....3.12.89.........................

Office Address ....Kinord House, West Road, Duncairn..

....

Surname(s) (include maiden name) ....BALFOUR.................... Date of Birth ...23.11.69......

Christian or Forename(s) ....David............................... Marital Status ..Single.............

Home Address ....19 Gairn Street, Duncairn...

....

Present Address ....

.... Occupation ....Unemployed...........

Court ....Duncairn Sheriff Solemn........................ Date of Court ...5.12.89.............

Offence ......Assault by Stabbing..

.............Bail (Scotland) Act 1980..

....

Disposal ....

....

BASIS OF REPORT

David Balfour was interviewed on two occasions, once in the company of his parents and once on his own.

FAMILY

Father:	David Balfour	Aged 43 years
Mother:	Anne Balfour	Aged 41 years
Brother:	Peter Balfour	Aged 16 years
Subject:	David Balfour	Aged 20 years

The family occupy a three apartment semi-detached local authority house in an area where delinquency is not unknown. The house is comfortably furnished and maintained to a high standard. They have occupied their present home for seventeen years but did apply for a transfer eighteen months ago as they were concerned about David and felt a change of environment would be beneficial to him. So far they have been unsuccessful.

Mr Balfour is a plumber and has been so employed all his working life. Mrs Balfour is presently employed in a part-time capacity as a school cleaner.

Peter left school in June of this year having gained 5 'O' grades and immediately started work as an apprentice motor mechanic. He attends college on a day release scheme one day per week.

- 2 -

PERSONAL:

David attended local schools, Duncairn Primary and then the academy. He was seen as
a likeable boy who appeared to be well adjusted and an average scholar. This continued
until his final year at school when, seemingly for no reason, he lost all interest in
school and he began truanting on a regular basis. He left school in December 1985
having gained no certificates.

On leaving school he was unemployed until June 1986 when he gained employment in the
fish industry. Unfortunately he was made redundant in December 1988 and has been
unemployed since although he informs he goes for a job interview on December 1st and
should know the result when he appears in court on the 5th. Again it is for a job in
the fish.

During the period of unemployment David has been in receipt of £54.80 per fortnight
income support. While unemployed his parents have been taking no board money. They
felt if he had money in his pocket he would be less likely to get into trouble.

When David was interviewed alone his sudden loss of interest in school was discussed
and it quickly became apparent he had negative feelings towards his parents. It seems
that Peter contracted an illness and David felt his parents concentrated their attention
on him and he felt neglected. This feeling has persisted as David feels his parents
have been over protective towards Peter since then. His self esteem suffered a further
blow when Peter did reasonably well at school and "got himself a good job". Unfortunately
David had never spoken to his parents about his feelings and they seem totally bemused
by his behaviour.

When discussing his previous offences David stated the offensive weapon mentioned was
a piece of wood he picked up when he felt threatened by a group he encountered in the
street. Of the other offences, while denying he had a drink problem, admits they
occurred after he had been drinking.

Of the present offence David agrees he had taken some drink but does not see that as a
factor. His explanation is that he saw a man running towards him apparently to attack
him and his one thought was to defend himself which he did with the pen knife which he
habitually carried. On reflection he agrees he could have run away.

ASSESSMENT & RECOMMENDATION:

David is a young man who appears to have been brought up in a stable home and no problems
of note appeared until he was in his last year at school. He presents as an angry young
man who feels neglected by his parents, but they in turn are somewhat bemused as they
had no idea, until now, of David's feelings. His anger is further compounded because his
brother is seemingly doing well. It is possible until Peter's illness David had been the
one to receive the most attention and has reacted badly when this was removed.

Another possible area of concern is his alcohol intake. He states he drinks little and
will not consider he could have a problem but this is the third court appearance following
his consuming alcohol.

The writer feels the areas highlighted should be investigated and it is felt this could
best be done by way of a probation order.

- 3 -

ASSESSMENT & RECOMMENDATION (Cont'd.)

The offence that David has committed is recognised to be extremely serious and made more so because it was committed while on bail on a deferred sentence and there is little doubt the court will consider the possibility of a custodial sentence. Because of that the writer arranged to have David assessed as to his suitability for community service and thus, hopefully, to offer an alternative to custody. I have to advise the court he is considered a suitable candidate and work would be available. The conditions governing community service and the commitment necessary to complete an order have been explained to David and he has signified his understanding and would consent to participate if given the opportunity.

With the above in mind and the areas of concern highlighted earlier, which the writer feels should be further investigated, it is felt this could best be achieved by the imposition of a probation order with an added condition that he perform unpaid work for the benefit of the community.

The court is therefore respectfully asked to consider the above recommendation as being a suitable disposal in this case.

Signature: *Donald Angus.*

(Donald Angus)
Social Worker

reference to severity of injury, and they also found that the accused had been provoked.

As your lordship sees, the report recommends a period of probation with a condition of community service. I submit, with respect, that that would be a disposal which would do justice to the accused on the one hand and to the interests of society on the other.

SHERIFF: Thank you, Miss McKenzie. (*After taking time to consider*) Stand up please, Mr Balfour. You have been found guilty of a serious crime, but I accept that there were mitigating factors to which I am entitled to give weight. As I am sure you are aware, anyone who carries and uses a knife can usually expect to receive a sentence of custody. However, in your case, because of the mitigating factors to which I have referred, I am prepared to accept the recommendations in the report. I intend to make a probation order for a period of two years with the standard conditions and certain extra ones as well. The standard conditions are that, throughout the period of probation, you will be under the supervision of a social worker. You must obey any directions given to you by the social worker. You must attend for appointments with him or her as required. You must notify your social worker of any change of address. You must not commit any offence while on probation. The additional conditions are that, firstly, you will perform 120 hours unpaid work, and, secondly, you will find security of £250 for your good behaviour during the period of probation. As far as the unpaid work is concerned, you will be told where and when to attend for your work appointments. You must attend promptly, and you must perform the work efficiently. You must also keep your supervising social worker informed of the hours when you are working at your normal job and of any changes therein. This is so that your unpaid work may be fitted in with your paid work. If you are in breach of probation by failing to abide by any of the conditions which I have described to you, you will be brought back to court and dealt with as if you had not been placed on probation, and that, in your case, would almost certainly mean a custodial sentence. Do you understand?

ACCUSED: Yes.

SHERIFF: And do you accept probation on that basis?

ACCUSED: Yes.

MISS McKENZIE (*after consulting with the accused*): My lord, my client asks for eight weeks within which to lodge his security.

SHERIFF: Yes, I think that that is reasonable.

CLERK OF COURT: David Balfour, you have been placed on probation for two years with a condition of performing 120 hours unpaid work and also of finding security of £250 for your good behaviour. You must pay the £250 within eight weeks from today.

Chapter 2

The Case of Nicol Jarvie

THE PROCURATOR FISCAL, DUNCAIRN v NICOL JARVIE: SEARCH, ARREST, FIRST COURT APPEARANCE

On Saturday 3 June 1989 Mr James Todd left his second floor flat at 56 Constitution Street, Duncairn at 11 am. He returned home about 5 pm to find that the door had been forced open. The only thing missing was a video cassette recorder which Mr Todd had bought only one week previously. Mr Todd called the police. A uniformed officer came to see him very quickly and, later the same evening, he was interviewed by Detective Constables John Reid and Stephen Watson. DC Reid noted Mr Todd's statement in his notebook.

During the afternoon of 8 June DC Reid received an anonymous telephone call to the effect that the stolen video cassette recorder was in a flat at 10B Duncry Close, Duncairn, the occupier of which was Nicol Jarvie. DC Reid had had some previous acquaintance with Mr Jarvie, who was aged 26 and had a record for crimes of dishonesty including more than one conviction for theft by housebreaking, so he was not all together surprised by the information given to him. He decided to request the procurator fiscal's office to apply to the sheriff for a warrant to search the Jarvie flat. He completed the standard form (see p 55) and took it to the duty procurator fiscal depute who, having seen the police report on the case, signed the application for the warrant. DC Reid went straight from the fiscal's office to the sheriff court and there saw Sheriff Lawson in his chambers. He explained the circumstances of the case to the sheriff, who agreed to grant the search warrant.

At about 6 pm the same day DC Reid and DC Watson went to 10B Duncry Close. They knocked at the door, and it was opened by Mr Jarvie. DC Reid showed him the search warrant and Mr Jarvie asked the officers to come into the house. There they carried out a thorough search. Underneath the bed in the only bedroom of the flat they found a video cassette recorder which they were able to identify from its serial number as that stolen from Mr Todd. DC Reid told Mr Jarvie that he believed the VCR to be stolen, and cautioned him that he was not obliged to say anything but that, if he did, it would be noted and could be used in evidence. He then asked him if he had any explanation for the presence of the VCR under the bed. To this Mr Jarvie replied 'It's just a spare in case my other one packs up'. DC Reid then asked Mr Jarvie how he had got it, and Mr Jarvie said 'I bought it from a guy in a pub'. Thereafter he refused to say anything more. In the living room of the flat there was a VCR attached to the television set. That VCR appeared to be reasonably new, but the police did not test it to see whether it worked.

F9   PF Ref:—

Under the Criminal Procedure (Scotland) Act, 1975

IN THE SHERIFF COURT OF   GRAMPIAN, HIGHLAND AND ISLANDS AT DUNCAIRN

.. 8 June 19 89

THE PETITION OF   GEORGE WILLIAM BROWN

Procurator Fiscal of Court for the public interest.

HUMBLY SHEWETH

    THAT   from credible information which the Petitioner has received
it appears that there are reasonable grounds for suspecting that a video
cassette recorder stolen by theft by housebreaking at 56 Constitution
Street, Duncairn on 3 June 1989, are in the possession of or under the
control of:

NICOL JARVIE (26) b. 15.03.63
Unemployed
10b Duncry Close
Duncairn

The Petitioner therefore craves the Court to   grant Warrant to Officers of Law to
enter the said premises at 10b Duncry Close, Duncairn, and to search
said premises including any outhouses and sheds, and any person found
therein, and to take possession of such property as above mentioned,
and for these purposes to open all shut and lockfast places, if necessary
by force.

ACCORDING TO JUSTICE

Susan Stewart

O U N C A I R N   8 J U N E   19 89 . — The Court having considered the foregoing

Petition Grants Warrant as craved.

Sorley Lawson

Sheriff

DC Reid then told Mr Jarvie that he was being arrested on a charge of theft by housebreaking on 3 June 1989 at 56 Constitution Street, Duncairn. He again cautioned him and asked if he had anything he wished to say in reply to the charge. Mr Jarvie replied that he did not. He was then taken to Divisional Police Headquarters in Duncairn and locked up in a cell overnight.

The following morning the police report of the case (which consisted at this stage of only a summary of the evidence) went to the procurator fiscal's office, where Susan Stuart, the procurator fiscal depute dealing with custody cases that day, decided that it should be the subject of a summary complaint in the sheriff court. The complaint was prepared (see p 57) and about 11 am Mr Jarvie, who had been taken to the sheriff court, was served with the complaint together with a notice of previous convictions (see p 58).

The legal aid duty solicitor in the sheriff court was Kenneth Liberton, the court partner in a small firm in Duncairn. He had a brief interview with Mr Jarvie, who instructed him that he wished to plead not guilty. Mr Liberton asked him if he had a lawyer of his own. Mr Jarvie said that his regular lawyer was Robert Seymour and that he was wanting Mr Seymour to appear for him at his trial. Mr Liberton knew that Mr Seymour was a partner in the firm in Duncairn which did more criminal defence work than any other. He told Mr Jarvie that he would appear for him in court that day, and Mr Jarvie could then contact Mr Seymour in order to arrange for him to appear at his trial. Mr Jarvie asked Mr Liberton to apply for bail on his behalf. Mr Liberton said that he would do so, but advised Mr Jarvie not to be too optimistic in view of his previous record. However, when Mr Liberton spoke to Miss Stuart just before the case called in court, she said that the Crown was not opposing bail.

About noon Mr Jarvie was taken into court handcuffed to a police officer. Sheriff Walter Scott was on the bench, and Miss Stuart was the depute fiscal taking the court. Matters proceeded as follows:

CLERK OF COURT: Are you Nicol Jarvie?

ACCUSED: Yes.

MR LIBERTON: My lord, I appear for the accused as duty solicitor. He has instructed me to tender a plea of not guilty. I should say that, in any further proceedings, Mr Jarvie will be represented by Mr Seymour.

CLERK OF COURT: Mr Jarvie, do you confirm that you wish to plead not guilty?

ACCUSED: Yes.

PROCURATOR FISCAL DEPUTE: My lord, I move your lordship to fix a diet of trial. I also move that you fix an intermediate diet. I have no objection to the accused being granted bail.

SHERIFF: Mr Liberton, have you any objection to an intermediate diet?

MR LIBERTON: No, my lord, and I move for bail.

SHERIFF: Very well. Mr Jarvie, you will be released on bail on the following conditions. Firstly, you must attend court on the dates which you will be told. You will be given two dates, and you must attend on the first of these dates. If the case is not then disposed of, you must attend on the second date also. The second condition is that you do not commit any offence while on bail, and the third condition is that you do not interfere with witnesses or in any way obstruct the course of justice. Do you understand these conditions?

ACCUSED: Yes.

SHERIFF: Do you accept them?

F. 1	89009457	A18956/89	SS/CG		C......................
	Names of Accused		Date of Disposal		Sentence (if any)

Duncairn
9 June 1989

Under the Criminal Procedure (Scotland) Act, 1975

IN THE SHERIFF COURT OF   GRAMPIAN, HIGHLAND & ISLANDS AT DUNCAIRN

THE COMPLAINT OF THE PROCURATOR FISCAL AGAINST

NICOL JARVIE
Unemployed   Date of Birth: 15.3.63
10b Duncry Close
Duncairn

The charge against you is that   on 3 June 1989 <u>YOU DID BREAK INTO</u> the dwellinghouse occupied by James Todd at 56 Constitution Street, Duncairn, and there <u>STEAL</u> a video cassette recorder.

Susan Stuart

Procurator-Fiscal Depute

Apprehension and Search   19   .—The Court grants Warrant to apprehend the said
Accused and grants warrant to search the person, dwellinghouse, and repositories of said Accused and any place where they may be found and to take possession of the property mentioned or referred to in the Complaint and all articles and documents likely to afford evidence of   guilt or of guilty participation.

Sheriff.

Dd 8848228 100M 11/86 22314 (14892) 244   **(Over)**

F. 19

NOTICE OF PREVIOUS CONVICTIONS APPLYING TO   NICOL JARVIE

In the event of your being convicted of the charge(s) in the Complaint it is intended to place before
the Court the following previous conviction(s) applying to you.

	Date	Place of Trial	Court	Offence	Sentence
1.	17 June 1981	Duncairn	District	Theft	Admonished
2.	20 October 1981	Duncairn	District	Theft	Fined £50
3.	19 August 1982	Duncairn	Sheriff Summary	Theft by opening lock-fast places Theft	Probation 1 year On 18.2.83 Breach of Probation – Admonished
4.	7 January 1983	Duncairn	Sheriff Summary	Theft Con: Police (S) Act 1967 Section 41(1)(a)	Fined £50 Fined £50
5.	15 August 1983	Duncairn	District	Breach of the Peace	Fined £40
6.	25 May 1984	Duncairn	Sheriff Summary	Con: Road Traffic Act 1972 Section 175(1)(a)	Fined £100, licence endorsed
7.	24 August 1984	Duncairn	Sheriff Summary	Theft by housebreaking	60 hours CSO
8.	14 June 1985	Duncairn	Sheriff Summary	Theft by housebreaking and opening lockfast places	90 days imprisonment
9.	12 February 1986	Duncairn	District	Breach of the Peace Assault	Fined £75
10.	30 September 1987	Duncairn	Sheriff Summary	Theft Fraud	Fined £100 Fined £50 + £100 Compensation Order
11.	6 June 1988	Duncairn	Sheriff Summary	Attempted housebreaking and opening lockfast places with intent	60 days imprisonment
12.	14 October 1988	Duncairn	Sheriff Summary	Theft by housebreaking	6 months imprisonment

Dd 8037094 100M 7/87 22314 (16084) 244

ACCUSED: Yes.

CLERK OF COURT: (*After having confirmed with Miss Stuart that the trial date did not coincide with the leave dates of the police witnesses, which were noted in the police report.*) Intermediate diet 1 September 1989 and trial diet 6 October 1989, both at 10 am. Bail granted.

Mr Jarvie was then taken back to the court cells where, in due course, he was served with his bail order. He was then released from custody.

Outside the court Mr Liberton spoke briefly to Mr Jarvie. He told him that he (Mr Liberton) would give Mr Seymour the service copy complaint and notice of previous convictions. He advised Mr Jarvie to contact Mr Seymour as soon as possible. 'Remember that you've got to apply for legal aid within fourteen days from today.'

On Miss Stuart's return to the office she took steps to instruct the officer in charge of the case, DC Reid, to prepare full witness statements, and this was done. As this was only a summary case the Crown witnesses were not precognosced. The fiscal conducting the trial would do so on the basis of the police statements.

THE PROCURATOR FISCAL, DUNCAIRN v NICOL JARVIE: DEFENCE PREPARATION, INTERMEDIATE DIET

As soon as he left the court Mr Jarvie made an appointment to see Mr Seymour on Tuesday 13 June. At this meeting Mr Seymour (who had meanwhile received the service copy complaint and notice of previous convictions from Mr Liberton) took a brief statement from Mr Jarvie. He also completed a legal aid application form which he got Mr Jarvie to sign (see pp 60–66B). In his statement Mr Jarvie said that he knew nothing about the housebreaking on 3 June. He had not even been in Duncairn that day as he had been visiting a friend in Edinburgh. As for the VCR, he had, as he had told the police, bought it from a man in a pub. The date of the transaction was, so far as he could remember, 3 June. He did not know the name of the seller, but had been assured by him that the sale was legitimate. He had paid £100. It was true that he already had a VCR, but it was rather old and had not been working very well. He had been thinking of replacing it.

Mr Seymour submitted the legal aid application to the Scottish Legal Aid Board together with a copy of the complaint, the notice of previous convictions, Mr Jarvie's statement, and a copy of Mr Jarvie's UB40 form to prove that he was unemployed. Some two weeks later he received a legal aid certificate. He then wrote to the procurator fiscal's office and requested a list of the Crown witnesses in Mr Jarvie's case. Shortly afterwards he received the list which contained only three names: Mr James Todd (the owner of the VCR), DC John Reid and DC Stephen Watson. Mr Seymour decided to interview the two police officers first. He thought that they might provide him with enough information to make it unnecessary for him to interview Mr Todd. He was well aware of the reluctance of many victims of crime to co-operate with defence lawyers.

Mr Seymour, following the usual practice, wrote to the Chief Constable to request permission to precognosce the two police witnesses. This permission

SLAB/CR/1

> **BEFORE COMPLETING THIS FORM, PLEASE READ
> CAREFULLY THE NOTES OVERLEAF.**

THE SCOTTISH LEGAL AID BOARD

APPLICATION FORM

FOR

LEGAL AID

IN

SUMMARY CRIMINAL PROCEEDINGS

> **DO NOT DELAY IN TAKING THIS FORM TO A
> SOLICITOR WHO MAY BE ABLE TO ASSIST IN ITS
> COMPLETION.**

SCOTTISH LEGAL AID BOARD
LEGAL AID (SCOTLAND)
LEGAL AID IN SUMMARY CASES

> **DO NOT DELAY IN TAKING THIS FORM TO A SOLICITOR WHO MAY BE ABLE TO ASSIST YOU IN COMPLETING IT.**

Notes on Completion of Form

PLEASE READ THESE NOTES **BEFORE** COMPLETING THE APPLICATION FORM

Before the Scottish Legal Aid Board can approve your Application, it needs to be satisfied that:—

(a) You do not have any rights or other facilities available for payment of your defence (e.g. when under an Insurance Policy or from a Motoring Organisation or Trade Union).

(b) You will be unable to meet the expenses of the case without undue hardship to you or your dependants.

(c) It is in the interests of justice that Legal Aid should be made available to you.

(d) Your Application has been submitted within the time limits, unless there are special reasons.

2. Your Application must be lodged with the Board not later than 14 days from the first diet at which you tendered a plea of **NOT GUILTY**. This date should be entered at question 11. If your Application is lodged more than 14 days after the date entered, you may not get Legal Aid.

3. You must answer all the questions. The completed form must be submitted with a copy of the Complaint. It may be in your interests to supply a copy of the convictions attached to the Complaint. Insufficient information may result in refusal of your Application.

4. Use this form to apply for Legal Aid for a Summary case in which you are pleading **NOT GUILTY** to all or part of the proceedings. It must **not** be used for any other type of case.

5. Submit your last wage/salary slip or, if your are unemployed, evidence of your DHSS Benefit (e.g. Supplementary Benefit/Pensions) or Unemployment Benefit. **DO NOT** submit Pension or DHSS order books.

6. If the Application is by, or on behalf of, a child under 16 years of age, the child's name should appear at Part A of the form. The income of the parent should be shown on the financial Part — C — of the form.

7. Your Solicitor must complete Part F, and will assist you in completing question 7 in Part A. You **must** sign the form and it **must** also be signed by or on behalf of your Solicitor.

8. If the Court in which your case is being heard is in Strathclyde Region, send this form to Scott House, 12/16 South Frederick Street, Glasgow, G1 1HT. If the Court in which your case is being heard is anywhere else in Scotland, send this form to 44 Drumsheugh Gardens, Edinburgh, EH3 7SW.

SCOTTISH LEGAL AID BOARD

BEFORE COMPLETING THIS FORM, PLEASE READ CAREFULLY THE NOTES OPPOSITE.	**FOR OFFICIAL USE**
DO NOT DELAY IN TAKING THIS FORM TO A SOLICITOR WHO MAY BE ABLE TO ASSIST IN ITS COMPLETION.	Reference Number: ....
	Date of Receipt: ....

All information will be treated in confidence, in terms of Section 34 of the Legal Aid (Scotland) Act 1986.

Part A: Applicant Details (BLOCK LETTERS PLEASE — TICK BOXES WHERE APPROPRIATE)

1. Surname: ...... JARVIE ......
   Forename(s): ... NICOL ...
   MR [✓]   MRS [ ]   MISS [ ]   OTHER [ ] SPECIFY

2. Date of Birth (actual date must be given)
   Date ... 15 ... Month ...... 3 .. Year 1963 ......

3. Home Address: ....
   .... 10B .. DUNCRY .CLOSE ....
   .... DUNCAIRN ....

4. If in Custody, please state place of detention:
   ....

5. Occupation: state **all** present jobs, or whether unemployed:
   .... UNEMPLOYED ....

6. Have you any rights or other facilities available to you for payment of your defence (e.g. under an Insurance Policy or as a member of a Motoring Organisation or Trade Union?)
   YES [ ]   NO [✓]
   If YES, state details: ....
   ....
   ....

7. The Solicitor who has agreed to act for me if Legal Aid is granted is:
   ...... R. .SEYMOUR ....
   LEGAL AID CODE NUMBER: ... 12345 ....

Part B: Proceedings Details

8. My case will be heard at ..... DUNCAIRN ....
   Sheriff Court or ....
   ~~District Court~~ --

9. Procurator Fiscal's Reference Number (if shown on complaint):
   .... 89009457 ....

10. Brief description of charges:
    .... Theft .by .Housebreaking ....
    ....
    ....

11. Date of NOT GUILTY Plea:
    Date ...... 9 ..... Month .. 6 .... Year 1989

12. Date of next Court appearance:
    Date .... 1 .... Month .... 9 .... Year 19. 89 (/D)
    6   10   89(/D)

13. Names of Co-accused (if any)
    ....
    ....

14. Did you receive assistance from a Duty Solicitor in this case?   YES [✓]   NO [ ]

15. (a) Have you received advice and assistance on this case?   YES [ ]   NO [✓]
    (b) If YES, did it include assistance by way of representation?   YES [ ]   NO [✓]
    If YES, state Reference Number:
    ....

16. Have you previously applied for Legal Aid in this case?   YES [ ]   NO [✓]
    If YES, state Reference Number:
    ....

17. State any charge(s) to which you have pleaded NOT GUILTY: ....
    .... As .Libelled ....

18. State any charge(s) to which you have pleaded GUILTY: ...... NONE ....
    ....

19. Have you been granted Legal Aid in another Criminal case which has not yet finished?
    YES [ ]   NO [✓]
    If YES, state Reference Number:
    ....

SLAB CR/1

¯Page 2

Part C: Financial Details

Give details of your net income (i.e. after the deduction of tax and National Insurance), from all sources. If you are married and living with your wife or husband, then you have to provide details of his or her income as well. You may be asked to provide proof of the information.

If you are applying for Legal Aid for a child under sixteen, you must give details of **your** financial circumstances.

20. Do you receive Supplementary Benefit?   YES [ ]   NO [✓]

    If YES, give the address of the Social Security Office dealing with your claim.

    ```
    ...........................................................................
    ...........................................................................
    ...........................................................................
    ```

21. Do you receive Family Income Supplement?   YES [ ]   NO [✓]

    If YES, give weekly amount: —   £   ____

22. Give details of your INCOME in the table below.

Description of Income	Amount		OFFICIAL USE
	Your Income	Income of Husband/ Wife	
(a) Weekly earnings or salary, including overtime, commission or bonuses. (Give **net** figures). Attach **your last wage slip**. If you or your spouse are self-employed, state your weekly drawings from the business.	---;	---	
(b) Income from any part-time job not included at (a) above. (Give **net** figures).	---	---	
(c) Income from State Benefits — e.g. Pensions, Unemployment Benefit, Sickness Benefit, Child Benefit. Specify: Unemployment benefit.	£27.50	---	
(d) Any other Income — give details.	---	---	
(e) If in business of your own, attach the most recent accounts available.	---	---	

Allowances and Deductions

In assessing your means, the Board will make allowances for the cost of supporting your husband or wife, children and any other dependant relatives, and also for your accommodation costs. If there are any other expenses which you think the Board should make allowance for, give details at question 26.

23. Give the NUMBER of dependants who are LIVING WITH YOU.

Husband or Wife	Children 18 and over	Children 16 and 17	Children 11 to 15	Children Under 11	Other (specify below)	OFFICIAL USE
--	--	--	--	--	--	

24. If you pay maintenance to a dependant who does not live with you, state the amounts you pay.

Name of Dependant	Your relationship to him or her	Amount you pay per week
--	--	--

25. You may claim for the HOUSING EXPENSES of you and your wife or husband. State the amounts you pay each week. If you own more than one house, give details relevant to the house in which you live.

Description of Payment	Amount per week
Rent	Paid direct
Mortgage Repayment	
Feu Duty or Ground Annual	
Service Charge	
Rates	
Board and Lodging	
Bed and Breakfast	

26. Please give details of any OTHER EXPENSES which you meet from income.

Description of Expenditure		Amount spent per week
Hire Purchase	£6	
Community charge	£6	£17
Insurance/credit	£5	

Page 4

Capital and Savings

Give details of all your capital and savings. If you are married and living with your husband or wife, give details of his or her capital and savings. State particulars of savings with the National Savings Bank or any other Banks, Building Societies, National Savings Certificates, cash stocks and shares, or any other investments. Also give details of any property and/or land you own, such as houses or flats, apart from the house or flat in which you live.

27. State details of your CAPITAL and SAVINGS in the table below.

Description of Capital and Savings	You	Husband/ Wife	
(a) Do you own a house and/or property (apart from your main dwelling?)	YES ☐ NO ✓	YES ☐ NO ☐	

	Amount		
	You	Husband/ Wife	Remarks
(b) If YES, state:			
(i) the value (i.e. the approximate selling price):			
(ii) the amount of any outstanding mortgage:			
(c) Give details of savings, institutions, (e.g. Bank, Building Society).			

28. State details of any EXPENSES you or your husband or wife meet from Capital.

Description of Expenditure	Amount spent per week
None	

29. If the Application has been completed on behalf of a child, please state below any Income or Capital of the child.

N/A

Page 5

> **IT MAY BE IN YOUR INTERESTS TO OBTAIN
> ADVICE BEFORE COMPLETING THIS PART.**

Part D

Interests of Justice

Indicate by ticking the appropriate box whether any of the following might apply in your case.

Provide a brief explanation in the space provided to any questions to which you answer YES.

30. (a) The offence is such that, if proved, it is likely that the Court would impose a sentence which would deprive you of your liberty or lead to the loss of your livelihood.

YES [✓]   NO [　]

> I have a large number of previous convictions and have
> been sentenced to prison before for analagous offences
> (copy list of previous convictions attached

(b) The case involves consideration of a substantial question of law or evidence of a complex and difficult nature.

YES [✓]   NO [　]

> I have a special defence of alibi. Even if court does not
> find me guilty of theft by housebreaking   I am not even
> guilty of reset as I bought the item in good faith at a fair
> price.

(c) It is in the interests of someone else that you should be legally represented.

YES [　]   NO [✓]

> ....
> ....
> ....

(d) (i) Are you in custody?

YES [　]   NO [✓]

> ....
> ....
> ....

(ii) Is it in connection with the offence for which Legal Aid is now sought?

YES [　]   NO [✓]

> ....
> ....
> ....

31. Indicate the nature of the defence to be advanced to the charge.

> I was offered the vcr in a public house.   The seller told
> me he was in possession of it legitimately.   I was not
> involved in the housebreaking.   All I did was pay £100 for
> the item referred to

OFFICIAL
USE

Page 6

32. Are there any other factors, e.g. are you on Bail, which should be taken into account in determining this Application. If so, give full particulars.

> .. I am. on. bail .and .therefore .in. accordance .with .the .conditions
> .. of .the. order .I. can .not. .contact. .the .Crown .witnesses .direct....
> ....

YOU MUST ATTACH A COPY OF THE COMPLAINT AND IT MAY BE IN YOUR INTERESTS ALSO TO SUPPLY A COPY OF THE CONVICTIONS, IF ANY, ATTACHED TO THE COMPLAINT.

Part E

Further Information (Page 8 may also be used)

This part of the form is set aside for any further information you think the Board should have when deciding upon your Application. You may also use this part of the form to tell the Board of any future changes in circumstances that might alter your financial position. .

DECLARATION BY APPLICANT

I certify that the foregoing information is correct and I authorise the Scottish Legal Aid Board or its officials to take such steps as may be necessary to verify same, including making any approach to Third Parties, including the Department of Health and Social Security, and I authorise such Third Parties, including the Department of Health and Social Security, to release such information to the Board as may be required by the Board. I do this in the knowledge that Section 35 of the Legal Aid (Scotland) Act 1986 provides that any person seeking or receiving Legal Aid who wilfully fails to comply with any Regulations as to the information to be furnished by him, or for the purpose of obtaining Legal Aid knowingly makes any false statement or false representations, shall be guilty of an offence and liable on Summary convictions to a fine not exceeding level 4 on the standard scale, or imprisonment for a term not exceeding 60 days, or both.

I undertake to pay into the Scottish Legal Aid Fund any monies recovered or receivable by me from any Third Party in connection with the costs of this case.

Date .... 13/6/89 ....   *Niol Jarvie*
                                                     Applicant's Signature.

Page 7

Part F

To be completed by the Applicant's Solicitor.

33. Do you consider:

(a) that the applicant will be unable to understand the proceedings or state his/her case because of age, inadequate knowledge of English, Mental Illness, other mental or physical disability or otherwise?

YES ☐   NO ☑   If YES, give brief explanation.

> ....
> ....
> ....

(b) that the defence to be advanced appears to be frivolous?

YES ☐   NO ☑   Brief explanation, if appropriate.

> Complete defence to the charge libelled.   Even if Crown were to suggest a
> plea to reset the accused would adhere to his not guilty plea.   With regard
> to the libel accused has stated special defence of alibi which if accepted
> will result in him being acquitted.

34. Please provide any information you feel will be of assistance.

> If convicted accused will almost certainly be sent to prison having already
> had a C.S.O.   It would be in everyones best interests for accused to be
> legally represented as his alibi is spoken to by a friend and to allow for
> the proper legal procedure to be adopted it is in my opinion essential the
> accused has the benefit of legal representation

I did/~~did not~~ act as a Duty Solicitor in this case.

I agree to act on behalf of the Applicant if Legal Aid is granted.

..........13/6/89....................................   *Robert Seymour*........................
Date   *Solicitor's Signature.*

PLEASE ENSURE THAT THE APPLICANT SUBMITS WITH THE APPLICATION FORM A COPY OF THE COMPLAINT AND, IF APPROPRIATE, A LIST OF PREVIOUS CONVICTIONS AND ANY OTHER SUPPORTING DOCUMENTS.

was granted, and on 2 August Mr Seymour interviewed the two detectives and obtained precognitions from them. DC Reid's precognition was as follows:

Precognition of John Turnbull Reid

I am John Turnbull Reid. I am a detective constable in the Grampian Police stationed at Duncairn. I am 29 years old and have ten years' police service.

On 3 June 1989 at 7 pm I attended at the second floor flat at 56 Constitution Street, Duncairn occupied by James Todd. I was accompanied by DC Watson. I saw that the front door had been forced open, apparently by bodily pressure. The lock was broken. Mr Todd informed me that the only item missing was a VCR which he had bought one week previously. He showed me the receipt for it which gave the serial number of the VCR. I took possession of the receipt. I arranged for members of the Identification Bureau to attend and examine the premises for fingerprints. I understand that this examination proved negative.

On 8 June about 3 pm I was at Divisional Headquarters when I received a telephone call from a man who refused to give his name. He said that he had heard that I was dealing with the break-in at 56 Constitution Street and that the stolen VCR was in Nick Jarvie's flat at 10B Duncry Close. I asked him how he knew, but he rang off.

I obtained a search warrant and at 6 pm on the same day, accompanied by DC Watson, I went to Jarvie's flat. We were admitted by Jarvie who was alone in the flat. It consists of one bedroom, living room, bathroom and kitchen. We carried out a search and found a VCR under the bed in the bedroom. I checked the serial number and found that it corresponded with that on the receipt given to me by Mr Todd. I had already seen that there was another VCR in the living room. It was attached to the television. I did not check that it was working, but it looked reasonably new to me. I cautioned Jarvie and asked him to account for his possession of the VCR under the bed. He said: 'It's just a spare in case my other one packs up'. I then asked Jarvie where he had got it and he said that he had bought it from a guy in a pub. He refused to answer any further questions. I cautioned and charged him with theft by housebreaking, to which he made no reply. I then arrested him and took him to Divisional Headquarters where he was locked up. I took possession of the VCR.

I can identify Jarvie.

DC Watson gave a similar precognition.

Mr Seymour decided that he did not require to interview Mr Todd. He wrote to Mr Jarvie asking him to make an appointment to see him as soon as possible, and in due course an appointment was made for 9 August.

At that meeting Mr Seymour went over with Mr Jarvie the statements which he had taken from the police officers and told him that the prosecution had a strong case against him.

'You were in possession of this VCR fairly soon after it had been stolen, and the fact that it was under the bed may be sufficient in the way of suspicious circumstances to raise a presumption that you stole it.'

'I've told you already that I know nothing about the break-in. I was in Edinburgh all that day.'

Mr Seymour asked for the name and address of the friend in Edinburgh whom Mr Jarvie had been visiting, and was given the name Stewart Green of 65 Niddrie Mains Road. Mr Jarvie was certain that Mr Green would be willing to give evidence on his behalf.

Having discussed the case further, Mr Seymour prepared a precognition for Mr Jarvie as follows:

Precognition of Nicol Jarvie

I am Nicol Jarvie. I live at 10B Duncry Close, Duncairn. I am 26 years old. I am unemployed.

I know nothing about the housebreaking at 56 Consitution Street, Duncairn on 3 June 1989.

On 2 June 1989 I travelled to Edinburgh by bus to visit my friend, Stewart Green, 65 Niddrie Mains Road. I arrived in Edinburgh about 7 pm and went immediately to Stewart's house. We both then went out for a drink. We started off in a pub and ended up at a party somewhere. I don't know the address. We got back to Stewart's house about 1 am. The next morning we did not get up until 10. Stewart and I had something to eat and then went out for a drink and to the bookie's. We were in the pub until about 4 pm. I then caught the bus back to Duncairn.

When I got back to Duncairn I went to my local, the Rowan Tree. I got there about 9 pm. I got talking to a guy I'd never met before. He told me he had a VCR to sell. He was needing money badly. My own VCR had been playing up a bit so I was interested in this one. I asked him if it was legit and he said it was. He asked for £120, and I said that I'd give him £100. I'd been lucky on the horses that afternoon, so I had the money. He agreed to accept £100. We then went outside to a van. The VCR was in the back of the van. I took it and gave him the £100. He then drove off in the van. I haven't seen him since.

I can't really describe the guy. He was quite ordinary looking, aged about 35. The van was green, I think. I don't remember what make it was.

I took the VCR home and put it under my bed. My old one seemed to be working OK, so I really didn't give it a thought until the police came round. I agree that I told the police that I'd bought it from a guy in a pub and that it was a spare in case my other one packed up.

I had no idea the VCR was stolen. If I had, I would not have touched it. I have been trying to go straight since I got out of jail in February.

Mr Seymour reminded Mr Jarvie that he had to be in court for the intermediate diet on 1 September and said that he would write to Mr Green in order to ask him for a statement. He did so, but had received no reply by 1 September.

Meanwhile Mr Seymour had written to Miss Stuart intimating that there was to be a defence of alibi, and that there would be one defence witness, whose name and address he gave. He had also spoken on the telephone with Miss Stuart, who gave him a brief summary of the evidence which Mr Todd (the owner of the VCR) was expected to give in court.

On 1 September Mr Jarvie was in court when his case was called.

CLERK OF COURT: Intermediate diet. Nicol Jarvie. Are you Nicol Jarvie?

ACCUSED: Yes.

MR SEYMOUR: My lord, I appear for Mr Jarvie. He adheres to his plea of not guilty. The case is fully prepared with the exception of a statement from one witness. As I have already informed my friend's colleague, Miss Stuart, I can at this stage indicate that my client will be pleading an alibi. He maintains that from about 7 pm on 2 June until about 4 pm on 3 June he was in Edinburgh and that from about 4 pm until 8 pm he was on a bus between Edinburgh and Duncairn. A witness, Stewart Green of 65 Niddrie Mains Road, Edinburgh, will be called to prove the alibi. I move your lordship to continue bail.

SHERIFF LAWSON: Thank you Mr Seymour. (*Addressing Kenneth Patrick, the procurator fiscal depute*) Mr Patrick, I assume that you wish the case to be continued to the trial diet.

PROCURATOR FISCAL DEPUTE: Indeed, my lord. That is on 6 October.

SHERIFF: Very well.
CLERK OF COURT: Case continued to the trial diet on 6 October at 10 am.
  Bail continued.

After leaving court Mr Seymour spoke to Mr Jarvie and told him he had not
heard from Mr Green. Mr Jarvie said that Green was not very good at
answering letters, but that he (Jarvie) had spoken to him on the telephone and
he had confirmed that he would be willing to attend as a witness. Mr
Seymour said that he would issue him with a citation to attend and would
have an interview with him before the trial started.

THE PROCURATOR FISCAL, DUNCAIRN V NICOL JARVIE: TRIAL, VERDICT AND SENTENCE

On 6 October at 10 am the 'call over' of cases set down for summary trial that
day took place before Sheriff Walter Scott. There were eight all together as
well as three intermediate diets. Of the eight cases for trial four pleaded guilty
and were disposed of. In two others the accused had failed to turn up, so the
Crown moved for a warrant to apprehend. In the case of Mr Jarvie and one
other case the pleas of not guilty were adhered to. The other trial proceeded
first, which was a great relief to Mr Seymour as he had not yet had an
opportunity to interview Mr Green, although the latter *had* appeared in
response to his citation.

While the other trial was proceeding Mr Seymour spoke to Mr Green and
obtained a brief statement from him. This confirmed what Mr Jarvie had said
about the time of his arrival in and departure from Edinburgh, although Mr
Green was somewhat vague about what had happened during the period in
between.

Mr Seymour had already prepared a 'list of defence witnesses' as a courtesy
for the court, and he now gave four copies of this list to the court officer, so
that he, the sheriff, the fiscal and the clerk could each have one. The 'list'
contained only the one name, that of Mr Green.

At noon the other trial finished and Mr Jarvie went into the dock. The
Crown was represented by Susan Stuart, the depute fiscal who had originally
dealt with the case (although this was purely coincidental), and Mr Jarvie
was, of course, represented by Mr Seymour. The clerk of court was Mr
Harrison. The trial proceeded as follows:

CLERK: Trial of Nicol Jarvie. Are you Nicol Jarvie?
ACCUSED: Yes.
SOLICITOR: My lord, my client adheres to his plea of not guilty. I would
  remind your lordship that, at the intermediate diet, I gave notice of a
  special defence of alibi. (*Mr Seymour repeated the terms of the alibi.*)
PFD: My lord, my first witness is Mr James Todd.

JAMES THOMSON TODD (SWORN)
EXAMINED BY THE PROCURATOR FISCAL DEPUTE: Is your full
  name James Thomson Todd, do you live at 56 Constitution Street,
  Duncairn, and are you 45 years of age?—I'm now 46, but my name and
  address are correct.
  What sort of house is it that you live in?—It's a second floor flat.

Can the door from the street be locked?—No.

On Saturday 3 June this year did you leave your house in the morning about 11 o'clock?—I did.

Did you lock the door to your flat?—Yes. It was a Yale lock.

What time did you return to your flat?—About 5 pm.

What state was it in?—The front door was open. The lock had been burst. The house itself was OK except that my new video was missing.

What did you do?—I phoned for the police.

When the police came did you give them this document, Production 1? (*The witness was shown the receipt for the VCR.*)—Yes. That's the receipt for the video. I had bought it just about a week earlier.

Is there a serial number shown on the receipt?—Yes. It's 08577.

Now please look at Label No 1. Do you recognise that? (*The witness was shown the VCR*)—Yes. That's my video.

Can you find the serial number on it?—Yes, it's on the side here. It's the same as in the receipt.

How much did you pay for the VCR?—£430.

NO CROSS-EXAMINATION

JOHN TURNBULL REID (SWORN)
EXAMINED BY THE PROCURATOR FISCAL DEPUTE: Are you John Turnbull Reid, a detective constable of Grampian Police?—Yes.

What are your age and length of service?—29 years old and ten years' police service.

In the evening of Saturday 3 June this year were you instructed to attend at a flat at 56 Constitution Street, Duncairn in connection with an alleged theft by housebreaking?—I was.

What time did you get there?—About 7 pm.

What did you find?—The front door of the flat had clearly been forced. The Yale lock was broken. The jamb had been torn away from the woodwork. I saw the householder, Mr Todd, who informed me that a VCR was missing. He gave me the receipt for it.

Please look at Production 1. Is that the receipt?—Yes.

Did you arrange for a search to be made for fingerprints?—Yes. It proved negative.

What was your next involvement with the case?—I received certain information as a result of which I obtained a search warrant for the flat at 10B Duncry Close. That was on 8 June. I went there about 6 pm.

Please look at Production 2. Is that the search warrant?—It is.

Was anyone with you?—Yes, my colleague, DC Watson. He had also been with me at the flat on the 3rd.

What happened when you went to Duncry Close?—We knocked at the door, and it was opened by the accused.

When you say 'the accused', is that someone who is in court?—Yes. That's him there. (*The witness pointed at the accused.*)

What happened then?—I showed him the search warrant, and he let us in. We then searched the flat.

Did you find anything of significance?—Yes. Under the bed in the bedroom we found a VCR with the same serial number as was on the receipt.

Please look at Label 1. Is that the VCR you found?—Yes.

Was there any other VCR in the flat?—Yes. There was one attached to the television in the living room.

What did you do when you found the VCR under the bed?—I cautioned the accused and asked him if he could account for it being there.

Did he say anything?—May I be allowed to refer to my notebook?

Did you make the note at the time?—Yes.

SHERIFF: Mr Seymour, have you any objection?

MR SEYMOUR: No, my lord.

SHERIFF: Please do consult your book.

THE WITNESS: The accused said: 'It's just a spare in case my other one packs up.' I then asked him where he had got it, and he said: 'I bought it from a guy in a pub.' He refused to say anything more.

What happened then?—I cautioned and charged the accused, and he made no reply. I then arrested him and took him to police headquarters.

CROSS-EXAMINED BY MR SEYMOUR: Was Mr Jarvie obstructive in any way?—Oh no. Not at all.

Was the VCR concealed?—Well, it was right under the bed. You couldn't see it without either getting down on the floor or moving the bed.

Did you test the other VCR, the one attached to the TV?—No.

So far as you know, it may have been on its last legs?—I suppose so, but it looked fairly new and, if it wasn't working properly, I don't understand why it was still attached to the TV and the other one was under the bed.

Is it the case that, apart from finding the VCR in his flat, you found no other evidence to connect my client with this crime?—That's correct.

There is no suggestion that he was seen hanging around the locus on the 3rd?—No, sir.

DC Watson was then called to give evidence, and his examination in chief and cross-examination proceeded in virtually the same way as that of DC Reid. At the conclusion of DC Watson's evidence Miss Stuart closed the Crown's case.

MR SEYMOUR: My lord, I have a submission to make in terms of section 345A of the 1975 Act. In my submission there is no case to answer in respect that there is insufficient evidence in law to prove that my client committed the crime charged or any other crime of which he could competently be found guilty on this charge. The only evidence implicating him is that the stolen VCR was found in his flat. No doubt my friend will seek to found on the doctrine of recent possession, but, in my submission, while the property may indeed have been recently stolen, there is nothing in the way of criminative circumstances surrounding my client's possession, and, as your lordship is well aware, the existence of such circumstances is essential before the doctrine can be prayed in aid.

SHERIFF: What about the fact that the VCR was found under a bed? Is that not suspicious?

MR SEYMOUR: In my submission, no. That is neutral. I don't think that I can usefully add anything to what I have said.

PFD: My lord, in my submission there are criminative circumstances here. There is, as your lordship has said, the fact that the VCR was found under a bed. That is surely an unusual place to keep such an object. There is also the fact that there was another VCR in the house, apparently being used normally as it was attached to the TV. I think that I am also entitled to found on the explanation given by the accused as to how he came into possession of it. Buying from a man in a pub is just about as hackneyed an excuse as saying it fell off the back of a lorry. Certainly, I submit that the three factors taken together are more than ample to provide criminative circumstances, which, together with the possession, raise a presumption of guilt. It is, of course, open to the accused to rebut that presumption.

MR SEYMOUR: I have nothing to add.

SHERIFF: In my opinion there is a case to answer here. I agree that the place where the VCR was found together with the fact that there was another VCR apparently in use in the house amount to criminative circumstances. I have reservations about founding on the explanation given by the accused as to how it came into his possession, but there is enough without that. I reject the defence submission. Mr Seymour, do you wish to lead evidence?

MR SEYMOUR: Yes, my lord. Might I suggest that, that as it is now 12.50, your lordship hears the defence case after lunch?

SHERIFF: Certainly. I shall adjourn until two o'clock.

When the court resumed after lunch Mr Seymour called Mr Jarvie to give evidence.

NICOL JARVIE (SWORN)

EXAMINED BY MR SEYMOUR: Is your full name Nicol Jarvie, do you live at 10B Duncry Close, Duncairn, and are you 26 years old?—Yes, sir.

Mr Jarvie, where were you on Saturday, 3 June this year?—I was in Edinburgh until about four. I had gone there the night before. I didn't get back to Duncairn until about eight.

Where were you staying in Edinburgh?—With my friend, Stewart Green. He lives in Niddrie.

Were you with him the whole time you were in Edinburgh?—Yes. We went to a pub and then a party the night I got there. We went to the pub again at dinner time on the Saturday and stayed there until I left apart from going to the bookie's next door.

What time did you leave Edinburgh?—My bus was about 4.15.

What time did you get back to Duncairn?—About 8.30.

What did you do when you got back to Duncairn?—I went home and then went out to the Rowan Tree. That's my local.

What happened there?—A man spoke to me and asked me if I wanted to buy a video. I was interested because mine wasn't working very well. He wanted £120, but I offered him £100 and he accepted. He had the video in his van. We went out and I collected it and took it home.

Do you know this man's name?—No.

Had you seen him before?—No, I don't think so.

Have you seen him since?—No.

How did you come to have £100 on you?—I'd had a bit of luck with the horses that afternoon in Edinburgh.

Why did you put the VCR under the bed?—I didn't want it to be too obvious in case anybody saw it and decided to pinch it. I found that my old one was still working OK.

Did you have no suspicion about being offered the VCR in a pub by a stranger?—Oh no. People often buy and sell things in that pub. I asked the guy if it was legit, and he assured me it was. The only reason he was selling it was that he was hard up.

CROSS-EXAMINED BY THE PROCURATOR FISCAL DEPUTE: What did you do in Edinburgh on the Friday night?—We went to a pub and then to a party.

Which pub?—I don't know.

Where was the party?—I don't know. I don't know Edinburgh that well.

When did you get back to your friend's house?—About one.

What time did you get up the next day?—About ten.

What was the name of the pub you went to on the Saturday?—I can't remember.

Was it the same one as the night before?—No.

Which betting shop did you go to?—William Hill.

What horses did you back that day?—I don't remember.

What sort of bet was it?—A three horse accumulator.

What did you put on?—About a fiver.

How much did you win?—I can't remember exactly, but it was about £150.

Are you surprised to hear that the VCR had been bought only a week previously for £430?—I don't really know the value of these things.

If that was the price, then you were getting it very cheaply paying only £100, weren't you?—I suppose so.

How much did you pay for your own VCR?—I don't remember. I think it was about a couple of hundred quid.

And you weren't at all suspicious?—No.

Aren't you just making all this up?—No.

Isn't it the case that you came into possession of that VCR by breaking into Mr Todd's flat and stealing it?—No. As God's my witness I was in Edinburgh that day.

Or, if you didn't steal it, didn't you get it from the thief knowing very well that it was stolen?—I had no idea it was stolen. If I had, I wouldn't have touched it.

Miss Stuart sat down pretty well satisfied with her cross-examination. She felt that, by concentrating on the details of the alleged alibi, she had exposed Mr Jarvie's rather patchy knowledge of what he had been supposed to be doing in Edinburgh. Mr Seymour did not re-examine. He also realised that Miss Stuart's cross had been effective, and he had no desire to get Mr Jarvie into deeper trouble.

STEWART GREEN (SWORN)

EXAMINED BY MR SEYMOUR: Is your full name Stewart Green, do you live at 65 Niddrie Mains Road, Edinburgh, and are you 27 years old?—Yes.

Do you have a job?—I'm a dealer.

Do you know Mr Jarvie, who is sitting there? (*Indicating the dock*)—Yes.

How long have you known him?—About five years.

Does he ever come to visit you in Edinburgh?—Yes. Quite often.

Please take your mind back to a Friday at the beginning of June this year. Did Mr Jarvie come to see you then?—Yes. He came to my house about quarter past seven.

What did you do then?—We went out to the pub and then on to a party.

What time did you get home?—About five o'clock.

What did you do the next day?—We got up about twelve, had something to eat and went out to the pub.

Did you go anywhere else apart from the pub?—Yes. The bookie's.

What time did Mr Jarvie leave to go home?—About four.

CROSS-EXAMINED BY THE PROCURATOR FISCAL DEPUTE:

What pub did you go to on the Friday night?—The Edinburgh Arms.

What pub did you go to on the Saturday?—The same one. It's my local.

What bookie did you go to?—Harrower's.

Did Mr Jarvie have a bet?—Yes. He won some money.

How much?—About £25 I think.

What sort of bet did he have?—I think it was a double.

Are you sure you're remembering the right weekend?—Yes.

Are you an honest man?—I think so.

Have you been convicted of perjury?—Yes, but that was a long time ago. I told a lie in court because I was scared of getting beaten up.

Aren't you telling lies now in order to protect your friend?—No. I'm telling the truth. He was with me that weekend.

What sort of dealer are you, Mr Green?—General dealer.

Do you ever deal in video cassette recorders?—Sometimes.

RE-EXAMINED BY MR SEYMOUR: When were you convicted of perjury?—When I was sixteen.

What was the sentence?—I had sentence deferred for a year for good behaviour, and then I was admonished.

MR SEYMOUR: My lord, that is the case for the defence.

PFD: My lord, in my submission there is sufficient evidence here for your lordship to infer that the accused is guilty as libelled. I found on the doctrine of recent possession. Your lordship has already held that there is enough evidence for that doctrine to operate. In my submission the accused's explanation of his possession should be rejected as utterly incredible. I would remind your lordship of the discrepancies between the evidence of the accused and that of his witness. They differed as to times, names of places and the nature of bets. I suggest that the whole alibi is simply concocted. It is not without significance, perhaps, that Mr Green is a dealer who deals occasionally in VCRs. I invite your lordship to find the charge proved. At the very least, if your lordship is not satisfied that there is sufficient evidence of the accused's involvement in the actual theft, I submit that your lordship must find him guilty of reset of the VCR, which your lordship is aware is a competent verdict on a charge of theft. I would press, however, for a verdict of guilty as libelled.

SHERIFF: Thank you Miss Stuart. Mr Seymour.

MR SEYMOUR: My lord, in my submission you should accept my client and Mr Green as witnesses worthy of credit. It is true that there were discrepancies between them, but does this not demonstrate that they have not put their heads together to concoct a story? Had they done so, surely they would have made a better job of it. I suggest that your lordship should have no difficulty in accepting that my client could not have committed the housebreaking as he was in Edinburgh at the time. So far as the circumstances of his coming into possession of the VCR are concerned, again surely he would have made up a better story if he had been trying to manufacture one. It may seem strange for him to buy a VCR in a pub, but, as your lordship knows, strange things do happen. And if he paid £100 for it, that is still a substantial amount of money. If he had said that he paid only £10, then that really would have been incredible. On the whole matter I urge your lordship to find my client not guilty or, at the very least, to find the charge not proven.

SHERIFF (*after a few minutes consideration*): I accept that there are cases where discrepancies between the evidence of witnesses reinforces credibility, but that is when the discrepancies are relatively few and of a minor character. In the present case the discrepancies between the accused and Mr Green are so numerous that I cannot accept their evidence as credible. I accordingly reject the alibi. Equally, I have found unworthy of belief the accused's evidence of how he came into possession of the VCR. I accordingly reject that evidence also. This means that the accused has completely failed to rebut the presumption of guilt created by his possession of the recently stolen VCR in criminative circumstances. Although there may be nothing else to connect him with the actual housebreaking, I am entitled under the doctrine of recent possession to find him guilty of the crime charged. I have rejected his alibi as false, and this reinforces my view that I should find him guilty as libelled, which I now do.

PFD: My lord I produce a schedule of previous convictions.

MR SEYMOUR: These are admitted. I must accept, my lord, that my client has a bad record for dishonesty. However, he has kept out of trouble, apart from the present offence, since his release from prison in February.

SHERIFF: That's not very long, Mr Seymour.

MR SEYMOUR: Not perhaps for you or me, my lord, but quite long for my client. I would remind your lordship that, contrary to what happens all too often in housebreaking cases, there was no suggestion here of the house being ransacked or vandalised. My client is unfortunately unemployed. He is single and has no dependants. He receives benefit of £55 per fortnight. His rent is paid direct. He has the usual household expenses. I appreciate that a custodial sentence must be a possibility, but I would strongly urge your lordship to consider a financial penalty or, alternatively, to ask for a community service report.

SHERIFF (*after some consideration*): Stand up please, Mr Jarvie. You have been found guilty of a serious crime. You have previous convictions for dishonesty. In my opinion a fine would be an unrealistic disposal. Given your limited resources, you could not pay a fine of any substantial amount. In any event, with your record and the gravity of the offence, a fine would be quite inappropriate. You have already had community service not that long ago, and it is relatively unusual for someone to receive a second chance of community service, given that it is the last resort before custody. I'm afraid that I can see no alternative to a sentence of imprisonment. Looking to your record and the gravity of the crime, I should be perfectly justified in imposing a sentence of six months. I am perhaps being unduly lenient when I restrict it to a period of four months.

Chapter 3

From Crime to Court

INTRODUCTION

The investigation of crime in Scotland is carried out by the police. The public prosecution of crime is the responsibility of the Lord Advocate, who acts, at the local level, through the procurator fiscal service. In theory the police act on the instructions of the procurator fiscal in investigating crime[1], but, nowadays it is relatively rare for the fiscal to be personally concerned in the investigation of a case except for such serious crimes as murder.

The first part of this chapter is concerned with the powers which the police have to question, detain, arrest and search, all or any of which may be a preliminary to an accused person's appearing before a court. It should, however, be remembered that the great majority of criminal cases are summary prosecutions where the accused is simply cited to attend court without having been detained or arrested, and where there has been no search carried out. A person may be cited without ever having been charged, although the majority of those cited will have been charged. Citation will be described below in the chapter dealing with summary prosecution (chapter 6). The second part of this chapter is concerned with the role of the solicitor prior to a case actually coming to court.

PART 1: THE POLICE INVOLVEMENT

Questioning by the police

The police have a right to ask questions of any person whom they believe to be a witness to a crime[2]. If police inquiries are only at the stage of investigation, and suspicion has not focussed on any person, the police do not require to administer any form of caution to a person questioned by them. While it is the moral duty of a citizen to assist the police, a person is under no legal obligation to answer questions apart from the obligation of a potential witness to give his name and address[3].

Once suspicion has focussed on a particular person he will probably be

---

1 See *Smith v HMA* 1952 JC 66 at 71, 1952 SLT 286 at 288, per Lord Justice-Clerk Thomson.
2 *Bell v HMA* 1945 JC 61, 1945 SLT 204: *Chalmers v HMA* 1954 JC 66, 1954 SLT 177; *Thompson v HMA* 1968 JC 61, 1968 SLT 339.
3 1980 Act, s 1(1)(b). See below at pp 80, 81.

detained under s 2 of the Criminal Justice (Scotland) Act 1980 (for which see the next section of this chapter), but it is possible that a suspect may be questioned without having been detained. In any event, the common law rules about the admissibility in evidence of answers to questions apply equally whether or not the suspect has been detained[1]. These rules will therefore be examined now.

It used to be thought, on the basis of *Chalmers v HMA*, that the law made inadmissible any answers given by a suspect to police questioning[2]. If that was indeed ever the law, it is clear that it is no longer so. Recent cases have emphasised that the only test of admissibility is 'fairness', by which is meant both fairness to the accused person and fairness to the interests of the public[3]. A statement made in answer to a question will be admissible if it was fairly obtained. Whether questioning has been fair in any particular case depends on its own facts. Factors which, it has been suggested, may be relevant, are: the age of the suspect[4]; his mental capacity[5]; his physical state[5]; the length of time during which he has been in a police station[6]; whether or not he has been cautioned[7]; and, the nature of the questioning[8]. The fact that the person asked questions *is* a suspect is only one other factor to be taken into account in assessing fairness[9]. Although all these factors may have to be considered, it can probably reasonably be said that, nowadays, there is a presumption in favour of the admissibility of a suspect's answers to questioning. Evidence of answers to questions will be excluded only if the police have clearly indulged in intimidation, threats, inducement or cross-examination[10]. As we shall see when the procedure in a jury trial is examined, the law now favours the jury being the arbiter of what is fair or unfair and not the judge[11].

A person who is to be charged should always be cautioned to the effect that he is not obliged to say anything in answer to the charge, but that anything he does say will be noted and may be used in evidence. An answer to the charge made following upon such a caution is normally admissible in evidence.

Once a suspect has been charged he should not be further questioned by the police, and answers given to questioning at that stage are inadmissible in evidence[12]. However, anything said by an accused person which is truly voluntary is admissible[12]. If an accused indicates that he wishes to make a voluntary statement, it is accepted practice that the statement should be noted by an officer who is unconnected with the case[13]. The statement should be

---

1 1980 Act, s 2(5)(a).
2 *Chalmers v HMA* 1954 JC 66, 1954 SLT 177.
3 *Miln v Cullen* 1967 JC 21, 1967 SLT 35; *Hartley v HMA* 1979 SLT 26.
4 *Chalmers v HMA* 1954 JC 66, 1954 SLT 177.
5 *Hartley v HMA* 1979 SLT 26; *HMA v Gilgannon* 1983 SCCR 10.
6 *Hartley v HMA* 1979 SLT 26; *HMA v Gilgannon* 1983 SCCR 10; *Thompson v HMA* 1968 JC 61, 1968 SLT 339.
7 *Tonge v HMA* 1982 JC 130, 1982 SCCR 213, 1982 SLT 506; *Wilson v Heywood* 1989 SCCR 19.
8 *Lord Advocate's Reference No 1 of 1983* 1984 JC 52, 1984 SCCR 62, 1984 SLT 337; *HMA v Mair* 1982 SLT 471.
9 *Miln v Cullen* 1967 JC 21, 1967 SLT 35; *Tonge v HMA* 1982 JC 130, 1982 SCCR 213, 1982 SLT 506.
10 *Lord Advocate's Reference No 1 of 1983* 1984 JC 52, 1984 SCCR 62, 1984 SLT 337: *HMA v Mair* 1982 SLT 471 is a relatively rare recent example of answers being held to be inadmissible on the ground that the questioning by the police was improper.
11 See below at p 144.
12 *Stark and Smith v HMA* 1938 JC 170, 1938 SLT 516; and see below at p 84.
13 *Tonge v HMA* 1982 JC 130 at 147, 1982 SCCR 313 at 350, 1982 SLT 506 at 517, per Lord Cameron.

written out by the officer, read over to or by the accused, and then signed by him and by the officer.

Detention under section 2 of the Criminal Justice (Scotland) Act 1980

Until the coming into force of s 2 of the Criminal Justice (Scotland) Act 1980 on 1 June 1981 a police officer had generally no legal right to detain a person suspected of committing a crime unless he had arrested him, although a person who was asked to 'assist the police with their inquires' may very well have been unaware of this fact. Section 2 gives a constable[1] limited powers of detention where he has 'reasonable grounds for suspecting that a person has committed or is committing an offence punishable by imprisonment'[2]. Having detained the person the constable must take him 'as quickly as is reasonably practicable to a police station or other premises'[3].

Detention is for a maximum period of six hours and must conclude at the end of that period or (if earlier) when the detainee is either arrested, or detained in pursuance of some other enactment or subordinate instrument, or where the constable no longer has grounds for suspecting that he has committed or is committing an offence punishable by imprisonment[4]. The detainee must be informed that his detention has been terminated immediately that in fact happens[4]. If a person is in fact detained for more than six hours, that does not invalidate anything lawfully done during the six hour period[5].

Once a person has been released from detention under s 2 he may not again be detained on the same grounds or grounds arising out of the same circumstances[6]. Similarly, if a person has been detained under some other enactment or subordinate instrument, he may not be detained under s 2 on the same grounds or on grounds arising from the same circumstances as those which led to his earlier detention[7].

When a person is detained under s 2 the detaining officer must inform him of his suspicion, of the general nature of the offence of which he is suspected and of the reason for his detention[8].

Certain matters must be recorded. These are: (a) the place where detention begins and the police station or other premises to which the detainee is taken; (b) the general nature of the suspected offence; (c) the time when detention begins and the time of arrival at the police station or other premises; (d) the time when the detainee is informed of his right to refuse to answer questions and to request (under s 3(1)(b) of the Act) intimation of his detention to be given to a solicitor and another person; (e) the time when such request is (i)

---

1 'Constable' means any police officer up to and including a chief constable: Police (Scotland) Act 1967, ss 3(1), 51(1), as applied by the 1980 Act, s 81(1).
2 1980 Act, s 2(1). For an example of 'reasonable grounds for suspicion', see *Wilson v Robertson* 1986 SCCR 700.
3 1980 Act, s 2(1).
4 1980 Act, s 2(2).
5 *Grant v HMA* 1989 SCCR 618, 1990 SLT 402.
6 1980 Act, s 2(3).
7 1980 Act, s 2(3A).
8 1980 Act, s 2(4).

made and (ii) complied with; (f) the time of his departure from the police station or other premises, or, if appropriate, of his arrest[1]. The Act contains no provisions as to how these matters should be recorded. In practice police forces have forms which are used[2], but it has been held that entries in police notebooks are sufficient[3]. In the same case the High Court specifically reserved its opinion on what the legal effect would be of a failure to record.

A constable may ask a detainee questions relating to the suspected offence, but the general rules of admissibility of evidence apply to any answers given[4]. In the case of serious crime a tape recorder is now normally used to record the interrogation of a person who has been detained (as in the case of *David Balfour*). The type of recorder used includes a time injection system and provides for two copies of the tape of the interview. The recording is therefore virtually immune from being tampered with. A transcript of a recording of an interview between an accused person and a police officer, if appropriately certified by the transcriber, is sufficient evidence of the making of the transcript and of its accuracy, provided that it has been served on the accused not later than fourteen days prior to the trial and he has not challenged its accuracy[5]. If the accuracy of the transcript is disputed, the jury may listen to the tape being played. Even if the accuracy of the transcript is not in question, it may be to the advantage of the defence to insist on the tape being played in order that the jury may hear how police actually asked the questions and how the accused answered them. A tape recorder is commonly listed as a Crown production and produced in court, so that it may be used for playing the tape.

Although a constable is empowered to ask questions of a detainee, the latter has the right not to answer any question other than to give his name and address. The constable must inform him of this right both on detaining him and on arrival at the police station or other premises[6]. If the detainee *is* to be questioned, it is not sufficient simply to advise him of this right. He should also be given the normal common law caution, ie that he is not obliged to answer any question, and that, if he does so, his answer will be noted down and may be used in evidence[7].

A detainee is subject to the same powers of search as he would be if he had been arrested[8]. Although it is not specifically stated, this almost certainly means search of the individual rather than search of premises. It is an open question whether the right to search includes a right to put the detainee on an identification parade[9]. In any case where an identification parade is held, the

---

1 1980 Act, s 2(4).
2 See the case of *David Balfour* at pp 2, 3.
3 *Cummings v HMA* 1982 SCCR 108, 1982 SLT 487.
4 1980 Act, s 2(5)(a). For the general rules of admissibility in evidence of answers to police questions see the first section of this chapter.
5 1987 Act, s 60.
6 1980 Act, s 2(7).
7 *Tonge v HMA* 1982 JC 130, 1982 SCCR 213, 1982 SLT 506.
8 1980 Act, s 2(5)(b). For powers to search on arrest see below at p 83.
9 RW Renton and HH Brown *Criminal Procedure according to the Law of Scotland* (5th edn, 1983) at para 5–30 consider that an identification parade is an extension of the right to search. CHW Gane and CN Stoddart *Criminal Procedure in Scotland: Cases and Materials* (1983) at pp 148–9 disagree, arguing that, if parading a suspect had been intended to follow detention, it would have been specifically provided for as is the taking of fingerprints. It is submitted that the latter view is to be preferred.

suspect (whether a detainee under s 2 or not) is entitled to have the legal aid duty solicitor attend on his behalf[1].

The detainee may have his fingerprints and palmprints taken and 'such other prints and impressions as the constable may, having regard to the circumstances of the suspected offence, reasonably consider appropriate'[2]. It is provided that the records of such prints and impressions must be destroyed immediately following a decision not to institute criminal proceedings or on the conclusion of such proceedings otherwise than on a finding of guilt[2]. However, there is no sanction provided for a failure to destroy the records.

A constable is entitled to use reasonable force in detaining a person and in searching him under s 2(5)(b) or obtaining prints or impressions under s 2(5)(c)[3].

Certain rights are given to the detainee under s 3 of the 1980 Act. If he is an adult (ie over sixteen years old), he is entitled to have intimation of his detention and of the place where he is being detained sent to a solicitor and one other person reasonably named by him[4]. The reference to reasonableness probably means that the police are not obliged to contact a person unless he is in the reasonably close vicinity of the police station. Such intimation must be made without delay or 'where some delay is necessary in the interest of the investigation or the prevention of crime or the apprehension of offenders, with no more delay than is so necessary'[4]. Although it is not explicitly stated, it seems to be clearly implied that it is the police officer responsible for the detention who is to be the judge of when delay is necessary. As has already been noted, the detainee must be informed of this entitlement on detention and on arrival at the police station or other premises[4].

There are also provisions in s 3 relating to the detention of a child (defined as a person under sixteen years of age)[5]. These will be discussed below in chapter 10.

The Prevention of Terrorism (Temporary Provisions) Act 1984 provides for what it calls 'detention' of suspected persons under s 12 or orders made under s 13, although 'detention' appears to be used here to mean custody following arrest. The 1980 Act provides[6] rules relating to intimation to solicitors and others in respect of arrest and detention under the 1984 Act, but the details of these are outwith the scope of a textbook such as this.

Detention under section 1 of the Criminal Justice (Scotland) Act 1980

Before we leave the subject of detention it should be noted that, under s 1 of the 1980 Act, there is conferred on a constable what might be described as a very limited right of detention, to enable identification of a suspect or witness to a crime. Section 1(1) empowers a constable to require a person to give his name and address if the constable has 'reasonable grounds for suspecting that

---

1 Legal Aid (Scotland) Act 1986, s 21(4)(b) and Criminal Legal Aid (Scotland) Regulations 1987, SI 1987/307, reg 5(1)(a).
2 1980 Act, s 2(5)(c).
3 1980 Act, s 2(6).
4 1980 Act, s 3(1)(b).
5 1980 Act, s 3(5).
6 1980 Act, ss 3A, 3B, 3C and 3D.

(he) has committed or is committing an offence"[1]. There is a similar power in respect of a potential witness to the offence[2]. The constable must explain to the suspect or witness the general nature of the offence[3]. In both cases the power may be exercised either at the locus of the offence or at any place where the constable is entitled to be. The constable may require a suspect to remain with him while he notes any explanation given by the suspect and/or until his name and address have been verified provided that this can be done quickly[4]. He may use reasonable force to ensure that the suspect remains with him[5], so to that extent may detain him. There is no power to 'detain' a potential witness. The suspect or the potential witness who fails without reasonable excuse to provide his name and address is guilty of an offence[6]. The provisions of s 1 (unlike those of s 2) are not confined to offences punishable by imprisonment.

Arrest

(a) General

A person is arrested when he is forcibly detained (using that word in a non-technical sense), which may or may not involve actual physical restraint. Arrest is, at least in legal theory, a more drastic step than detention. As has been described above, there is a strict time limit to detention under s 2 of the 1980 Act. A person who has been arrested must be brought before a court with due expedition, but there is no general statutory limit[7]. Arrest is generally considered to require more in the way of evidence against a suspect than detention, where only 'reasonable grounds for suspecting' are necessary, but it is common for a person merely to be detained where there is ample evidence to justify arrest.

(b) Arrest with warrant

A warrant to arrest is most commonly granted in respect of a crime which is likely to be tried under solemn procedure. The initiating writ in such a case is the petition (see the case of *David Balfour* at pp 7, 8). It runs in the name of the procurator fiscal, narrates the crime alleged to have been committed, and craves the court to grant a warrant to apprehend and, usually, also to search. The petition is almost invariably presented to a sheriff, although any magistrate having jurisdiction in the area where the crime was committed has

1 1980 Act, s 1(1)(a).
2 1980 Act, s 1(1)(b).
3 1980 Act, s 1(4).
4 1980 Act, s 1(2).
5 1980 Act, s 1(3).
6 1980 Act, s 1(5). The offence is punishable, in the case of a suspect, by a fine not exceeding level 3 on the standard scale, and, in the case of a potential witness, by a fine not exceeding level 2 on the standard scale.
7 Police (Scotland) Act 1967, s 17(1) provides that it is the duty of any police officer 'to take every precaution to ensure that any person charged with an offence is not unreasonably and unnecessarily detained in custody'. The 1975 Act, s 321(3) provides that a person arrested under a summary warrant in terms of the Act, at common law or under other statutory powers, must, where practicable, be brought before a competent court not later than the first day after arrest which is not a Saturday, Sunday or court holiday.

power to grant a warrant[1]. The sheriff usually grants the warrant without further inquiry as the procurator fiscal (or, more commonly, the depute fiscal dealing with the case) who has signed the petition is presumed to be acting responsibly and to have satisfied himself that there is sufficient evidence to justify arrest. If an accused person is arrested without a warrant (see below), a petition is presented to the sheriff as soon as possible, usually when the accused first appears before the sheriff. The warrant is then granted.

A warrant may also be granted in respect of a summary complaint, but this is relatively rare as most summary complaints proceed by way of citation of the accused. The Criminal Procedure (Scotland) Act 1975 provides that a judge of the court in which a complaint is brought (who may be a sheriff or a justice in the district court) has power, on the motion of the prosecutor, 'to grant warrant to apprehend the accused where this appears to the judge expedient'[2]. Typical situations where a warrant to apprehend might be granted in a summary prosecution are: where the accused's whereabouts are unknown; where the accused has failed to respond to citation; where the case would be time-barred if citation proceeded in the normal course; or where the accused is in custody in another jurisdiction.

(c) Arrest without warrant

Arrest without warrant has long been accepted as part of the common law of Scotland, although its scope and limitations are somewhat ill-defined. Contrary to the situation in England and Wales, offences in Scotland are not divided between 'arrestable' (ie those where arrest without warrant is permitted) and 'non-arrestable' or between felonies and misdemeanours. Arrest itself being a serious step, it might have been thought that arrest without warrant required especial justification and that the onus of proof would be on the arrester. However, it has recently been held in the Outer House of the Court of Session that the onus is on a person alleging unlawful arrest to prove that it was unreasonable and unnecessary[3].

A private citizen has a right to arrest without warrant if he witnesses a serious crime[4], but must hand the arrested person over to a police officer as soon as possible[5].

A constable may arrest without warrant where, for example, he has seen a crime committed or where the suspect is pointed out to him running from the locus. Other circumstances which may justify arrest without warrant are the gravity of the offence, the fact that the suspect is in hiding and about to abscond or if he is of no fixed abode[6]. If the suspect can simply be charged and then released for citation, or if there is no prejudice caused by the officer's waiting until a warrant to apprehend has been obtained, arrest is not justified[7].

---

1 Hume *Commentaries* II, 77; Alison *Practice of the Criminal Law of Scotland* p 121; JHA Macdonald *The Criminal Law of Scotland* (5th edn) p 198.
2 1975 Act, s 314(1)(b).
3 *Henderson v Moodie* 1988 SCLR 77, 1988 SLT 361, sub nom *Henderson v Chief Constable, Fife Police*.
4 *Hume* II, 76; Alison *Practice* p 119; *Macdonald* p 197. For recent examples of a case where the concept of arrest by a private citizen is discussed, see *Codona v Cardle* 1989 SCCR 287, 1989 SLT 791 and *Bryans v Guild* 1989 SCCR 569, 1990 SLT 426.
5 *McKenzie v Young* (1902) 10 SLT 231.
6 *Peggie v Clark* (1868) 7M 89.
7 *Leask v Burt* (1893) 21R 32; *Somerville v Sutherland* (1899) 2F 185, 7 SLT 239.

Arrest without warrant is in certain circumstances authorised in respect of a large number of statutory offences. Probably that most frequently encountered in practice is a contravention of the Road Traffic Act 1988, s 5 (where arrest is usually for the limited purpose of subjecting the suspect to a breath test or of obtaining a sample from him), but there are other offences under the Road Traffic Act and under such statutes as the Misuse of Drugs Act 1971 and the Civic Government (Scotland) Act 1982[1]. An arrest without warrant for a statutory offence is legal if the constable has reasonable grounds for belief that the offence has apparently been committed, provided that that conclusion is honestly reached[2].

(d) Procedures after arrest

As has already been noted, an arrested person should be brought before a court as soon as possible[3]. He may, pending his appearance in court, be detained in a police station house, police cell or other convenient place[4]. He has a right to have intimation of his arrest and whereabouts sent to a solicitor and to have a private interview with the solicitor prior to his appearance at judicial examination or in court; and he must be informed of these rights[5]. An arrested adult is also entitled to have intimation of his arrest and whereabouts sent to one other named person but that is subject to a proviso that such intimation may be delayed if delay is 'necessary in the interest of the investigation or the prevention of crime or the apprehension of offenders'[6]. The time of the making of the request for intimation and the time of compliance with it must be recorded[7]. It may be noted that there is no sanction against a failure to comply with any of these rights of intimation. No doubt the general rule of 'fairness' would be applied, and evidence following a failure to intimate would be admissible if it were considered by the court that it had not been unfairly obtained[8]. A person arrested on a charge of murder, attempted murder or culpable homicide has the right to call on the services of the duty solicitor under the legal aid scheme, and the duty solicitor must act for him until he is released on bail or fully committed[9].

At common law an arrested person may be searched by the police[10], and this can include physical examination[11] and the taking of fingerprints[12]. The corollary of these rights of the police after arrest is that such searches are

---

1 For a fuller, although not completely comprehensive, list see *Renton and Brown* para 5–23.
2 *McLeod v Shaw* 1981 SCCR 54, 1981 SLT (Notes) 93 – a case of an alleged offence under the Road Traffic Act 1972, s 5(2), ie being drunk in charge of a motor vehicle.
3 See p 81, note 7 above.
4 1975 Act, s 321(2), which applies to summary cases. Although there is no specific provison in the 1975 Act for cases on petition, the usual form of petition warrant provides for detention in a police station or other convenient place.
5 1975 Act, s 19 (petition case); s 305 (summary case). In a petition case judicial examination may be delayed for up to 48 hours after arrest to allow time for the attendance of a solicitor (s 19(3)).
6 1980 Act, s 3(1)(a). As has already been noted, the provision about delay applies also in the case of persons detained under s 2 – see p 80 above, note 4.
7 1980 Act, s 3(2).
8 Cf the comments on 'fairness' in connection with the admissibility of statements to the police at p 77 above. See also *Bell v Hogg* 1967 JC 49, 1967 SLT 290.
9 Criminal Legal Aid (Scotland) Regulations 1987, SI 1987/307, reg 5(1)(b).
10 *Jackson v Stevenson* (1897) 2 Adam 255, 24R(J) 38, 4 SLT 277.
11 *Forrester v HMA* 1952 JC 28, 1952 SLT 188.
12 *Adair v McGarry* 1933 JC 72, 1933 SLT 482.

usually unlawful before arrest, although an exception may be made in a case of emergency, in which case the test of 'fairness' will be applied[1].

An arrested person may not be interrogated by the police. Answers to questions asked by the police after arrest are not admissible in evidence[2]. However, an admission made by an arrested person to the police, if made voluntarily, is admissible in evidence. 'It is not the law that after a man has been cautioned and charged, there must be no contact whatever between him and police officers. What the law seeks to do is to protect the arrested person against unfair pressure and against the inducement to emit statements against his interest'[3].

(e) Release after arrest

An arrested person normally remains in custody until his appearance in court, but the police have powers, in the case of a charge which is likely to be tried summarily, to release following arrest. The person who is to be released may give an undertaking that he will attend a specified court on a given date[4]. Alternatively, he may be released without any undertaking[4], in which case he might be put on honour to attend a specified court at a specified time, but more probably would simply be cited to attend court in normal course. A person who has been released on undertaking and who fails to attend court is guilty of an offence[5].

If an 'undertaker' fails to appear in the specified court at the specified time the case will not call, and the court will almost certainly subsequently grant a warrant for his arrest so that the case will commence as a custody case.

Search

(a) General

As a general rule a person may not be searched (unless he has been detained or arrested) nor may premises be searched, unless a court has granted a warrant for that purpose. The same principles apply to both searches of persons and searches of premises.

(b) Search without warrant

Certain statutes[6] make provision for search of premises and persons without warrant. Such statutes usually provide that, before carrying out a search, the police officer concerned must have 'reasonable grounds for suspecting' that an offence under the statute is being or has been committed.

---

1 *Bell v Hogg* 1967 JC 49, 1967 SLT 290.
2 *Stark and Smith v HMA* 1938 JC 170, 1938 SLT 516; *Wade v Robertson* 1948 JC 117; 1948 SLT 491.
3 *Fraser and Freer v HMA* 1989 SCCR 82 at 91 per Lord Justice-General Emslie.
4 1975 Act, ss 294(2), 295(1).
5 1975 Act, ss 294(3), 295(2).
6 Eg Misuse of Drugs Act 1971, s 23(2) (illegal drugs); Civic Government (Scotland) Act 1982, s 60 (stolen property); Criminal Justice (Scotland) Act 1980, s 4(1) (offensive weapon). For a detailed examination see *Renton and Brown* paras 5–35 to 5–36b.

At common law search of premises (and of persons) without warrant may be justified on the ground of urgency[1].

(c) Search with warrant

At common law a search warrant may be granted by any magistrate (which includes a sheriff). Some statutes specify that only a sheriff may grant a warrant[2]. Under certain statutes a magistrate must take evidence on oath before he grants a search warrant[3].

A search warrant must be dated[4] and signed by the person granting it[5]. There is no need for anyone to have been charged or arrested before a search warrant can be granted[6]. All that is necessary is that the person applying for the warrant (usually the procurator fiscal) should have reasonable grounds for suspecting that a crime has been committed. The application for the warrant should state what the crime is and, if known, the name of the alleged perpetrator. It is competent for the procurator fiscal to apply for a search warrant to recover evidence relating to a statutory offence without anyone having been charged, unless the statute concerned excludes this expressly or by necessary implication[7]. When the warrant is to search premises it must adequately identify the premises, but this may be done by reference to a designation in the application for the warrant[8].

Where an ex facie valid warrant is founded upon as grounds for a search, a sheriff cannot review the granting of it, although the High Court has power to suspend an illegal search warrant[9]. Where, therefore, it is desired to challenge the validity of a search warrant in a trial in the sheriff court, whether solemn or summary, an application would have to be made to the High Court for that purpose.

As a general rule, once a person has been committed for trial under solemn procedure or had a trial diet fixed under summary procedure, the prosecutor cannot carry out any further search of the accused's person or of premises in connection with the crimes or offences charged. However, a warrant for further search will be granted in exceptional circumstances[10]. In such cases intimation of the application for the warrant should be made to the accused in

---

1 *HMA v McGuigan* 1936 JC 16, 1936 SLT 161; *Bell v Hogg* 1967 JC 49, 1967 SLT 290.
2 Eg Public Order Act 1936, s 2(5).
3 Eg Misuse of Drugs Act 1971, s 23(3).
4 *Bulloch v HMA* 1980 SLT (Notes) 5; *HMA v Welsh* 1987 SCCR 647, 1988 SLT 402.
5 *HMA v Bell* 1984 SCCR 430. It is probably not essential that the granter of the warrant be named or designed in it: *HMA v Strachan* 1990 SCCR 341 (Sh Ct).
6 *Stewart v Roach* 1950 SC 318, 1950 SLT 245.
7 *MacNeill Petr* 1984 JC 1, 1984 SCCR 450, 1984 SLT 157.
8 *Bell v HMA* 1988 SCCR 292, 1988 SLT 820.
9 *Allan v Tait* 1986 SCCR 175.
10 *HMA v Milford* 1973 SLT 12 (warrant granted after full committal to take blood sample in case of alleged rape); *Lees v Weston* 1989 SCCR 177, 1989 SLT 446 (warrant granted after full committal to take fingerprints in case of allegedly being concerned in the supply of Class A drugs); *Currie v McGlennan* 1989 SCCR 466, 1989 SLT 872 (warrant granted to hold an identification parade after full committal in a case of murder); cf *McGlennan v Kelly* 1989 SCCR 352, 1989 SLT 832, where, in a case of alleged rape, a warrant to obtain samples of pubic hair was refused partly because of the lapse of time between samples having previously been obtained and the presentation of the petition to obtain the further samples.

order that he may be heard on the matter. Failure to intimate may result in any evidence recovered being held to be inadmissible at the trial[1].

(d) Evidence obtained by irregular search

If evidence has been obtained irregularly, either without a warrant or by the officer exceeding the scope of the warrant, it may not necessarily be inadmissible. It is a question of circumstances in each individual case and of fairness. 'Whether any given irregularity ought to be excused depends upon the nature of the irregularity and the circumstances under which it was committed'[2]. If, in the course of a search under a warrant granted in respect of an offence, a suspicious article is found which appears to implicate the accused in a different offence, that article may be admissible in evidence at a trial for the latter offence. However, it will be admissible only provided that the search was not random[3].

(e) Intimate body searches

There are no reported cases in Scotland dealing with intimate body searches, but there seems to be no good reason why the general principles explained above should not apply to such searches. By analogy with the case of *Hay v Her Majesty's Advocate*[4] a warrant authorising the search should be obtained unless the matter is one of great urgency.

PART 2: THE SOLICITOR'S INVOLVEMENT

General

In most cases, whether under solemn or summary procedure, a solicitor is unlikely to become involved until after the case is in court. However, as we have already seen, a person who has been arrested has a right to have a solicitor informed of that fact and a right to have a private interview with the solicitor[5]. A person detained under s 2 of the 1980 Act has a right to have a solicitor informed of that fact[6], although he has no right to a private interview with the solicitor. In these cases the solicitor is under no obligation to attend on the accused or detainee or to act for him. A person charged with murder, attempted murder or culpable homicide has a right to call on the services of the duty solicitor under the legal aid scheme, and, in this case, the duty solicitor *must* act for him until he is released on bail or fully committed[7].

---

1 *Smith v Innes* 1984 SCCR 119 (Sh Ct) in which a warrant to take fingerprints was granted after a summary trial had been fixed. No intimation of the application for the warrant was made to the accused. Evidence obtained as a result of the warrant was held inadmissible by the sheriff at the trial. The Crown marked an appeal but did not proceed with it.
2 *Lawrie v Muir* 1950 JC 19 at 27, 1950 SLT 37 at 40 per Lord Justice-General Cooper. See also *MacNeil v HMA* 1986 SCCR 288 and *Innes v Jessop* 1989 SCCR 441, 1990 SLT 211.
3 *Tierney v Allan* 1989 SCCR 334, 1990 SLT 178; *Innes v Jessop* 1989 SCCR 441, 1990 SLT 211.
4 *Hay v HMA* 1968 JC 40, 1968 SLT 334, in which it was held competent to take impressions of a suspect's teeth, a warrant having been granted by a magistrate prior to arrest.
5 1975 Act, ss 19, 305.
6 1980 Act, s 3(1)(b).
7 Criminal Legal Aid (Scotland) Regulations 1987, SI 1987/307, reg 5(1)(b).

Another situation where the duty solicitor *must* become involved is where a person is to be placed on an identification parade. The duty solicitor must attend the parade on behalf of the suspect if called upon to do so by him[1]. A suspect may also have the solicitor of his choice attend an identification parade under the legal aid scheme[2].

The solicitor and the detainee

If a solicitor is told that a detained person has asked that he be informed of his detention and whereabouts, he may very well decide to attend at the police station or other premises where the detainee is being held. What should he do when he gets there?

As a general rule the solicitor should try to speak to the officer in charge of the case in order to find out from him as much as possible about it: what the alleged crime is and where, when and how it was perpetrated. He should find out if the detainee has said anything to the police, whether incriminating or exculpatory. He should inquire whether any real evidence incriminating his client has been found. How much information the solicitor will actually be given will depend on the attitude of the officer concerned. Many policemen are extremely reluctant to say more than they absolutely have to. Having obtained such information as he can, the solicitor should, if permitted to do so, interview his client.

The advice which the solicitor will give to his client will obviously depend on the circumstances. If the client confesses his guilt to the solicitor, the latter may very well advise him to make a full statement to the police. If the detainee denies guilt, the solicitor may wish to inquire whether there is any particular line of defence, eg alibi, incrimination or self defence. In the event that there is, he may again advise his client to make a full statement to the police. If the solicitor advises his client to make a statement, the advice should include a recommendation that the statement should, if possible, be tape-recorded. On the other hand, he may advise that, as he is fully entitled to do, the detainee should say nothing beyond giving his name and address.

The solicitor should ensure that his client is not detained for longer than permitted under s 2.

The solicitor and the client who has been charged

The above comments about what the solicitor should do on arrival at the police station apply equally in the case of a solicitor called to see someone who has been arrested and charged.

When a person has been charged, the police should, as we have seen, ask him no further questions[3]. However, it may still be in his interests, having received legal advice, to make a full statement to the police. If the solicitor advises him to do so, and that advice is accepted, the solicitor should inform the officer in charge of the case of his client's wish. He should request that an

---

1 Legal Aid (Scotland) Act 1986, s 21(4)(b), and Criminal Legal Aid (Scotland) Regulations 1987, SI 1987/307, reg 5(1)(a).
2 Legal Aid (Scotland) Act 1986, s 21(4)(b).
3 *Stark and Smith v HMA* 1938 JC 170, 1938 SLT 516.

officer who is not connected with the case note his client's statement[1], and that, if possible, the statement should be tape-recorded. There is no reason, in principle, why the solicitor should not be present when his client makes his statement. Unwillingness on the part of the police for the solicitor to be present or to have a statement tape-recorded may be a matter for adverse comment by the defence at a later stage.

The solicitor and the identification parade

If there is an eye-witness to a crime, the police may wish to hold an identification parade in order to see whether the witness is able to identify the suspect. The suspect is placed in a line with a number of other persons, and the parade is viewed by the witness. It is common nowadays for the parade to be viewed by means of a one-way screen, so that the suspect does not see the witness.

An arrested person may be placed on an identification parade[2]. He has no legal right to refuse, but, for obvious practical reasons, if he were unwilling, there would be little point in holding a parade. If an arrested person were to refuse, the police would be entitled to have him viewed by witnesses in circumstances which might very well be less favourable to him than those of an identification parade.

The function of the solicitor attending a parade on behalf of his client is to ensure that the parade is conducted fairly and that his client is not prejudiced, whether because of the composition of the parade or for any other reason. The solicitor is also present as an observer, and, in the event of any dispute about the conduct of the parade, he would be able to give evidence of what occurred. Legal representation is especially important if a one-way screen is used as then the witnesses cannot be seen by the suspect.

The Scottish Home and Health Department has laid down rules for the conduct of identification parades[3]. Although these rules have no statutory force, a failure to observe them would be a matter for comment by the defence, and might well render any identification made less valuable to the Crown case.

The solicitor attending a parade should check that those in the line-up are, so far as possible, similar in age and build to his client. He should ensure that his client is not wearing any particularly distinctive clothing. If his client has facial hair, he should request that as many of the stand-ins as possible are similarly adorned.

The solicitor should satisfy himself that a witness who has viewed the parade has no opportunity to communicate with a witness who has still to do so. He should note carefully what words, if any, are used by a witness who points out his client or any other person on the parade.

If the solicitor is in any way dissatisfied with the parade, he should inform the officer in charge of the parade of his dissatisfaction and should request that his comments be recorded in the report of the parade. He should, of course,

---

1 See p 77 note 13 above.

2 *Adair v McGarry* 1933 JC 72, 1933 SLT 482. In exceptional circumstances a warrant to hold an identification parade may be granted even after full committal: *Currie v McGlennan* 1989 SCCR 466, 1989 SLT 872.

3 The rules for the conduct of identification parades are conveniently set forth in *Gane and Stoddart* at pp 150–2.

make a note himself of such matters as well as keeping a full record of what happened at the parade.

Although strictly outwith the scope of this chapter as it would normally occur after an accused person has appeared in court, it is convenient here to note that an accused (in practice his solicitor) has a right to ask the sheriff to direct the prosecutor to hold an identification parade[1]. The sheriff has a discretion whether to grant the application and may do so only if (a) an identification parade has not already been held at the prosecutor's instance, and (b) the prosecutor has refused or unreasonably delayed holding a parade after being requested to do so by the accused[2]. Accordingly, the necessary preliminary to an application to the sheriff is a formal request to the fiscal that he hold a parade. In the only case under this section which has been reported to date[3] the sheriff held that an identification parade took place only when the accused was actually placed in a line-up, whether or not any witnesses actually attended. Two abortive attempts to hold parades which had been cancelled because witnesses refused to attend were therefore not parades within the meaning of the section.

1 1980 Act, s 10.
2 1980 Act, s 10(2).
3 *Wilson v Tudhope* 1985 SCCR 339 (Sh Ct).

Chapter 4

Solemn Procedure: Before the Trial

INTRODUCTION

Solemn procedure is the name given to the form of criminal procedure in which an accused, if he goes to trial, is tried before a jury. Other names for the procedure are 'petition procedure' and 'procedure on indictment'. These are used because the initiating writ in solemn procedure is a petition, and an indictment is the document containing the charge(s) on which the accused goes to trial. The case of *Her Majesty's Advocate v David Balfour* described in chapter 1 is an example of such procedure. The trial may take place in the High Court of Justiciary or in a sheriff court. The initial procedure is, however, identical, whichever court the accused is ultimately tried in. Solemn procedure is governed by Part I of the Criminal Procedure (Scotland) Act 1975. The other form of procedure, which involves trial without a jury, is called summary procedure. It is illustrated by the case of *Nicol Jarvie* described in chapter 2, and will be the subject of a later chapter.

In this chapter and the next we shall examine the progress of a solemn case from the time when the accused first appears before a sheriff to the conclusion of the trial when the jury returns its verdict. First, however, it is appropriate to discuss the composition, jurisdiction and powers of the two courts of solemn jurisdiction.

THE HIGH COURT OF JUSTICIARY

The High Court is both a court of first instance and a court of appeal. In this chapter we are concerned only with its original jurisdiction, ie as a court of trial.

The High Court can try any crime triable under solemn procedure, unless its jurisdiction is specifically excluded by statute. Its powers of punishment are unlimited, unless defined by statute.

The judges of the High Court (Lord Commissioners of Justiciary) are the same individuals as the judges of the Court of Session[1], headed by the Lord Justice-General (who is, in his civil capacity, Lord President of the Court of Session). For the purposes of a criminal trial a High Court judge will normally preside alone, but, in cases of difficulty or importance, it is competent for more than one judge to sit for part or the whole of a trial[2].

---

1 1975 Act, s 113(1).
2 1975 Act, s 113(4).

At the time of writing only members of the Faculty of Advocates have the right of audience in the High Court, although this may change if the Law Reform (Miscellaneous Provisions) (Scotland) Bill 1990 becomes law. The prosecution case is conducted by Crown Counsel (usually an advocate depute but, on occasions, one of the Crown Officers).

The High Court, as a court of first instance, may sit anywhere in Scotland[1].

Only in the High Court may cases of treason, murder, rape, deforcement of messengers and breach of duty of magistrates be tried[2]. The High Court also has exclusive jurisdiction in the case of certain statutory offences.

The territorial jurisdiction of the High Court extends throughout Scotland, and to its territorial waters (including ships in these waters). In cases of cross-border crimes (eg a fraud perpetrated in one country and taking effect in another) the High Court has jurisdiction if the 'main act' took place in Scotland[3].

In certain cases, both at common law and by statute, the High Court has jurisdiction over crimes committed outwith Scotland. The most important[4] of these are as follows:

(1) Piracy. This is a crime according to the law of nations (*jure gentium*). It is triable wherever the pirates are found[5].

(2) Treason. This may be tried in Scotland irrespective of where the treasonable acts were committed[6].

(3) 'Any British subject who in a country outside the United Kingdom does any act or makes any omission which if done or made in Scotland would constitute the crime of murder or culpable homicide shall be guilty of the same crime and subject to the same punishment as if the act or omission had been done or made in Scotland'[7]. Under this section a person may be proceeded against in any sheriff court district in which he is arrested or is in custody[8].

(4) 'Any British subject employed in the service of the Crown who, in a foreign country, when acting or purporting to act in the course of his employment, does any act or makes any omission which if done or made in Scotland would constitute an offence punishable on indictment shall be guilty of the same offence, and subject to the same punishment, as if the act or omission had been done or made in Scotland'[9]. Again the accused may be proceeded against in any sheriff court district in which he is arrested or is in custody[10].

(5) Crimes committed on British ships on the high seas irrespective of the nationality of the accused, and crimes committed by a British subject on a British ship in a foreign port[11].

---

1 1975 Act, ss 112, 114(1).
2 Hume *Commentaries* II, 58; Alison *Practice of the Criminal Law of Scotland* pp 20–30; JHA Macdonald *The Criminal Law of Scotland* (5th edn) p 193.
3 *Macdonald* p 192. In the case of *Laird v HMA* 1984 SCCR 469, 1985 SLT 298, the High Court appears to have gone further and held that it is sufficient for jurisdiction in Scotland in a fraud case that the initial fraudulent pretence was made in Scotland, even although the practical consequences occurred in England.
4 For an exhaustive list see RW Renton and HH Brown *Criminal Procedure according to the Law of Scotland* (5th edn, 1983) paras 1–08 to 1–22.
5 *Hume* II, 48; *Macdonald* p 192.
6 *Hume* II, 50.
7 1975 Act, s 6(1).
8 1975 Act, s 6(3).
9 1975 Act, s 6(2).
10 1975 Act, s 6(3).
11 Merchant Shipping Act 1894, s 686.

(6) A thief who has committed theft in any other part of the United Kingdom may be tried in Scotland for that crime if he is found in Scotland in possession of the stolen property[1]. Similarly, if a person receives in Scotland property stolen elsewhere in the United Kingdom, he may be dealt with (for reset) in the same way as if the property had been stolen in Scotland[2].

THE SHERIFF COURT

Scotland is divided into six sheriffdoms[3]. With the exception of the sheriff-dom of Glasgow and Strathkelvin (in which there is only the one sheriff court) every sheriffdom is divided into a number of sheriff court districts. In each district is a sheriff court which is manned by one or more sheriffs. In each sheriffdom there is also a sheriff principal. Although the sheriff principal has an appellate function in civil cases, his criminal jurisdiction is identical with that of a sheriff.

Both solicitors and advocates have the right of audience in the sheriff court. The prosecution case is conducted usually by the procurator fiscal or one of his deputes, although on very rare occasions Crown Counsel may appear.

The court in which proceedings in any particular case will be commenced is normally that for the district in which is situated the place where the crime is alleged to have been committed. The 1975 Act contains detailed rules governing the territorial jurisdiction of the sheriff in cases where the normal rule does not apply[4]. These are not entirely easy to understand, and there is a certain amount of apparent duplication between one section and another. The following are the most important rules:

The territorial jurisdiction of the sheriff includes 'all navigable rivers, ports, harbours, creeks, shores and anchoring grounds in or adjoining' the sheriff-dom[5]. In certain cases two or more courts may have concurrent jurisdiction[6]. If a crime is committed partly in one sheriff court district and partly in another, the accused may be indicted in the court of either district[7]. If crimes connected with each other are committed in different sheriff court districts, the accused may be indicted in the sheriff court of any of these districts[8]. A similar rule applies if several crimes are committed in succession in different sheriff court districts[8]. These provisions apply equally whether the sheriff court districts are in the same or different sheriffdoms. Indeed, it is strongly arguable that, if the districts are within the same sheriffdom, the provisions

---

1　1975 Act, s 7(1).
2　1975 Act, s 7(2).
3　The sheriffdoms are: Grampian, Highland and Islands; Tayside, Central and Fife; Lothian and Borders; Glasgow and Strathkelvin; North Strathclyde; South Strathclyde, Dumfries and Galloway.
4　1975 Act, ss 3, 4, 5.
5　1975 Act, s 3(1).
6　When sheriffdoms are separated by a stretch of water, both have jurisdiction over the stretch of water (1975 Act, s 3(3)). Section 4(1) contains a similar provision applying to sheriff court districts. Under s 4(2) both courts have jurisdiction if a crime is committed on or near the boundary of their districts. In the case of a crime committed on a moving vehicle or vessel, any court through whose district the vehicle or vessel has passed has jurisdiction (s 4(3)).
7　1975 Act, s 5(1). Although the section uses the word 'indicted', its provisions are clearly intended to apply also to the procedure prior to actual indictment.
8　1975 Act, s 5(1). See also s 4(4).

are unnecessary, as a sheriff has jurisdiction throughout the whole sheriffdom and not only in the district of the court to which he is appointed[1].

We have already noted that, in the case of certain crimes committed abroad, proceedings may be taken in Scotland, and that these proceedings are commenced in the court of the district where the accused is arrested or is in custody[2].

Any crime triable on indictment may be tried in the sheriff court with the exception of those for which the High Court has exclusive jurisdiction, either at common law or by statute[3]. The sentencing powers of the sheriff are limited. The maximum sentence which he may impose is one of three years' imprisonment[4], although the maximum sentence for a statutory offence may be less, in which case it is the statutory maximum which applies. However, the sheriff may remit a convicted person to the High Court for sentence if he considers that his powers of punishment are inadequate[5]. On indictment a sheriff has power to impose an unlimited fine, unless, of course, a maximum fine is prescribed by statute.

FIRST EXAMINATION

The charge in a case brought under solemn procedure is almost invariably first formulated in a petition at the instance of the procurator fiscal[6]. The accused may be arrested on the basis of the warrant contained in the petition, or he may have been arrested previously without a warrant, or he may simply have been asked to attend court on a specified date, having been served with a copy of the petition. This latter procedure is common in cases where there has been a long period of investigation, for example embezzlement.

The accused's first appearance on petition is always before the sheriff, even although the case may ultimately be tried in the High Court. It is in private[7]. This is known as 'first examination', and any subsequent appearance is known as 'further examination'. If there is more than one accused on the petition, each must appear separately before the sheriff[7].

An accused appearing on petition is entitled to the services of the duty solicitor under the legal aid scheme up until the time when he is released on bail or fully committed, or his application for legal aid is granted or refused, whichever of these events is the earlier[8]. An accused is, of course, under no obligation to be represented by the duty solicitor. He may choose to have his own solicitor. As we shall see below, an accused is entitled to apply for legal aid, nominating a solicitor of his choice, as soon as he has been committed or released on bail. If legal aid is applied for and granted at first examination, it

1 Sheriff Courts (Scotland) Act 1971, s 7; *Kelso District Committee v Fairbairn* (1891) 3 White 94; *Tait v Johnston* (1891) 18R 606.
2 1975 Act, s 6. See above at p 91 and notes 7–10 at p 91.
3 See above at p 91.
4 1975 Act, ss 2(2), 221(1).
5 1975 Act, s 104.
6 See the case of *David Balfour* at pp 7, 8. A petition is not strictly necessary (*O'Reilly v HMA* 1984 SCCR 352, 1985 SLT 99), but it is very rare for an accused who is a natural person to be indicted without having first appeared in court on petition.
7 1975 Act, s 20(3C).
8 Legal Aid (Scotland) Act 1986, s 22(1)(b).

will cover everything which the solicitor has done that day, including interviewing the accused and appearing at first examination and any further examination.

At first examination the accused is entitled to make a 'declaration' if he wishes, but he is not obliged to do so[1]. A declaration is a statement by the accused, saying anything which he may wish to say about the crime with which he is charged. It must be in the accused's own words and not prepared for him by his solicitor, although the accused may read from a statement prepared by himself[2]. In practice it is rare for an accused to make a declaration, but there are advantages in his doing so, if he wishes to put forward a particular line of defence and the procurator fiscal does not wish to ask him questions in terms of s 20A of the 1975 Act[3]. The procurator fiscal must provide for a shorthand writer to take a *verbatim* record of any declaration made by the accused[4].

In the great majority of cases the first examination is formal and brief. The accused's solicitor intimates that the accused does not wish to make any plea or declaration, and the fiscal moves that he be committed either for trial or for further examination.

Committal for trial, which is properly called committal 'until liberated in due course of law', is also known as 'full committal'. It means that the accused (unless released on bail) is committed to prison until either released as a result of some legal process, or acquitted or sentenced. The accused must receive a copy of the warrant committing him to prison after full committal[5].

If the accused is committed for further examination and is not released on bail, he must be brought before the court again for full committal. This should probably be within eight days, excluding both the day of committal for further examination and the day of full committal. Very surprisingly this time limit has never been authoritatively determined[6]. In practice the appearance for full committal is usually within one week of first examination.

BAIL

Under solemn procedure bail may competently be granted by the sheriff to persons accused of all crimes except murder and treason[7], but a person serving a prison sentence may not be granted bail, even if just about to be released[8]. Even in the case of murder and treason the Lord Advocate or the High Court may release a person on bail[9].

An application for bail may be made immediately after an accused has been

---

1 1975 Act, s 20(1).
2 *Carmichael v Armitage* 1983 JC 8; 1982 SCCR 475; 1983 SLT 216.
3 See below at pp 98–101.
4 1975 Act, s 20B(1), and see also Act of Adjournal (Consolidation) 1988, SI 1988/110, r 16(1) discussed below at p 100.
5 1975 Act, s 22(3).
6 *Dunbar Petr* 1986 SCCR 602.
7 1975 Act, ss 26(1), 28(1).
8 *Currie v HMA* (1980) SCCR Supp 248.
9 1975 Act, s 35. For a modern example of an application for bail in a charge of murder see *McLaren v HMA* 1967 SLT (Notes) 43.

brought before a sheriff for examination[1]. If the accused is released on bail prior to full committal (ie when only committed for further examination), he does not require to be fully committed before an indictment may be served on him[2]. If bail is refused at the stage of first examination, the accused may again apply when brought before the court for full committal[3]. An application for bail at the stage of full committal must be disposed of within 24 hours of its first being placed before the sheriff, failing which the accused must be released[4]. This does not of course mean that the accused cannot thereafter be indicted, simply that he may no longer be detained.

An application for bail is normally made by petition for which there is no statutory form, although a standard form has been developed. This narrates inter alia that the accused is innocent of the crime charged[5]. Bail application forms are usually available from the sheriff clerk's office. An application for bail may also be made orally.

The prosecutor must be given an opportunity to be heard on an application for bail, whether before or after full committal[6]. If the prosecutor does not oppose bail, the sheriff should grant it[7].

Before full committal an accused has no right of appeal against a sheriff's refusal to grant bail[8]. However, at that stage as well as after full committal, the Crown has a right to appeal against a grant of bail[9]. After full committal the accused has a right of appeal against refusal of bail or a condition of bail[10].

There is a presumption in favour of granting bail[11].

In *Smith v M*[12] Lord Justice-Clerk Wheatley laid down guidelines about the criteria to be applied by a sheriff when deciding whether or not to grant bail. For the pre-trial stage these were: (1) Bail may be refused if the accused has a significant record for crimes analogous to the offence charged, especially if the accused has recently been released from prison, (2) unless there is a cogent reason to the contrary, bail should be refused when the acused is alleged to have committed the offence charged while in a position of trust, eg awaiting trial (whether on bail or not), on licence or parole, on probation or deferred sentence, or performing a community service order, (3) bail may be refused when possible intimidation of witnesses is alleged, when the accused is of no fixed abode, when there are reasonable grounds for expecting that he will not attend for trial, or, in very special circumstances, because of the nature of the offence.

1 1975 Act, s 26(2).
2 1975 Act, s 26(4). An accused released on bail prior to full committal, who thereafter fails to attend court to answer an indictment properly served on him, has no statutory right to apply for bail as s 28(1) applies only to a person who has been fully committed. However, he may apply for bail to the *nobile officium* of the High Court: *Campbell Petr* 1989 SCCR 722.
3 1975 Act, s 27.
4 1975 Act, s 28(2). The 24 hour period is mandatory: *Gibbons Petr* 1988 SCCR 270, 1988 SLT 657.
5 This on occasions sits rather unhappily with the declaration in a legal aid application presented at the same time to the effect that the accused intends to plead guilty!
6 1975 Act, ss 26(2), 28(1).
7 *G v Spiers* 1988 SCCR 517; *Maxwell v McGlennan* 1989 SCCR 117, 1989 SLT 282 sub nom *Spiers v Maxwell*.
8 1975 Act, s 31(1), which confers a right of appeal *after* full committal.
9 1975 Act, s 31(2).
10 1975 Act, s 31(1), read in conjunction with the Bail etc (Scotland) Act 1980, s 1(4)(c).
11 *G v Spiers* 1988 SCCR 517.
12 *Smith v M* 1982 JC 67, 1982 SCCR 517, 1982 SLT 421.

For some time after the guidelines in *Smith* had been published procurators fiscal were rigorous in opposing bail applications, especially on the basis of guideline (2). If a sheriff dared to grant bail against such opposition, and the Crown appealed, the wrath of the Lord Justice-Clerk (who dealt with most bail appeals) was likely to descend on the head of the sheriff. In recent years less attention appears to have been paid to the guidelines by fiscals, who oppose bail less frequently, and the displeasure of the High Court has been reserved for sheriffs who have refused bail in the absence of opposition by the Crown, albeit they have done so on grounds which seemed adequate to them (and followed the guidelines)[1]. However, *Smith* still offers a reasonable guide to the sort of reasons why a sheriff may, if so moved by the fiscal, refuse bail. As in so many situations in the field of the criminal law, it is a question of balancing the public interest against the interests of the individual accused.

Money bail has been virtually abolished in Scotland. Bail may now be granted only on conditions, and these should not include a pledge or deposit of money except in special circumstances[2]. The conditions which may be imposed are stated in the Act[3] to be such as:

'the court or the Lord Advocate considers necessary to secure that the accused –

(a) appears at the appointed time at every diet relating to the offence with which he is charged of which he is given due notice;

(b) does not commit an offence while on bail;

(c) does not interfere with witnesses or otherwise obstruct the course of justice whether in relation to himself or any other person; and

(d) makes himself available for the purposes of enabling inquiries or a report to be made to assist the court in dealing with him for the offence with which he is charged.'

The provisions of this subsection have come to be considered as the four 'standard conditions' which are mandatory in all bail orders[4]. Although of only academic interest, it may be observed that what the Act says is only that the conditions imposed must *secure* what is stated in the subsection, and not that these are the conditions themselves. Other conditions may be added, eg that the accused surrenders his passport, or that he stays away from a particular person or place. The accused will not be released on bail until he has accepted the conditions[5]. It is not unknown for a person to refuse to accept bail conditions. In that event he must either be remanded in custody or released without conditions and ordained to appear.

Breach of a bail condition is an offence, normally punishable by imprisonment for not more than three months and/or a fine not exceeding £200[6]. Failure to appear at a diet in respect of solemn proceedings is an offence carrying a particularly heavy penalty[7]. A charge alleging breach of a bail condition may be added to an indictment at any time before trial[8].

1 See eg *G v Spiers* 1988 SCCR 517 and *Maxwell v McGlennan* 1989 SCCR 117, 1989 SLT 282 sub nom *Spiers v Maxwell*.

2 Bail etc (Scotland) Act 1980, ss 1(1)(a), 1(3).

3 Bail etc (Scotland) Act 1980, s 1(2).

4 *MacNeill v Milne* 1984 SCCR 427.

5 Bail etc (Scotland) Act 1980, s 1(4)(c).

6 Bail etc (Scotland) Act 1980, ss 3(1)(b), 3(2). If the conviction for breach of the bail condition is in the district court, the maximum period of imprisonment is 60 days.

7 Bail etc (Scotland) Act 1980, s 3(3): imprisonment for two years and/or an unlimited fine.

8 Bail etc (Scotland) Act 1980, s 3(4).

After full committal an accused may apply to the sheriff for a review of his decision to refuse bail or to grant bail subject to conditions[1]. An application for review (which is to be distinguished from an appeal) may be made not earlier than the fifth day after the original decision and thereafter not earlier than the fifteenth day after any subsequent decision[2].

As has already been noted[3], both the accused and the Crown have a right of appeal against a sheriff's decision on bail. Written notice of appeal must be given to the other party[4]. If the appeal is by the Crown against a grant of bail, the accused is not released until the appeal has been disposed of[5], provided that the appeal is heard within 72 hours (or 96 hours if bail was originally granted in the Western or Northern Isles)[6]. A bail appeal is usually heard in chambers by a single judge of the High Court, although it may be heard in open court by more than one judge[7]. The accused is not normally present at a bail appeal.

LEGAL AID

Whether or not an accused has been represented by the duty solicitor at examination before the sheriff, he may apply to the sheriff for legal aid[8]. Such an application is usually made at first examination. It must be in writing and 'in such form as the court may require'[9]. In practice a standard form has been devised, and it is in common use[10]. This provides for the accused to give details of his financial situation (income, capital, outlays) and of his dependents, and to state how he intends to plead or that he has not yet decided how to plead. These forms are available from the Scottish Legal Aid Board (SLAB), although, occasionally, the sheriff clerk's office may be able to provide one.

In solemn proceedings legal aid may be refused only on financial grounds. The sheriff must grant the application if he is satisfied, after consideration of the accused's financial circumstances, that the expenses of the case cannot be met by the accused himself without undue hardship to him or his dependants[11]. This is subject to the proviso that legal aid will be available only on special cause shown if the accused has available rights and facilities making it unnecessary for him to obtain legal aid, or has a reasonable expectation of receiving financial or other help from a body of which he is a member[12]. This is intended to meet the situation if the accused is a member of a trade union, motoring organisation or the like, which might pay for legal representation.

An accused may be required to make a statement on oath in connection with his application for legal aid[13].

1 1975 Act, s 30.
2 1975 Act, s 30(3).
3 See above at p 95 and notes 8–10 on p 95.
4 1975 Act, s 31(3).
5 1975 Act, s 31(2).
6 1975 Act, s 33.
7 1975 Act, s 31(4).
8 Legal Aid (Scotland) Act 1986, s 23.
9 Criminal Legal Aid (Scotland) Regulations 1987, SI 1987/307, reg 6.
10 See the case of *David Balfour* at pp 10, 11.
11 Legal Aid (Scotland) Act 1986, s 23.
12 Criminal Legal Aid (Scotland) Regulations 1987, SI 1987/307, reg 7.
13 AA(C) 1988, r 165.

When assessing whether the accused could meet the expenses of the case without undue hardship the sheriff should take account of whether or not it is likely to go to trial. If an accused is fully committed in custody, it is unlikely that legal aid would be refused unless he has a reasonable amount of capital.

There is no right of appeal against a refusal of legal aid[1], but it may be that an application could be made to the *nobile officium* of the High Court if a sheriff could be shown to have failed completely to apply his mind to the issue of undue hardship[2]. If a legal aid application is refused, the accused may reapply if there has been a change of circumstances, or if it becomes apparent that the trial is likely to be of exceptional length or complexity.

Legal aid, once granted, continues until the accused is acquitted or sentenced (including a remit to the High Court for sentence)[3]. However, it may be discontinued by the court on the ground of the accused's misconduct[4].

As we have seen, it is usually the sheriff who considers a legal aid application. However, if an accused who is being tried before the High Court has not previously received legal aid, he may apply for it to the High Court, which may grant it[5] or remit to the sheriff for him to consider the application[6].

JUDICIAL EXAMINATION

Strictly speaking 'judicial examination' includes any appearance on petition before a sheriff, whether for first or further examination. If an accused emits a declaration, that too is part of his judicial examination[7]. However, since 1980, the term has been commonly used to describe the form of questioning introduced by s 6(2) of the 1980 Act, which added ss 20A and 20B to the 1975 Act. In this section of the chapter 'judicial examination' will be used in this restricted sense.

The 1980 procedure provides that, when an accused is brought before a sheriff for examination (first or further), he may be questioned by the prosecutor (ie the procurator fiscal or one of his deputes):

'in so far as such questioning is directed towards eliciting any denial, explanation, justification or comment which the accused may have as regards –
(a) matters averred in the charge:
  Provided that the particular aims of a line of questions under this paragraph shall be to determine –
  (i) whether any account which the accused can give ostensibly discloses a category of defence (as for example alibi, incrimination, or the consent of the alleged victim); and

---

1 This is not stated in terms in the current legislation as it was under the previous legal aid legislation in the Act of Adjournal (Rules for Legal Aid in Criminal Proceedings) 1964, SI 1964/1409, para 9. There are, however, no provisions for appeal in the 1986 Act, the 1987 Regulations (SI 1987/307) or the 1988 Act of Adjournal (SI 1988/110).
2 By analogy with *Rae Petr* 1981 SCCR 356, 1982 SLT 233; but see also *McLachlan Petr* 1987 SCCR 195.
3 Criminal Legal Aid (Scotland) Regulations 1987, SI 1987/307, reg 4.
4 AA(C) 1988, r 164.
5 Legal Aid (Scotland) Act 1986, s 23(2)(a)(ii).
6 AA(C) 1988, r 163.
7 Although a declaration, if made at all, is usually made at first examination, an accused may make one at any time on intimating to the fiscal his desire to do so: 1975 Act, s 20(3).

(ii) the nature and particulars of that defence;
(b) the alleged making by the accused, to or in the hearing of an officer of police, of an extrajudicial confession (whether or not a full admission)[1] relevant to the charge;

Provided that questions under this paragraph may only be put if the accused has, before the examination, received from the prosecutor or from an officer of police a written record of the confession allegedly made; or

(c) what is said in any declaration emitted in regard to the charge by the accused at the examination'[2].

There are certain principles to which the fiscal must have regard in framing questions. These are:

(a) the questions should not be designed to challenge the truth of anything said by the accused;
(b) there should be no reiteration of a question which the accused has refused to answer at the examination; and
(c) there should be no leading questions[3].

The sheriff must ensure that the questions are fairly put to and understood by the accused[3]. The accused is not put on oath[4].

Section 20A(1)(b) of the 1975 Act provides that either the prosecutor *or* a police officer may provide the accused with a written record of any alleged extrajudicial confession. However, the detailed rules of procedure provide that it must be the *prosecutor* who does so, otherwise the accused may not be questioned about the confession[5].

If the accused is represented by a solicitor (as he almost invariably is), he is entitled to confer with his solicitor before answering any question, and the sheriff must inform him of this entitlement[6]. Such consultation usually takes place in the room where the judicial examination is being held, and is in the form of a whispered conversation between the solicitor and his client. There is no reason why, if the accused or his solicitor requests it, they should not be permitted to consult in private, although there would be obvious disadvantages if this happened every time the fiscal asked a question.

An accused and his solicitor will, of course, have had an opportunity to consult together prior to the judicial examination. The solicitor will have received a copy of the petition and the written record of any alleged extrajudicial confession.

The solicitor should advise the accused of the purpose of the judicial examination. He should advise him that, if there is any particular line of defence upon which the accused is founding (eg self defence or alibi), he should describe that clearly at the judicial examination.

The solicitor should go through any alleged extrajudicial confession in

---

1 'Confession' means any statement clearly susceptible of being regarded as incriminating: *McKenzie v HMA* 1983 JC 13, 1982 SCCR 545, 1983 SLT 304. The statement here which was held to be susceptible of being so regarded was: 'Just my break, I knew I'd be picked out'. It should be noted that the fiscal may seek a judicial examination on the basis of an alleged confession even after an accused has been fully committed, provided that he has not previously been examined about that confession: 1975 Act, s 20(3A).
2 1975 Act, s 20A(1).
3 1975 Act, s 20A(2).
4 AA(C) 1988, r 18(3).
5 AA(C) 1988, r 18(1), (2).
6 1975 Act, s 20A(3).

detail with the accused and should question him about the circumstances in which it was made. If there is anything untoward about these circumstances, the solicitor should advise the accused to mention this at the judicial examination.

The solicitor should write nothing on the accused's own copy of the petition and other documents as this might be misinterpreted as 'coaching'.

An accused at judicial examination is not obliged to answer any question asked by the fiscal. However, if he declines to answer a question, the fact of his so declining may be commented upon at his trial by the prosecutor, the judge or a co-accused, where, in giving evidence at the trial, the accused says something which he could have said in answer to that question[1].

Some solicitors invariably advise the accused not to answer any questions at judicial examination. The accused then tells the sheriff that, acting on legal advice, he is not going to answer any question. This may be sound advice in some cases, but not if there is a definite line of defence which should be put forward as soon as possible[2].

The accused's solicitor has a very limited right to ask questions at the judicial examination. He requires the permission of the sheriff, and the purpose of his question must be confined to clarifying any ambiguity in an answer given by the accused to the fiscal, or to give the accused an opportunity to answer any question which he has previously refused to answer[3]. The solicitor is given no specific right to object to any question asked by the fiscal, but it is suggested that he is entitled to and should object if the fiscal clearly goes beyond the bounds of what is permitted by the statute, and the sheriff himself has not stepped in.

There are very detailed rules laid down for the recording of what happens at a judicial examination[4]. The fiscal must provide a shorthand writer to make a *verbatim* record of the proceedings including any declaration made by the accused[5]. If the shorthand writer is of a standard such that he or she would be acceptable to a court to note evidence at a trial or proof, then it is not necessary that the proceedings should be tape-recorded[6]. If, as is much more common, the shorthand writer is not of such a standard, then a tape recording of the proceedings must also be made[6]. At the beginning of the judicial examination the shorthand writer must make a solemn declaration that he or she will faithfully discharge the duties of shorthand writer to the court[7]. The whole proceedings must be recorded by the shorthand writer[8] with the exception of any question disallowed by the sheriff and answers to such questions[9]. The shorthand writer must make a transcript of the proceedings[10], and, as soon as possible after their conclusion, deliver the transcript, signed and certified as correct, to the fiscal[11].

If a tape-recorder is used, it must record on two tapes simultaneously[12].

1 1975 Act, s 20A(5).
2 See eg *McEwan v HMA* 1990 SCCR 401.
3 1975 Act, s 20A(4).
4 1975 Act, s 20B and AA(C) 1988, rr 15–17.
5 1975 Act, s 20B(1) and AA(C) 1988, r 16.
6 AA(C) 1988, r 16(1).
7 AA(C) 1988, r 16(2).
8 AA(C) 1988, r 16(4).
9 AA(C) 1988, r 16(5).
10 AA(C) 1988, r 16(4).
11 AA(C) 1988, r 16(7).
12 AA(C) 1988, r 17(1).

One of the tapes is given to the fiscal[1], and the other is sealed in an envelope and retained by the sheriff clerk until the fiscal informs him that the proceedings against the accused have come to an end[2]. The sheriff clerk must then return the tape to the fiscal[3].

Within fourteen days of the date of the examination the fiscal must serve a copy of the transcript on both the accused and his solicitor (if he has one)[4]. The 1975 Act and the 1988 Act of Adjournal make provision for rectification of errors in the transcript[5]. The ultimate decision on whether there has been an error and what rectification of it should be made is for the sheriff[6].

If the case proceeds to trial, the list of productions appended to the indictment must include the record of any judicial examination[7].

PRECOGNITION

Once an accused has been fully committed the procurator fiscal must have the case against him precognosced in order that Crown counsel may consider what, if any, proceedings are appropriate.

A witness's precognition is a statement taken from him (in the case of the Crown) by the fiscal, one of his deputes or, more usually, a precognition clerk in the fiscal's office. A precognition should, so far as possible, use the witness's own words. It should not include evidence which would be inadmissible, eg hearsay. The precognoscer may append to the precognition a comment on the impression which the witness is likely to make in court. If the witness has some physical or mental defect (for example is of low intelligence, deaf or blind), this should be indicated in the precognition.

Most witnesses attend for precognition as a result of a request from the fiscal. However, if a witness is reluctant to attend, he may be compelled to do so by means of citation. The usual warrant granted in the original petition includes a warrant to cite witnesses for precognition[8], but if, for some reason, this has not been granted, the fiscal may make a separate application to the sheriff for a warrant.

The fiscal sometimes considers it appropriate that a witness should give his precognition on oath. This might, eg, occur if it were expected that the witness was likely to renege on his precognition when he came to give evidence at the trial. A precognition on oath is taken before a sheriff. The witness, having taken the oath, is questioned by the fiscal. The questions and the witness's answers are recorded by a shorthand writer. The precognition is then transcribed, and the witness must appear before the sheriff again in order to sign the transcript.

It is not competent to put to a witness the terms of an unsworn precognition made by him, notwithstanding the terms of ss 147 and 349 of the 1975

---

1 AA(C) 1988, r 17(4)(a).
2 AA(C) 1988, rr 17(4)(b), 17(5).
3 AA(C) 1988, r 17(8).
4 1975 Act, s 20B(3).
5 1975 Act, s 20B(4) and AA(C) 1988, r 19.
6 1975 Act, s 20B(8).
7 1975 Act, s 78(2).
8 See the case of *David Balfour* at p 7.

Act (which permit a witness at a trial to be asked about a statement previously made which contradicts the evidence which he is giving). This is because the precognition is considered to be the words of the precognoscer rather than those of the witness. However, a precognition on oath (where the words are indisputably those of the witness) may be put to a witness[1].

Once the precognition of the witnesses is complete, the full precognition, together with documentary productions, is sent to the Crown Office in Edinburgh. There it is read by Crown counsel (usually one of the advocates-depute, but, if the case is one of great importance or difficulty, possibly one of the law officers) who will direct whether proceedings are to be taken and, if so, of what sort. The nature of the proceedings and the court in which they take place usually depend on the gravity of the charge. Crown counsel will have in mind the maximum powers of sentencing possessed by a sheriff. The Lord Advocate may have issued directions that certain types of case are to be prosecuted in a particular forum.

If the decision is that no proceedings are to be taken, the accused must be liberated forthwith if he is in custody. If he is on bail, he must be informed. For a case to be marked 'no pro' does not necessarily preclude proceedings at a later date if new evidence emerges. However, further proceedings will be incompetent if the Crown is, by its actings, personally barred from taking further action against an accused, for example by informing him that no further steps would be taken in the matter[2], or by issuing a general statement of policy[3].

If it is decided to indict the case in the High Court, the indictment will be prepared in the Crown Office, and it will be signed by an advocate-depute. If it is decided to indict in the sheriff court, the precognition is returned to the fiscal with instructions to him to prepare an indictment. The indictment is then signed by the fiscal or one of his deputes 'by authority of Her Majesty's Advocate'[4]. If the decision is that summary prosecution is appropriate, the precognition is returned to the fiscal with instructions to him to prepare the appropriate summary complaint.

THE INDICTMENT

General

The indictment is the document which contains the charge(s) against an accused who is to be tried before a jury. The accused is indicted 'at the instance of the Lord Advocate, although, if there is no Lord Advocate at the time, the indictment may proceed in the name of the Solicitor General[5].'

The essentials of an indictment are that it should name the accused, it should state the time when and the place where the crime was committed, and it should set forth the way in which the crime was committed. Styles for the more usual common law crimes are set forth in Schedule A of the

1 *Coll Petr* 1977 JC 29.
2 *Thom v HMA* 1976 JC 48, 1976 SLT 23; *HMA v Stewart* 1980 JC 84.
3 Such a statement is, however, given a restricted interpretation: *Lockhart v Deighan* 1985 SCCR 204, 1985 SLT 549.
4 1975 Act, s 41.
5 1975 Act, s 42.

Criminal Procedure (Scotland) Act 1887, which is applied to modern procedure by s 41 of the 1975 Act. These styles should be adhered to unless there is good reason to the contrary.

An indictment may be written or printed or a combination of both[1]. In practice most indictments in both the High Court and the sheriff court are typewritten.

Sections 43–56 of the 1975 Act contain provisions (originating in the 1887 Act) intended to simplify the form of indictment as compared with the pre-1887 form.

The accused

An accused may be named and designed according to the name and designation (ie address and occupation, although the latter is frequently omitted nowadays) which he gave at examination or full committal, and it is not necessary to set forth any other name or designation by which he may be known[2]. In practice, however, if an accused has an alias, it is common to state it in the indictment. Thus the libel might be against 'David Balfour also known as John Smith'. The designation of an accused is usually 'prisoner in the prison of X' if he is in custody, or 'whose domicile of citation has been specified as 1 Y Street, X' if he is on bail. The domicile of citation is the address at which an accused who is on bail will be cited[3].

Naming the crime

It is not necessary to specify the crime charged in an indictment by any particular legal name. It is enough that the indictment sets forth facts relevant and sufficient to constitute an indictable crime[4].

Multiple accused

If two or more persons are charged together with committing a crime, it is implied that they acted jointly and/or severally[5].

Accession

It is implied that a person charged is guilty actor (ie as principal) or art and part (ie as accessory)[6]. However, there are occasions when greater specification is required. For example, a woman might be charged with rape, a crime of which she clearly could not be the principal. However, she could be guilty as an accessory because she assisted in overcoming the victim's

1 1975 Act, s 57.
2 1975 Act, s 43.
3 Bail etc (Scotland) Act 1980, s 2(3).
4 1975 Act, s 44.
5 1975 Act, s 45.
6 1975 Act, s 46.

resistance while her male co-accused had intercourse. In such a situation it would be necessary to specify what part each accused played in the commission of the crime.

Time

The indictment must specify the time when the crime was alleged to have been committed. Usually it is only the date which is given, but there are certain crimes where the exact time of day may be crucial to the charge, in which case it too must be set forth[1]. If a single date is stated, there is an implied latitude of three months, ie covering the month libelled, the previous month and the month after[2]. If the crime is charged as having been committed between two specified dates, the prosecutor is confined to the period between these dates, and there is no further latitude[3].

If the period of time libelled is greater than three months, the exceptional latitude must be justified by the prosecutor[4]. In many cases an exceptional latitude has been allowed, and it is difficult to generalise about the circumstances which have justified it. Sexual offences against children are one field where a wide latitude is commonly permitted[5]. That the crime was committed at some time during a period when the accused was in a particular occupation, or that, because of the lapse of time since it was committed, witnesses cannot be expected to remember exact dates, are reasons why the latitude may be extended.

It is unnecessary to set forth in the indictment the circumstances which justify an exceptional latitude[6], but evidence must be led at the trial to show that it is not unfair to the accused[7].

An exceptional latitude of time may, of course, prejudice an accused if he is seeking to put forward a defence of alibi. However, this is not a reason for dismissing an indictment, provided that the Crown has exercised due diligence. The appropriate remedy for the accused is to seek an adjournment during the course of the trial as the evidence emerges[8].

Place

Specification of the place where the crime was committed is essential as it is that which usually determines the jurisdiction of the court[9]. The words 'or near' or 'in the near neighbourhood of' are implied in all descriptions of the locus unless the actual place is of the essence of the charge[10]. The libel of place

---

1 Eg night poaching, which is committed between 'the expiration of the first hour after sunset' and 'the beginning of the last hour before sunrise' (Night Poaching Act 1828, s 12).
2 *Hume* II, 221; Alison *Practice* p 251; 1975 Act, s 50(1).
3 *Creighton v HMA* (1904) 4 Adam 356, 6F(J) 72, 12 SLT 36; *Andrew v HMA* 1982 SCCR 539.
4 Alison *Practice* p 256, quoted with approval by Lord Russell in *Ogg v HMA* 1938 JC 152 at 154.
5 Eg *HMA v AE* 1937 JC 96, 1938 SLT 70; *HMA v Hastings* 1985 SCCR 128, 1985 SLT 446.
6 1975 Act, s 50(3). See *Hunter v Guild* 1989 SCCR 717, dealing with the equivalent summary provision, s 312(f).
7 *HMA v Mackenzie* (1913) 7 Adam 189, 1913 SC(J) 107, 1913 SLT 48.
8 *Murray v HMA* 1987 SCCR 249.
9 See above at p 92.
10 1975 Act, s 50(2).

should be as specific as possible in order to give the accused fair notice. However, there are cases where, because of the nature of the charge, the prosecutor cannot be more specific than to say something along the lines of 'or elsewhere in Glasgow to the prosecutor unknown'[1].

The facts of the crime

The indictment must libel facts and circumstances which constitute a crime known to the law of Scotland. Thus, to charge that an accused attempted to cause a woman to abort, libelling only a belief that she was pregnant and not that she actually *was* pregnant, was held to be irrelevant, as the crime of attempted abortion requires a foetus *in utero*[2].

Qualifying words

Certain words from which wicked intention or guilty knowledge could be inferred and which previously had to be inserted in a charge, are now implied where necessary[3]. However, it should be noted that, in the case of fire raising, it is still necessary to specify whether the crime was committed 'wilfully' or 'culpably and recklessly' as these are two different crimes.

Statutory charges

If the crime charged is a statutory contravention, it is not necessary to quote the words of the statute. It is sufficient to libel that the crime was committed contrary to the Act of Parliament, referring to the appropriate section of the Act[4].

Descriptions

Words such as 'or thereby' in relation to quantities or 'to the prosecutor unknown' in relation to the 'perpetration of any act regarding persons, things or modes' are now implied where necessary[5]. That property (heritable or moveable) is not the property of the accused is to be implied where that is essential to the criminality of the charge[6]. In the case of persons, the words 'now or lately' residing at a particular address are to be implied[7]. It is not necessary to specify the material of which an article is made[7]. Nor is it necessary to specify the form of a sum of money; all that requires to be libelled is the amount and that it consists of money[8]. The contents of a document need

---

1 *Gold v Neilson* (1907) 5 Adam 423, 1908 SC(J) 5, 15 SLT 458, which is a summary case, but the principle is the same. The charge was reset of 44 different articles.
2 *HMA v Anderson* 1928 JC 1, 1927 SLT 651.
3 1975 Act, s 48.
4 1975 Act, s 49.
5 1975 Act, s 51.
6 1975 Act, s 52.
7 1975 Act, s 53.
8 1975 Act, s 54.

not be narrated at length. It is sufficient to describe the document and, where it is a production, to refer to the number given to it in the list of productions[1].

LISTS OF PRODUCTIONS AND WITNESSES

There are appended to the indictment a list of the productions upon which the Crown intends to found and a list of the witnesses whom the Crown intends to lead in support of the charge(s) against the accused.

The list of productions is divided into two parts, the first being documentary productions (referred to as 'productions'), and the second being other articles (referred to as 'labels' because an article normally has a label attached to it for identification purposes).

The list of witnesses should give the full name and address of each witness[2]. It is no objection to the admissibility of a witness that he has ceased to live at the specified address, provided that he has lived there some time during the six months before the trial[2]. In recent years there has grown up a practice of giving the address of some witnesses (especially the victims of crime) as 'care of' the local police force. This is no doubt intended for the protection from intimidation of such witnesses. Although this practice is prima facie contrary to the terms of s 79(1) of the 1975 Act, which clearly implies that the address given should be that of the witness's residence, there is no reported case of any objection having been taken to it. In the case of many witnesses it is their professional or business address, rather than that of their residence which is given. Police witnesses are usually described by their rank, the force to which they belong and the place where they are stationed.

TIME LIMITS

For many years the prosecution of crime in Scotland under solemn procedure has been governed by strict time limits. These are intended, primarily, to prevent an accused being detained for unnecessarily long periods without receiving an indictment or being brought to trial. They are now contained in s 101 of the 1975 Act, which also includes a general time limit on the prosecution of cases on indictment.

The twelve-month rule

A jury trial of an accused must be commenced[3] within twelve months of the accused's first appearance on petition[4]. If the trial does not begin within that period, the accused must be discharged and is 'for ever free from all question or process for that offence'[4]. The time limit does not apply to an accused for

---

1 1975 Act, s 55.
2 1975 Act, s 79(1).
3 A trial commences, for the purposes of this section, when the jury is sworn: 1975 Act, s 101(6).
4 1975 Act, s 101(1). If the charge is reduced to summary proceedings, the twelve-month rule does not then apply: *MacDougall v Russell* 1985 SCCR 441, 1986 SLT 403.

whose arrest a warrant has been granted in respect of his failure to appear at a diet of the case[1].

The court has power 'on cause shown' to extend the twelve-month period. An application for extension is normally made to the sheriff, but, if the accused has already been served with a High Court indictment, the application must be made to a High Court judge[2].

The leading case on extension of the twelve-month limit is *Her Majesty's Advocate v Swift*[3]. In that case the High Court, on appeal, refused to grant an extension and laid down the following principles: (1) an extension is to be granted only if sufficient reason for it is shown and the judge is prepared to exercise his discretion in favour of the Crown; (2) fault on the part of the Crown is not an absolute bar to the extension being granted, but the nature and degree of that fault are relevant factors in assessing sufficient reason and in the exercise of discretion under principle (1); (3) the gravity of the charge(s) is not in itself a sufficient reason for granting an extension; (4) the shortness of the extension sought and the fact that the accused is not prejudiced are not relevant in assessing the sufficiency of the reason for granting the extension, but they may be relevant factors in the question of exercising discretion when sufficient reason *has* been demonstrated.

It has been emphasised that mere pressure of business is not enough to justify an extension[4], but pressure of business has been somewhat narrowly interpreted in later cases[5].

An extension of the twelve-month limit may be applied for and granted even after the period has already expired[6].

An application for an extension is an independent proceeding and is not affected by any question of the competency of an indictment which is called on the same day, as it is always open to the Crown to serve a fresh indictment if the extension is granted[7].

An extension may be applied for where the accused has disappeared[8]. If the application cannot be served on the accused himself because he cannot be traced, it should be intimated to his solicitor, if known[9].

Both the accused and the Crown have a right of appeal to the High Court against the sheriff's or judge's decision on an application for an extension of the twelve-month limit[10].

---

1 1975 Act, s 101(1), proviso (i). This proviso does not apply if a warrant is granted erroneously on the basis that an accused was absent when in fact he was present: *HMA v Campbell* 1987 SCCR 536, 1987 SLT 72.

2 1975 Act, s 101(1), proviso (ii).

3 *HMA v Swift* 1984 JC 83, 1984 SCCR 216, 1985 SLT 26.

4 *McGinty v HMA* 1984 SCCR 176, 1985 SLT 25.

5 *Dobbie v HMA* 1986 SCCR 72, 1986 SLT 648: *Rudge v HMA* 1989 SCCR 105, 1989 SLT 591 (note the critical comment by Sheriff G H Gordon (editor of SCCR) at 1989 SCCR 108).

6 *HMA v M* 1986 SCCR 624, 1986 SLT 475 sub nom *HMA v Mullen*, a rather unusual case where an appeal from a preliminary diet caused the trial, which had been fixed just within the twelve months, to be discharged.

7 *McDonald v HMA* 1988 SCCR 298, 1988 SLT 693.

8 *Watson v HMA* 1983 SCCR 115, 1983 SLT 471.

9 *Campbell v HMA* 1986 SCCR 573, 1987 SLT 399.

10 1975 Act, s 101(5). Procedures are provided for by AA(C) 1988, r 50 which specifies that Form 23 should be used in an appeal by the accused.

The 80-day rule

An accused who has been committed for trial in custody may not be detained for a total period of more than 80 days from full committal without having been served with an indictment[1]. If no indictment has been served within that period, the accused must be liberated forthwith[1]. This does not mean that he cannot thereafter be served with an indictment, but simply that he may no longer be detained in custody pending his trial.

If an indictment is served within the 80 days but then falls because the accused is not called to answer it in court on the specified date, he must be released unless a new indictment is served before the 80-day period has expired[2].

The Crown may apply to a single judge of the High Court for an extension of the 80-day limit, and the judge may extend it 'for any sufficient cause', but should not do so if he is satisfied that, 'but for some fault on the part of the prosecutor', the indictment could have been served within the period[3]. The power to extend may be exercised even after the period has actually expired[4].

Both the accused and the Crown have a right of appeal to the High Court against the decision of the single judge[5].

The 110-day rule

An accused who has been committed for trial in custody must be brought to trial and the trial commenced[6] within 110 days from full committal[7]. If the trial is not begun within that period, then the accused must be liberated forthwith, and he is thereafter 'for ever free from all question or process for that offence'[7].

The Crown may apply to a single judge of the High Court to extend the period on the following grounds: (a) the illness of the accused or of a judge; (b) the absence or illness of any necessary witness; (c) any other sufficient cause which is not attributable to any fault on the part of the prosecutor[8]. Clearly this last ground leaves a great deal to the discretion of the judge. In *Her Majesty's Advocate v McTavish*[9] an extension was refused when the reason advanced by the Crown for seeking it was to enable the carrying out of tests which might have resulted in different, more serious charges. In *Gildea v Her Majesty's Advocate*[10] an extension was allowed when the reason for seeking it was that a previous trial in the circuit had lasted longer than had been foreseen.

1 1975 Act, s 101(2)(a).
2 *HMA v Walker* 1981 JC 102, 1981 SCCR 154, 1981 SLT (Notes) 3.
3 1975 Act, s 101(3).
4 *Farrell v HMA* 1984 JC 1, 1984 SCCR 301, 1985 SLT 58.
5 1975 Act, s 101(5). Procedures are provided for by AA(C) 1988, r 50 which specifies that Form 24 should be used in an appeal by the accused.
6 A trial commences, for the purposes of this section, when the jury is sworn: 1975 Act, s 101(6).
7 1975 Act, s 101(2)(b).
8 1975 Act, s 101(4). For an exceptional case where two extensions were granted (making the total period 186 days), see *Young v HMA* 1990 SCCR 315.
9 *HMA v McTavish* 1974 JC 19, 1974 SLT 246.
10 *Gildea v HMA* 1983 SCCR 144, 1983 SLT 458 (note the critical comment by Sheriff G H Gordon (editor of SCCR) at 1983 SCCR 148).

Both the accused and the Crown have a right of appeal to the High Court against the decision of the single judge[1].

Computation of time limits under the 80-day and 110-day rules

The time limits apply only to periods spent in custody as a result of the committal warrant. A sentence imposed on a different charge interrupts the running of the period[2]. If the accused having been fully committed, is liberated after having been detained for a period and is then fully committed on a second warrant on different charges, any time in custody following thereon will be attributed to the second warrant and not to the earlier one[3]. However, if the accused is fully committed on a second warrant *without* having been liberated, the time spent in custody is still computed from the date of the first warrant so far as the charges covered by that warrant are concerned[4].

CITATION OF THE ACCUSED

When any sitting of a court has been appointed to be held for a jury trial or trials, the sheriff clerk (in the case of sheriff court trials) or the Clerk of Justiciary (in the case of High Court trials) issues a warrant to cite accused persons, witnesses and jurors[5]. The warrant is authority to cite for the first day of the sitting 'with continuation of days'[5].

The record copy of the indictment (ie the copy which will form part of the official record of the court) must be lodged with the clerk of the appropriate court on or before the date of service of the indictment[6]. Copies of the lists of witnesses and productions must be lodged not less than ten clear days before the trial diet[7].

Service of the indictment on the accused

The accused *must* be served with an indictment[8]. If he is not so served, the proceedings are incompetent[9].

Service of an indictment may be effected by any officer of law[10], which includes any macer, messenger-at-arms, sheriff officer or other person

---

1 1975 Act, s 101(5). Procedures are provided for by AA(C) 1988, r 50 which specifies that Form 25 should be used in an appeal by the accused.
2 *Wallace v HMA* 1959 JC 71, 1959 SLT 320: *Brown v HMA* 1988 SCCR 577, in which it was held that the prison practice of releasing on Friday a prisoner whose release date should truly have been the following Sunday, should be ignored in computing a period of imprisonment which interrupts the 110 days.
3 *HMA v Boyle* 1972 SLT (Notes) 16.
4 *Ross v HMA* 1990 SCCR 182.
5 1975 Act, s 69; AA(C) 1988, r 10, Form 3.
6 1975 Act, s 78(1). Failure to lodge the record copy timeously does not amount to a fundamental nullity: *HMA v Graham* 1985 SCCR 169, 1985 SLT 498.
7 1975 Act, s 78(1).
8 1975 Act, s 70.
9 *McAllister v HMA* 1985 SCCR 36, 1985 SLT 399, in which it was held that there had been no service, although an execution of service, bearing that the accused had been personally served at his domicile of citation was produced. This was conceded by the Crown to be inaccurate as there had in fact been no personal service.
10 1975 Act, s 71.

having authority to execute a warrant of the court; any constable within the meaning of the Police (Scotland) Act 1967; and (only in the case of an accused who is in prison) a prison officer[1].

Service may be effected in four separate ways:

(a) delivering the document to the accused personally;
(b) leaving the document in the hands of a member of the family of the accused or other occupier or employee at *the proper domicile of citation of the accused*;
(c) affixing the document to the door of, or depositing it in, *the proper domicile of citation of the accused*;
(d) where the officer of law serving the document has reasonable grounds for believing that an accused, *for whom no proper domicile of citation has been specified*, is residing at a particular place but is unavailable –
    (i) leaving the document in the hands of a member of the family of the accused or other occupier or employee at that place; or
    (ii) affixing the document to the door of, or depositing it in, that place[2].

Note that paragraph (d) applies only in the rare case where no proper domicile of citation has been specified. This would be only when the accused has neither been remanded in custody nor been released on bail.

Where the accused is in custody service should be made personally. If the accused is on bail, the indictment should be served at his proper domicile of citation, ie the address stated in his bail order[3], by an officer of law[4] using one of the methods specified in paragraphs (b) and (c) of the 1988 Act of Adjournal. Citation of the accused at that address by one of these methods will be presumed to have been duly carried out[5]. In a case decided under the previous bail legislation[6] the High Court held that, even if an accused had been detained on another charge following his release on bail and was actually in prison, service by leaving the indictment at his domicile of citation was good. This was at a time when it was common to specify the sheriff clerk's office as the domicile of citation (as was done in this case), which meant at least that the accused's solicitor could receive the service copy indictment from the sheriff clerk. It might have been hoped that the court would not take an equally strict view under the modern bail legislation where the domicile of citation is normally the accused's residence. This would, however, have been too optimistic a view[7].

Documents served with indictment

Along with the indictment are served the lists of productions[8] and witnesses[9].

There must also be served at the same time any notice of previous convictions which the prosecutor intends to place before the court in the event of

---

1 1975 Act, s 462(1).
2 AA(C) 1988, r 167(2).
3 Bail etc (Scotland) Act 1980, s 2(1)(b).
4 See note 1 above and p 109, note 10 above.
5 Bail etc (Scotland) Act 1980, s 2(3).
6 *Bryson v HMA* 1961 JC 57, 1961 SLT 289.
7 In *Jamieson v HMA* 1990 SCCR 137, another case where the accused was in prison at the time of service at his domicile of citation, *Bryson v HMA* (above) was approved and followed. In *Welsh v HMA* 1986 SCCR 233, 1986 SLT 664, in which the address specified as the proper domicile of citation had been demolished, but sticking the indictment on a remaining main door was held to be a good service. See also *McAllister v HMA* 1985 SCCR 36, 1985 SLT 399.
8 This must include the record of the transcript of the judicial examination (1975 Act, s 78(2)).
9 1975 Act, s 70.

conviction[1]. Convictions contained in such a notice, duly served, are held to apply to the accused unless he gives written notice of objection at least five clear days before the trial diet[2]. If the accused is going to plead guilty, notice of objection to a previous conviction must be made at least two clear days prior to the diet at which he so pleads[3].

With the indictment the accused must also receive a notice calling upon him to appear for the trial diet[4]. This stipulates the court, the date and the time of his appearance. The date must be no less than 29 clear days from service of the indictment[5]. However, service on a date less than 29 clear days from the trial diet does not amount to a fundamental nullity[6].

Body corporate

If an accused is a body corporate, service is effected by delivering a copy of the indictment together with a notice to appear to its registered office or (if there is no registered office in the United Kingdom) to its principal place of business in the United Kingdom[7]. This delivery may be made by registered post or recorded delivery[7].

Correction of errors prior to service

Prior to service any error in the indictment may be corrected by deletion or alteration on the record copy and service copies, and such a deletion or alteration is sufficiently authenticated by the initials of any person authorised to sign the indictment[8]. In the case of the service copy any correction is also sufficiently authenticated by the initials of the person serving it, and this applies also to any notice served on an accused[9].

Lodging of productions

There is no statutory provision about the lodging of Crown productions, although it is clear that productions for a sheriff court trial should be lodged with the sheriff clerk and that those for a High Court trial should be lodged with the Clerk of Justiciary[10]. The productions should be lodged at a time which provides the accused (or more probably his solicitor) with sufficient opportunity to examine them before the start of the trial[11]. If productions are

1 1975 Act, s 68(2).
2 1975 Act, s 68(3) – the notice must be given to the Crown Agent in the case of a High Court trial, and to the procurator fiscal in the case of a trial in the sheriff court.
3 1975 Act, s 68(3). This does not apply to a plea of guilty under s 102 procedure (for which see below at pp 124–126).
4 1975 Act, s 75.
5 1975 Act, s 75, and see also s 111A, which makes provision for the situation when the last day falls on a Saturday, Sunday or holiday.
6 *HMA v McDonald* 1984 JC 94, 1984 SCCR 229, 1984 SLT 426.
7 1975 Act, s 74(1).
8 1975 Act, s 58(1).
9 1975 Act, s 58(2).
10 This is implicit in the terms of the 1975 Act, s 83.
11 *Hume* II, 388; Alison *Practice* p 594.

lodged late, they may still be admissible in evidence. The accused's remedy is to seek an adjournment of the trial in order to examine them if he so wishes[1]. The proper time for the accused to take objection to the late lodging (or a complete failure to lodge) is before the jury is sworn[1]. In practice documentary productions are usually lodged along with the record copy of the indictment.

CROWN WITNESSES

All the witnesses on the list appended to the indictment should be cited by the Crown. A witness may be cited by any officer of law[2]. The officer need not be accompanied by a witness, and his own evidence is sufficient to prove citation[3].

Although the Crown must append a list of witnesses to the indictment, it is not limited to leading evidence from only the witnesses named in that list. Additional witnesses may be examined provided that written notice has been given to the accused not less than two clear days before the date on which the jury is sworn to try the case[4]. The notice should contain the name and address of each witness[4]. A similar provision applies to productions which are not on the Crown list[4]. Copies of such notices are usually sent also to the accused's solicitor.

The Crown may also call a witness or put in evidence a production included in any list or notice lodged by the accused[5].

PREPARATION BY THE DEFENCE

It is only with service of the indictment (a copy of which is also usually sent to the accused's solicitor) that the accused is officially informed of the exact charge against him and of the witnesses and productions. In practice, however, it is probable that the defence solicitor has already had informal discussions with the fiscal and has been given some information about these matters. The solicitor will almost certainly also have had at least one consultation with his client since full committal.

It is strongly recommended that a solicitor should begin preparing for a trial, insofar as he is able, prior to service of the indictment, but, for the purposes of this section only, we shall assume that the solicitor has had no contact with either the fiscal or his client between full committal and service. This means that the defence must move very fast as the trial may be as early as 29 days after service of the indictment.

---

1 *MacNeil v HMA* 1986 SCCR 288.
2 1975 Act, s 71. For the definition of 'officer of law', see above at pp 109, 110.
3 1975 Act, s 72.
4 1975 Act, s 81.
5 1975 Act, s 82A.

Precognition of crown witnesses by the defence

The first thing which the defence solicitor should do is to have precognitions taken from the Crown witnesses. It may not be necessary to precognosce all the witnesses on the Crown list. In some cases it will be obvious that precognition is unnecessary, eg witnesses speaking to the contents of uncontroversial reports. If the solicitor has had a preliminary discussion with the fiscal, that may have given him some indication of which witnesses need not be precognosced.

A solicitor may take precognitions himself, and it is advisable in the case of a particularly sensitive witness, such as the alleged victim in a rape case, that he should. However, the more common practice nowadays is to use a private inquiry agency. The employees of such agencies are very often former police officers and should therefore be familiar with the technique of taking statements from witnesses. Precognoscers should be informed of what the line of defence is and whether there are any particular points to be put to witnesses.

There is no legal obligation on a Crown witness to give a precognition to the defence, although there is judicial authority for the proposition that it is his civic duty to do so[1]. Crown witnesses are notoriously reluctant to give statements to the defence. It may sometimes prove beneficial to remind a witness that it is only by precognition that an accused may be made fully aware of the strength of the case against him, and that this might result in a plea of guilty.

The defence is entitled to apply to have a witness cited for precognition on oath[2]. There has been a difference of shrieval opinion on the scope of this entitlement. On the one hand the opinion has been expressed that an accused should be allowed to precognosce a witness on oath only in the same exceptional circumstances as those in which the Crown would do so, and not just where it is desired to obtain a precognition from a witness who is being unco-operative[3]. On the other hand it has been held that the object of the statutory provision is to place the defence on equal terms with the Crown in preparation of the case, and that the words 'on oath' do not restrict such precognition by the defence to exceptional circumstances[4]. It is submitted that the latter view is to be preferred and that the true purpose of the provision is to enable the defence to obtain a precognition from a reluctant or recalcitrant witness. The fact that the precognition is on oath is, as the sheriff in *Brady* put it, 'so that the exercise can be a meaningful one, and of some value to the defence'[5].

If the defence solicitor suspects that a Crown witness has a criminal record, he should ask the fiscal about it. The fiscal will usually co-operate by providing a copy of any record.

1 *HMA v Monson* (1893) 1 Adam 114 at 135, 21R(J) 5 at 11, per Lord Justice-Clerk Macdonald.
2 1980 Act, s 9; AA(C) 1988, rr 5–9, Forms 1, 2.
3 *Low v Macneill* 1981 SCCR 243 (Sh Ct); *Cirignaco v Lockhart* 1985 SCCR 157 (Sh Ct), 1985 SLT (Sh Ct) 11.
4 *Brady v Lockhart* 1985 SCCR 349 (Sh Ct).
5 *Brady v Lockhart* 1985 SCCR 349 at 351 per Sheriff Lunny.

Identification parade

As has already been noted[1], the accused is in certain circumstances entitled to apply to the sheriff to have the fiscal ordered to hold an identification parade with the accused in it[2].

Examination of crown productions

The defence solicitor will normally receive copies of the documentary productions for the Crown, such as forensic science reports and transcripts of tape recorded interviews.

The accused (or his solicitor) is entitled to examine and inspect the productions which have been lodged[3]. If the accused has difficulty in obtaining access to any production, he may apply to the court in which his trial is to take place for a warrant, and this may include an application to submit the production to tests[4].

Defence witnesses and productions

The accused is entitled to lead evidence from any witness on the Crown list and also to put in evidence any production on the Crown list.[5] However, if the defence wishes to lead evidence from any other witness (apart from the accused himself who is entitled to give evidence without notice), or to found on any other production, written notice of these must be given to the fiscal or the Crown Agent, as the case may be, at least three clear days before the day on which the jury is sworn to try the case[6]. This three-day period may be shortened if the accused can show that he was unable to give the full notice[6]. In practice the Crown very often consents to late notice being given by an accused. A copy of the note of defence witnesses and productions must be lodged, at or before the trial diet, with the sheriff clerk or the Clerk of Justiciary, as the case may be[7].

A defence witness should be cited by officer of law (sheriff officer or messenger at arms)[8], although in practice citation by recorded delivery post is common.

It is competent for the accused to apply to the High Court for commission and diligence for the recovery of documents. As in a civil case, a specification of documents is lodged. The accused must satisfy the court that there is a connection between the document sought to be recovered and the defence which is to be put forward[9]. If commission and diligence is granted, it is executed in exactly the same way as in a civil case. Only the High Court has

1 See above at p 89.
2 1980 Act, s 10; AA(C) 1988, r 13, Forms 8 and 9.
3 1975 Act, s 83.
4 *Davies Petr* 1973 SLT (Notes) 36.
5 1975 Act, s 82A.
6 1975 Act, s 82(2).
7 1975 Act, s 82(3).
8 1975 Act, s 71.
9 *Hasson v HMA* 1971 JC 35, 1971 SLT 199.

the power to grant commission and diligence, even although the trial may be in the sheriff court[1].

Consultation

When the defence solicitor has obtained precognitions of all the witnesses who he considers require to be precognosced and has examined the productions, he should arrange a consultation with his client, in order to discuss the case. The solicitor should advise the accused of the strength of the Crown case, and it may be that, being confronted with this, the accused will decide to plead guilty to all or part of the indictment. In practice the solicitor is likely to have more than one consultation with his client. The solicitor should take the opportunity to explain the court procedure to the accused – assuming, of course, that the latter is not already well versed in it!

Counsel

If the trial is to be in the High Court, the defence solicitor must take steps to instruct counsel. This should be done as early as possible. Counsel should have at least one consultation with his client, even although the solicitor may already have seen the accused several times. For a High Court case the granting of legal aid automatically covers the employment of one junior counsel, but the employment of more than one junior or of senior counsel (whether with or without a junior) requires the approval of the Scottish Legal Aid Board except in cases of murder[2]. Even if the trial is to be in the sheriff court, the solicitor may consider that counsel should represent the accused. If the accused is on legal aid, an application must be made to the Scottish Legal Aid Board for approval of the employment of counsel in the sheriff court[3].

In order to instruct counsel the defence solicitor makes contact with one of the advocates' clerks employed by Faculty Services Ltd at Parliament House in Edinburgh. The clerk will advise on the availability of counsel. When it has been decided which advocate is to be employed, the solicitor sends him a full set of instructions, including the indictment, precognitions and copies of productions.

Discussion with the prosecution

Following the consultation, if the trial is to be in the sheriff court, the solicitor should make contact with the procurator fiscal depute who is to conduct the trial. If the accused has decided to offer a partial plea, the fiscal's view on the acceptability of this must obviously be sought. If there are real possibilities of negotiating a plea, there may be several meetings between the fiscal and the defence solicitor. It is clearly advantageous to agree a plea as far in advance as possible, in order that witnesses and potential jurors may be informed that

1 *HMA v Ashrif* 1988 SCCR 197, 1988 SLT 567.
2 Criminal Legal Aid (Scotland) Regulations 1987, SI 1987/307, reg 14(1)(a).
3 Criminal Legal Aid (Scotland) Regulations 1987, SI 1987/307, reg 14(1)(b). For the form of application, see the case of *David Balfour* at p 26.

they need not attend court. Even if the accused still intends to go to trial, the solicitor should discuss with the fiscal the possibility of agreeing or admitting non-controversial evidence. The agreement or admission is incorporated into a minute, which is lodged with the clerk of the appropriate court[1], and, during the trial, is read out to the jury before the party lodging it closes his case.

If the trial is to be in the High Court, defence counsel should speak to the advocate depute on the same basis as suggested above, although there is likely to be less in the way of negotiation in this situation.

Special defences

There are certain defences of which the accused must give advance notice to the Crown. These are known as 'special defences'. Although the matter is not entirely free from doubt, it can be stated with reasonable confidence that there are only four special defences which are recognised today. These are: alibi; incrimination; self-defence; and insanity.

Alibi means that the accused maintains that, at the time when the crime was committed, he was not at the locus libelled, but at some other specified place. The notice of special defence should give the exact times between which an accused maintains he was at the specified place.

Incrimination (sometimes rather dubiously called 'impeachment') means that the accused maintains that the crime was committed not by him but by some other named person. If the accused alleges that the crime was committed by a co-accused, this is not, strictly speaking, a special defence, but the accused must lodge a notice of intention to lead evidence incriminating the co-accused in exactly the same way as if it were a special defence[2]. For practical purposes this notice amounts to a special defence.

Self-defence means that the accused maintains that he was defending himself against an attack by the alleged victim of the crime. It is a complete defence to a charge of assault or homicide. It is to be distinguished from provocation, which is not a complete defence but which goes only towards mitigation.

Insanity means that the accused's reason was impaired by some mental disorder and that he was thereby rendered incapable of exerting his reason to control his conduct and reactions. If proved, the defence results in a verdict of not guilty by reason of insanity. It is to be distinguished from diminished responsibility, which is not a special defence, and which, if proved, has the effect of reducing a charge of murder to one of culpable homicide.

There is no onus of proof on an accused in respect of the special defences of alibi, incrimination or self-defence[3]. In the case of insanity there is an onus on the accused to prove, on balance of probabilities, that he was insane at the time the crime was committed[4].

A special defence must be lodged not less that ten clear days before the trial diet[5]. If the special defence is not lodged timeously, it may be lodged late

1 1975 Act, s 150. Although the section refers both to minutes signed by only one party and to joint minutes signed by both parties, in practice the latter is almost always what is used.
2 1975 Act, s 82(1), which applies also to special defences.
3 *Lambie v HMA* 1973 JC 53, 1973 SLT 219.
4 See *Jessop v Robertson* 1989 SCCR 600 (Sh Ct), for a rare example of a case where the question of onus was raised.
5 1975 Act, s 82(1).

provided that the accused satisfies the court that there is a good reason why it was not lodged at the proper time. It must, in any event, be lodged before the jury is sworn[1]. The written notice of special defence must be lodged with the clerk of the court in which the trial is to take place and, at the same time, a copy of the notice must be sent to the Crown and to any co-accused or his solicitor[2].

The usual form of a special defence of self-defence is: 'McKenzie for the panel[3] (*or* accused) David Balfour pleads not guilty and specially and without prejudice to said plea, that, on the occasion libelled in charge one of the indictment, he was acting in self defence, he having been assaulted by the said John Henry Starr'. The other special defences run in a similar vein. The special defence is signed by the accused's solicitor or, in the High Court, by his counsel.

Attack on character

If the accused intends to attack the character of his alleged victim, he must give notice of this intention to the Crown and to the court[4]. There is no statutory provision for this. It is suggested that the notice should be in writing.

Objection to witness

An accused is entitled to object to any misnomer or misdescription of any person named in the indictment or of any witness in the list of Crown witnesses. The objection must be in writing and should be intimated to the court, the prosecutor and to any co-accused not less than ten clear days before the trial diet[5]. If no such intimation is made an objection will be allowed only on cause shown[5]. If the court considers the objection to be well founded, it may grant 'such remedy by postponement, adjournment or otherwise' as it considers appropriate[6].

POSTPONEMENT OF TRIAL

On occasions, as in the case of *David Balfour*, either the defence or the Crown may wish to have the trial postponed until a later date. It is also possible that the Crown and the defence are both agreed that there should be a postponement. It is provided by statute[7] that an application for

1 1975 Act, s 82(1).
2 AA(C) 1988, r 68, which applies also to notices of intention to lead evidence incriminating a co-accused.
3 'Panel', sometimes spelt 'pannel', is the old Scots word for an accused person in a jury trial. It is still in fairly common use.
4 Alison *Practice* p 533; *Macdonald* p 304.
5 1975 Act, s 80(1).
6 1975 Act, s 80(2).
7 1975 Act, s 77A(1).

postponement of a trial diet may be made to the court before which the trial is to take place at any time prior to that diet.

The application is made by way of a minute lodged with the sheriff clerk or the Clerk of Justiciary, as the case may be[1].

If the application is by only the one party, the court fixes a date for the hearing of it and appoints intimation to all the other parties[2]. Having heard the parties in open court, the court may refuse the application or, if it grants it, fix a new trial diet or give leave to the prosecutor to serve a notice fixing a new trial diet[3]. The accused should be present at the hearing unless the court permits it to proceed in his absence[4].

If all parties make a joint application[5], the court may dispose of it without hearing parties. In that event it is dealt with by a judge or sheriff in chambers[6].

PRELIMINARY DIET

Although there are no longer two diets in every solemn case, as there used to be before the coming into force of s 12 of the 1980 Act, there are some circumstances in which the accused or the Crown *must* apply for what is called a 'preliminary diet', and some circumstances in which they *may* so apply.

If an accused wishes to take a plea to the competency or relevancy of the indictment or any part of it, he must apply for a preliminary diet[7]. A similar rule applies if an accused wishes to take objection to the validity of the citation against him on the ground of any discrepancy between the record copy of the indictment and the copy served on him, or on account of any error or deficiency in the service copy or in the notice of citation[8]. An accused must make an application concerning these matters within fifteen clear days after service of the indictment[9]. On receipt of such an application the court *must* order that a preliminary diet be held[10]. In both cases, even although no timeous application for a preliminary diet has been made, the plea or objection may be taken later by leave of the court and on cause shown[11].

If an accused wishes to submit a plea in bar of trial or apply for separation or conjunction of charges or trials, he must apply for a preliminary diet[12], and must do so no later than ten clear days before the trial diet[13]. On receipt of such an application the court *may* order that a preliminary diet be held[14]. Again, if no application for a preliminary diet has been made timeously, the plea or

---

1   AA(C) 1988, r 42. An application by one party is in Form 20. A joint application is in Form 21.
2   AA(C) 1988, r 43.
3   1975 Act, s 77A(2). Detailed rules are contained in AA(C) 1988, rr 44–47.
4   1975 Act, s 77A(4).
5   AA(C) 1988, r 42(2), Form 21.
6   1975 Act, s 77A(3), AA(C) 1988, r 48.
7   1975 Act, s 108(2).
8   1975 Act, s 108(1).
9   1975 Act, s 76(7)(a).
10   1975 Act, s 76(1)(a).
11   1975 Act, s 108(1), (2).
12   1975 Act, s 108(2)(b), (c).
13   1975 Act, s 76(7)(b).
14   1975 Act, s 76(1)(b).

application may be entertained later by leave of the court and on cause shown[1].

If either the Crown or the defence wishes to move the court to refuse to allow part of the record of the judicial examination[2] to be read to the jury, an application must be made for a preliminary diet subject to the same limitations as in the preceding paragraph[3]. In practice the Crown and the defence usually agree about this, and there is no need for a preliminary diet.

If either the Crown or the defence considers that there is some matter, other than those mentioned in the three preceding paragraphs, which could with advantage be resolved before the trial diet, they may apply to the court to hold a preliminary diet[4]. The application may be made at any time between service of the indictment and the trial diet[5]. The court *may* grant such an application[6].

All applications for a preliminary diet must be made by minute of notice lodged with the Clerk of Justiciary or the sheriff clerk as the case may be[7]. There are detailed rules for the procedure following the lodging of such a minute[8].

When it orders that a preliminary diet is to take place, the court may postpone the trial diet for a period not longer than 21 days[9]. This period may be extended by the High Court[10]. Any postponement, whether of 21 days or more, does not count towards any time limit in respect of the case[11].

The accused should attend a preliminary diet, but the diet may proceed in his absence if the court permits[12]. A shorthand writer must be present at a preliminary diet, and a shorthand note is taken of all proceedings at the diet, which are to treated as proceedings at the trial[13]. Any matter which could have been the subject of a preliminary diet, notice of which was not timeously given, may still be considered by the court at a preliminary diet (fixed to deal with another matter) provided that notice has been intimated to the court and to the other parties at least 24 hours prior to the preliminary diet[14].

APPEAL FROM PRELIMINARY DIET

Either party may appeal to the High Court against a court's decision at a preliminary diet, provided that leave to appeal has been obtained from the court concerned[15]. Leave must be applied for immediately after the decision

---

1 1975 Act, s 108(2)(b), (c).
2 See above at pp 98–101.
3 1975 Act, s 76(1)(b) referring to an application under s 151(2).
4 1975 Act, s 76(1)(c).
5 1975 Act, s 76(7)(c).
6 1975 Act, s 76(1)(c).
7 AA(C) 1988, r 24. The minute is in Form 15.
8 AA(C) 1988, rr 25–33.
9 1975 Act, s 76(4).
10 1975 Act, s 76(5).
11 1975 Act, s 76(4).
12 1975 Act, s 76(6).
13 AA(C) 1988, r 33(2).
14 1975 Act, s 76(3).
15 1975 Act, s 76A(1).

of the court has been given[1], and the note of appeal[2] must be lodged within two days thereafter[3]. The judge against whose decision an appeal is taken has power to postpone the diet of trial if he grants leave to appeal[4], and the High Court has a similar power of postponement[5]. In the case of an appeal from a sheriff's decision, the sheriff must furnish the High Court with a report, which is made available to the parties[6]. There is no provision for the making of a report by a High Court judge, although no doubt the appeal court could call for a report if it considered it to be necessary. After hearing the appeal the High Court may affirm the decision of the court of first instance or, if allowing the appeal, remit to the court of first instance with such directions as it thinks fit[7]. If the court of first instance has dismissed the indictment or any part of it, the High Court may reverse that decision and direct that a trial diet be fixed[7].

MATTERS TO BE RAISED AT A PRELIMINARY DIET

We shall now briefly consider the various matters which must or may be raised at a preliminary diet.

Competency and relevancy

The same principles governing competency and relevancy apply in criminal as in civil cases.

A case is incompetent if it cannot be tried by the court before which it is brought. Examples of incompetency are: lack of jurisdiction (whether because of the territorial limitations of the court or because it is a crime which cannot be tried in that court, for example rape in the sheriff court); that the prosecutor has no title to prosecute; that the charge is time barred; that the 110-day rule has been broken. If the case is held to be incompetent, that is usually an end of the matter as incompetency cannot be cured by amendment.

A charge is irrelevant if what is libelled does not correspond with the requirements of the law relating to such a charge. A libel that set forth facts not amounting to a crime for example, would be irrelevant. Irrelevancy may very often be cured by amendment, and, if the amendment is allowed, the case may proceed to trial[8].

Plea in bar of trial

A plea in bar of trial is a plea to the effect that the trial should not take place at

1 AA(C) 1988, r 34(1).
2 AA(C) 1988, r 35, Form 17. The note of appeal is lodged with the Clerk of Justiciary or the sheriff clerk as the case may be.
3 1975 Act, s 76A(1).
4 AA(C) 1988, r 34(2).
5 1975 Act, s 76A(2); AA(C) 1988, r 38.
6 AA(C) 1988, rr 36(2)(b), 37.
7 1975 Act, s 76A(3).
8 For amendment, see below at pp 149, 150.

that particular time and place (or perhaps not at all, in which case the plea is indistinguishable from a plea to the competency). The following are examples of circumstances in which a plea in bar of trial may be taken: (1) the accused is insane and unable to plead or to give instructions for his defence; (2) the accused has 'tholed his assize', ie has already been tried for the crime concerned; (3) the accused has been a witness for the Crown in the trial of another person on the same charge; (4) the prosecutor is personally barred from proceeding[1]; (5) there has been undue delay amounting to oppression in bringing the accused to trial[2]; (6) the accused cannot have a fair trial because of pre-trial publicity[3].

Separation of charges

If there is more than one charge on an indictment, the accused may move the court to have the charges separated so that each would be tried before a different jury. Although the test has been said to be one of fairness to the accused[4], the modern law is that separation of charges will not be granted unless there is a material risk of real prejudice, which does not arise merely because the charges are of different kinds of crime committed at different times in different places and circumstances[5]. A motion for separation of charges is relatively rarely granted[6]. The decision whether to grant such a motion is essentially one for the discretion of the judge of first instance, and leave to appeal against such a decision should be granted only if the matter is finely balanced[7].

Separation of trials

The Crown has a wide discretion to place more than one accused together in an indictment, provided that there is some connection between the accused and/or the crimes[8]. If two or more persons are charged on the one indictment, each may move the court to separate the trials so that he is tried before a different jury from that which tries the other(s). As with separation of charges the test is fairness, but a motion to separate trials is seldom granted[9]. The decision is very much one for the judge of first instance. 'A decision to separate trials is one peculiarly within the discretion of the trial judge . . . It has been said that an appeal court will interfere only if oppression

1 See eg *Thom v HMA* 1976 JC 48, 1976 SLT 23: *HMA v Stewart* 1980 JC 84.
2 See eg *McGeown v HMA* 1989 SCCR 95, 1989 SLT 625.
3 For a full discussion of this see *X v Sweeney* 1982 JC 70, 1982 SCCR 161, 1983 SLT 48 sub nom *H v Sweeney. Kilbane v HMA* 1989 SCCR 313 is a recent example of a case in which the plea was taken and was unsuccessful.
4 *HMA v McGuiness* 1937 JC 37, 1937 SLT 274.
5 *Reid v HMA* 1984 SCCR 153, 1984 SLT 391.
6 *HMA v Maitland* 1985 SCCR 166, 1985 SLT 425, is a rare modern example of the granting of a motion to separate charges.
7 *Reid v HMA* 1984 SCCR 153, 1984 SLT 391.
8 *Hume* II, 177. *HMA v Granger* 1985 SCCR 4, 1985 SLT 496, is perhaps a fairly extreme example. Two accused were charged on the same indictment with perjury, and there was no suggestion of concert. It was held that, as the purpose of each accused's perjury was the same, viz to defeat the ends of justice, their trials should not be separated.
9 *Sangster v HMA* (1896) 2 Adam 182 at 189, 24R(J) 3 at 7, 4 SLT 135 at 136 per Lord Moncrieff.

is demonstrated. It is perhaps more accurate to say that an appeal court will not interfere unless there is shown to have taken place a palpable failure of justice'[1].

Conjunction of trials

If several accused are charged on separate indictments, they may move the court to be tried together. Such a motion is relatively rare, but will be granted if the court considers that the defence of the accused would be so prejudiced by separate trials that a miscarriage of justice might result[2].

Other matters which may be raised at a preliminary diet

There is no limit to the matters which may be the subject of a preliminary diet under s 76(1)(c) of the 1975 Act, but most applications have concerned the admissibility of evidence[3]. Evidence may be led at such a preliminary diet[4].

JURORS

Potential jurors are selected from the list of those qualified and liable to serve which must be kept for each sheriff court district[5].

Every person up to the age of 65, who is registered as a parliamentary or local government elector is eligible for jury service, provided that he has been ordinarily resident in the United Kingdom, Channel Islands or Isle of Man for at least five years since attaining the age of thirteen, and provided that he is not disqualified or ineligible[6].

A person who has served a prison sentence (or the equivalent for a young offender) of three months or more is disqualified for jury service unless rehabilitated under the Rehabilitation of Offenders Act 1974[7]. A person who has been sentenced to imprisonment (or the equivalent for a young offender) for five years or more is permanently disqualified for jury service[7].

The list of those who are ineligible for jury service is long[8]. It consists mainly of those concerned in the administration of justice. Certain other categories, such as members of either House of Parliament, servicemen and members of the medical and allied professions, are eligible for jury service, but are entitled, as of right to be excused[9].

Either the Crown or the defence may apply to the court to have a jury consisting of members of only one sex[10]. The trial judge may also of his own

---

1 *Davidson v HMA* 1981 SCCR 371 at 376 per Lord Justice-General Emslie.
2 *HMA v Clark* 1935 JC 51, 1935 SLT 143.
3 See eg *HMA v Cumming* 1983 SCCR 15 (Sh Ct), *McDonald v HMA* 1989 SCCR 165, 1989 SLT 627 (a case where the Crown challenged the competency of witnesses cited for the defence).
4 *HMA v Bell* 1984 SCCR 430, 1984 SLT 349.
5 Jurors (Scotland) Act 1825, s 3.
6 Law Reform (Miscellaneous Provisions) (Scotland) Act 1980, s 1(1).
7 Ibid, Sch 1, Part II.
8 Ibid, Sch 1, Pt I.
9 Ibid, Sch 1. Pt IV.
10 1975 Act, s 100(1).

volition decide to have a single sex jury[1]. An application by a party for a single sex jury must be made at least fifteen clear days prior to the trial diet and is heard in chambers[2]. The judge's decision thereon is final[3].

The clerk of the trial court is responsible for preparing the list of assize, that is the list of potential jurors who will be cited to attend court and from whom the jury will be selected[4]. The names are taken in rotation from the list of jurors[5]. If the trial is in the sheriff court, the potential jurors are taken from the list for the sheriff court district concerned[6]. If the trial is in the High Court, the potential jurors may be drawn from a wider area than the district in which the trial is being held[7].

It should be noted that, although throughout this section reference has been made to trial in the singular, it is more likely that jurors will be summoned to attend at a sitting of the court where several trials may take place.

Jurors are cited by recorded delivery or registered post[8].

Any person cited for jury service may be excused for a good reason by the clerk of court[9] or the judge[10]. There is still in force the rather sexist provision that a woman may be exempted from service on a jury for a particular case 'by reason of the nature of the evidence to be given or the issues to be tried'[11], although it is unlikely that much use is made of it nowadays. A woman may also apply to be exempted 'on account of pregnancy or other feminine condition or ailment'[12].

Any person who is cited as a juror and who fails to respond to the citation is guilty of an offence and may be fined up to £200[13].

1 1975 Act, s 100(1).
2 1975 Act, Sch 3, para 2.
3 1975 Act, Sch 3, para 3.
4 1975 Act, Sch 3, para 1.
5 1975 Act, s 90.
6 1975 Act, s 89.
7 1975 Act, s 87.
8 1975 Act, s 98.
9 Law Reform (Miscellaneous Provisions) (Scotland) Act 1980, s 1(5).
10 Ibid, s 1(6); 1975 Act, s 133. Under the latter provision the ground for excusing the juror must be stated in open court.
11 1975 Act, s 100(1).
12 1975 Act, Sch 3, para 8.
13 1975 Act, s 99(1).

Chapter 5

Solemn Procedure: The Trial

ACCELERATED TRIAL UNDER SECTION 102 OF THE 1975 ACT

Before the procedure at a normal trial is discussed, notice must be taken of what is called (in the headnote to the section) an 'accelerated trial'. The use of the word 'trial' in this context is rather misleading as, from the very nature of the procedure, the case does not in fact go to trial in the accepted sense, there being no evidence led.

Section 102 of the 1975 Act provides that an accused may intimate in writing to the Crown Agent an intention to plead guilty, in which case an accelerated procedure is followed. The section does not specify when a 's 102 letter' (as the intimation is usually called) may be submitted, but it is clear from the terms of one of the prescribed forms of notice[1] that it may be at any time after full committal. Although the section states that intimation is to be made to the Crown Agent, in practice the s 102 letter is usually delivered to the fiscal, who forwards it to Crown Office. It is then for Crown Counsel to instruct whether the s 102 procedure should be followed.

The actual plea offered in a s 102 letter may be the result of negotiation between the defence and the Crown, and it may well not completely reflect the charges in the petition. It is usually in the interests of the accused that a plea be negotiated as early as possible.

A s 102 letter may be submitted by an accused even if he has already been served with an indictment for trial in normal course. The advantage of having the case brought forward in such a situation is unlikely to be very great unless the indictment has been served a long time prior to the trial diet. Of course it is always beneficial to give advance information of a plea of guilty in order that witnesses and prospective jurors may be told that they need not attend court. This can, however, be done simply by the defence informing the prosecutor without going through the formality of s 102 procedure. In practice most s 102 letters come before any indictment has been served.

If the Crown agrees to accept the s 102 letter, and an indictment has not already been served, a special s 102 indictment is served on the accused. This does not have any list of witnesses or productions appended[2]. With the indictment is served a notice telling the accused where and when to appear, which must be not less than four clear days after the date of the notice[2]. If the accused has already received an indictment, only a notice is served on him.

1 AA(C) 1988, Form 6.
2 1975 Act, s 102(1).

124

The form of notice will depend on whether the accused has already been served with an indictment[1]. A copy of the s 102 indictment with intimation of the date of calling is usually sent by the fiscal to the defence solicitor as a matter of courtesy.

The s 102 indictment may be accompanied by a list of previous convictions. Any objection to a conviction on that list must be intimated in writing to the fiscal within two days after service of the indictment[2].

If the accused submits his s 102 letter prior to service of an indictment, the Crown may indict him in either the sheriff court or the High Court[3]. If he has already been served with a sheriff court indictment, then the s 102 diet will be held in the court specified in the notice served with that indictment[4]. However, if the accused has already been indicted in the High Court, the s 102 diet may take place in Edinburgh, notwithstanding that the notice served with the indictment indicates a different venue[5].

When the s 102 diet calls, the accused usually pleads guilty as he has intimated in his letter. However, sometimes he has changed his mind and pleads not guilty or tenders a plea of guilty to only part of the indictment. In that event, unless the prosecutor is prepared to accept the plea tendered, the diet is deserted *pro loco et tempore* (ie for that particular time and place), and the case proceeds as if there had been no s 102 letter[6]. If the accused has already been served with an indictment prior to the s 102 letter, and a trial has therefore been fixed, the court may postpone that trial diet, and the period of postponement will not count towards any time limit which would otherwise apply to the case[7]. If the Crown receives advance warning that the accused has changed his mind, the s 102 indictment may simply not be called in court. Matters will then proceed as if no s 102 letter had been submitted.

If the accused does plead guilty at the s 102 diet, he must sign the plea, and the judge countersigns it[8]. The court then proceeds to sentence in exactly the same way as if the accused had been found guilty after trial. The prosecutor moves for sentence, gives a summary of the facts of the case and informs the court of the period, if any, during which the accused has been in custody. Counsel or the solicitor for the accused makes a plea in mitigation, and the judge either proceeds to sentence or adjourns in order to obtain reports. If the version of the facts given by the Crown is disputed by the defence, the court should ascertain whether there is any possibility of reconciling the discrepancies. If this is not possible, either the disputed facts should be ignored or a proof in mitigation may take place[9]. In that event evidence is led by the defence, and the Crown may then lead evidence to refute the defence case. The judge decides which version of the facts he prefers, and he sentences on

1 AA(C) 1988, r 12, Forms 6, 7.
2 1975 Act, s 68(4). The section specifically states 'procurator fiscal' and does not indicate that, if the case is being indicted in the High Court, the intimation should be sent to the Crown Agent, although AA(C) 1988, r 166 would normally imply this.
3 1975 Act, s 102(2)(a). If in the High Court, the diet will usually be in Edinburgh, but could be at any other place where the High Court is sitting.
4 1975 Act, s 102(2)(b).
5 AA(C) 1988, r 12(3).
6 1975 Act, s 102(3).
7 1975 Act, s 102(3). AA(C) 1988, r 12(3)–(6).
8 1975 Act, s 103(1). This rule applies even when the accused tenders a plea of guilty to only part of the indictment and the prosecutor is not prepared to accept the restricted plea. If the prosecutor does not accept the restricted plea, this fact must be recorded (s 103(2)).
9 *Barn v Smith* 1978 JC 17, 1978 SLT (Notes) 3. If the prosecutor concurs in the request for a proof in mitigation, the court should allow it: *Kyle v McNaughton* 1990 SCCR 450.

the basis of that version. Alternatively, in the event of the discrepancies between Crown and defence not being reconciled, the court may permit the accused to withdraw his plea of guilty, and the case can then proceed to trial in due course as if a plea of not guilty had originally been tendered[1].

If it is apparent that reports will be required before sentence can be passed, the court may very well adjourn the case for reports without having heard the facts. In that event the case may be dealt with by a different judge when it next calls.

Even although the case has been brought in the sheriff court, it may be remitted to the High Court for sentence if the sheriff considers his powers to be inadequate[2].

A plea of guilty, whether tendered at a s 102 diet or at a diet of trial in normal course, may be withdrawn in certain very limited circumstances, eg if the plea was tendered under a substantial error or misconception, or if it was a plea to an incompetent or irrelevant charge[3].

JURY TRIAL

The procedure at a jury trial will now be discussed so far as possible in chronological order of events.

PRELIMINARY MATTERS

Shorthand note

The whole proceedings at the trial must be taken down in shorthand[4]. The shorthand writer takes an oath that he will faithfully perform his duties (the oath *de fideli administratione*).

Calling of the diet

The first thing which happens at a trial diet is that the clerk of court calls the diet[5] and asks the accused to confirm his identity.

It is essential that the accused be present at the trial diet[6], as must the prosecutor[7]. If the accused is not present, the court usually grants a warrant

---

1 See CGB Nicholson *The Law and Practice of Sentencing in Scotland* (1981, with Suppt 1985) para 8–03.
2 1975 Act, s 104. See below at p 157.
3 *HMA v Black* (1894) 1 Adam 312; *HMA v Robertson* (1899) 3 Adam 1, 1F(J) 74, 7 SLT 10. It is competent to allow the plea to be withdrawn in the sheriff court: *Healy v HMA* 1990 SCCR 110.
4 1975 Act, s 274.
5 See the case of *David Balfour* at p 30 above.
6 1975 Act, s 145(1). The subsection continues: 'Provided that, if during the course of his trial an accused so misconducts himself that in the view of the court a proper trial cannot take place unless he is removed, the court may order him to be removed for so long as his conduct may make necessary and the trial to proceed in his absence; but if he is not legally represented the court shall appoint counsel or a solicitor to represent his interests during such absence'.
7 *Walker v Emslie* (1899) 3 Adam 102, 2F(J) 18, 7 SLT 281.

for his arrest, if satisfied that he has been properly cited to attend the diet. Alternatively the diet may be adjourned under s 77 of the 1975 Act, or the accused may be cited to a fresh diet under s 127 of the same Act[1].

A body corporate, being an artificial person, cannot physically appear at a trial diet. If the case is actually proceeding to trial the body corporate must be represented by counsel or a solicitor, but, if the case is not going to trial, it may appear by a 'representative'[2]. The representative may appear to state objection to the competency or relevancy of the indictment, to tender a plea of guilty or not guilty, or to make a plea in mitigation[3]. If, at a trial diet, a body corporate is not represented by anyone, the court may hear and dispose of the case in its absence, provided that it is satisfied that the body corporate has been properly cited[4].

Pleading

Counsel or the solicitor for the accused intimates that the accused is pleading guilty or not guilty. If the accused in unrepresented, the clerk or the judge will ask him how he pleads. If the plea is one of guilty (whether to all or part of the indictment), it must be signed by the accused himself and counter-signed by the judge[5]. If the plea is guilty to the whole indictment, or if the prosecutor accepts a restricted plea, there is no need to empanel a jury, and the court may proceed to deal with the case as if the accused had been found guilty after trial[6]. The procedure is then the same as that described for a plea of guilty under the s 102 procedure[7].

If the plea is one of not guilty, the accused may seek to give late intimation of a special defence or of the incrimination of a co-accused, or to be allowed to lodge a list of witnesses or productions[8].

A restricted plea of guilty, which it is known the Crown will not accept, should be tendered outwith the presence of potential jurors if at all possible. This is so that the jurors will be unaware of the fact that the accused is guilty of any offence.

The jury

If the accused has pleaded not guilty or has tendered a restricted plea of guilty which the prosecutor has not accepted, the case will go to trial. Accordingly a

---

1 1975 Act, s 77 provides for the case being adjourned to a later sitting of the court within one month (sheriff court) or two months (High Court). Section 127 provides for the accused being served with another copy of the indictment within nine clear days of the abortive trial diet, along with a notice to appear to answer the indictment at another diet (which may be in the same court or a different court), that diet to be not less than nine clear days after the date when notice was given.
2 1975 Act, s 74(2). 'Representative' is defined as 'an officer or servant of the body corporate duly appointed by it for the purpose of those proceedings' (s 74(8)).
3 1975 Act, s 74(2).
4 1975 Act, s 74(4).
5 1975 Act, ss 103(1), 124. Refusal by a prosecutor to accept a restricted plea must be recorded (s 103(2)).
6 1975 Act, s 124.
7 See above at pp 125, 126.
8 See above at pp 114, 115 and 116, 117.

jury must be empanelled. The name of each person summoned to the diet as a potential juror will have already been written on a piece of paper together with his or her number on the list of assize. The folded papers will have been put into a box or jar, from which (subject to challenges and objections) fifteen are now drawn by the clerk of court[1].

Jury vetting does not exist in Scotland[2].

The prosecutor and the defence solicitor or counsel (or the accused himself if unrepresented) will have been furnished with a copy of the list of assize, which gives the name, address and occupation of each potential juror. The accused should be told by his legal representative to indicate if there is any person called to serve on the jury to whom he may take exception, perhaps, eg because he knows him.

The prosecutor and every accused are each entitled to challenge three jurors without giving any reason[3]. Such a challenge is sometimes called a 'peremptory' challenge or objection. It is usually exercised by the challenger saying, 'Needn't come', in a quiet and undramatic manner. The challenge must be made as soon as the juror's name is called, otherwise it will not be allowed[4]. Such a challenge automatically disqualifies the juror from participating in the trial[5].

There is no limit to the number of objections to jurors 'on cause shown'[6]. 'Cause shown' is interpreted fairly narrowly.

'It is not a sufficient cause for a juror to be excused that he is of a particular race, religion or political belief or occupation, or indeed that the juror might or might not feel prejudice one way or the other towards the crime itself or to the background against which the crime has been committed. A juror can, of course, be excused on limited personal grounds. If he is personally concerned in the facts of the particular case, or closely connected with a party to the proceedings or with a witness, or if he suffers from some physical disability such as deafness or blindness or dumbness, there would be special cause for excluding him. Personal hardship or conscientious objection to jury service by itself may also be a ground for excusing a juror, at the discretion of the trial judge. The essence of the system of trial by jury is that it consists of fifteen individuals chosen at random from amongst those who are cited for possible service'[7].

General questioning of potential jurors in advance of balloting is not appropriate[7], although it may be appropriate to ask jurors, after they have been balloted, whether there are any reasons known to them which make it desirable that they should not take part in that particular trial[8].

After the jury has been sworn to try the case no objection to a juror is competent[9]. However, a juror, even although sworn, may be excused by the judge for good reason (for example familiarity with the case), provided that

---

1 1975 Act, s 129.
2 *McCadden v HMA* 1985 SCCR 282 at 286, 1986 SLT 138 at 141, per Lord Justice-Clerk Wheatley.
3 1975 Act, s 130(1).
4 1975 Act, s 130(2).
5 1975 Act, s 130(3).
6 1975 Act, s 130(4).
7 *M v HMA* 1974 SLT (Notes) 25, per Lord Justice-General Emslie.
8 *Spink v HMA* 1989 SCCR 413.
9 1975 Act, s 130(6).

this is done prior to the first Crown witness being sworn. In that event another person is balloted to take his place. In the light of this statutory provision (introduced in 1987)[1] Lord Justice-General Emslie issued a note to judges about the practice which should be followed. This is that unempanelled jurors should be discharged only after the first witness for the Crown has entered the witness box and taken the oath[2]. This accounts for the rather strange procedure which was followed in the case of *David Balfour*, when the first witness was sworn and the trial was then immediately adjourned[3].

Once the jury has been selected (subject to the possibility of a juror's being replaced as just described), the clerk usually reads over the whole indictment to the jurors, substituting the third person for the second person throughout[4]. If the indictment is long and complex, the clerk may read a summary approved by the judge[4]. In some courts it is the practice, if the indictment is lengthy, to provide the jurors with copies of it, so that they may follow it as it is read to them by the clerk. It is suggested that this may in many cases be preferable to attempting to summarise it. After the charge has been read to the jurors they take the oath (or affirmation) that they will 'well and truly try the accused and give a true verdict according to the evidence'[5]. If a juror is replaced after the jury has been sworn (as described in the previous paragraph), the indictment is read out to the new juror and he or she takes the oath as an individual. After the jury has been sworn any special defence or notice of intention to incriminate a co-accused, which has been lodged by an accused, is usually read to them, although there is no statutory requirement for this to be done. It has recently been specifically held by the High Court that there is no need for a notice incriminating a co-accused to be read to the jury[6]. The court seemed to imply that a special defence should be read out, but gave no authority for this proposition.

If a juror dies or becomes ill in the course of the trial or is 'for any other reason unfit to continue to serve as a juror', the court may, in its discretion, on the application of either the Crown or the defence, direct that the trial continue with the remaining jurors, provided that their number is not less than twelve[7]. If the number of jurors is thus reduced below fifteen, at least eight are still required for a majority verdict of guilty[7]. 'Any other reason' leaves much scope for the discretion of the trial judge, although a sheriff has held that the need to cancel a holiday because of the length of the trial did not fall into that category[8].

In exceptional circumstances something (such as an impropriety involving a juror) may occur which requires the whole jury to be discharged and the diet deserted *pro loco et tempore*, but this is a last resort. Usually any

---

1 1975 Act, s 129. All fifteen jurors may be excused and a completely new jury empanelled in terms of this provision: *Hughes Petr* 1989 SCCR 490, 1990 SLT 142.

2 Note to Judges dated 22 January 1988.

3 See above at p 32.

4 1975 Act, s 135. This section also provides that the jury may have copies of the indictment at the discretion of the judge. If the jury receive copies of the indictment, they should not include any charge to which the accused has pleaded guilty and which is therefore not proceeding to trial before the jury.

5 1975 Act, s 135. AA(C) 1988, r 69, Form 33 (Parts 1, 2).

6 *McShane v HMA* 1989 SCCR 687.

7 1975 Act, s 134.

8 *Farrell v HMA* 1985 SCCR 23, 1985 SLT 324.

impropriety should be dealt with by discharge of the juror concerned and appropriate directions to the remaining jurors[1].

Introduction by the judge

There are no opening speeches by either the Crown or the defence in a criminal jury trial in Scotland. It used to be the case that, the jury having been sworn, the prosecution evidence was led without any more ado. Since about the 1970s, however, the practice has grown up among the majority of judges in both the High Court and the sheriff court of making some brief introductory remarks to the jury, partly in order to give them some idea of what is going to happen, and also partly to provide them with an opportunity to settle down.

The usual procedure is thus as follows: the jury is empanelled and sworn; the first Crown witness is called and sworn[2]; the court adjourns for a few minutes so that the jurors may make themselves comfortable; after the adjournment the judge makes his introductory remarks; the evidence of the first Crown witness is taken.

In his remarks the judge usually introduces those appearing in the case and describes the procedure in outline[3]. It must be emphasised that the practice of giving an introduction has no statutory authority, and there is no obligation on a judge to follow it. However, it is submitted that in most cases it makes good sense.

THE EVIDENCE

Evidence for the Crown is led first. There is no obligation on the defence to lead evidence, but defence evidence is frequently led. This section will deal with various aspects of evidence. Much of what will be said applies equally to both the Crown and the defence.

Oath or affirmation

Each witness must give his evidence after taking an oath or, if he objects to being sworn, making a solemn affirmation[4]. If practical, a witness is entitled to take an oath according to the forms of his own religion. Thus a Jew takes the oath with his head covered. If it is impractical for a witness to take a particular form of oath, he must affirm[5].

---

1 *Stewart v HMA* 1980 JC 103, 1980 SLT 245; *McCadden v HMA* 1985 SCCR 282, 1986 SLT 138; *Hamilton v HMA* 1986 SCCR 227, 1986 SLT 663.
2 See notes 1 and 2 above, at p 129.
3 See the case of *David Balfour* at pp 32, 33.
4 Oaths Act 1978, s 5(1). The form of oath and affirmation are in AA(C) 1988, Form 33, Parts 3, 4.
5 Oaths Act 1978, s 5(2).

Child witnesses

If a witness is a child of twelve or under, he will not be asked to take the oath. The judge must ascertain by questioning whether he understands the difference between truth and untruth[1]. If the judge is satisfied that he does understand the difference, the judge should tell him that he must tell the truth[1]. If the child does not understand the difference, he is not a competent witness.

A child between twelve and fourteen may be put on oath if the judge is satisfied that he understands the meaning of the oath. A cynic might wonder how many adult witnesses would be able to satisfy a judge that *they* understood the meaning of the oath, if they were asked.

When a child, especially a very young child, is a witness, the court usually adopts a degree of informality in order to put the witness at his ease[2]. The judge may remove his wig and gown and either have the child beside him on the bench or sit at the clerk's table with the child. Counsel and solicitors will very often also abandon their wigs and gowns. Both the examiner and the witness may remain seated during the taking of evidence. On occasions, especially in the case of alleged sexual abuse of a child, a screen may be used to ensure that the child witness is unable to see the accused, although this may create problems if the identification of the accused by the witness is a vital issue. The public may be excluded while a child witness is giving evidence in a case with sexual connotations[3].

Witnesses requiring interpretation

If a witness does not speak or understand English, or is deaf and unable to speak, an interpreter will be required. It is the responsibility of the fiscal to provide an interpreter. The interpreter takes an oath that he will faithfully perform his duties as interpreter (the oath *de fideli administratione*). He must translate every word of the witness's evidence.

If an accused does not speak or understand English or is deaf and mute, the whole proceedings must be translated for his benefit.

Presentation of evidence

In many cases insufficient thought is given in advance as to how evidence should be presented. It must be borne in mind that the jury knows nothing about the case other than what is contained in the indictment and what has been disclosed by evidence already led. The same also applies to the judge, except that he will probably have seen and read copies of the productions prior to the commencement of the trial. Accordingly, evidence should be presented in a way which makes it easy for the jury to understand and follow. Careful thought must be given to the order in which witnesses should be called and about the order in which questions should be asked of each witness. Before any question is asked of a witness the examiner should reflect on exactly what

1 *Rees v Lowe* 1989 SCCR 664.
2 See Memorandum by Lord Justice-General Hope, 26 July 1990.
3 1975 Act, s 166.

evidence he hopes to obtain from the witness and frame his questions accordingly. This will inevitably involve a good deal of time being devoted to preparation of the case, but it will be time well spent.

The actual technique of asking questions will of course vary from case to case and from witness to witness, but there are certain principles which apply to all cases and every witness.

Firstly and most importantly, the examiner must ensure that the witness's evidence is audible to the jury and the judge. A convenient way of achieving this is usually for the examiner to stand beside the jury rather than next to the witness box. The witness is then encouraged to project his voice towards the jury. The examiner should observe the jurors in order to see whether any of them has apparent difficulty in hearing the witness. If the judge has difficulty in hearing, he is unlikely to keep quiet about it.

Questions should be as brief as possible. Only one question should be asked at a time. There is a great temptation, especially in cross-examination, to ask a series of questions together. This is usually a waste of time.

So far as possible, technical language should be avoided in asking questions. If the witness is giving evidence about technical matters, he should always be asked to explain the technicalities in everyday language. These comments apply equally to legal technicalities. The use of legal jargon should, in any event, be avoided if at all possible.

Leading questions

A leading question is one which suggests its own answer. Such questions often begin with such words as 'Isn't it the case that' or 'Do you agree that'. The general rule is that leading questions are not permitted in examination-in-chief (ie when a witness is being examined on behalf of the party calling him)[1], but are permissible in cross-examination (ie examination on behalf of the other party or parties in the case). However, this rule is subject to certain exceptions.

Preliminary matters, such as a witness's name and designation, may be the subject of leading questions in chief. If it is clear that part of a witness's evidence is not in dispute, that may be led on. It is good manners for an advocate (using the word here to mean any lawyer presenting a case in court) to indicate to his opponent if there is an area of evidence on which he has no objection to leading questions being asked in chief.

If a witness appears to be 'hostile' (a term which has no technical meaning in Scotland), by going back on his precognition or prevaricating, it is generally accepted that leading questions may be asked of him, although the authority for this proposition is somewhat sparse[2]. What is certainly the case is that a witness may be asked if he has, on a previous occasion, made a statement about a matter which is different from the evidence which he has given about it at the trial. If he denies having made such a statement or its terms, the

---

1 The reason for this rule is fairly obvious. It is the witness's evidence and not that of the examiner, which the jury is entitled to hear.
2 *Frank v HMA* 1938 JC 17 at 22, 1938 SLT 109 at 110, per Lord Justice-Clerk Aitchison: AG Walker and NML Walker *The Law of Evidence in Scotland* pp 364–5: RW Renton and HH Brown *Criminal Procedure according to the Law of Scotland* (5th edn, 1983) para 10–40.

making of it and its contents may be proved[1]. Of course, if the witness denies the accuracy of the previous statement or denies having made it, his only *evidence* in the case remains what he has said from the witness box at the trial, although his credibility may be put in question.

Hearsay

Hearsay evidence is evidence of what a person has said. It is sometimes asserted that such evidence is inadmissible in a criminal trial, but that is not completely accurate. Hearsay evidence is generally inadmissible insofar as it is relied upon to prove the accuracy of the statement spoken to. For example, if a witness says, 'John Smith told me that he had been threatened by the accused', this is not admissible evidence of the fact that John Smith was threatened. However, it *is* perfectly good evidence of the fact that John Smith made the statement that he had been threatened, and may be admissible for that purpose.

There are many circumstances in which hearsay evidence may in fact be admissible, and some of the most important are noted here.

Evidence of a statement made by an accused is admissible subject to the general rules of admissibility of incriminating statements[2]. However, a statement by one accused is not evidence against another accused, unless made in the presence of the latter[3].

A statement which is part of the *res gestae* (ie part of what actually happened at the time the crime was committed) is normally admissible. For example, if a witness depones that he heard someone at the scene of the crime cry out, 'My God, Jim's got a knife', and this was immediately followed by a stabbing, this would be admissible. The person who shouted out the remark should be led as a witness if he can be found.

Evidence of what the victim of a crime said shortly after the commission of the crime may be admissible. This is known as 'a *de recenti* statement'. It is admissible only as fortifying the credibility of the victim's evidence.

As has already been noted, evidence of a statement previously made by a witness may be admissible under s 147 of the 1975 Act[4].

If hearsay is the best evidence available, it may be admissible not only as evidence that a statement was made but also of the contents of that statement. Thus, if a person is dead, and his death is proved or admitted, evidence of what he has said about a matter would be evidence on that matter, if it were otherwise competent evidence[5]. The weight to be given to the evidence may be affected by the fact that there can be no cross-examination on it, but weight and admissibility are two different things.

Evidence of a previous identification of the accused by a witness who, in court, cannot or will not identify him is admissible[6].

Business records may in certain circumstances be sufficient evidence of

1 1975 Act, s 147. This applies only if the previous statement is admissible in evidence. A precognition (other than a precognition on oath), eg, is not admissible, as it is the statement of the witness in the words of the precognoscer rather than of the witness himself.
2 See above at pp 77, 84.
3 See eg *McIntosh v HMA* 1986 SCCR 496, 1987 SLT 296.
4 See note 1 above.
5 See eg *HMA v Docherty* 1980 SLT (Notes) 33.
6 *Muldoon v Herron* 1970 JC 30, 1970 SLT 228; *Smith v HMA* 1986 SCCR 135.

their contents, if the person who supplied the information from which the records have been compiled is unavailable[1].

Examination-in-chief

The purpose of examination-in-chief is to lead evidence of facts favourable to the examiner's side. The limitation on leading questions has already been noted[2].

Cross-examination[3]

After the party leading a witness has finished his examination-in-chief, the other parties have the right to cross-examine. If there are several accused, they usually cross-examine in the order in which they appear on the indictment, although the judge may permit a different order, if he considers that any accused might be prejudiced by following the normal practice. If an accused or other defence witness gives evidence, the prosecutor always cross-examines last, ie after cross-examination for any other accused has been completed.

There are two main purposes of cross-examination: (1) to cast doubt on the credibility or reliability of the witness; and (2) to elicit evidence of facts favourable to the cross-examiner's side. In the case of some witnesses only one of these purposes will be relevant. If it is not necessary to achieve either of these purposes with the witness, then he should not be cross-examined at all.

As has already been noted[4], leading questions are permitted in cross-examination.

In civil cases failure to cross-examine a witness on a particular matter may entitle the court to draw the inference that the witness's evidence on that matter is accepted by the cross-examiner as true. No such inference may be drawn from failure to cross-examine in a criminal trial[5].

'Ordinarily, there is no burden on the accused and he is entitled to sit back and leave the Crown to it. Of course, if he sits back too far and too long, he may come to grief, but that is his own affair. He may leave the Crown evidence severely alone, in the hope that it does not reach the standard of reasonable certainty, or he may intervene at points where he is hopeful of raising a reasonable doubt. It follows that the procurator for the accused may be as selective as he chooses in cross-examination. The worst that can happen to him is that his selection may be criticised and his omissions commented on'[6].

1 Criminal Evidence Act 1965, s 1.
2 See above at pp 132, 133.
3 For a specialised examination of cross-examination in relation to criminal cases see Stone *Cross Examination in Criminal Trials* (1988). For a rather old fashioned but nonetheless valuable and reasonably concise discussion on the technique of cross-examination in general see Lees *A Handbook of Written and Oral Pleading* (2nd edn of 1920 reprinted in 1988 by Caledonian Books) pp 91–102. Although dealing mainly with civil cases, the comments there made apply, on the whole, equally to criminal trials.
4 See above at p 132.
5 *McPherson v Copeland* 1961 JC 74, 1961 SLT 373 (a summary case, but the principle is the same in both solemn and summary cases).
6 *McPherson v Copeland* 1961 JC 74 at 78, 1961 SLT 373 at 375, per Lord Justice-Clerk Thomson.

Although there is no doubt that this is the law, it is generally rash, if not foolish, for the defence agent or counsel to fail to cross-examine a witness who has given strong evidence against his client – especially before a jury.

If the defence intends to lead evidence of a particular fact, then, notwithstanding what was said in *McPherson*, it is advisable, and probably necessary, to put that fact to the Crown witnesses in cross-examination, if they have given evidence which is incompatible with it. This is known as 'laying a foundation in cross'. The first reason for the rule is to give the Crown witness an opportunity of commenting on the defence version of the facts – it is not impossible that he may agree with it! Secondly, if the matter has been put in cross-examination, it cannot be suggested by the Crown that the accused has only just thought it up when he himself gives evidence about it. If, of course, the accused has not informed his solicitor of something and then comes out with it for the first time in his own evidence, there is not much that can be done about it.

It has been held in a summary case that failure on the part of a prosecutor to cross-examine an accused did not bar the prosecutor from seeking a conviction[1]. In a jury trial a prosecutor who did not cross-examine an accused but nevertheless asked the jury to convict would almost certainly occasion remarks of disapproval from the bench.

In cross-examination, as in so much else, moderation is advisable. Hectoring and bullying are seldom productive and may antagonise the jury. If the cross-examiner obtains the answer he wants, he should stop there and not ask further questions which may result in answers which undermine any good already done.

Re-examination

After all the parties have cross-examined, the party calling the witness has a limited right to ask questions in what is called re-examination. The right to ask questions is limited to dealing with new matters raised in cross-examination or to clarify any ambiguities arising from cross-examination. It is not a proper use of re-examination to introduce new matters which could properly have been raised in examination-in-chief. However, such questions may be permitted subject to the right of other parties to ask further question in cross-examination relating to these matters only. As the sheriff reminded the depute fiscal in the case of *David Balfour*[2], leading questions should not be asked in re-examination[3].

Questions by the judge

The judge may ask questions of any witness. According to the strict procedural rule, after re-examination *only* the judge may ask questions: any party who wishes to have further questions put must do so through the judge. However, this rule has been relaxed to some extent in recent years so that

1 *Young v Guild* 1984 SCCR 477.
2 See above at p 36.
3 ID Macphail *A Revised Version of a Research Paper on the Law of Evidence in Scotland* (1987) para 8.33.

judges sometimes permit further questions with a limited right of further cross-examination as described in the previous paragraph.

If the judge does ask questions, he must do so circumspectly and ensure that he is not usurping the function of the advocate. 'I must deprecate the practice of . . . constant interruptions by a presiding judge. Basically his function is to clear up any ambiguities that are not being cleared up either by the examiner or the cross-examiner. He is also entitled to ask such questions as he might regard relevant and important for the proper determination of the case by the jury, but that right must be exercised with discretion, and only exercised when the occasion requires it. It should not result in the presiding judge taking over the role of examiner or cross-examiner. Normally the appropriate time to put such relevant questions as he may think necessary for the proper elicitation of the truth is at the end of the witness's evidence, and not during the course of examination or cross-examination'[1].

Release of witness

The Crown should not release any witness without the consent of the defence. This is because the defence has the right to call any witness who is on the Crown list or is in a notice of additional witnesses.

Recall of witness

At common law the judge has power to recall any witness at any time in order to clarify an ambiguity[2]. It has been held by the High Court that, in a summary case, the power may be exercised even during the defence speech to the court[3]. It is very doubtful whether a judge in a jury trial would be justified in recalling a witness during the defence speech to the jury. He should instead tell the jury that, if their recollection of the evidence differs from that of counsel or the solicitor for the defence, it is their recollection upon which they must rely.

If a judge does recall a witness in exercise of his common law power, he himself asks the witness whatever questions he considers appropriate. No doubt, if his questions elicited new matter from the witness, he would permit parties to ask further questions restricted to this new matter.

There is now also a statutory right for a party to recall a witness with the leave of the judge[4]. The purpose of the recall is not confined to correcting omissions or clarifying ambiguities[5]. Although it is not specifically stated in the section, it is probably implicit in it that recall of a witness thereunder must be before the close of the case of the party seeking the recall[6].

1 *Livingstone v HMA* (1974) SCCR Supp 68 at 69–70, per Lord Justice-Clerk Wheatley.
2 *McNeilie v HMA* 1929 JC 50 at 53, 1929 SLT 145 at 147, per Lord Justice-General Clyde.
3 *Rollo v Wilson* 1988 SCCR 312, 1988 SLT 659 – the ambiguity was whether or not a Crown witness had identified the accused.
4 1975 Act, s 148A.
5 *Thomson v HMA* 1988 SCCR 354, 1989 SLT 22, in which a witness who prevaricated was detained after giving her evidence. At a later stage she indicated her willingness to tell the truth, and the sheriff permitted her recall. This was approved by the High Court on appeal.
6 *Thomson v HMA* 1988 SCCR 354 at 360 (note by Sheriff G H Gordon, editor of SCCR).

Additional evidence

At any time before the commencement of the speeches to the jury the judge may permit the prosecutor or the defence to lead additional evidence notwithstanding that the witness to be called or the production to be referred to is not included in the list appended to the indictment or in any notice lodged under s 81 (notice of additional witness or production for the Crown) or s 82(2) (notice of witnesses or productions for the defence) of the 1975 Act, or that a witness must be recalled[1]. Such additional evidence will be allowed, however, only when the judge (a) considers that it is prima facie material, and (b) accepts that, at the time when the jury was sworn, the evidence was not available, or the materiality of the evidence could not have been foreseen by the party seeking to call the evidence[2]. If a motion to lead additional evidence is granted, the judge may adjourn or postpone the trial before permitting the evidence to be led[3].

Evidence in replication

After the close of the defence case and before the commencement of speeches to the jury, the judge may permit the prosecutor to lead additional evidence for the purpose of (a) contradicting evidence given by any defence witness which could not reasonably have been anticipated by the prosecutor, or (b) providing proof of a statement made by a witness on a previous occasion (under s 147 of the 1975 Act)[4].

As with the additional evidence mentioned in the preceding section, it is no bar to calling evidence under this section that the witness or production are not on any list or in any notice, or that a witness must be recalled[5]. Again, the judge may adjourn or postpone the trial before permitting the additional evidence to be led[6].

Evidence in replication is competent even where the evidence which it is sought to rebut has been elicited in cross-examination by a co-accused rather than in chief by the accused himself[7].

Evidence of accused's criminal record

There is a general prohibition against the leading of evidence about the criminal record (if any) of an accused[8]. Although the statutory provision does not say so explicitly, it is well established that the prohibition does not apply to the defence, and that there is nothing to stop an accused giving evidence about his own criminal record or eliciting evidence of it from some other

1 1975 Act, s 149(2).
2 1975 Act, s 149(1).
3 1975 Act, s 149(3).
4 1975 Act, s 149A(1).
5 1975 Act, s 149A(2).
6 1975 Act, s 149A(3).
7 *Sandlan v HMA* 1983 JC 22, 1983 SCCR 71, 1983 SLT 519. At the trial in this case the accused was himself permitted to be recalled in order to rebut evidence in replication (using the power to permit additional evidence under s 149(1)).
8 1975 Act, s 160(1).

witness, if he so desires[1]. There are special rules governing the accused himself being asked questions about his character and criminal record, and these will be examined below[2].

There are exceptions to the general rule. It is always competent to prove a previous conviction if it is necessary to do so in order to establish part of the charge on which the accused is being tried[3], or if the accused has led evidence of his own good character[4]. There are also cases where the fact that an accused has a previous conviction may be referred to in the course of the evidence, although it is not necessary for the proof of the crime being tried as such, but is evidence of an incidental matter which is an essential part of the Crown case. So, where articles which an accused had been given on his release from prison were left by him on the same day at the scene of a crime, it was held admissible to lead evidence from the prison officer who had given him the articles (thus making it clear to the jury that he had just served a prison sentence)[5].

The effect of a breach of the prohibition on disclosure of previous convictions depends on the circumstances in which it occurs. If the prosecutor deliberately leads evidence that an accused has a criminal record, and the accused is convicted by the jury, the conviction will be quashed on appeal, even although the trial judge has directed the jury to ignore the disclosure[6]. However, if the disclosure has been the result of inadvertence or is accidental, then the conviction may be allowed to stand, provided that the judge has adequately directed the jury and there appears to have been no miscarriage of justice[7].

If previous convictions are disclosed and the trial judge concludes that the matter is too serious for him to remedy in his charge, he should probably desert the trial diet *pro loco et tempore*, reserving the right of the Crown to bring fresh proceedings against the accused[8]. If a conviction is quashed on appeal because of disclosure, it may be appropriate to allow a new trial[8].

Evidence of the accused

The accused is always a competent witness in his own defence[9]. If he is the only defence witness who is to speak to the facts of the case, he should be called as the first witness for the defence[10]. His failure to give evidence must

---

1 See below at p 140.
2 See below at pp 139, 140.
3 1975 Act, s 160(2). This would apply, eg, in a charge of driving while disqualified, as it is necessary to prove that the accused has been disqualified. Such a charge is, however, tried separately from other charges in order that the jury may not be prejudiced.
4 1975 Act, s 106(2).
5 *HMA v McIlwain* 1965 JC 40, 1965 SLT 311. See also *Carberry v HMA* 1975 JC 40, 1976 SLT 38 and *Murphy v HMA* 1978 JC 1 (but note Lord Kissen's strong dissent in the latter case).
6 Eg *Graham v HMA* 1983 SCCR 314, 1984 SLT 67.
7 *Binks v HMA* 1984 JC 108, 1984 SCCR 335, 1985 SLT 59; *Deeney v HMA* 1986 SCCR 393. In certain special circumstances a conviction may be allowed to stand even if the trial judge has not dealt with the disclosure in his charge: *Fyfe v HMA* 1989 SCCR 429, 1990 SLT 50.
8 *Binks v HMA* 1984 JC 108, 1984 SCCR 335, 1985 SLT 59. For desertion *pro loco et tempore*, see below at p 149.
9 1975 Act, s 141(1).
10 1975 Act, s 142.

not be commented upon by the prosecutor[1], but it will not necessarily be fatal to a conviction that comment has been made, provided that the judge deals adequately with the comment in his charge[2]. The judge himself *is* entitled to comment on the accused's failure to give evidence, but must do so with discretion[3].

The accused who gives evidence on his own behalf may be asked any question in cross-examination, notwithstanding that 'it' (by which is presumably meant the answer thereto) would tend to incriminate him of the offence charged[4].

The accused should give his evidence from the witness box and not the dock unless the judge directs otherwise[5]. Such a direction is likely to be given only if the judge were satisfied that there would be a serious security risk if the accused left the dock.

The accused has no right to make an unsworn statement but must give evidence on oath or affirmation[6]. If he gives evidence, then, like every other witness, he may be cross-examined on behalf of the other parties.

The accused should not be asked and is not required to answer questions tending to show that he has been convicted of any offence other than that for which he is being tried, or is of bad character unless:

'(i) the proof that he has committed or been convicted of such other offence is admissible evidence to show that he is guilty of the offence with which he is then charged; or
(ii) the accused or his counsel or solicitor has asked questions of the witnesses for the prosecution with a view to establish the accused's good character, or the accused has given evidence of his own good character, or the nature or conduct of the defence is such as to involve imputations on the character of the prosecutor or of the witnesses for the prosecution; or
(iii) the accused has given evidence against any other person charged in the same proceedings'[7].

Exceptions (i) and (iii) are self explanatory. There can obviously be no question of the court being asked to exercise a discretion whether or not to allow questioning in the case of exception (i). It has been held that the court has no discretion to refuse to allow the accused to be asked questions in the case of exception (iii)[8]. The court has, however, a discretion whether or not to allow cross-examination of the accused in the case of exception (ii). The first two parts of this exception (accused asking questions to establish his own good character, and himself giving evidence of his own good character) cause no difficulties. However, the interpretation of the remainder of this exception (nature or conduct of defence) and the exercise of discretion thereunder have been the subject of much judicial discussion. Matters have now been clarified, relatively speaking, by the decision in the seven judge case of

---

1 1975 Act, s 141(1)(b).
2 *Clark v HMA* (1977) SCCR Supp 162; *Upton v HMA* 1986 SCCR 188, 1986 SLT 594.
3 *Scott v HMA* 1946 JC 90.
4 1975 Act, s 141(1)(e).
5 1975 Act, s 141(1)(g).
6 *Gilmour v HMA* 1965 JC 45, 1966 SLT 198.
7 1975 Act, s 141(1)(f).
8 *McCourtney v HMA* 1977 JC 68, 1978 SLT 10.

Leggate v Her Majesty's Advocate[1]. This case established the following propositions:
(1) If the nature or conduct of an accused's defence involves imputations on the character of Crown witnesses, the accused may be cross-examined as to his character. It is irrelevant whether or not it was necessary for the accused to conduct his defence in this way in order to establish it fairly.
(2) The accused may not be cross-examined as to his character when he merely asserts that a Crown witness was lying.
(3) The trial judge has a wide discretion to refuse to allow the accused to be cross-examined on character, and the fundamental test in exercising that discretion is fairness, having regard to the position of the accused on the one hand and the public interest in bringing wrongdoers to justice on the other. It is a significant factor in the exercise of that discretion whether the questions asked of the Crown witnesses were integral and necessary to the defence or were a deliberate attack on their character.
(4) When seeking permission to cross-examine on character, the prosecutor may refer to the date and general nature of the accused's criminal record, even although the judge is not normally entitled to have any knowledge of the accused's criminal record until the prosecutor moves for sentence following conviction at the trial[2].

The bar on questioning an accused about his character or record does not apply to questions asked in examination-in-chief by his own counsel or solicitor. It may sometimes be advantageous for an accused to make no secret of the fact that he has a record. For example, he may wish it to be known that, in the past, he has always pleaded guilty and ask the jury to infer his innocence from the fact that he is pleading not guilty on this occasion. Again, if he is a person with a record for dishonesty only and is on trial for a crime of violence, he may consider it beneficial to put before the jury that he is just a simple thief who would not harm anyone. It is often a question calling for nice judgment on the part of the advocate representing an accused whether or not to take from him that he has a record.

If the accused has no criminal record and is a person of good character, that should be brought out in evidence unless there is some very pressing reason to the contrary, and it is difficult to envisage what such a reason could be.

If an accused's bad character or criminal record *is* improperly disclosed to the jury as a result of questioning by the prosecutor, the same principles will apply as when his criminal record is disclosed in any other way[3]. The trial judge probably has the option of deserting the diet *pro loco et tempore* or carrying on and attempting to repair the damage when he comes to charge the jury[4].

In parenthesis it may be noted that, if an accused has a record, it is very unwise for the defence to leave the notice of previous convictions lying around where it may be visible to an observant member of the jury. Jury boxes in some courts are very close to the table where the defence advocate sits!

1 *Leggate v HMA* 1988 SCCR 391, 1988 SLT 665.
2 1975 Act, s 161(1).
3 See above at p 138.
4 *Binks v HMA* 1984 JC 108, 1984 SCCR 335, 1985 SLT 59.

Evidence of the accused's spouse

The spouse of an accused is a competent and compellable witness for the accused[1]. The spouse is also a competent witness for a co-accused and for the prosecutor[2], but cannot be compelled to give evidence for them unless that could have been done at common law[3]. There are in fact at common law no circumstances where the spouse of one accused could be a compellable witness for a co-accused. In the case of the Crown, however, the spouse of an accused is a compellable witness if the accused is charged with a crime committed against the spouse. This has been interpreted broadly to include not only acts of violence against the spouse, but also offences against the spouse's property[4]. If there are two accused and the Crown calls the spouse of one of them, he or she cannot be compelled to give evidence against *either* accused[5].

Even if the spouse is a compellable witness, he or she is entitled to refuse to disclose any communication made between the spouses during the marriage[6].

The prosecutor is not entitled to comment on the failure of an accused's spouse to give evidence[7]. The same principles apply as in the case of the accused himself as a witness[8].

If an accused wishes to call his or her spouse as a witness, notice of this must be given as with any other defence witness[9].

Evidence of a co-accused

One co-accused is a competent witness for another co-accused, but is not compellable[10]. If one of two or more co-accused gives evidence on his own behalf, he may be cross-examined by the other accused[11]. However, if an accused gives evidence on his own behalf and is cross-examined by a co-accused, that co-accused is not then entitled also to call him as a witness[11].

It is now settled that it is proper for the Crown to cross-examine one accused in order to obtain from him evidence incriminating another accused[12]. The co-accused who is thus incriminated is entitled to cross-examine the witness further on the evidence elicited by the Crown[12].

When one of two or more accused on the same indictment has pleaded guilty (even although not sentenced) or been acquitted or had the diet against him deserted, he is a competent and compellable witness for either the prosecutor or any other accused[13]. No notice of intention to call such a

---

1 1975 Act, s 143(1)(a). *Hunter v HMA* 1984 JC 90, 1984 SCCR 306, 1984 SLT 434.
2 1975 Act, s 143(1)(b).
3 1975 Act, s 143(2)(a).
4 *Harper v Adair* 1945 JC 21.
5 *Bates v HMA* 1989 SCCR 338, 1989 SLT 701.
6 1975 Act, s 143(2)(b).
7 1975 Act, s 143(3).
8 See above at p 139.
9 1975 Act, s 144.
10 1975 Act, s 141(2)(a).
11 1975 Act, s 141(2)(b).
12 *Todd v HMA* 1984 JC 13, 1983 SCCR 472, 1984 SLT 123.
13 1975 Act, s 141(3).

witness need be given, but the court may grant to any party an adjournment or postponement of the trial if it seems just to do so[1]. A co-accused is a competent witness under this provision, even although his plea of guilty was tendered at a s 102 diet prior to the trial diet, provided of course that he appears on the same indictment as that with which the trial is concerned[2]. It is no bar to a co-accused being called as a witness under this provision that he has heard part of the evidence in the case[3].

Evidence in trials of sexual offences

By an amendment to the 1975 Act introduced in 1985[4] there is a general prohibition against an attack by the defence on the character of the complainer[5] in a trial where the accused is alleged to have committed a sexual offence against the complainer. The actual offences to which the section applies are listed[6] and include offences against persons of either sex. The prohibition is against the defence asking questions designed to elicit or leading evidence tending to show that the complainer:
(a) is not of good character in relation to sexual matters;
(b) is a prostitute or an associate of prostitutes; or
(c) has at any time engaged with any person in sexual behaviour not forming part of the subject matter of the charge[7].
The prohibition does not apply to questioning and evidence adduced by the Crown[8].

The general prohibition is subject to certain exceptions. The defence may apply to the court for permission to ask questions or lead evidence which would otherwise be forbidden by s 141A, and the court must grant the application if it is satisfied:
(a) that the questioning or evidence . . . is designed to explain or rebut evidence adduced, or to be adduced, otherwise than by or on behalf of (the accused):
(b) that the questioning or evidence . . . (i) is questioning or evidence as to sexual behaviour which took place on the same occasion as the sexual behaviour forming the subject-matter of the charge, or (ii) is relevant to the defence of incrimination, or
(c) that it would be contrary to the interests of justice to exclude the questioning or evidence[9].
Such an application by the defence must be made in court but in the absence of the jury, the complainer, any witness and the public[10]. Even if the application is granted, the court may limit the extent of the questioning or the evidence[11].

1 1975 Act, s 141(3).
2 *Monaghan v HMA* 1983 SCCR 524.
3 *HMA v Ferrie* 1983 SCCR 1.
4 1975 Act, s 141A.
5 Ie the person against whom the offence is alleged to have been committed (s 141A(3)).
6 1975 Act, s 141A(2). They are: rape, sodomy, assault with intent to rape, indecent assault, indecent behaviour, an offence under s 106(1)(a) or s 107 of the Mental Health (Scotland) Act 1984, various offences under the Sexual Offences (Scotland) Act 1976, and an offence under s 80(7) of the Criminal Justice (Scotland) Act 1980.
7 1975 Act, s 141A(1).
8 1975 Act, s 141A(4).
9 1975 Act, s 141B(1).
10 1975 Act, s 141B(3).
11 1975 Act, s 141B(2).

The judge may exclude the public from the court while the complainer is giving evidence in a trial of a sexual offence, in order to spare the complainer embarrassment and, as a result, make him or her more willing to give detailed evidence.

Presence of witness in court

An expert witness (ie a witness called to give his opinion on a matter relevant to the case rather than to speak to a fact in the case) is usually permitted to remain in court while evidence of the facts is being given, if either party so moves[1]. However, the court always has a discretion in the matter. One expert should not be in court while another expert is giving evidence[1].

Witnesses to facts should not normally be in court before giving their evidence, but a witness may be permitted, on the motion of any party, to be in court prior to giving evidence 'if it appears to the court that the presence of the witness would not be contrary to the interests of justice'[2]. An example of this would be the mother of the complainer in a child abuse case, who was allowed to be present with her child while he was giving evidence, notwithstanding that she herself was subsequently to be called as a witness.

Even if a witness has, without permission, been in court prior to giving evidence, and a party is objecting to his being allowed to testify, the trial judge has a limited discretion whether to allow him to do so[3]. The discretion may be exercised in the witness's favour 'where it appears to the court that the presence of the witness was not the result of culpable negligence or criminal intent, and that the witness has not been unduly instructed or influenced by what took place during his presence, or that injustice will not be done by his examination'[3].

Accused's solicitor as witness

The solicitor of an accused is a competent witness for any party, but, if called by a party other than his own client, he cannot be compelled to disclose anything which he has learned in preparing the case[4]. The privilege of confidentiality is that of the accused and not of the solicitor, so that the solicitor must disclose information if his client wishes him to do so[4].

If an accused's solicitor is called as a witness on behalf of his own client, the confidentiality referred to above flies off[5].

The fact that the accused's solicitor has been in court and has heard the evidence in the case is no bar to his being called as a witness[6].

Under solemn procedure the solicitor should, of course, have advance warning of the fact that he may be called as a witness. He should therefore be able to arrange that another solicitor or counsel will act for the accused at the trial concerned. It is certainly undesirable that a solicitor who is conducting a

---

1 JHA Macdonald *The Criminal Law of Scotland* (5th edn) p 295.
2 1975 Act, s 139A.
3 1975 Act, s 140.
4 *Macdonald* p 295.
5 1975 Act, s 138(4).
6 *Macdonald* pp 294–5.

trial should be a witness in it, and this should be avoided unless the circumstances are most exceptional.

Objections to admissibility of evidence

If a witness is asked a question the answer to which is considered inadmissible by one of the parties in the case, that party must object to the question. If the questioner wishes to persist with his question, the judge directs the jury to withdraw. He then hears submissions from the objecting party and from the questioner and reaches a decision on the issue of admissibility. The jury is then brought back, and the examination of the witness continues.

An objection may be to a specific question, eg, if the accused were to be asked a question about his character by the prosecutor. The objection may also be to a 'line of examination' rather than to a single question. Thus, if it were sought to lead evidence about a search of premises which the defence maintained was illegal, it would be the line of examination in the sense of all questions about the search which would be objected to.

If an objection is not taken timeously, the jury will of course hear the evidence, and it will be virtually impossible to argue at an appeal that it was inadmissible. An objection should be taken by a party, but, in the case of a particularly blatant attempt to lead inadmissible evidence, the judge may, of his own volition, refuse to allow a line of questioning to be pursued.

In certain circumstances the judge may require to hear evidence outwith the presence of the jury in order to decide whether or not evidence is admissible. This is what is known as a 'trial within a trial'. The cases in which it has occurred have been concerned almost exclusively with the admissibility of a statement allegedly made by an accused to the police, and the dispute has been as to whether the statement was fairly obtained. The procedure of a trial within a trial was introduced into Scotland by the case of *Chalmers v Her Majesty's Advocate*[1]. It has been much criticised in recent years[2], partly because of the amount of time it allegedly wastes and partly because it is said to involve the judge in usurping the jury's function as the arbiter of facts. It is nevertheless still part of our procedure[3]. It is rare for a judge to exclude evidence following a trial within a trial, and the circumstances in which he is entitled to do so are limited. 'A judge who has heard the evidence regarding the manner in which a challenged statement was made will normally be justified in withholding the evidence from the jury only if he is satisfied on the undisputed relevant evidence that no reasonable jury could hold that the statement had been voluntarily made and had not been extracted by unfair or improper means'[4].

Record of proceedings at judicial examination

The record of proceedings at any judicial examination of an accused must be

1 *Chalmers v HMA* 1954 JC 66, 1954 SLT 177.
2 Eg in *Hartley v HMA* 1979 SLT 26; *HMA v Whitelaw* 1980 SLT (Notes) 25; *HMA v Mair* 1982 SLT 471.
3 It was used eg in *Aiton v HMA* 1987 SCCR 252.
4 *Balloch v HMA* 1977 JC 23 at 28, 1977 SLT (Notes) 29 at 30, per Lord Justice-Clerk Wheatley.

on the Crown list of productions[1]. This record includes any declaration made by the accused as well as the questions and answers forming part of what is commonly called the judicial examination[2].

The record is usually read out to the jury by the clerk of court. It need not be sworn to by witnesses[3]. The record is almost invariably read to the jury before the prosecutor closes his case. If, for any reason, the Crown decided not to have it read, then it could be introduced as part of the defence case, the accused being entitled to put in evidence any Crown production[4].

Both the Crown and the defence have the right to apply to the court at a preliminary diet[5] to have part of the record of the proceedings at a judicial examination excluded from what is read to the jury[6]. In practice there is usually agreement about what should be excluded (eg reference to a previous conviction), and there is no need for a preliminary diet.

The evidential value of what an accused says at a judicial examination was considered in the case of *Hendry v Her Majesty's Advocate*[7]. The court (a bench of five judges) held that any self-incriminating statement was competent evidence against an accused, but that anything which was self-exonerating could not be used by the defence as evidence of the accused's innocence. However, even a self-exonerating statement might be relevant evidence for the jury to consider. For example, it could demonstrate that the accused had made a statement consistent with innocence at an early stage of proceedings, or it could add to the weight and credibility of other exculpatory evidence in the case[8].

The fact that an accused did not answer any questions at a judicial examination is not something which should go against him at his trial[9] unless he has put forward a defence which he could have mentioned in answer to a question at the judicial examination[10]. In that event the prosecutor, the judge and any co-accused are entitled to comment on his failure to answer, and the jury is entitled to take account of it when weighing the evidence[11].

Evidence by certificate

Apart from evidence which is admitted or agreed by the parties[12], the normal rule is that the only evidence which a jury may consider is oral evidence given in court. However, there is statutory provision for evidence of certain routine matters to be presented to the jury in the form of a certificate[13]. This provision applies only to a limited number of specified statutory offences[14]. A certificate

1 1975 Act, s 78(2).
2 See above at pp 98–101.
3 1975 Act, s 151(1).
4 1975 Act, s 82A.
5 See above at pp 118, 119.
6 1975 Act, ss 76(1)(b), 151(2).
7 *Hendry v HMA* 1985 SCCR 274, 1986 SLT 186.
8 *Hendry v HMA* 1985 SCCR 274 at 279–80, 1986 SLT 186 at 190.
9 *Walker v HMA* 1985 SCCR 150.
10 *McEwan v HMA* 1990 SCCR 401.
11 1975 Act, s 20A(5). See *Alexander v HMA* 1988 SCCR 542, 1989 SLT 193.
12 1975 Act, s 150. See above at p 116.
13 1980 Act, s 26(1).
14 The statutes concerned are listed in the 1980 Act, Sch 1.

is admissible in evidence on behalf of the Crown only if a copy of it has been served on the accused not less than fourteen days before the trial[1]. If the accused serves notice on the prosecutor, not less than six days before the trial (or later as the court may in special circumstances allow), that he is challenging anything in the certificate, then the certificate will not be sufficient evidence[2], and the prosecutor must lead oral evidence in the usual way.

Evidence by letter of request or evidence on commission

There are two further exceptions to the general rule that only oral evidence is admissible in a criminal jury trial. Firstly, if a witness is abroad, the court in Scotland may issue a letter of request to a court or tribunal in the foreign country for it to examine the witness[3]. Secondly, if a witness in the United Kingdom, Channel Islands or the Isle of Man is too ill or infirm to attend court, or is normally resident abroad and is unlikely to be present in the United Kingdom, Channel Islands or Isle of Man at the time of the trial, the court may appoint a commissioner to take his evidence[4].

An application for a letter of request or a commission is made by way of petition[5] to the court in which the trial is to take place (or the High Court if that is not yet known)[6]. The application must be intimated to all the other parties in the case[7]. The judge has a discretion whether or not to grant the application[8], but may grant it only if he is satisfied that (a) the evidence which it is averred the witness is able to give is necessary for the proper adjudication of the trial, and (b) there would be no unfairness to the other party were such evidence to be received in the form of the record of an examination conducted by the foreign court or the commissioner[9]. The opinion has been expressed in the High Court that letters of request should be granted only if the evidence to be obtained is formal[10].

The application may be made at any time before the jury is sworn[11] or even, in exceptional circumstances, during the trial[11].

The record of the examination or commission, as the case may be, is read out to the jury by the clerk of court after the party seeking to found on the evidence has so moved the court[12], and the judge may direct that the jury is to be provided with copies of the evidence[12].

---

1 1980 Act, s 26(3)(a).
2 1980 Act, s 26(3)(b).
3 1980 Act, s 32(1)(a). Detailed procedural rules are contained in AA(C) 1988, rr 51–56.
4 1980 Act, s 32(1)(b). Detailed procedural rules are contained in AA(C) 1988, rr 57–61.
5 AA(C) 1988, rr 51, 57.
6 1980 Act, s 32(1).
7 AA(C) 1988, rr 51(4), 61.
8 AA(C) 1988, rr 52(1), 61.
9 1980 Act, s 32(2).
10 *Muirhead v HMA* 1983 SCCR 133, 1983 SLT 545 (Lord Cameron). Contrast *HMA v Lesacher* 1982 SCCR 418 (Sh Ct) in which a letter of request was granted for evidence which was very far from formal.
11 1980 Act, s 32(5).
12 AA(C) 1988, rr 56(1), 61.

SUBMISSION OF NO CASE TO ANSWER

At the end of the Crown case the defence may submit to the judge that the accused has no case to answer in respect of both (a) an offence charged in the indictment and (b) any other offence of which he could be convicted under the indictment were the offence charged the only offence so charged[1].

It should be noted that a submission will be successful only if there is insufficient evidence to convict the accused of *any part* of a charge. Thus, in an indictment charging assault with intent to rape, if there were no evidence from which the jury would be entitled to infer the libelled intent, but there were sufficient evidence of assault, a submission would be rejected. It should also be noted that, for a submission to succeed, there must be no case to answer under both heads (a) and (b) of the subsection. Thus, if an accused were charged with robbery and there were insufficient evidence of that but there were sufficient evidence of theft, a submission would be rejected as a verdict of guilty of theft is competent on a charge of robbery[2].

The submission is heard by the judge outwith the presence of the jury[3]. The judge must hear argument from the party making the submission[4].

If the judge is satisfied that the evidence led by the Crown is insufficient in law to justify the accused being convicted under either head (a) or head (b) of the subsection he must acquit him of the offence in respect of which the submission has been made[5]. If there are any other charges in the indictment, the trial will proceed in respect of these[5].

There is no reported case on the interpretation of 'insufficient evidence in law' in the context of solemn proceedings, but the High Court has held, in construing the equivalent (and in this respect identical) provision relating to summary trials[6], that the only question is whether there is no evidence which, if accepted would entitle the court to proceed to conviction[7]. In other words, the court is concerned not with credibility, reliability or the acceptability of the evidence, but only with its sufficiency – not with its quality but with its quantity.

If the submission is rejected by the judge, the trial proceeds exactly as if no submission had been made[8].

The High Court has reserved its opinion on what the position would be if a judge wrongly rejected a submission of no case to answer, the trial proceeded, and the accused were convicted as a result of evidence given by himself, by a co-accused, or by some other defence witness[9].

---

1 1975 Act, s 140A(1). For alternative verdicts see below at pp 155, 156.
2 1975 Act, s 60(2).
3 1975 Act, s 140A(2).
4 *Taylor v Douglas* 1983 SCCR 323, 1984 SLT 69. This was a summary case, but the principle is the same.
5 1975 Act, s 140A(3). Note that the acquittal is by the judge himself. He does not direct the jury to acquit the accused, as would be the case if the Crown accepted a plea of not guilty in the course of the trial.
6 1975 Act, s 345A(2).
7 *Williamson v Wither* 1981 SCCR 214.
8 1975 Act, s 140A(4).
9 *Little v HMA* 1983 JC 16, 1983 SCCR 56, 1983 SLT 489.

ABANDONMENT OF CHARGE BY THE CROWN

The Crown is master of the instance in a criminal trial, and the prosecutor has an unfettered discretion to abandon a charge and accept an accused's plea of not guilty to all or part of an indictment at any stage of a case. The judge has no authority to interfere in the exercise of the prosecutor's discretion. In practice the prosecutor may very well refer the question of whether or not to accept a plea of not guilty to some higher authority (the procurator fiscal in the case of a depute fiscal, or the Home Advocate Depute or one of the law officers in the case of an advocate depute).

If a charge is abandoned after a jury has been sworn, the jury must return a verdict of not guilty on that charge. If there are no other charges proceeding to trial against the accused, the judge will there and then direct the jury to return a verdict of not guilty, the verdict will be recorded and read back to the jury, and the accused will be discharged. If there are other charges proceeding to trial, the judge will usually reserve his direction to the jury to find the accused not guilty until he comes to charge them on the remainder of the indictment. There is, however, no reason why he should not, if so minded, have the not guilty verdict taken and recorded at once.

On the same basis, if an accused changes his plea to guilty at any stage of the trial after a jury has been sworn, the jury must be directed to find him guilty 'in terms of his own confession'.

ADJOURNMENT OF TRIAL AND DESERTION OF DIET

Adjournment

Every trial must proceed from day to day until concluded unless it is adjourned over a day or days[1]. Whether or not to adjourn is within the discretion of the presiding judge[2]. If a trial is adjourned, it must be to a specified time and place. An adjournment to a later time on the same day need not be minuted, but an adjournment to another date must be contained in an interlocutor duly signed[3].

If a trial is interrupted without being adjourned, the instance falls immediately[4]. However, this rule is subject to certain statutory exceptions. For example, a trial may be interrupted to take the verdict of a jury in another case[5], or to deal with a plea of guilty in another case[6].

---

1 1975 Act, s 136.
2 1975 Act, s 136; *Kyle v HMA* 1987 SCCR 116.
3 *Renton and Brown* para 10–12, founding on *Ross* (1848) Arkley 481 and *John Martin* (1858) 3 Irv 177.
4 *Law and Nicol v HMA* 1973 SLT (Notes) 14. The particular situation which arose in this case is now covered by AA(C) 1988, r 74.
5 1975 Act, s 156.
6 1975 Act, s 157.

Desertion *pro loco et tempore*

The court may desert a diet of trial *pro loco et tempore* (ie for that particular time and place). The effect of such desertion is that the Crown may raise a fresh indictment against the accused or may, in certain circumstances, proceed against him at a later date on the same indictment[1].

The prosecutor is entitled to move the court to desert *pro loco et tempore* before the jury is sworn[2]. The court may, of its own volition, desert *pro loco et tempore* at any stage of the trial, and whether or not to do so is within the discretion of the presiding judge[3]. Circumstances in which such desertion is appropriate are, eg, the illness of an accused[4] or of a witness[5].

Desertion *simpliciter*

When the court wishes, exceptionally, to bring the entire proceedings to an end, it may desert the diet *simpliciter*. The prosecutor is then barred from raising a fresh libel, unless the court's decision has been reversed on appeal[6]. However, a private prosecution may be brought against the accused[7].

Death or illness of presiding judge

If the presiding judge dies or is unable to proceed with a case because of illness, the clerk of court is given certain powers. If the diet has not been called, he may convene the court and adjourn the diet to a later sitting[8]. If the diet has been called but no evidence has been led, he may adjourn the diet to a later sitting[9]. If evidence has been led, he may desert the diet *pro loco et tempore*[10]. In this last case specific power is given to the Lord Advocate to raise a fresh indictment[11].

AMENDMENT OF INDICTMENT

It quite frequently occurs that the Crown seeks to amend the indictment either prior to the leading of evidence or, more commonly, in the course of the trial. The basic principle is clear:

---

1 1975 Act, s 127. The accused must be served with another copy of the indictment within nine clear days after the date of the abortive trial diet, along with a notice to appear to answer the indictment at another diet (which may be in the same court or a different court), that diet to be not less than nine clear days after the date when notice was given.
2 *Renton and Brown* para 10–15.
3 *Mallison v HMA* 1987 SCCR 320.
4 *HMA v Brown and Foss* 1966 SLT 341.
5 *Farrell v HMA* 1984 JC 1, 1984 SCCR 301, 1985 SLT 58.
6 1975 Act, s 127(1A).
7 *X v Sweeney* 1982 JC 70, 1982 SCCR 161, 1983 SLT 48 (sub nom *H v Sweeney*). For private prosecution, see chapter 11.
8 1975 Act, s 128(1)(a).
9 1975 Act, s 128(1)(b).
10 1975 Act, s 128(1)(c).
11 1975 Act, s 128(2).

'No trial shall fail or the ends of justice be allowed to be defeated by reason of any discrepancy or variance between the indictment and the evidence'[1].

This principle is amplified in the following subsection:

'It shall be competent at any time prior to the determination of the case, unless the court see just cause to the contrary, to amend the indictment by deletion, alteration or addition, so as to cure any error or defect therein, or to meet any objection thereto, or to cure any discrepancy or variance between the indictment and the evidence'[2].

It is further provided that no amendment is permitted which changes the character of the offence charged[3].

It is clear that amendment will not be allowed in order to attempt to cure a fundamental nullity in an indictment or a charge. Thus, if no locus is stated for the offence, the prosecutor is not permitted to amend to insert one, a locus being essential in order to establish jurisdiction[4]. However, where the name of one of several accused was radically misstated in one of three charges in an indictment (having been correctly stated in the preamble and the remaining charges), the Crown was allowed to amend to correct the error[5].

Whether or not to allow an amendment is within the discretion of the trial judge, and the accused may be granted an adjournment or some other remedy if the judge considers that the accused may be prejudiced in his defence on the merits of the case as a result of the amendment[6].

A motion to amend may be made at a preliminary diet[7].

An amendment is sufficiently authenticated by being initialled by the clerk of court[8].

SPEECHES BY CROWN AND DEFENCE

At the conclusion of the evidence the prosecutor addresses the jury, followed by counsel or the solicitor for the accused, or the accused himself if he is unrepresented. The defence is always entitled to speak last[9]. If there are more than one accused, the normal practice is that the speeches follow the order in which they appear in the indictment.

It has already been noted that the prosecutor should not comment on the failure of the accused or his spouse to give evidence[10], but that the prosecutor may be permitted to comment on an accused's failure to answer a question at a judicial examination[11].

The speech to the jury is important as it enables each party to put forward

---

1 1975 Act, s 123(1).
2 1975 Act, s 123(2).
3 1975 Act, s 123(3).
4 *Stevenson v McLevy* (1879) 4 Couper 196, 6R(J) 33. This was a summary case, but the principle is the same.
5 *Keane v HMA* 1986 SCCR 491, 1987 SLT 220.
6 1975 Act, s 123(3).
7 *Keane v HMA* 1986 SCCR 491, 1987 SLT 220.
8 1975 Act, s 123(4).
9 1975 Act, s 152.
10 1975 Act, ss 141(1)(b), 143(3). See above at pp 139, 141.
11 1975 Act, s 20A(5). See above at p 145.

to the jury the points most favourable to his case. Care should be taken in the preparation of a speech in order to ensure that it is presented in a logical and comprehensible way. It should not, of course, mention matters which were not led in evidence. As a general rule brevity is to be commended.

As the judge will direct the jury on the law, speeches should say as little about the law as possible, although some comment thereon is almost unavoidable. For example, it is usual for a prosecutor to tell the jury about the burden and standard of proof. Then too the jury is unlikely to understand what is involved in a special defence of self-defence unless some attempt to deal with the legal concept is made by the parties in their speeches[1]. It is good practice and good manners for an advocate to remind the jury that they *will* be directed on the law by the judge and that it is his direction which they must follow even if it differs from the view of the speaker.

It is of, course, open to either party to ask the judge to give a particular direction in law to the jury, eg, to the effect that part of a charge has not been proved. Nowadays, this is usually done in the absence of the jury prior to the speech by the prosecutor. It is helpful if the judge indicates whether or not he is prepared to give the requested direction, so that the parties may adapt their speeches accordingly. However, the judge is under no obligation to give such an indication. If an application for a direction is made before the prosecutor addresses the jury, there is an opportunity for a legal debate on the matter, provided that the judge is prepared to hear submissions from the parties. If, however, as sometimes happens, the defence does not make an application until after the prosecutor has spoken, there should be no debate as the prosecutor is *functus* (ie he has had his say).

THE JUDGE'S CHARGE

The judge's primary task in charging the jury is to tell them what is the law which they must apply to the case[2]. He should tell the jury that the facts are for them.

It seems now to be well settled that there is no duty on a judge to sum up the evidence.

> 'In our Scottish procedure the judge does not give a summing up, as is the practice south of the border, by rehearsing all the evidence. All that the judge is required to do is to make reference to such of the evidence as is necessary for the determination of the issues in the case, and he may do so on a broad canvas. All that is required in that situation is that he does it in an even-handed fashion so as not to give an advantage one way or the other'[3].

There is, it is true, a reference in an old statute to the judge's summing up the evidence[4], but it is suggested that this was probably an English importation which no longer has any place in our modern procedure.

The judge must tell the jury that the onus of proof is on the Crown, and he should direct them that the standard of proof is 'beyond reasonable doubt'. It

1 See the case of *David Balfour* above at pp 42–44.
2 *Hamilton v HMA* 1938 JC 134 at 144, 1938 SLT 333 at 337, per Lord Justice-General Normand.
3 *King v HMA* 1985 SCCR 322 at 328, per Lord Justice-Clerk Wheatley.
4 Justiciary and Circuit Courts (Scotland) Act 1783, s 5.

is for each individual judge to decide how to tell the jury what is meant by reasonable doubt, but examples of commercial transactions are unlikely to be helpful, and it is advisable that judges should adhere to 'the traditional formula'[1]. It is not perhaps so easy to determine what *is* the traditional formula, but it is suggested that the sheriff in the case of *David Balfour*[2] dealt with the matter in a sufficiently traditional way[3].

The judge should tell the jury that they cannot find an accused guilty without corroborated evidence of the essential facts. He should direct them as to which are the essential facts and what evidence is capable of affording corroboration of them. It may, however, not be fatal for the judge to omit a direction about corroboration[4].

Where a particular piece of evidence is vital to the Crown case, the judge must so direct the jury and tell them that, if they do not accept that piece of evidence, they must acquit[5]. It is not proper for the judge to direct the jury that it is for *them* to decide which facts are crucial[6].

The judge should direct the jury on the legal meaning of the crime with which the accused is charged.

If inadmissible evidence has, through inadvertence, been heard by the jury, the judge should direct them to ignore it, although the omission of such a direction may not be fatal to a conviction[7].

If an accused gives evidence which is consistent with innocence, the jury should be told that, if they believe him or his evidence causes them to have a reasonable doubt, they must acquit. However, it may be sufficient if the jury is told that they must acquit if *any* evidence raises a reasonable doubt in their minds[8]. If an accused gives evidence in support of a special defence, the jury *must* be directed that, if they believe the accused, they must acquit[9].

In so far as a judge deals with the facts of the case, he must ensure that he does so accurately. A factual error in a charge may result in the conviction being quashed on appeal, notwithstanding that the judge has told the jury that it is *their* recollection of the evidence and not his which counts[10].

If there is more than one charge on the indictment, the judge must direct the jury that they should consider each charge separately and reach a verdict in respect of it. If there is more than one accused, the jury must be directed to consider the case against each accused separately.

The judge should take care not to make remarks in his charge which are prejudicial to the defence[11].

If the judge reaches the conclusion that there is insufficient evidence in law to support a finding of guilt on any charge, he must direct the jury to acquit the accused of that charge, even though the defence has not made a sub-

1 *Shewan v HMA* 1989 SCCR 364.
2 See above at p 45.
3 See also *McKenzie v HMA* 1959 JC 32 at 37, 1960 SLT 41 at 42, per Lord Justice-Clerk Thomson.
4 *Wilson v HMA* (1976) SCCR Supp 126.
5 *McIntyre v HMA* 1981 SCCR 117.
6 *Dorrens v HMA* 1983 SCCR 407.
7 *Jones v HMA* 1981 SCCR 192.
8 *Dunn v HMA* 1986 SCCR 340, 1987 SLT 295.
9 *Dunn v HMA* 1986 SCCR 340. See also *King v HMA* 1985 SCCR 322.
10 *Larkin v HMA* 1988 SCCR 30.
11 As in *Cooney v HMA* 1987 SCCR 60, where the sheriff made derogatory remarks about defence witnesses. The conviction was quashed. See also *McArthur v HMA* 1989 SCCR 646, 1990 SLT 451, and *Crowe v HMA* 1989 SCCR 681.

mission of no case to answer. Similarly, if there are any parts of a charge for which, in the opinion of the judge, there is insufficient evidence, he must direct the jury to delete these parts of the charge from any verdict of guilty which they may return.

The jury should be told that there are three verdicts open to them: guilty, not guilty and not proven. The High Court has on several recent occasions remarked on the undesirability of attempting to explain to a jury the difference between not guilty and not proven as verdicts of acquittal[1]. This is quite astonishing. It displays an extraordinary lack of willingness on the part of the High Court to grasp the nettle of the inherent illogicality of two separate verdicts of acquittal in a legal system where the accused is presumed innocent until proved guilty[2].

The judge should direct the jury that they may reach a verdict either unanimously or by a majority, but that, if their verdict on any charge is to be guilty, there must be at least eight of them in favour of that verdict[3]. It is inappropriate to direct a jury that they should spend a reasonable time trying to reach a unanimous verdict as there is no obligation on them to reach such a verdict[4].

Although it is not essential, it is good practice for a judge to tell a jury that they should elect one of their number as foreman (or chancellor, to use the old Scottish term). The foreman will act as chairman while the jury discuss their verdict, and will also give the verdict to the clerk when they return to court.

It is not uncommon for a judge, at the end of his charge, to ask the prosecutor and the defence lawyer whether they wish any further direction[5]. This practice has been criticised by the High Court as undesirable[6].

SECLUSION OF THE JURY

When the jury retire, they are enclosed in a room by the clerk of court[7], and communication with them is excluded except in certain limited circumstances until they have reached their verdict[8]. Communication with the jury is confined to contact between them and the judge (or someone acting on his behalf, who would usually be the clerk of court) for certain specified purposes[8].

The judge may communicate with the jury for the purpose of giving them a further direction[9]. If the jury are to be given such a direction, they must be brought back into court. The clerk may not simply go to the jury room and give them the appropriate direction, even if he is acting on the judge's

1 *Affleck v HMA* 1987 SCCR 150; *Macdonald v HMA* 1989 SCCR 29, 1989 SLT 298; *Fay v HMA* 1989 SCCR 373, 1989 SLT 758.
2 See the critical comment by Sheriff G H Gordon, editor of SCCR, at 1989 SCCR 378.
3 *Affleck v HMA* 1987 SCCR 150; *Glen v HMA* 1988 SCCR 37, 1988 SLT 369.
4 *Crowe v HMA* 1989 SCCR 681.
5 Eg *Alexander v HMA* 1988 SCCR 542, 1989 SLT 193 (a High Court judge); *Ralston v HMA* 1988 SCCR 590, 1989 SLT 474 (although the part of the charge concerned is not there reproduced) (a sheriff).
6 *Thomson v HMA* 1988 SCCR 534, 1989 SLT 170.
7 1975 Act, s 153(2).
8 1975 Act, s 153(3).
9 1975 Act, s 153(3)(a)(i).

instructions[1]. This is because the whole trial must take place in the presence of the accused[2].

No juror may leave the jury room after the jury has been enclosed, other than to receive or seek a further direction from the judge, or to make a request about a matter relevant to the case or about certain other matters relating to the welfare of the jury[3]. An example of a matter relevant to the case would be a request to see one of the productions. Whether or not the jury should be allowed to see a production is a matter for the judge, whose discretion must be exercised in the interests of justice[4].

The jury may be provided with food and drink while enclosed[5]. They may send and receive (through the medium of the judge or someone authorised by him) personal messages unconnected with the case[6]. They may be provided with medical treatment or other assistance which is immediately required by them[7]. A juror is entitled to make a request to the judge with regard to any of these matters[8], and the judge may give the appropriate instruction[9].

A jury may be accommodated overnight if necessary, and the judge may give directions for their seclusion in such accommodation[10] (which is usually a hotel). Whether or not to arrange for the jury to be accommodated overnight is a matter for the judge's discretion. He should ask the jury whether they are likely to reach a verdict within a reasonable time, after having explained that no pressure is being put upon them to reach a verdict speedily, and that the interests of justice require that they should be given as much time as they need to decide on their verdict[11].

If the prosecutor or any other person enters the jury room while the jury is enclosed, or communicates with them in any way other than one of those authorised by the provisions discussed above, the accused must be acquitted[12].

The jury indicate that they have reached a verdict by ringing a bell or giving some other signal which is audible outside the jury room.

A juror must not give and should not be asked for information about anything which occurred while the jury was enclosed[13]. Any disobedience to this rule, whether by a juror or anyone else, is a contempt of court[13] which is punishable by imprisonment for a maximum period of two years or a fine or both[14].

---

1 *Cunningham v HMA* 1984 JC 37, 1984 SCCR 40, 1984 SLT 249; *McColl v HMA* 1989 SCCR 229, 1989 SLT 691.
2 1975 Act, s 145(1).
3 1975 Act, s 153(3)(b).
4 See eg *McMurdo v HMA* 1987 SCCR 343, 1988 SLT 234; *Bertram v HMA* 1990 SCCR 394.
5 1975 Act, s 153(3A)(a).
6 1975 Act, s 153(3A)(c).
7 1975 Act, s 153(3A)(d).
8 1975 Act, s 153(3)(b)(i).
9 1975 Act, s 153(3A).
10 1975 Act, s 153(3A)(b).
11 *McKenzie v HMA* 1986 SCCR 94, 1986 SLT 389.
12 1975 Act, s 153(4).
13 Contempt of Court Act 1981, s 8(1).
14 Contempt of Court Act 1981, s 15(2).

VERDICT

A jury may give their verdict without retiring[1], but in practice they usually retire to deliberate unless the verdict is a formal one directed by the judge.

When the jury return to court having indicated that they have reached a verdict, the clerk will ask: 'Who speaks for you?'. The foreman of the jury will identify himself or herself and will be asked by the clerk to stand up. The clerk will then ask the foreman whether the jury have reached a verdict. On receiving an affirmative answer, he will ask the foreman what the verdict is, separately in respect of each charge against each accused, and whether the verdict is unanimous or by a majority[2].

If the verdict is by a majority, it is competent for the judge to inquire what the majority is, and the opinion has been expressed by the High Court that, when there is a majority verdict of guilty, the jury ought to be asked how many of them voted for guilty[3]. Despite the fact that this opinion was expressed by a bench of three judges presided over by the Lord Justice-Clerk, such an inquiry seems seldom to be made. The sheriff in the case of *David Balfour* did, however, think fit to make it[4].

A verdict must be consistent with the indictment. A jury may delete certain parts of a charge and return a verdict of guilty to the remainder, provided that what is left is still a crime[5]. A jury may not, however, amend a charge. Thus, where an indictment charged an accused with assault by 'pulling' a quantity of hair and skin tissue from a woman's head, a verdict of guilty of assault by 'removing' the hair and skin tissue was held to be incompetent, as it proceeded upon an assumption that an instrument had been used, and that was not charged[6]. However, it is competent for a jury to substitute 'a sum of money' for a specific sum, or to reduce quantities of articles. Both are considered to amount to deletions of part of the charge.

By statute certain alternative verdicts are open to a jury, and they should, where appropriate, be directed about any such alternative in the course of the judge's charge. The more important alternatives[7] are:

(1) On a charge of robbery, theft, embezzlement or fraud the accused may be convicted of reset[8].

(2) On a charge of robbery, embezzlement or fraud the accused may be convicted of theft[9],

(3) On a charge of theft an accused may be convicted of embezzlement or fraud[10],

(4) On a charge of a completed crime the accused may be convicted of an attempt to commit that crime[11],

(5) On a statutory charge the accused may be convicted of a common law

---

1 1975 Act, s 155.
2 1975 Act, s 154. The section provides for the possibility of a written rather than an oral verdict, but the former is, in modern practice, unknown.
3 *McCadden v HMA* 1985 SCCR 282, 1986 SLT 138.
4 See above at p 48.
5 1975 Act, s 61(2), (3). *Sayers v HMA* 1982 JC 17, 1981 SCCR 212, 1982 SLT 220.
6 *Blair v HMA* 1989 SCCR 79, 1989 SLT 459.
7 For a comprehensive list see *Renton and Brown* para 10–61.
8 1975 Act, s 60(1).
9 1975 Act, s 60(2).
10 1975 Act, s 60(3).
11 1975 Act, s 63(1).

crime, if the facts proved amount to the common law crime but not to the statutory charge[1], provided, of course, that the facts libelled in the charge are capable of amounting to a common law crime.

(6) On a charge of rape an accused may be convicted of indecent assault or of various statutory sexual offences[2].

When the foreman of the jury has announced their verdict, the clerk of court records it. This may take some time, if the indictment is lengthy and there are several accused. The jury may be given a meal while their verdict is being recorded[3]. When the verdict has been recorded, the clerk reads it out, and the jury are asked to confirm that that is a 'true record of your verdict'.

After the jury's verdict has been recorded, if it is a verdict of acquittal, the accused is discharged and is free to leave the dock.

Once the verdict has been recorded, the jury may be discharged, although it is common practice to postpone this until after the accused has been sentenced or the case has been adjourned for reports. If there are other cases to be tried at the sitting, the jurors may be told to return later to be available to be balloted for a further trial. When discharging a jury the judge usually thanks them for their services and may tell them where to go in order to claim any expenses to which they are entitled.

SENTENCE

If an accused is found guilty, the prosecutor moves for sentence.

> 'Even when a verdict of guilt has been returned and recorded, it still lies with the Lord Advocate whether to move the court to pronounce sentence, and without that motion no sentence can be pronounced or imposed'[4].

Thus, an accused was convicted of two charges in an indictment (murder and attempted murder), and the prosecutor moved for sentence on only the murder charge (as was then the practice if an accused were convicted of murder and another charge). The conviction on the murder charge was quashed on appeal. The accused went free as no sentence had been, or could be, passed on the remaining charge[5].

The exact words used by the prosecutor when moving for sentence are immaterial, provided that he makes it clear that he is inviting the court to pass sentence[6].

As the court must have regard to any period of time spent in custody on remand by an accused[7], it is proper for the prosecutor, when moving for sentence, to inform the judge of the date on which the accused was remanded and how long he has spent in custody. Under solemn procedure, differing in this respect from summary procedure, there is no notice of penalties for

1 1975 Act, s 64.
2 Sexual Offences (Scotland) Act 1976, s 15.
3 As in *Sayers v HMA* 1981 SCCR 312 (also reported on other matters in 1982 JC 17 and 1982 SLT 220).
4 *Boyle v HMA* 1976 JC 32 at 37, 1976 SLT 126 at 129, per Lord Cameron.
5 *Paterson v HMA* 1974 JC 35.
6 *Noon v HMA* 1960 JC 52, 1960 SLT (Notes) 51.
7 1975 Act, s 218.

statutory offences produced to the judge. The prosecutor should therefore be in a position to inform the judge what is the maximum penalty for any statutory offence of which the accused has been convicted. This is both a courtesy and a help to the judge, and it is unfortunate that it is a practice which appears to have fallen into desuetude, at least in the sheriff court.

After the prosecutor has moved for sentence and produced any notice of previous convictions[1], counsel or the solicitor for the accused, or the accused himself if he is unrepresented, may address the court in mitigation of sentence. If the accused has pleaded not guilty and gone to trial, it is usual, and advisable, that the plea in mitigation should not refer to the facts of the crime. The personal circumstances of the accused should be given to the court. The accused's representative should, so far as possible, obtain independent confirmation of such matters as employment. Most courts are, without such confirmation, somewhat sceptical about the job due to start next Monday, not to mention the pregnant girlfriend or the ailing mother. Evidence in mitigation is competent, although not frequently led. There has in recent years grown up a practice in some sheriff courts of the sheriff being asked to read a letter from the accused himself. Although the judge is always entitled to have regard to such a letter, it is suggested that this is a practice which should not be followed. The accused's advocate is there to speak for him, and he can usually say much more effectively than the accused himself what requires to be said.

Before passing sentence the judge may order reports, in which case the proceedings are adjourned for a period which must not exceed three weeks[2]. The accused may be remanded in custody for this purpose, may be released on bail or may simply be ordained to appear[3]. An accused who is remanded in custody may appeal against the refusal of bail within 24 hours of being remanded[4]. The court may also remand an accused for an inquiry into his physical or mental condition[5]. The remand may be in custody, or the accused may be placed on bail with a condition of attending for medical examination or residing in a particular institution[6]. Again there is a right of appeal against refusal of bail[7].

The accused must be present when sentence is passed[8], and the sentence must be pronounced in open court[9]. As has already been noted[10], a sheriff may remit an accused to the High Court for sentence if he considers that his powers are inadequate (ie that the sentence should be longer than three years' imprisonment)[11]. If two accused appear on the same indictment, and the sheriff considers that his powers of punishment are inadequate for the one but not for the other, he should nevertheless remit both in order that both may be sentenced by the same judge[12].

The subject of sentencing will be examined in detail in chapter 7.

---

1 1975 Act, s 161(1). See above at pp 110, 111.
2 1975 Act, s 179(1). *HMA v Clegg* 1990 SCCR 293.
3 1975 Act, s 179(1).
4 1975 Act, s 179(2).
5 1975 Act, s 180(1).
6 1975 Act, s 180(2).
7 1975 Act, s 180(5).
8 *Hume* II 470; Alison *Practice* p 653; *Macdonald* p 349.
9 1975 Act, s 217(1).
10 See above at p 93.
11 1975 Act, s 104.
12 *HMA v Duffy* 1974 SLT (Notes) 46.

Chapter 6

Summary Procedure

INTRODUCTION

Summary procedure is the name given to the form of criminal procedure in which an accused, if he goes to trial, is tried by a judge or judges without a jury. The case of *Nicol Jarvie* described in chapter 2 is an example of summary procedure in the sheriff court. The two courts of summary jurisdiction are the sheriff court and the district court. The procedure is essentially the same in both courts. Summary procedure is governed by Part II of the Criminal Procedure (Scotland) Act 1975.

In this chapter we shall examine the progress of a summary case from the time when the police make a report to the procurator fiscal to the conclusion of the trial. First, however, it is appropriate to discuss the composition, jurisdiction and powers of the courts of summary jurisdiction.

THE SHERIFF COURT

The organisation, composition and territorial jurisdiction of the sheriff court in relation to solemn procedure were described in chapter 4[1]. What was said there applies equally to summary procedure save that the territorial jurisdiction is governed by different sections of the 1975 Act[2].

Any common law crime may be prosecuted summarily in the sheriff court apart from those crimes for which the High Court has exclusive jurisdiction[3]. The crimes of uttering a forged document, wilful fire-raising, robbery, and assault with intent to rob, which were formerly triable only on indictment, may now be prosecuted summarily in the sheriff court[4]. Any statutory offence may be tried summarily in the sheriff court unless the statute specifically provides that it may be tried only on indictment[5].

The maximum power of sentence of a sheriff under summary procedure is usually what governs whether a case is brought summarily or on petition.

1 See above at pp 92, 93.
2 Section 287 is the equivalent of s 4, s 288 is the equivalent of s 3, and s 292 is the equivalent of s 7.
3 These are murder, rape, deforcement of messengers and breach of duty of magistrates. Treason is also in the exclusive jurisdiction of the High Court, but it is strictly speaking statutory rather than common law.
4 1975 Act, s 291.
5 1975 Act, s 457A.

The sheriff's powers (unless extended by statute) are: (a) to impose a fine not exceeding the prescribed sum (£2,000 at the date of writing)[1]; (b) to order the accused to find caution (ie a sum of money as a guarantee) not exceeding the prescribed sum for his good behaviour for a period not exceeding twelve months[1]; (c) to impose a sentence of imprisonment in the event of the accused failing to pay a fine or find caution[2]; and (d) to impose a sentence of imprisonment of not more than three months[2]. The maximum period of imprisonment is extended to six months where a person is convicted of '(a) a second or subsequent offence inferring dishonest appropriation of property, or attempt thereat, or (b) a second or subsequent offence inferring personal violence'[3]. Of course, the sheriff also has power to pass many other forms of sentence, as will be discussed in the next chapter.

THE DISTRICT COURT

District courts were established by the District Courts (Scotland) Act 1975 to replace the burgh courts, justice of the peace courts and various other courts of summary jurisdiction. The Act provided for the establishment of a district court in the area of each district or islands council (local authorities created by the Local Government (Scotland) Act 1973) unless the Secretary of State directed that no court should be established because of a likely lack of business[4]. The district or islands area is known as the 'commission area'[5].

The judges of the district court are the justices of the peace for the relevant commission area or a stipendiary magistrate[6]. Justices of the peace are appointed by the Secretary of State[7]. A court may consist of one or more justices[8]. A stipendiary magistrate may be appointed by the local authority for the commission area[9]. He must be an advocate or solicitor of at least five years' standing[10]. At the time of writing Glasgow is the only commission area with a stipendiary magistrate.

A clerk of court must be appointed by the local authority. He must be an advocate or solicitor and acts as legal assessor as well as clerk[11].

The territorial jurisdiction of a district court is confined to its commission area, subject to a provision similar to s 287(4) of the 1975 Act to cover offences committed in several different commission areas[12]. Section 292 of

---

1 1975 Act, s 289. In terms of s 289B(6) the 'prescribed sum' may be altered by an order made by the Secretary of State under s 289D.
2 1975 Act, s 289. The maximum period of imprisonment which may be imposed as an alternative in respect of various sums is provided in s 407.
3 1975 Act, s 290.
4 District Courts (Scotland) Act 1975, s 1(1).
5 Ibid, s 26(1).
6 Ibid, ss 2(2) and 26(1).
7 Ibid, s 9(2).
8 Ibid, s 2(2).
9 Ibid, s 5(1).
10 Ibid, s 5(2).
11 Ibid, s 7(1).
12 Ibid, s 3(4). See the comments on the equivalent solemn provision (1975 Act, s 4(4)) above at p 92.

the 1975 Act (thefts committed outside Scotland) applies to the district court as well as to the sheriff court[1].

The type of common law crime which may competently be prosecuted in a district court consisting of justices is defined in a negative way, the relevant section of the 1975 Act specifying crimes which may not be tried in 'a court of summary jurisdiction other than the sheriff court'[2]. The excluded crimes are: murder; culpable homicide; robbery; rape; wilful fire-raising or attempt thereat; stouthrief[3]; theft by housebreaking; housebreaking with intent to steal; theft, reset, fraud, or embezzlement where the amount involved exceeds £1,000; assault involving fracture of a limb; assault with intent to rape; assault to the danger of life; assault by stabbing; uttering forged documents; uttering forged banknotes; and offences under the Acts relating to coinage[4]. If one of the excluded crimes comes before a district court, it should be remitted to the sheriff court[5]. The district court may also remit a case which *is* within its competence, if it considers that, 'in view of the circumstances of the case', it should be dealt with by the sheriff[5].

Statutory offences other than road traffic offences may be tried in a district court consisting of justices, if the maximum penalty does not exceed 60 days' imprisonment or a fine of level 4 on the standard scale or both[6]. So far as road traffic offences are concerned, a district court may try any offence for which a fixed penalty may be imposed and any other offence in respect of which a conditional offer may be sent[7]. Apart from that, a district court may not try any offence involving obligatory endorsement of a driving licence[8]. A district court may disqualify from driving under the 'totting up' procedure only[9].

The maximum powers of punishment of a district court consisting of justices (unless extended by statute) are: (a) to impose a sentence of imprisonment not exceeding 60 days[10]; (b) to impose a fine not exceeding level 4 on the standard scale (£1,000 at the date of writing)[11]; (c) to ordain the accused to find caution of an amount not exceeding level 4 on the standard scale for his good behaviour for a period not exceeding six months[11]; (d) to impose a sentence of imprisonment in the event of the accused failing to pay a fine or find caution[11].

It must be emphasised that the foregoing limitations on jurisdiction and powers apply only to courts consisting of justices. If a district court consists of a stipendiary magistrate, it has the same jurisdiction and powers as a sheriff court sitting summarily[12].

---

1 See the comments on the equivalent solemn provision (1975 Act, s 7) above at p 92.
2 1975 Act, s 285.
3 Stouthrief was a form of aggravated robbery and is now in desuetude (GH Gordon *The Criminal Law of Scotland* (2nd edn, 1978) para 16–01, note 5).
4 1975 Act, s 285.
5 1975 Act, s 286. The section does not actually specify the sheriff court, referring only to 'a higher court', but the sheriff court is the only other court of summary jurisdiction.
6 1980 Act, s 7(1). For the standard scale see note 11 below.
7 Road Traffic Offenders Act 1988, s 10(1).
8 Ibid, s 10(2).
9 Ibid, s 35(6).
10 1975 Act, s 284.
11 1975 Act, s 284. The standard scale is set forth in s 289G. It may be altered by an order made by the Secretary of State under s 289D(1).
12 District Courts (Scotland) Act 1975, s 3(2).

REPORT OF CRIME TO THE PROCURATOR FISCAL

The procurator fiscal is the prosecutor in both the sheriff court and the district court. All cases which are to proceed in either of these courts are reported by the police to the fiscal. The report may relate to an accused who has been arrested and detained in custody, or to one who has been arrested and released on an undertaking or on honour to attend a specified court[1]. Rather exceptionally it may relate to a case where, for some reason, the accused has not been in custody but will require to be arrested on a so-called 'initiating warrant' following preparation of a complaint[2]. However, by far the great majority of summary cases are those in which the accused has simply been told by the police that the circumstances of the alleged offence will be reported to the fiscal, and that, if proceedings are taken, the accused will be cited to attend court.

The police report as initially sent to the fiscal contains only a summary of the case against the accused, together with a note of the accused's criminal record, if any. On the basis of this information the fiscal who receives the report must decide whether to prosecute the accused, and, if so, in which court to do so. The decision whether to prosecute may depend on a number of factors. The most important is likely to be the sufficiency of the evidence, but, if the offence is very trivial, a decision may be taken that it would not be in the public interest to launch a prosecution. If an offence is triable in the district court, the decision whether to bring it there or in the sheriff court may depend on how serious an example of that type of offence it is and on the accused's criminal record.

Having taken a decision to prosecute, the fiscal prepares a complaint.

THE COMPLAINT

The complaint is the document which contains the charge(s) against the accused under summary procedure. The form of complaint is standard[3]. The heading specifies the court in which the case is being brought. The complaint continues: 'The complaint of the Procurator Fiscal against . . .'. The accused is then named and his address stated (and/or the fact that he is in custody). His date of birth is also usually stated. The next part of the complaint is the actual charge: 'The charge against you is . . .'. Styles for most common law crimes and many (mostly out of date) statutory offences are given in Schedule 2, Part II of the Summary Jurisdiction (Scotland) Act 1954[4]. A common law charge should be as nearly as may be in the form shown in the Schedule, and no further specification is required[5]. The complaint is signed by the procurator fiscal or one of his deputes[6].

1 1975 Act, s 295. See above at p 84.
2 1975 Act, s 314(1)(b) provides for the granting of an initiating warrant. See above at p 82.
3 1975 Act, s 311(1); AA(C) 1988, r 87, Form 45. See the complaint in the case of *Nicol Jarvie* (at p 57 above).
4 This Schedule is one of the few parts of the 1954 Act which is still in force. Its terms are referred to specifically in the 1975 Act, s 312 and AA(C) 1988, Form 45.
5 1975 Act, s 312. *Anderson v Allan* 1985 SCCR 399: this case makes no reference to the principle of giving an accused fair notice. See the commentary by Sheriff G H Gordon (editor of SCCR) at 1985 SCCR 401. Contrast the position in the case of a statutory charge – see note 3 below at p 162.
6 1975 Act, s 311(2). In *Lowe v Bee* 1989 SCCR 476 (Sh Ct), it was held that an unsigned complaint was a nullity.

Part II of the 1975 Act contains provisions relating to the detailed contents of summary complaints[1] in terms identical with ss 43–55 of Part I relating to solemn procedure, and the comments made earlier about these sections should be referred to[2].

In the case of statutory offences the 1975 Act provides that 'the description of any offence in the words of the statute or order contravened, or in similar words, shall be sufficient'[3], and 'where the offence is created by more than one section of one or more statutes or orders, it shall be necessary to specify only the leading section or one of the leading sections'[4].

CITATION

If an accused is in custody or attends as an 'undertaker' or on honour[5], he is served with the complaint and any other documents[6] by being handed them by a police officer[7]. However, the great majority of accused are cited to attend, and it is therefore appropriate to examine now the process of citation.

The court does not require to grant a warrant to cite. The 1975 Act is itself sufficient warrant[8]. The 1988 Act of Adjournal provides for various forms to be used in connection with citation: the citation itself[9]; the form of notice of previous convictions[10]; the notice of penalty for statutory offences[11]; the form of reply which an accused may use to respond to the complaint in writing rather than attending court[12]; and the means form in which an accused may provide information about his financial position, which will enable the court to fix an appropriate fine[13].

The 'form of citation' provides for a statement of the date when the case is to be heard[14] and the court in which the accused is to appear. It also contains advice about how to respond to the citation, indicating three possible ways: (1) to attend court personally; (2) to arrange for a lawyer or some other person to attend; (3) to write to the court, using the reply form and envelope provided. The form warns an accused that failure to respond at all may result in a warrant being issued for his arrest.

1 1975 Act, s 312.
2 For ss 43–55, see above at pp 103–106. The equivalence is as follows: 43/312(a); 44/312(b); 45/312(c); 46/312(d); 48/312(e); 49/312(s); 50/312(f); 51/312(g); 52/312(h); 53/312(i); 54/312(j); and 55/312(k).
3 1975 Act, s 312(p). But an accused is still entitled to fair notice of the case against him. See eg *Blair v Keane* 1981 JC 19, 1981 SLT (Notes) 4.
4 1975 Act, s 312(r).
5 1975 Act, s 295(1)(a).
6 A notice of penalty in respect of a statutory offence in terms of s 311(5) and a notice of previous convictions in terms of s 357(1) of the 1975 Act.
7 Strictly speaking, service is not necessary. It is sufficient that the terms of the complaint are read out to the accused when he first appears in court (1975 Act, s 334(1)(b)). In practice, however, an accused is always served with a complaint.
8 1975 Act, s 315(1).
9 AA(C) 1988, r 87, Form 47.
10 AA(C) 1988, r 87, Form 48.
11 AA(C) 1988, r 87, Form 46.
12 AA(C) 1988, r 88, Form 49.
13 AA(C) 1988, r 88, Form 50.
14 The omission of the date of appearance makes the citation invalid: *Beattie v McKinnon* 1977 JC 64.

The 'form of reply to complaint' provides spaces for the accused to indicate whether he is pleading guilty or not guilty. If he is pleading guilty, it gives him an opportunity to admit or deny any previous convictions of which he has been given notice, although, if he does not expressly deny a conviction, he is deemed to have admitted it[1]. It provides a space for him to give any explanation which he may wish about the case. Although the form is relatively simply set out and should be easy to understand, it is remarkable how often it is wrongly or misleadingly completed.

The means form emphasises that there is no obligation to provide the information requested. It contains spaces for details of the accused's income and expenditure to be stated together with details of his employment and dependents.

An accused must be cited at least 48 hours before he is due to appear in court[2].

There are various methods of citation, all of which may be effected by an officer of law[3]. An accused may be cited by having the citation delivered to him personally or left for him at his dwelling-house or place of business with some person resident or employed there, or, where he has no known dwelling-house or place of business, at any other place in which he may at the time be resident[4]. If the accused is employed on a vessel, the citation may be left with a person on board and connected with the vessel[5]. If the accused is a company, association or corporation, the citation may be left at their ordinary place of business with a partner, director, secretary or other official, or they may be cited in the same way as if the proceedings were in a civil court[6]. If the accused is a body of trustees, the citation may be left with any one of them who is resident in Scotland or with their known solicitor in Scotland[7].

As an alternative to citation by an officer of law, the citation, signed by the prosecutor, may be sent by registered or recorded delivery post to the accused's dwelling-house or place of business, or if he has no known dwelling-house or place of business, to any other place where he may at the time be resident[8]. If citation is by post, the provisions for trial in absence of a statutory offence[9] and granting a warrant for the accused's arrest on his failure to appear[10] do not apply, unless it is proved to the court that the accused actually received the citation or that the contents thereof came to his knowledge[11]. The accused's knowledge may be proved by production in court of any letter or other communication purporting to be written by him 'in such terms as to infer' (by which is surely meant 'in terms such as it may be inferred therefrom') that the contents of the citation came to his knowledge[12].

In the case of postal citation the period of notice (*induciae*) runs from 24

1 1975 Act, s 357(1)(c)(i).
2 1975 Act, s 315(2). The term *induciae* used in the section means a period of notice.
3 1975 Act, s 326(1). For the definition of 'officer of law' see s 462(1) discussed above at pp 109, 110.
4 1975 Act, s 316(2)(a).
5 1975 Act, s 316(2)(b).
6 1975 Act, s 316(2)(c). For citation of a company in a civil court see ID Macphail *Sheriff Court Practice* (1988), ch 6, especially para 6–40.
7 1975 Act, s 316(2)(d).
8 1975 Act, s 316(3).
9 1975 Act, s 338(1)(b). See below at p 184 for trial in absence.
10 1975 Act, s 338(1)(c).
11 1975 Act, s 316(3), proviso.
12 1975 Act, s 316(4).

hours after the time of posting[1]. If the citation is actually received by the accused, it is the posting itself and not receipt by the accused which is the execution of citation[2]. However, if an attempted postal citation is returned by the post office marked 'not known at this address', then there has been no valid execution of citation[3]. Postal citation is proved by production of a written execution signed by the person who signed the citation together with the relevant post office receipt[4].

TIME LIMITS IN STATUTORY CASES

Some statutes provide for the commencement of proceedings within a certain time after the commission of the alleged offence[5], or after information sufficient to justify proceedings has come to the knowledge of the prosecutor or some other person[6]. If there is no time limit imposed for a statutory offence by the statute creating the offence, a general time limit applies of six months after the date of the contravention concerned, or, in the case of a continuous contravention, within six months after the last date of such contravention[7]. In the case of a continuous contravention, if proceedings are commenced within six months after the last date, then the whole period of the offence may be included in the prosecution[7]. Proceedings in respect of any offence involving bodily injury to a child under the age of seventeen years must be commenced within six months of the commission of the offence, and the same rule about a continuous offence applies[8].

For the purpose of the six-month time limit proceedings are deemed to commence on the date when a warrant to apprehend 'or to cite an accused' is granted, provided that the warrant is executed without undue delay[9]. However, as has already been noted, a warrant to cite is unnecessary as the 1975 Act itself is sufficient warrant[10]. This provision has been interpreted as meaning the date when a diet is assigned (ie a date fixed when the case will call in court), to which the accused is then cited[11].

What constitutes 'undue delay' in executing a warrant is a question of fact, circumstances and degree, which is very much within the province of the

---

1　1975 Act, s 319(1).

2　*Lockhart v Bradley* 1977 SLT 5.

3　*Keily v Tudhope* 1986 SCCR 251, 1987 SLT 99.

4　1975 Act, s 319(2). Although this subsection refers to 'the appropriate form contained in an Act of Adjournal', there is at the time of writing no prescribed form.

5　Eg, Misuse of Drugs Act 1971, s 25(5), (twelve months); Sexual Offences (Scotland) Act 1976, s 4(1), (one year).

6　Eg, Road Traffic Offenders Act 1988, s 6 (six months from the date when evidence sufficient to warrant proceedings comes to the knowledge of the prosecutor); Social Security Act 1986, s 56(5)(a) (three months from the date on which evidence sufficient in the opinion of the Lord Advocate to justify proceedings comes to his knowledge, or twelve months from the commission of the offence, whichever is the later).

7　1975 Act, s 331(1).

8　1975 Act, s 331(2).

9　1975 Act, s 331(3).

10　1975 Act, s 315(1).

11　Ie, under 1975 Act, s 314(1)(a), which gives power to the court to assign a diet to which the accused may be cited.

court of first instance[1]. Much will depend on whether there has been any fault on the part of either the prosecutor or the accused. It has been held that a delay of only six days in citing an accused after the fixing of an assigned diet was 'undue' in the absence of any explanation by the Crown[2]. In another case, however, it was held that a similar delay of six days was *not* undue, the local practice with regard to citation having been followed[3]. At the other end of the scale a delay of fifteen months in executing a warrant to apprehend was held to be not undue where the delay was entirely due to the accused's own conduct[4].

The period to be looked at in assessing whether there has been undue delay is the period between the grant of the warrant and its execution, and not the period between the end of the six months and the date of execution[5].

If a warrant to apprehend has been granted within the six months, and (as happens quite frequently) the accused attends court by arrangement without actually having been arrested, the requirement about undue delay does not apply as there has been no execution of the warrant[6].

WARRANT TO APPREHEND OR TO SEARCH

Relatively rarely, once a complaint has been prepared but before any further action has been taken on it, the prosecutor may seek to have the accused arrested rather than cited. The prosecutor may apply to a judge of the appropriate court for a warrant to apprehend[7]. The judge may grant a warrant if he considers it expedient[7].

The prosecutor may also apply to a judge of the appropriate court at the same stage of proceedings for a warrant to search the accused's person, his dwelling-house and repositories and any place he may be found, for anything likely to afford evidence of his guilt[8]. This power is not frequently used, but, if an application is made, the judge concerned should satisfy himself that there is good reason for granting the warrant. The legislation provides no criteria for assessing whether or not it is appropriate to grant a search warrant.

FIRST CALLING IN COURT (FIRST DIET)

If the accused is in custody, he will, of course, be brought to court. If he is an undertaker[9], he must attend at the specified time. If he, without reasonable

---

1 *Beattie v Tudhope* 1984 SCCR 198, 1984 SLT 423. See also *Smith v Peter Walker & Son (Edinburgh) Ltd* 1978 JC 44; *McNeillie v Walkinshaw* 1990 SCCR 428. If the facts are disputed, evidence should be heard: *McCartney v Tudhope* 1985 SCCR 373, 1986 SLT 159.
2 *Carmichael v Sardar & Sons* 1983 SCCR 433 (Sh Ct), a case in which the Crown marked an appeal, but did not proceed with it.
3 *Beattie v Tudhope* 1984 SCCR 198, 1984 SLT 423.
4 *Nicolson v Skeen* (1976) SCCR (Supp) 74.
5 *MacNeill v Cowie* 1984 SCCR 449, 1985 SLT 246.
6 *Young v Smith* 1981 SCCR 85, 1981 SLT (Notes) 101.
7 1975 Act, s 314(1)(b).
8 1975 Act, s 314(1)(c). See above at pp 85, 86 for search warrants.
9 Under the 1975 Act, s 295(1)(a).

excuse, does not do so, he is guilty of an offence[1]. Those in custody and undertakers are entitled to the services of the legal aid duty solicitor, irrespective of their means[2]. Representation by the duty solicitor continues until the conclusion of the first diet (including any application for liberation) or, if the accused pleads guilty, until the case is finally disposed of[2]. An accused in custody or an undertaker is, of course, entitled to employ his own solicitor rather than the duty solicitor, if he wishes, but he will require to pay for the privilege.

A person who has been cited to a court need not attend in person. He may respond in writing[3], or he may be represented by a solicitor or by some other person 'who satisfies the court that he is authorised by the accused'[4].

An objection to the competency or the relevancy of the complaint[5], or a denial that the accused is the person charged by the police with the offence[6], may be stated by the accused himself[7], or by counsel or a solicitor on his behalf[8], but not, it is implied, by any other person, or in writing. Such a preliminary plea may be disposed of at the first diet, but it is more usual for the case to be put down for a hearing at a later date. There is a right of appeal to the High Court against the court's decision on a preliminary plea, but such an appeal requires the leave of the court and must be taken within two days after the decision of the court[9]. If the preliminary plea is repelled, the accused may apply for leave to appeal only after stating how he pleads to the charge[10]. If a preliminary plea is not stated at the first diet, it may be stated at a later time only with leave of the court on cause shown[11]. Whether to allow a plea to be stated at a later stage is entirely within the discretion of the judge[12]. The fact that the accused was unrepresented at the first diet is invariably considered to be sufficient cause to allow him to state a preliminary plea at a later date.

Assuming that there is no preliminary objection, the next stage is for the accused either to plead to the complaint or ask that it be continued without plea[13]. There is no provision for an accused to seek a continuation without plea in writing, but, in practice, it is common for the prosecutor to make such a motion at the request of the defence contained in a letter to the fiscal. If the accused is neither present nor represented when a case is continued without

---

1 1975 Act, s 295(2).
2 Legal Aid (Scotland) Act 1986, s 22(1)(c); Criminal Legal Aid (Scotland) Regulations 1987, SI 1987/307, reg 5(1)(d).
3 1975 Act, s 334(3)(a).
4 1975 Act, s 334(3)(b).
5 The same principles of competency and relevancy apply to complaints as to indictments. See above at p 120.
6 Under the 1980 Act, s 26(5) there is a presumption that the person who appears in answer to the complaint is the person charged with the offence by the police.
7 1975 Act, s 334(1).
8 1975 Act, s 334(2).
9 1975 Act, s 334(2A). Detailed rules for the appeal are provided in AA(C) 1988, r 128.
10 AA(C) 1988, r 128(1). For the confused situation which can arise when this rule is not observed see *Lafferty v Jessop* 1989 SCCR 451, 1989 SLT 846.
11 1975 Act, s 334(1).
12 *Henderson v Ingram* 1982 SCCR 135.
13 1975 Act, s 328 provides for continuation without plea for seven days from the date of apprehension of the accused, or 'on special cause shown' for 21 days. In practice, cited cases are continued without plea for three weeks as a matter of course. Not infrequently a case may be continued without plea on several occasions.

plea, the prosecutor must intimate the fact of the continuation and the date of the adjourned diet to him[1].

If the accused has responded by means of the form of response which he received along with his citation, he should have indicated clearly whether he is pleading guilty or not guilty. If the accused is not present and is represented by a solicitor or other authorised person, he makes the plea on the accused's behalf. If the accused is present, whether or not he is represented by a solicitor or counsel, the strict rule is that he is required to state his plea himself[2]. There is power given to the court to accept a plea from a solicitor or counsel if the judge is satisfied that the accused is not capable of pleading personally[3]. However, it is fair to say that, in some courts at least, the rule requiring personal pleading by a represented accused is more honoured in the breach than in the observance. In these courts, in practice, a represented accused makes his plea personally only if the defence solicitor is having difficulty with his client and specifically requests that the court should take the plea from the accused himself. Otherwise the defence solicitor makes the plea on behalf of the accused[4].

Plea of guilty

If the accused pleads guilty, a similar procedure is followed to that on a plea of guilty under solemn procedure[5], although neither the accused nor the judge signs the plea, and the prosecutor does not usually make any formal motion for sentence. He produces a notice of previous convictions, if any, and, in the case of a statutory offence, the appropriate notice of penalty.

In the case of certain road traffic offences where the accused's driving licence must be endorsed, the licence should be produced to the court[6]. This is, firstly, so that the court may see what, if any, endorsements are already on the licence and thus take them into account when passing sentence[7]. Secondly, it is in order that the appropriate endorsement in the instant case may be added to the licence. If the licence is not produced, then, unless the accused satisfies the court that he has applied for a new licence and has not yet received it, the licence is suspended[8]. In practice a court may accept an undertaking by an accused to produce his licence later the same day or at a later date. If an accused claims to have mislaid his licence, the court may give him an opportunity to apply for a duplicate. If the accused, for whatever reason, does not produce a licence in court, the court is entitled to have regard to a computer print-out of the accused's record from the Driving and Vehicle Licensing Centre (DVLC)[9]. The accused must be asked if he admits the accuracy of the record[10], and, if any part of it is disputed, the prosecutor must prove it[11]. The view has been expressed that reference to the DVLC print-out

1 AA(C) 1988, r 119(3).
2 AA(C) 1988, r 119(1).
3 AA(C) 1988, r 119(2).
4 This practice appears to be condoned by the High Court: *Crombie v Hamilton* 1989 SCCR 499.
5 See above at pp 125, 126.
6 Road Traffic Offenders Act 1988, s 27(1).
7 Ibid, s 31.
8 Ibid, s 27(3).
9 Ibid, s 32(2).
10 Ibid, s 32(3).
11 Ibid, s 32(5).

is permitted only where the accused is or has been the holder of a driving licence[1], but it is submitted that the terms of s 32 of the Road Traffic Offenders Act 1988 are in fact wide enough to cover even the person who has never held a licence.

Except in the circumstances described in the previous paragraph, the court may not take account of previous convictions unless they are contained in a notice which has been served on the accused[2]. If the accused does not admit a conviction, the prosecutor must prove it[3]. An erroneous notice of convictions may be amended[4].

In the case of a statutory charge the prosecutor must serve a notice of penalty along with the complaint[5]. A copy of the notice must be produced to the court before sentence is passed[6]. If no notice has been served, or if a copy is not produced to the court, no penalty may be imposed in respect of that offence[7]. A sheriff has held that, where the prosecutor had failed to serve a notice, the case should be deserted *pro loco et tempore* following a plea of guilty, in order that the prosecutor could commence fresh proceedings[8]. However, this decision has been the subject of critical comment[9]. An erroneous notice of penalty may be amended[10]. If the notice served relates to a different offence from that of which the accused is convicted, it may still be valid if the penalties are in fact identical[11].

After any necessary notices have been produced to the court the prosecutor usually narrates briefly the circumstances of the offence(s), although some statutory offences are so self-explanatory that little, if any, elaboration of the terms of the complaint is needed. The accused or his representative, if either of them is present, then makes a plea in mitigation. If the accused has pleaded guilty in writing, the court considers any explanation or mitigating circumstance which he may have provided and any information contained in his means form or other document. If there is any discrepancy between the account of events given by the Crown and that given by the defence, the same procedure should be followed as in a solemn case[12]. The court then usually proceeds to sentence. Alternatively, it may adjourn the case to obtain reports or (where the accused has not been present at the first diet) for the accused to appear personally at a subsequent diet. If the court wishes to obtain reports, the accused may be remanded in custody even although he has not previously been in custody in connection with the case[13]. Such a remand is, however, relatively rare.

1 Road Traffic Encyclopaedia (Sweet and Maxwell), para 1–499, founding on the case of *Anderson v Allan* 1985 SCCR 262.
2 1975 Act, s 357(1)(a).
3 1975 Act, s 357(1)(e).
4 1975 Act, s 335(1).
5 1975 Act, s 311(5). Service must be on the accused personally. Service on his solicitor, even in the presence of the accused, is not sufficient: *Geddes v Hamilton* 1986 SCCR 165, 1986 SLT 536. Service may be proved by producing the written execution of the police officer who effected it: *Muir v Carmichael* 1988 SCCR 79.
6 1975 Act, s 311(5).
7 See eg, *Tudhope v Eadie* 1984 JC 6, 1983 SCCR 464, 1984 SLT 178, and *Miller v Allan* 1984 SCCR 28, 1984 SLT 280.
8 *MacPhail v McCabe* 1984 SCCR 146 (Sh Ct).
9 Ie by Sheriff G H Gordon (editor of SCCR) at 1984 SCCR 147–8.
10 1975 Act, s 355(1). *Slater v Jessop* reported as a Note at 1989 SCCR 147.
11 *Donnachie v Smith* 1989 SCCR 144.
12 See above at pp 125, 126.
13 1975 Act, s 380(1).

An accused who has pleaded guilty may, in certain circumstances, be permitted to withdraw that plea and substitute a plea of not guilty[1]. It is, for example, not uncommon for an unrepresented accused to plead guilty, to have his case continued for a social enquiry report, and to give to the social worker an account of the offence which is inconsistent with guilt. In such a situation he would usually be allowed to change his plea. The court would also probably strongly advise him to consult a solicitor.

Plea of not guilty

If an accused pleads not guilty, the prosecutor will almost certainly move the court to fix a diet of trial, although there are rare circumstances where the not guilty plea will be accepted.

In theory a trial may take place immediately after an accused has pleaded not guilty[2], unless the accused has appeared from custody, in which case he is entitled to have the case adjourned for at least 48 hours prior to the trial[3]. In practice, however, a trial diet is fixed for some time ahead. If either the prosecutor or the defence has information to the effect that the trial is likely to be a long one, the clerk of court should be informed, in order that sufficient court time may be set aside.

Intermediate diet

As well as a trial diet the court may, at the request of either side or of its own volition, fix an intermediate diet. The purpose of such a diet is to ascertain '(a) the state of preparation of the prosecutor and of the accused with respect to the case; and (b) whether the accused intends to adhere to the plea of not guilty'[4]. At the intermediate diet the court may ask the prosecutor and the accused (or his representative) any question for the purpose of ascertaining these matters[5].

An accused is obliged to attend an intermediate diet[6]. It is therefore inadvisable to fix an intermediate diet in a case where the accused lives a long distance from the court.

The intermediate diet was introduced into summary procedure in 1980, mainly with the intention of reducing the number of cases in which pleas of guilty were tendered on the day of the trial diet causing great inconvenience to witnesses and a considerable waste of court time. Regrettably, in many courts this intention has not been fulfilled, and last minute changes of plea are still common even where there has been an intermediate diet. An intermediate diet is now less often requested by either side than it used to be, but may be useful in a case where the accused faces a large number of charges, and it seems likely that he will offer a plea to some of them which may be acceptable to the prosecutor.

---

1 *McClung v Cruickshank* 1964 JC 64; *Tudhope v Cullen* 1982 SCCR 276 (Sh Ct).
2 1975 Act, s 337(a).
3 1975 Act, s 337(c).
4 1975 Act, s 337A(1).
5 1975 Act, s 337A(2).
6 1975 Act, s 337A(3).

At an intermediate diet an accused may plead guilty, in which case matters proceed exactly as if he had pleaded guilty at the first diet[1].

Ordained, bailed or remanded

If a trial diet is fixed, whether with or without an intermediate diet, the question arises of what steps should be taken to ensure the accused's attendance at the later diet.

In the great majority of cases he is simply ordained to appear. This means that he is told the date and time of the trial or intermediate diet and that he must appear then. There are no conditions attached. If the accused fails, without reasonable excuse, to appear having been ordained, he is guilty of an offence punishable by a fine not exceeding level 3 on the standard scale and to imprisonment not exceeding 60 days (in the district court) or three months (in the sheriff court)[2]. These penalties may be imposed in addition to any other penalty which the court may impose for the offence originally charged, notwithstanding that the normal maximum powers of the court may thereby be exceeded[3]. The accused may be dealt with for the offence of failing to appear, either at the trial diet for the original offence or at a separate diet[4].

Alternatively, the accused may, provided that he is present in court, be released on bail[5]. In the case of accused who have appeared from custody the Crown usually moves the court to admit to bail rather than to ordain to appear. Breach of any bail condition in connection with summary proceedings (including failure without reasonable excuse to appear at a diet) is punishable with a fine not exceeding £200 and imprisonment for 60 days (in the district court) or three months (in the sheriff court)[6]. These penalties may be imposed in addition to any other penalty which the court may impose for the offence originally charged, notwithstanding that the normal maximum powers of the court may thereby be exceeded[7].

It is also competent, but only in the case of an accused appearing from custody, to remand him in custody for trial[8], although this is a relatively rare occurrence.

If an accused is remanded in custody for trial, his trial must be commenced[9] within 40 days after the first diet, failing which he must be liberated forthwith and 'shall be for ever free from all question or process for that offence'[10]. This period may be extended by a sheriff (whether the case is in the district court or the sheriff court), if he is satisfied that delay in the commencement of the trial is due to (a) the illness of the accused or of a judge; (b) the absence or illness of any necessary witness; or (c) any other sufficient cause which is not attribu-

1 1975 Act, s 337A(4).
2 1975 Act, s 338(2).
3 1975 Act, s 338(3).
4 1975 Act, s 338(4).
5 See the comments on bail in solemn procedure above at pp 94–97, which are generally applicable to summary procedure with the exception of those dealing with penalties for breach of a condition of bail. If a case, originally on petition, has been reduced to summary procedure, bail granted on the petition continues in force for the summary case: *McGinn v HMA* 1990 SCCR 170.
6 Bail etc (Scotland) Act 1980, s 3(1), (2).
7 Bail etc (Scotland) Act 1980, s 3(5).
8 1975 Act, s 337(d).
9 The commencement of the trial occurs when the first witness is sworn (1975 Act, s 331A(4)).
10 1975 Act, s 331A(1).

table to any fault on the part of the prosecutor[1]. Both the Crown and the defence have a right of appeal to the High Court against the sheriff's decision[2].

LEGAL AID

As we have seen, in a case under solemn procedure the decision whether or not to grant legal aid is for the court, and only the financial position of the accused is relevant[3]. In summary proceedings the situation is quite different. The duty solicitor has responsibility for those in custody and undertakers until the end of the first diet or, in the case of a plea of guilty, ultimate disposal[4]. However, in the case of an accused pleading not guilty, or an accused pleading guilty who does not appear from custody or as an undertaker, the general rule[5] is that neither the court nor the duty solicitor is concerned in the provision of legal aid. Instead, the body which determines eligibility for legal aid is the Scottish Legal Aid Board.

The general rules for legal aid in summary cases are to be found in s 24 of the Legal Aid (Scotland) Act 1986. This provides that legal aid is to be made available in summary proceedings if the Board is satisfied that the accused could not afford to pay for representation himself 'without undue hardship to him or his dependents'[6], and 'that in all the circumstances of the case it is in the interests of justice that legal aid should be made available to him'[7]. The 'interests of justice' are not defined as such, but the Board is directed that the factors to be taken into account in determining whether it is in the interests of justice to grant legal aid include[8]

(a) where the offence is such that if proved it is likely that the court would impose a sentence which would deprive the accused of his liberty or lead to loss of his livelihood;

(b) where the determination of the case may involve consideration of a substantial question of law, or of evidence of a complex or difficult nature;

(c) where the accused may be unable to understand the proceedings or to state his own case because of his age, inadequate knowledge of English, mental illness, other mental or physical disability or otherwise;

(d) where it is in the interests of someone other than the accused that the accused be legally represented;

(e) where the defence to be advanced by the accused does not appear to be frivolous;

(f) where the accused has been remanded in custody pending trial.

---

1 1975 Act, s 331A(2).
2 1975 Act, s 331A(3). AA(C) 1988, r 100 and Form 54 apply to such appeals.
3 See above at pp 97, 98.
4 See above at p 166.
5 Subject to one exception under the Legal Aid (Scotland) Act 1986, s 23(1)(b), which provides that the court may grant legal aid to a convicted accused who has not previously received a custodial sentence, and in respect of whom the court is now considering a custodial sentence. The financial criterion is the familiar one to the effect that the accused could not afford to pay for representation 'without undue hardship to him or his dependents'.
6 Legal Aid (Scotland) Act 1986, s 24(1)(a).
7 Ibid, s 24(1)(b).
8 Ibid, s 24(3).

An accused must apply for legal aid in writing on the appropriate form[1]. Most solicitors practising in the criminal courts will have a supply of forms. Because the form is long and complex it is usually completed by the solicitor rather than by the accused. The accused must sign the form. The application must normally be submitted to the Scottish Legal Aid Board within fourteen days after the accused has tendered a plea of not guilty[2]. This time limit does not apply if the Board considers that there is special reason to consider a late application[3]. Along with the form should be sent a copy of the complaint and evidence of the accused's income, whether a wages slip or a UB40 form.

If an accused is in custody and has actually applied for legal aid, then, even although his application has not yet been granted, legal aid is available to him up until the date when his application is finally determined by the Board[4] (and thereafter, of course, if his application is granted). Otherwise legal aid normally becomes available only from the date when the application is granted[5].

An accused whose application for legal aid has been refused may apply to the Board for a review[6].

If an accused, appearing unrepresented before a court for trial, has either not applied for legal aid or has been refused on the ground that it was not in the interests of justice, and the court considers that, owing to the exceptional circumstances of the case, it would be inequitable to proceed with the trial without the accused being represented, the court may adjourn the trial to enable the accused to apply for legal aid to the Board, and the Board must consider the application expeditiously[7]. In such a case legal aid is automatically available from the date of the making of the application until the date of its determination[8], so that the trial need not be adjourned for too long. The fourteen-day time bar on applying for legal aid does not affect such an application[9]. If, in such a case, the application is refused on the ground of means, the accused may be required to repay to the Board the whole or part of what the Board has paid for his representation[10].

Legal aid in a summary case normally covers only representation by a solicitor. If the accused wishes to employ counsel, he must apply for prior approval to the Board[11]. A similar rule applies if the accused wishes to make use of the services of an expert witness[12]. In either case, however, the Board may give retrospective approval, if it considers that there was special reason for prior approval not having been applied for[13].

---

1 Criminal Legal Aid (Scotland) Regulations 1987, SI 1987/307, reg 8(1)(a).
2 Ibid, reg 8(1)(b).
3 Ibid, reg 8(2)(b).
4 Legal Aid (Scotland) Act 1986, s 22(1). This provision exists in order to avoid summary trial of persons in custody having to be adjourned until the granting of a legal aid application.
5 But see also Legal Aid (Scotland) Act 1986, s 24(7).
6 Ibid, s 24(5).
7 Ibid, s 24(6).
8 Ibid, s 24(7).
9 Criminal Legal Aid (Scotland) Regulations 1987, SI 1987/307, reg 8(2)(a).
10 Legal Aid (Scotland) Act 1986, s 24(8).
11 Criminal Legal Aid (Scotland) Regulations 1987, SI 1987/307, reg 14(1)(b).
12 Ibid, reg 14(1)(c).
13 Ibid, reg 14(2).

PREPARATION BY THE CROWN

In a summary prosecution the Crown does not normally obtain precognitions. Instead, the statements which the police have taken from witnesses prior to reporting the case to the procurator fiscal are used for the conduct of the trial. However, a case may already have been precognosced before the decision is taken to proceed summarily. The case may, for example, originally have been on petition, or it may have involved a sudden death and therefore have been reported, with precognition, to the Crown Office. The fiscal also has power, even in summary proceedings, to apply to the court for a warrant to cite witnesses for precognition[1].

There is no obligation on the Crown to provide a list of prosecution witnesses to the defence, but, as a matter of courtesy, the fiscal will provide a list on request on the basis that the defence will reciprocate by providing a list of their witnesses to the Crown.

Under s 26 of the 1980 Act proof of certain matters may be effected by certificate without the necessity for oral evidence, provided that a copy of the certificate has been served on the accused not less than fourteen days before the trial[2]. The prosecutor must therefore make sure that the certificate is served in time if he wishes to avail himself of this facility. There are similar provisions for proof by certificate in certain statutes[3].

In the rare summary case where the accused has been the subject of a judicial examination the prosecutor must apply to the court if he wishes to have any part of the record thereof excluded from the evidence[4]. Except on cause shown, at least ten clear days notice must be given to the court and to other parties[5].

The prosecutor must cite his witnesses. Citation should be by personal service or by leaving the citation with someone at the witness's dwelling house or place of business, or at a place where he is resident if he has no dwelling house or place of business[6]. If the witness is employed on a vessel, he may be cited by leaving the citation with a person on board and connected with the vessel[6]. Crown witnesses are invariably cited by police officers.

The prosecutor should, of course, always be willing to discuss with the defence the possibility of agreeing any evidence and thus cutting down on the number of witnesses.

PREPARATION BY THE DEFENCE

Preparation by the defence for a summary trial should follow the same pattern as that for a solemn case[7].

---

1 1975 Act, s 315(3). The court may grant the warrant if it 'shall deem it expedient'.
2 See above at pp 145, 146. Section 26(2) which relates to reports by forensic scientists applies only to summary proceedings.
3 Eg Road Traffic Offenders Act 1988, s 16.
4 1975 Act, s 352(2).
5 1975 Act, s 352(4).
6 1975 Act, s 316(2). The form of citation is in the Summary Jurisdiction (Scotland) Act 1954, Sch 2, Pt IV.
7 See above at pp 112–116.

Section 10 of the 1980 Act, allowing the defence to apply to the sheriff to order the prosecutor to hold an identification parade, is relevant to both solemn and summary proceedings[1]. It should be noted that even if the trial is to be in the district court, the application must still be made to the sheriff.

There are provisions in Part II of the 1975 Act about agreement of evidence in summary proceedings similar to those in Part I relating to solemn procedure[2]. Any such agreement should, if possible, be reached prior to the trial.

The provision about applying to the court to precognosce a witness on oath on behalf of the accused[3] applies equally to summary as to solemn proceedings.

Like the prosecutor, the defence may apply to the court to have all or part of the record of a judicial examination excluded from the evidence[4], and must, except on cause shown, give at least ten clear days notice to the court and other parties of such an application[5]. As under solemn procedure such exclusion is usually agreed between prosecution and defence, and a formal application to the court is unnecessary.

If an intermediate diet has been fixed[6], the defence should make every effort to ensure that the case is fully prepared by the date of that diet, in order that it may be made clear to the court whether or not the trial is to proceed.

Defence witnesses should be cited in the same way as Crown witnesses[7], but the person serving the citation would normally be a sheriff officer. In practice it is common to cite defence witnesses by recorded delivery post although there is no statutory basis for this.

ALTERATION OF THE DIET

It quite frequently happens in a summary case that it is desired to change the date of a trial or other diet. The most common reason for this is that it is discovered, after a trial diet has been fixed, that an essential witness is to be unavailable on that date. The 1975 Act provides a convenient mechanism for changing a diet. All parties to a case (ie the fiscal and all accused) may apply to the court by written joint application to discharge a diet and fix an earlier diet in its place[8]. In practice a standard form of joint petition is signed by the fiscal and by the defence solicitor (or by the accused himself if he is unrepresented), and the case then calls in court as soon as possible. When the case does call either party may move the court to fix a fresh diet of trial or whatever other diet is appropriate.

This procedure for accelerating a diet is also, of course, appropriate if, after a trial has been fixed, the accused decides to tender a plea of guilty. At the accelerated diet in such a case the plea is tendered, and the case then proceeds as if the accused had pleaded guilty at the first diet.

1 The relevant rule for summary proceedings is AA(C) 1988, r 98.
2 1975 Act, s 354, which is the summary equivalent of s 150.
3 1980 Act, s 9(1). See above at p 113. AA(C) 1988, r 93 and Form 51 apply to summary proceedings.
4 1975 Act, s 352(2).
5 1975 Act, s 352(4).
6 See above at p 169.
7 Ie under 1975 Act, s 316(2). The form of citation is in the Summary Jurisdiction (Scotland) Act 1954, Schedule 2, Part IV.
8 1975 Act, s 314(3).

The prosecutor and the accused may also make a joint application to the court for postponement of a diet which has been fixed, and this may be made orally or in writing[1]. However, unlike the joint application for an accelerated diet described in the two preceding paragraphs, this application may be made only at a properly assigned diet of the case which has been duly called[2]. This may be either an intermediate diet or a trial diet. The application must be granted by the court unless there has been unnecessary delay on the part of one or more parties[3].

If the prosecutor wishes to postpone or accelerate a diet and and accused refuses to join with him in making a joint application[4], the prosecutor may apply to the court by way of an incidental application[5] for such a postponement or acceleration[6]. The court must give all parties an opportunity to be heard and may then discharge the diet and fix an earlier or later diet as the case may be[6].

An accused has a similar right to apply to the court for postponement or acceleration of a diet when the other parties are not prepared to join with him in an application[7]. Again, the court must give all parties an opportunity to be heard before deciding whether or not to grant the application[8].

TRIAL DIET

Plea in bar of trial

Many pleas in bar of trial[9] are really pleas to the competency of the proceedings (eg time bar) and should be treated as such[10]. However, a plea in bar of trial may depend on circumstances which have arisen only after service of a complaint, although the complaint itself is perfectly competent. For example, it may be submitted that there has been undue delay in actually bringing the case to trial, or that there has been prejudicial pre-trial publicity. It may be noted in passing that the court is less likely to sustain a plea in bar on the ground of pre-trial publicity in a summary case than it would be in a solemn case[11].

A plea in bar of trial should be stated when the case calls for trial, if it has not previously been stated.

1 1975 Act, s 314(4).
2 AA(C) 1988, r 99(1).
3 1975 Act, s 314(4).
4 Under either s 314(3) or s 314(4).
5 1975 Act, s 310.
6 1975 Act, s 314(5).
7 1975 Act, s 314(6).
8 1975 Act, s 314(6). AA(C) 1988, r 99(2) provides that Form 53 should be used for such an application.
9 See the comments on pleas in bar of trial in solemn procedure above at pp 120, 121, which apply equally to summary procedure.
10 See above at p 120.
11 *Aitchison v Bernardi* 1984 SCCR 88, 1984 SLT 343.

Defence of alibi

There is no general requirement to intimate a special defence in a summary trial. However, if an accused intends to found on an alibi, he must give notice to the prosecutor of the alibi, and of any witness who may be called to prove it, prior to the examination of the first prosecution witness[1]. The notice, which need not be in writing, should give particulars as to the time and place of the alibi[1]. It should be remembered that it is not a proper notice of an alibi to state the time as 'at the time when the crime was committed'. This begs the whole question. The notice should give specific times between which the accused was at a specific place or places. If notice of an alibi is given, the prosecutor is entitled, as of right, if he so desires, to an adjournment of the case[1].

Call-over of trials

There are usually several cases put out for trial on the one day. The normal practice is that a call-over of cases takes place as soon as the court convenes, in order to ascertain which of the trials is actually going to proceed. Pleas of guilty are disposed of at this time, and some cases may be adjourned to a later date. A number of cases will be left in which it is clear that the trial is going to proceed. The court then adjourns for what should be a short time so that the prosecution and the defence may discuss the order in which cases should be taken and any other preliminary matters. Following the adjournment, if all goes according to plan, the court is able to proceed with the trials without further interruption.

This call-over procedure has no statutory authority, but is now widely accepted. It enables witnesses in trials which are not to take place to be sent away rather than being kept waiting for the greater part of the day.

Conduct of the trial

The procedure in a summary trial is essentially the same as that in a solemn trial, although matters normally move somewhat more speedily. As in a solemn trial, there is no opening speech by the prosecutor.

The evidence

The comments about evidence under solemn procedure, which were made in chapter 5, are in the main equally applicable to summary proceedings except that the statutory references are different. This section will accordingly deal only briefly with the topic, and reference should be made to chapter 5.

Oath or affirmation

The form of oath or affirmation is the same as that under solemn procedure[2].

---

1 1975 Act, s 339.
2 AA(C) 1988, r 121. The 1975 Act, s 345, provides for a witness not having to take the oath repeatedly where he is giving evidence in a number of summary trials for statutory offences at the same diet. It is sufficient if he is reminded that he is on oath.

Child witnesses

As under solemn procedure the public may be excluded when a child witness is giving evidence in a case with sexual connotations[1].

Witnesses requiring interpretation

The same rules apply as under solemn procedure.

Presentation of evidence

Even where there is no jury, care should be taken in the presentation of the evidence in a case. Where the court consists of lay magistrates matters may have to be spelt out more carefully than where there is a professional judge (sheriff or stipendiary magistrate). Even with the professional judge, however, it must be borne in mind that all he has seen of the case is the complaint, and the evidence should be presented in a clear and comprehensible way.

The comments in the previous chapter about leading questions, hearsay[2], examination-in-chief, cross-examination, re-examination and questions by the judge are all relevant to summary procedure also.

Recall of witness

A judge has power at common law to recall any witness at any time in order to clarify an ambiguity. In a summary case this power may be exercised even during the submissions on the evidence by parties[3].

A judge may, on the motion of either party, permit a witness who has been examined already to be recalled[4].

Additional evidence

There is a provision for additional evidence in summary cases[5] in terms identical (*mutatis mutandis*) with those for additional evidence under solemn procedure[6]. The summary provision omits, of course, references to lists of witnesses and productions.

Evidence in replication

There is a provision for evidence in replication in summary cases[7] in terms

---

1 1975 Act, s 362 (equivalent of s 166).
2 The summary equivalent of 1975 Act, s 147 (making admissible evidence of a different statement previously made by a witness) is s 349.
3 *Rollo v Wilson* 1988 SCCR 312, 1988 SLT 659.
4 1975 Act, s 349A (equivalent of s 148A).
5 1975 Act, s 350.
6 1975 Act, s 149. See above at p 137.
7 1975 Act, s 350A.

identical (*mutatis mutandis*) with those for evidence in replication under solemn procedure[1]. The summary provision omits, of course, references to lists of witnesses and productions.

Evidence of accused's criminal record

Surprisingly there is no direct equivalent under summary procedure to the general prohibition which exists under solemn procedure against the leading of evidence about the criminal record of an accused[2]. However, it is implicit in the provisions which do exist[3] that no evidence of an accused's criminal record should be led prior to his conviction. An accidental disclosure of an accused's record is not fatal, as the record is then not 'laid before' the court[4]. Similarly, a conviction will not necessarily be set aside when the information about an accused's record is volunteered by a witness and not sought by the prosecutor[5].

Evidence of the accused

There are provisions about the accused as a witness in summary cases[6] in terms identical with those on the same subject under solemn procedure[7]. The decision in *Leggate v Her Majesty's Advocate*[8] applies equally to the summary provisions. When the accused puts forward his own good character the prosecutor should apply to the court for leave to attack his character in cross-examination[9].

All the comments made in chapter 5 about the accused as a witness should be read as applying also to summary procedure[10].

Evidence of the accused's spouse

There is a provision about the accused's spouse as a witness in summary cases[11] in terms identical with those on the same subject under solemn procedure[12]. The comments in the previous chapter on the solemn provisions[13] apply with the exception that no notice of an intention to call the spouse as a witness need be given.

Evidence of co-accused

There are provisions about a co-accused as a witness in summary cases[14] in

---

1 1975 Act, s 149A. See above at p 137.
2 1975 Act, s 160. See above at pp 137, 138.
3 1975 Act, ss 356(1), 357(1)(b).
4 *Johnston v Allan* 1983 SCCR 500, 1984 SLT 261; *O'Neill v Tudhope* 1984 SCCR 276, 1984 SLT 424.
5 *Carmichael v Monaghan* 1986 SCCR 598, 1987 SLT 338.
6 1975 Act, ss 346(1), 347.
7 1975 Act, ss 141(1), 142.
8 *Leggate v HMA* 1988 SCCR 391, 1989 SLT 665.
9 *McLean v Tudhope* 1982 SCCR 555.
10 See above at pp 138–140.
11 1975 Act, s 348.
12 1975 Act, s 143.
13 See above at p 141.
14 1975 Act, s 346(2), (3).

terms identical with those on the same subject under solemn procedure[1]. All the comments made in chapter 5 about a co-accused as a witness should be read as applying also to summary procedure[2].

Evidence in trials of sexual offences

There are provisions about evidence in summary trials of sexual offences[3] in terms identical (*mutatis mutandis*) with those on the same subject under solemn procedure[4]. The comments in chapter 5 on the solemn provisions[5] apply also to summary proceedings with the exception of references to the jury.

Presence of witnesses in court

As under solemn procedure[6], a summary court is given power[7] to permit a witness to remain in court before he has given evidence. There is a provision to cover the case of a witness who has been in court without permission in a summary case[8] in terms identical with those on the same subject under solemn procedure[9]. There is no reason why the rule which permits an expert witness to be in court while evidence of the facts is being given, should not apply in summary cases as it does under solemn procedure.

Accused's solicitor as witness

There is no specific authority on the subject of an accused's solicitor giving evidence in a summary trial, but it is submitted that there is no reason in principle why he should not, as in solemn procedure, be a competent witness, with the same restrictions on what he may be compelled to say[10]. If the solicitor is called as a witness on behalf of his own client, there is no confidentiality on a matter pertaining to the issue of the guilt of the accused[11].

A solicitor who is likely to be called as a witness should not, if at all possible, appear for the accused in the trial concerned.

Objections to admissibility of evidence

The same principles about objections to admissibility of evidence apply in summary as in solemn proceedings[12]. There is, of course, no question of a

1 1975 Act, s 141(2), (3).
2 See above at pp 141, 142.
3 1975 Act, ss 346A, 346B.
4 1975 Act, ss 141A, 141B.
5 See above at pp 142, 143.
6 1975 Act, s 139A. See above at p 143.
7 1975 Act, s 342A.
8 1975 Act, s 343.
9 1975 Act, s 140. See above at p 143.
10 See above at p 143.
11 1975 Act, s 341(4) (equivalent to s 138(4)).
12 See above at p 144.

trial within a trial. It is very important that an objection to the admissibility of evidence be stated timeously, as, if it is not, it cannot form the subject of a successful appeal[1]. If evidence is objected to, the court should not sustain the objection at that stage, but hear the evidence under reservation as to its competency[2].

Record of proceedings at judicial examination

It will not often happen that an accused in a summary trial has been the subject of a judicial examination, but, where he has been, the record of the judicial examination is received in evidence without being sworn to by witnesses[3]. As has been noted above[4], both the prosecutor and the accused are entitled to seek to have all or part of the record excluded from the evidence[5].

What was said in the previous chapter[6] about the evidential value of anything said at judicial examination is relevant to summary proceedings as well as to solemn.

Evidence by certificate

Reference has already been made[7] to the provisions of s 26 of the 1980 Act, and provisions of other statutes, regarding proof of certain matters by certificate. It is common practice for the prosecutor, before he leads his first witness, to produce the appropriate certificate together with an execution of service thereof on the accused. The advantage of producing these at this stage and not later is that, if there is any defect in the certificate or the service, the prosecutor may apply to the court to desert the diet *pro loco et tempore*, whereas he can make no such application after the first witness has been sworn[8].

Evidence by letter of request or on commission

In the sheriff court, but not in the district court, evidence by letter of request or on commission is competent as under solemn procedure[9]. There are detailed procedural rules for summary cases[10], but the same principles apply as under solemn procedure[11]. An application for a letter of request must be made before the first witness is sworn[12]. An application to appoint a commissioner to take evidence should normally be made at that time also, but may be made during the course of the trial in exceptional circumstances[12].

1 1975 Act, s 454. See *West v McNaughtan* 1990 SCCR 439.
2 *Clark v Stewart* 1950 JC 8 at 11, 1949 SLT 461 at 463, per Lord Justice-General Cooper.
3 1975 Act, s 352(1).
4 See pp 173, 174.
5 1975 Act, s 352(2).
6 See above at p 145.
7 See above at p 173.
8 1975 Act, s 338A(1).
9 1980 Act, s 32.
10 AA(C) 1988, rr 101–111.
11 See above at p 146.
12 1980 Act, s 32(5)(b).

Proof of official documents

Any letter, minute or other official document issuing from the office or in the custody of any of the departments of state or government in the United Kingdom is, in a summary prosecution, *prima facie* evidence of its contents without being spoken to by any witness, and a certified copy thereof is to be treated as equivalent to the original[1].

Any order by any of the departments of state or government or any local authority or public body made under statutory powers, or a print or copy of such an order, is to be received in a summary prosecution as evidence of the due making, confirmation and existence of the order without prejudice to the possibility of its being challenged as *ultra vires*[2].

Admissions by parties

Provided that an accused is legally represented, facts may be admitted by him without proof, the terms of documents may be agreed and copies of documents may be held to be the equivalent of originals[3]. It is provided that such admissions and agreements may be made by lodging a minute with the clerk of court[4]. While it is arguable that such admissions and agreements may also be made orally, it is probably the law that a minute should be lodged[5]. It is obviously desirable that as much as possible should be agreed in advance, in order to avoid the attendance of witnesses whose evidence is uncontroversial. For this reason it is very important that the defence solicitor and the fiscal discuss the case at an early stage.

Advance evidence by defence witnesses

Although the normal rule is that the prosecutor calls all his witnesses before any defence evidence is led, there is a rarely used provision entitling the accused to apply to the court for permission to examine a witness prior to the prosecution evidence being concluded[6]. This facility would be useful, for example, if a defence witness were about to go abroad for a period. The provision appears to be wide enough to enable the defence witness either to be heard before any Crown evidence has been led, or to be interposed in the course of the Crown case. The accused is still permitted to lead further evidence in normal course at the conclusion of the Crown case[6].

No case to answer

There is provision for the making of a submission of no case to answer in a summary trial[7], which is (*mutatis mutandis*) in identical terms with those of the

1 1975 Act, s 353(1).
2 1975 Act, s 353(2).
3 1975 Act, s 354(1).
4 1975 Act, s 354(2).
5 *Jessop v Kerr* 1989 SCCR 17 (Sh Ct).
6 1975 Act, s 337(h).
7 1975 Act, s 345A.

provision on the same subject under solemn procedure[1]. The comments on no case to answer in chapter 3[2] should be read as applying to summary procedure also.

Abandonment

The most common way for a prosecutor to abandon a complaint is to refrain from having it called in court. This has the same effect as if the complaint were deserted *pro loco et tempore*[3], ie the instance in the case falls, although the prosecutor may thereafter raise a fresh complaint, assuming that it is not time-barred. As a matter of courtesy, a prosecutor who intends not to have a case called in court should inform the accused of his intention and of whether he will be bringing a fresh complaint or whether he is content that the matter should proceed no further.

If the prosecutor decides to abandon a case after the trial has begun, he should do so by intimating to the court that he is not proceeding further and is prepared to accept a plea of not guilty. The court then returns a verdict to that effect.

Adjournment of trial

A trial diet may be adjourned on the motion of either party or by the court of its own volition[4]. An adjournment may be applied for either before the trial has actually started or after some evidence has been led.

Whether or not to adjourn a trial is a matter for the discretion of the court, but a motion by the Crown should be refused only 'in the most serious circumstances and for the most compelling reasons'[5]. This is because the consequence of such a refusal is that the instance falls, and the Crown is barred from bringing a fresh prosecution. 'But at the same time this (the power to refuse a Crown motion for an adjournment) is a power which, in view of the possible consequences of its exercise to parties and to the public interest, must be exercised only after the most careful consideration, on weighty grounds and with due and accurate regard to the interests which will be affected or prejudiced by that exercise'[6]. Even fault on the part of the Crown may not be a sufficient reason for refusing an adjournment[7].

Only in exceptional circumstances should a prosecutor anticipate an adjournment of a trial by countermanding his witnesses[8]. Wherever possible a case should be accelerated under the provisions of s 314(3) of the 1975 Act, in order that the motion to adjourn may be made in sufficient time to enable witnesses to be cited or not as the case may be.

The same principles of balancing the interests of the parties and the interests of the public apply where the motion to adjourn is made by the

1 1975 Act, s 140A.
2 See above at p 147.
3 See below at p 183.
4 1975 Act, s 337(f).
5 *Tudhope v Lawrie* 1979 JC 44 at 48, 1979 SLT (Notes) 13 at 13, per Lord Cameron.
6 *Tudhope v Lawrie* 1979 JC 44 at 49, 1979 SLT (Notes) 13 at 14.
7 *Tudhope v Mitchell* 1986 SCCR 45 (failure by Crown to cite witnesses).
8 *Skeen v Evans* 1979 SLT (Notes) 55.

defence. The conduct of the accused himself is a relevant factor. Thus, it is commonplace for a court to refuse to adjourn where the accused has done nothing about preparing for his defence, and then seeks an adjournment to enable him to do something about it. However, if he has instructed a solicitor and the latter is not immediately available when the trial diet calls, the court should at least adjourn until later in the day to give the solicitor an opportunity to be present[1].

If a trial has commenced and cannot be completed in one day, it must be adjourned to a later date. It is, unfortunately, not uncommon in the busier courts for such an adjournment to be over a period of weeks.

On occasions, after the call-over of trials, it will be apparent that all the trials set down for that day cannot possibly proceed. It is then appropriate to adjourn one or more trials to a later date. Such trials should be given priority on that date.

Desertion of the diet

As under solemn procedure[2], the court may desert a diet either *pro loco et tempore* or *simpliciter*.

The court may desert the diet *pro loco et tempore* of its own volition at any time, but the prosecutor may move for such a desertion only prior to the first witness being sworn[3]. Although a Crown motion to desert *pro loco et tempore* is normally granted without question, the decision is one for the discretion of the court, and such a motion may be refused if the court considers it inappropriate[4]. The effect of desertion *pro loco et tempore* is that the Crown may bring a fresh prosecution, provided that the case is not time-barred.

The power to desert the diet *simpliciter* of its own volition is rarely used by the court. It is appropriate only where it is desired to bring the case to an end for all time. If the diet is deserted *simpliciter*, the Crown may not bring a fresh prosecution.

If, at a trial diet, the Crown has moved the court to adjourn the trial or to desert the diet *pro loco et tempore*, and the court has refused to grant either motion, the court must desert the diet *simpliciter*[5], and the statute emphasises that the Crown may proceed no further[6]. This does not mean that, where the court has refused an adjournment, the Crown is not still entitled to move for desertion *pro loco et tempore*[7]. Whether such a motion would be granted is, however, a different question[7].

Death or illness of judge

Most surprisingly, there is no statutory provision in Part II of the 1975 Act (or in any other statute) for the eventuality of the judge in a summary trial

---

1 *Fraser v MacKinnon* 1981 SCCR 91; cf *Turnbull v Allan* 1989 SCCR 215, where an adjournment to a later date was refused, the case having been adjourned on three previous occasions.
2 See above at p 149.
3 1975 Act, s 338A(1).
4 *Jessop v D* 1986 SCCR 716 (Sh Ct), 1987 SLT (Sh Ct) 115.
5 1975 Act, s 338A(2).
6 1975 Act, s 338A(3).
7 *Tudhope v Gough* 1982 SCCR 157 (Sh Ct).

becoming ill or dying during the course of the trial. In such a situation the case should be called before another judge who should adjourn the proceedings to a date when the trial can begin again[1].

Amendment of complaint

There are provisions in Part II of the 1975 Act relating to amendment of the complaint, the notice of penalties and the notice of previous convictions[2], similar to those in Part I of the 1975 Act relating to amendment of an indictment[3]. The summary provisions have been interpreted as allowing a great deal of latitude to the Crown, although, even under summary procedure, an amendment cannot cure a fundamental nullity. Thus a new locus may be added to a complaint provided that a locus is already stated[4], but, if there is no locus at all, that is fatal[5]. Although a charge is irrelevant, it may still be cured by amendment[6]. This extends even to the omission of the date of the alleged offence[7] and to a charge brought under a repealed statute[8]. However, as under solemn procedure, amendment is not permitted if it changes the character of the offence charged[9].

Failure of accused to appear for trial

If an accused fails to appear for trial, the normal course is for the court to grant a warrant for his arrest on the motion of the prosecutor[10]. Alternatively, the court may fix a fresh trial diet, ordaining the accused to attend and appointing intimation of the diet to be made to him, which may be done by an officer of law, or by letter sent by registered or recorded delivery post[11].

Exceptionally, the trial may proceed in the absence of the accused. This is possible only when the accused is charged with a statutory offence which does not carry a sentence of imprisonment, or if the statute concerned authorises procedure in the absence of the accused[12]. The court, before proceeding to trial in absence, must be satisfied that the accused has been duly cited or has received intimation of the diet of trial[12]. Evidence against the accused must be led, unless the statute under which he is charged authorises conviction in default of appearance[12]. The court may allow the absent accused to be represented by an authorised solicitor, 'if it shall judge it expedient'[12], although it is difficult to envisage circumstances where it could be considered inexpedient for the accused to be represented. The provision for trial in absence is rarely used. Obvious difficulties would arise if the identity of the accused were in issue.

---

1 *Platt v Lockhart* 1988 SCCR 308, 1988 SLT 845.
2 1975 Act, s 335.
3 1975 Act, s 123. See above at pp 149, 150.
4 *Craig v Keane* 1981 SCCR 166, 1982 SLT 198.
5 *Stevenson v McLevy* (1879) 4 Couper 196, 6R(J) 33.
6 *Mackenzie v Brougham* 1982 SCCR 434, 1985 SLT 276.
7 *Duffy v Ingram* 1987 SCCR 286, 1988 SLT 226.
8 *Cook v Jessop* 1990 SCCR 211.
9 1975 Act, s 335(2). See eg *McArthur v MacNeill* 1986 SCCR 552, 1987 SLT 299.
10 1975 Act, s 338(1)(c).
11 1975 Act, s 338(1)(a).
12 1975 Act, s 338(1)(b).

Speeches

At the end of the evidence it is normal for both the prosecutor and the defence to address the court. Speeches in summary trials are usually much briefer than those in jury trials. They may deal with both the facts and the law, but care should be taken to distinguish between the two, especially when addressing a lay court.

Verdict

The court normally returns its verdict immediately after hearing the speeches. A lay court may adjourn to discuss the case if it consists of more than one justice. Again in the case of a lay court the justice or justices may wish to seek advice on the law from the clerk and adjourn for that purpose. Even a sheriff or stipendiary magistrate may wish to take time to consider the evidence or the law and may adjourn in order to do so, either until later in the same day or until a later date.

As in a case under solemn procedure, the court may find the accused guilty or not guilty or the charge not proven. The same alternative verdicts (eg guilty of theft on a complaint charging robbery) are open to a summary court as to a court of solemn jurisdiction[1].

If a summary court consists of more than one justice and the members of the court are evenly divided as to the guilt of the accused, the accused must be found not guilty[2].

Sentence

If the verdict is one of guilty, the court proceeds to sentence or adjourn for reports in the same way as if the accused had originally pleaded guilty[3], having considered any notice of penalties, notice of previous convictions and a plea in mitigation. As the court will have heard the evidence in the case, the prosecutor does not narrate the facts.

---

1 1975 Act, s 312(m), (o) and (t) are the summary equivalents of 1975 Act, ss 60(1), 60(2), 60(3), 63(1) and 64 for solemn cases. See above at pp 155, 156.
2 1975 Act, s 355.
3 See above at pp 167, 168.

Chapter 7

Sentencing

INTRODUCTION

Sentencing is one of the most difficult tasks which a judge has to carry out. Many judges would say that it was *the* most difficult. The task is difficult for a number of reasons. Firstly, judges receive very little in the way of training with regard to sentencing, although this has improved to some extent in recent years. Secondly, there is a very wide range of disposals available to a court. Thirdly, there is very often a delicate question involved of balancing the interests of the public (or of the victim) on the one hand against the interests of the accused on the other[1].

Another major factor which adds to the difficulty of the sentencer is that the High Court of Justiciary in its appellate capacity has been very reluctant to lay down general principles of sentencing, preferring to adopt an ad hoc approach to individual cases. In this regard its attitude is in marked contrast to that of the Criminal Division of the Court of Appeal in England. It is ironic that in one of the rare cases in which the High Court appears to have laid down a general principle it is the very opposite of that accepted in England[2]. To add to the difficulty of obtaining guidance on sentencing from the High Court, it is not unknown for that court to produce decisions which, on the face of it are quite irreconcilable with each other. This situation is well illustrated by recent cases on comparative justice. In 1985 the High Court held that, although the sentence on an appellant's co-accused had almost certainly been far too low, the court had to assume that it was appropriate, and that, by comparison, the appellant's sentence was far too high and should be reduced[3]. In 1988 the High Court (admittedly differently constituted) in two cases[4] in effect said that a sentence passed on a co-accused, whether by the same judge or a different judge, was not a relevant factor in assessing the appropriateness of the sentence on an appellant.

The purpose of this chapter is to examine the various disposals which are open to a court and to comment briefly on them[5]. However, before embark-

1 It is not proper for the sentencing court to seek the views of the victim of a crime on the sentence to be imposed, although the attitude of the victim may be a relevant factor in some cases: *HMA v McKenzie* 1989 SCCR 587, 1990 SLT 28.
2 *Strawhorn v McLeod* 1987 SCCR 413, in which the High Court stated that it was objectionable to give a more lenient sentence when an accused pleaded guilty at an early stage. The concept of a 'discount' for a plea of guilty is well established in England.
3 *Donnelly v McKinnon* 1985 SCCR 391.
4 *Lam v HMA* 1988 SCCR 347 and *Forrest v HMA* 1988 SCCR 481.
5 For a detailed examination of the subject of sentencing in Scotland see CGB Nicholson *The Law and Practice of Sentencing in Scotland* (1981, with Supp 1985).

ing on this exercise, it would be as well to recall the maximum powers of the various courts. These powers are of course, in the case of a statutory offence, always subject to any limitation imposed by the statute creating the offence.

The High Court's powers of sentencing are unlimited. It may impose imprisonment for any term up to and including life, and it may impose a fine of any amount.

The sheriff court, as a court of solemn jurisdiction, may impose imprisonment for a maximum period of three years[1], although a sheriff may remit an accused to the High Court for sentence if he considers that his powers of punishment are inadequate[2]. The sheriff in a solemn case may also impose an unlimited fine.

Sitting summarily a sheriff may normally impose a maximum period of three months' imprisonment[3]. However, this maximum period may be extended to six months, ie where the accused is convicted of '(a) a second or subsequent offence inferring dishonest appropriation of property, or attempt thereat, or (b) a second or subsequent offence inferring personal violence'[4]. The sheriff has power to impose a fine or to order the accused to find caution, in both cases for a sum not exceeding the 'prescribed sum'[5], which is £2,000 at the time of writing.

A district court consisting of a stipendiary magistrate has the same powers as those of a sheriff sitting summarily[6].

A district court consisting of one or more lay justices may imprison for a period not exceeding 60 days[7]. It may impose a fine or order the accused to find caution in a sum not exceeding level 4 on the standard scale[8], which is £1,000 at the time of writing.

IMPRISONMENT

General

Imprisonment is the only form of custodial sentence which may now be imposed on a person over 21 years of age[9]. No person under 21 can be sent to prison[10], but that does not of course mean that such a person cannot receive a custodial sentence[11]. A court of summary jurisdiction may not sentence a person to a period of imprisonment for less than five days[12], although there is a rarely used provision for offenders being detained for up to four days in authorised police cells[13].

1 1975 Act, ss 2(2), 221(1).
2 1975 Act, s 104.
3 1975 Act, s 289.
4 1975 Act, s 290.
5 1975 Act, s 289. The prescribed sum is discussed below at p 193.
6 District Courts (Scotland) Act 1975, s 3(2).
7 1975 Act, s 284.
8 1975 Act, s 284. The standard scale is discussed below at p 193.
9 1975 Act, s 221 provides that penal servitude and imprisonment with hard labour are no longer competent. Preventive detention and corrective training were abolished by the 1980 Act, Sch 8.
10 1975 Act, ss 207(1) and 415(1).
11 For custodial sentences for those under 21 see below at pp 191–193.
12 1975 Act, s 425(1).
13 1975 Act, s 425(2).

Restrictions on imprisonment

If a convicted person has not previously been sentenced to imprisonment or detention[1] by a court in any part of the United Kingdom, he may not have a sentence of imprisonment imposed on him unless the court considers that no other method of dealing with him is appropriate. For the purpose of determining whether any other method is appropriate, the court must obtain such information as it can about the offender's circumstances, and also must take into account any information which is before it concerning the offender's character and physical and mental condition[2]. For practical purposes the court obtains the necessary information by means of a social enquiry report (usually abbreviated to 'SER') prepared by a member of the local authority social work department, although the Act does provide that the information may be obtained 'otherwise'[2]. A court of summary jurisdiction must state its reason for holding that no sentence other than imprisonment is appropriate and that reason must be minuted in the record of proceedings[3].

If an offender such as is mentioned in the previous paragraph is not legally represented, there is a further restriction on a sentence of imprisonment being imposed on him. Such a sentence cannot be imposed unless he has either (a) applied for legal aid and had his application refused on financial grounds, or (b) having been informed of his right to apply for legal aid and having had the opportunity to apply, he has failed to do so[4]. It is not enough that the accused be offered an opportunity to seek legal advice, he must be informed of his right to apply for legal aid[5].

Length of sentence

The length of a sentence of imprisonment will depend on a number of factors, including the gravity of the crime, the circumstances of the accused and his previous criminal record. It is an irrelevant consideration that the case has been indicted in the High Court rather than the sheriff court[6]. A very short sentence of imprisonment has recently on occasions not found favour with the High Court[7].

Consecutive or concurrent

If an accused appears on a number of charges, each possibly carrying a sentence of imprisonment, a question may arise as to whether the sentences

---

1 Defined in 1980 Act, s 41(2). It excludes a suspended sentence of imprisonment (competent in England and Wales and in Northern Ireland but not in Scotland) which has not yet taken effect (s 41(2)(a)).
2 1980 Act, s 42(1).
3 1980 Act, s 42(2).
4 1980 Act, s 41(1).
5 *Milligan v Jessop* 1988 SCCR 137.
6 *Khaliq v HMA* 1984 SCCR 212.
7 *McKenzie v Lockhart* 1986 SCCR 663 (fourteen days): *Kinney v Tudhope* 1985 SCCR 393 (21 days – the offender was under 21, so the sentence was detention rather than imprisonment, but the principle (in so far as there is one) is the same. Cf *Stirling v Stewart* 1988 SCCR 619 (30 days upheld as appropriate – also a case of an offender under 21).

should run consecutively or concurrently. A similar question may arise if the accused is already serving a sentence of imprisonment – should any new sentence be consecutive to or concurrent with that already being served?

If an accused appears on several charges in the same indictment or complaint, he should normally be sentenced separately on each charge[1]. If the crimes or offences are all part of one incident or course of conduct, the sentences should run concurrently with each other, and this applies equally even if the charges are contained in separate indictments or complaints[2].

If charges relating to separate incidents appear on separate complaints all calling on the same date, the court may impose sentences in respect of each complaint and make them consecutive, notwithstanding that the court's normal maximum powers on summary complaint are thereby exceeded[3].

A sentence for a contravention of s 3 of the Bail (Scotland) Act 1980 in respect of committing an offence while on bail may be made to run consecutive to the sentence for the offence which constitutes the breach of bail, notwithstanding that the normal powers of the court are thereby exceeded[4].

If an accused has been sentenced to life imprisonment, any other sentence imposed at the same time or subsequently should be concurrent and not consecutive[5].

If an accused is already serving a sentence of imprisonment at the time of being sentenced, it is a matter for the judge's discretion whether the new sentence should be concurrent or consecutive[6]. The view is frequently expressed that, if a concurrent sentence is imposed, it is effectively no sentence at all. It should be noted that, at least in summary cases, a consecutive sentence is competent only when the earlier sentence precedes *conviction* on the later complaint and not merely sentence thereon[7]. A consecutive sentence imposed on someone already in prison should be expressed as 'consecutive to the total period of imprisonment to which the prisoner is already subject' or 'to take effect on the expiry of all sentences previously imposed'[8].

Backdating of sentence

A sentence of imprisonment normally runs from the date of its imposition, but it may be backdated. In both solemn and summary cases the court is directed to 'have regard to any period of time spent in custody . . . on remand awaiting trial or sentence' when determining the period of imprisonment to impose[9]. This does not mean that a sentence of imprisonment must always be

---

1 *Caringi v HMA* 1989 SCCR 223, 1989 SLT 714 (common law charges). The principle had been established for statutory charges much earlier (*Seaton v Allan* 1973 JC 24, 1974 SLT 234).
2 *Williamson v Farrell* 1975 SLT (Notes) 92; *Moore v HMA* 1989 SCCR 298, 1989 SLT 883.
3 *Thomson v Smith* and *Morgan v Smith* 1982 JC 40, 1982 SCCR 57, 1982 SLT 546; *O'Lone v Tudhope* 1987 SCCR 211.
4 Bail (Scotland) Act 1980, s 3(5).
5 *McRae v HMA* 1987 SCCR 36; *McPhee v HMA* 1990 SCCR 313.
6 1975 Act, s 430(4) makes specific provision for a consecutive sentence in summary cases. There is no equivalent provision in Part I of the Act, but the competence of a consecutive sentence under solemn procedure has never been questioned. In any event, even in a summary case the power to impose a consecutive sentence exists at common law: *Young v McGlennan* 1990 SCCR 373.
7 *Noble v Guild* 1987 SCCR 518.
8 *Moore v MacPhail* 1986 SCCR 169.
9 1975 Act, s 218 (solemn) and s 431 (summary).

backdated to the date of remand. All that is necessary is that the judge is informed of the period spent in custody and applies his mind to the question of how to take account of it. Whether to backdate or not is a question for the judge's discretion[1]. However, this is not to say that the High Court never interferes with a decision whether or not to backdate[2]. If an accused is convicted only of a charge to which he has all along been prepared to plead guilty, his sentence should be backdated[3]. If an accused is remanded in custody for a report to be obtained and the maximum sentence of imprisonment is then imposed, it should be backdated to the date of remand[4].

Imprisonment with another sentence

It is as a general rule very undesirable to impose a sentence of imprisonment at the same time as another non-custodial sentence. Thus imprisonment should not be imposed along with a probation order[5]. Nor is it appropriate to sentence an accused to imprisonment on one charge while at the same time deferring sentence on another charge[6]. However, in some cases the court may quite properly impose imprisonment on some charges and a fine on others for which imprisonment would be an incompetent disposal. In such circumstances it is usual for the accused to ask that no time be allowed for payment of the fine. This means that the alternative of imprisonment in default of payment may run concurrently with the sentence imposed on the other charges.

Release from prison

Every prisoner serving a determinate sentence, who has been of good behaviour in prison, receives an automatic remission of one third of his sentence[7].

A prisoner may be released on licence before that if he is granted parole by the Secretary of State on the recommendation of the Parole Board[8]. The period of the licence is until the prisoner would normally have been released with full remission. A prisoner on licence may be recalled to prison[9]. A prisoner on licence who is convicted in the High Court or sheriff court of an offence punishable by imprisonment may have his licence revoked by the court[10].

Sentence for murder

The sentence for murder in respect of a person over 21 is imprisonment for life[11]. When imposing such a sentence the judge is entitled to make a recom-

---

1 *Muir v HMA* 1985 SCCR 402.
2 Eg in *Callaghan v HMA* 1986 SCCR 563.
3 *Campbell v HMA* 1986 SCCR 403.
4 *Morison v Scott* 1987 SCCR 376 (a case of an offender under 21, but the principle is the same).
5 *Downie v Irvine* 1964 JC 52, 1964 SLT 205.
6 *Lennon v Copeland* 1972 SLT (Notes) 68.
7 Prisons (Scotland) Rules 1952, SI 1952/565 (amended by SI 1981/1222), r 37.
8 Prisons (Scotland) Act 1989, s 22(1).
9 Ibid, s 28(1), (2).
10 Ibid, s 28(6).
11 1975 Act, s 205(1).

mendation as to the minimum period which should elapse before the offender may be released on licence[1]. He must state his reasons for making such a recommendation[2]. Although a life sentence for murder, being a sentence fixed by law, is not normally appealable[3], an appeal is competent against any such recommendation[4].

A person sentenced to life imprisonment for murder may be released on licence at any time by the Secretary of State on the recommendation of the Parole Board[5], but his licence remains in force for the rest of his life and may be revoked in the same way as that of an ordinary parolee[6].

DETENTION OF YOUNG OFFENDERS

General

In the case of an offender aged not less than sixteen but under 21 the only custodial sentence which a court may impose is detention in a young offenders institution[7]. Such detention is the equivalent of imprisonment for an adult[8]. Borstal institutions[9] and detention centres[10] no longer exist. Any reference in a statute to borstal training is to be understood as a reference to detention in a young offenders institution[11].

Restriction on detention

As in the case of imprisonment, no person without legal representation may be sentenced to detention without either having been offered the opportunity to apply for legal aid or having been refused it on financial grounds[12].

There is a further restriction on detention. The court may not impose a sentence of detention unless it is of the opinion that no other method of dealing with the offender is appropriate[13]. The court must obtain such information as it can to enable it to form an opinion of this matter, and this may be obtained by means of a social inquiry report 'or otherwise'[14]. In practice a social enquiry report is invariably obtained. The court must also take into account any information before it concerning the accused's character and physical and mental condition[14]. The court must state the reason

1 1975 Act, s 205A(1).
2 1975 Act, s 205A(2).
3 1975 Act, s 228(1).
4 1975 Act, s 205A(3).
5 Prisons (Scotland) Act 1989, s 26(1).
6 See above at p 190.
7 1975 Act, s 207(2), (5), s 415(2), (5).
8 The same provisions about remission and release on licence apply (1975 Act, ss 207(11), 415(11)).
9 1980 Act, s 45(3).
10 Criminal Justice Act 1988, s 124.
11 1980 Act, s 45(4).
12 1980 Act, s 41(1).
13 1975 Act, ss 207(3), 415(3).
14 1975 Act, ss 207(4), 415(4).

why no other disposal is appropriate, and, except in the case of the High Court, the reason must be minuted in the record of proceedings[1].

Length of sentence, concurrent or consecutive, backdating of sentence, detention with another sentence

The comments made above[2] on all these topics with respect to imprisonment of adult offenders apply equally to the detention of young offenders.

Release from young offenders institution

A young offender is entitled to the same one-third remission of sentence as is an adult prisoner[3].

A young offender is entitled to be paroled and released on licence in the same way as an adult prisoner[4].

An offender released on licence is subject to recall in the same way as an adult parolee[4], and his licence may be revoked by a court[4].

A young offender who has been sentenced to be detained for six months or longer may be placed under supervision on his release. The statutory provisions about supervision[5] are complex and will not be discussed further here. An offender released under supervision who is, while still under supervision, convicted of an offence punishable by imprisonment may by order of the court be recalled to young offenders institution[6].

Sentence for murder

A person under eighteen who is convicted of murder is sentenced to be detained without limit of time and will be detained in such place and under such conditions as the Secretary of State may direct[7].

A person who is eighteen or over but under 21 who is convicted of murder is sentenced to be detained in a young offenders institution and is liable to be detained for life[8].

As in the case of an adult offender, the judge may recommend a minimum period during which a young offender should be detained before being released on licence[9].

---

1 1975 Act, ss 207(3), 415(3).
2 See above at pp 188–190.
3 Young Offenders (Scotland) Rules 1965, SI 1965/195, r 35.
4 1975 Act, ss 207(11), 415(11) applying the Prisons (Scotland) Act 1989, ss 18, 22, 24, 26, 28 and 29 to young offenders.
5 Prisons (Scotland) Act 1989, s 32.
6 1975 Act, ss 212, 421.
7 1975 Act, s 205(2).
8 1975 Act, s 205(3).
9 1975 Act, s 205A. See above at pp 190, 191.

FINES

General

A fine is the most common sentence in courts of summary jurisdiction and is also relatively common in the sheriff court sitting as a court of solemn jurisdiction. The provisions in Part II (the summary part) of the 1975 Act relating to fines have very largely been applied to Part I (the solemn part) also[1], so the comments in this section will, unless otherwise indicated, apply to both forms of procedure.

Like the length of a custodial sentence, the amount of a fine is governed by a number of factors, including the gravity of the offence, It is specifically provided that the court must take into consideration 'the means of the offender so far as known to the court'[2].

The standard scale and the prescribed sum

In order to avoid the necessity of regularly changing the actual amounts of the maximum fines for statutory offences as money loses its value, there was introduced the standard scale[3]. This lays down five levels of fine[4]. These are at present:

Level 1   £50
Level 2   £100
Level 3   £400
Level 4   £1,000
Level 5   £2,000

These sums may be altered by the Secretary of State by order if it appears to him that there has been a change in the value of money[5].

The same thinking is behind the fixing of 'the prescribed sum' as the maximum fine which may normally be imposed by a sheriff sitting summarily[6]. This is presently £2,000[7], and the sum may be altered by the Secretary of State by order if it appears to him that there has been a change in the value of money[8].

Fines for statutory offences

In the case of a statutory offence triable only on indictment, or triable either on indictment or summarily which is actually tried on indictment, the court has an unlimited power to fine, notwithstanding that the statute concerned may provide a maximum fine[9]. If the statute makes no provision for a fine,

1 1975 Act, s 194.
2 1975 Act, s 395(1).
3 1975 Act, s 289G(1).
4 1975 Act, s 289G(2).
5 1975 Act, s 289D(1), (1A).
6 1975 Act, s 289(a).
7 1975 Act, s 289B(6).
8 1975 Act, s 289D(1), (1A).
9 1975 Act, s 193A. This excludes offences normally triable only summarily but which may be tried on indictment by virtue of the 1975 Act, s 457A(4).

but provides only for imprisonment, the court nonetheless has power to impose a fine[1].

In the case of a statutory offence, triable either on indictment or summarily, which is actually tried summarily, the provisions for calculating the maximum permissible fine in respect of contraventions of statutes passed prior to the introduction of the standard scale are complex[2], and the details are beyond the scope of this book. The practical effect is that all such fines are now stated in terms of the standard scale. Any notice of penalties served in connection with such an offence should be scrutinised closely, and reference should be made to the relevant legislation.

If the statutory offence is triable only summarily, the maximum fine imposed is normally stated as a level on the standard scale. For contraventions of statutes passed prior to the introduction of the standard scale there are again complex statutory provisions for fixing the appropriate level on the standard scale[3], the details of which are beyond the scope of this book. The advice given in the previous paragraph to scrutinise the notice of penalties carefully applies equally here.

Remission of fines

All courts have power to remit a fine in whole or in part[4]. If a fine has been transferred for enforcement to a court other than that which imposed it[5], it is the court to which it has been transferred which has the power of remission[6]. Otherwise it is the court which imposed the fine[7], except if the fine was imposed by the High Court, in which case it is the court by which payment of the fine was first enforceable[8]. If the person fined is serving a custodial sentence for non-payment of the fine[9], the whole of the custodial alternative or a proportion thereof, as the case may be, is remitted if the fine or any part thereof is remitted[10]. An offender need not attend court to have his fine remitted[11]. Remission is normally the result of an application by an offender, but the court may remit a fine of its own volition.

Time for payment of fines

In the case of most fines the accused asks either for time to pay[12] or to be allowed to pay by instalments[13]. An offender may, of course, pay the whole fine at the time when it is imposed, if he wishes to do so. Payment by cheque

1   1975 Act, s 193(2).
2   1975 Act s 289B. See *Renton and Brown* para 12–22b, and *Nicholson* (Supp) para 2–75.
3   1975 Act, ss 289C, 289E, 289F, 289G, 289GA, 289GB, 289GC and 289H. See *Renton and Brown* paras 17–22c, 17–22d, and *Nicholson (Supp)* paras 2–75, 2–75A.
4   1975 Act, 395A.
5   See below at p 197.
6   1975 Act, s 395A(1)(a).
7   1975 Act, s 395A(1)(b).
8   1975 Act, s 395A(1)(b). For enforcement of fines imposed by the High Court see below at p 197.
9   See below at p 197, for custody for non-payment of a fine.
10   1975 Act. s 395A(2).
11   1975 Act, s 395A(3).
12   1975 Act, s 396(1).
13   1975 Act, s 399(1).

is accepted, but the court then normally allows seven days for payment in order that the cheque may be cleared. An offender must be allowed at least seven days to pay either the whole fine or the first instalment thereof[1], unless (a) he appears to the court to possess sufficient means to enable him to pay forthwith; or (b) he states to the court that he does not wish time to pay; or (c) he fails to satisfy the court that he has a fixed abode; or (d) the court is satisfied for any other special reason that no time should be allowed[2]. If no time to pay is allowed, the court may immediately exercise its power to imprison for non-payment[3], but the reason for not allowing time to pay must be stated and recorded in the extract of the finding and sentence[4]. An offender who is not legally represented and who has not previously been sentenced to imprisonment or detention must not have an immediate alternative of imprisonment imposed with no time to pay without having been given an opportunity of applying for legal aid[5]. The alternative of imprisonment cannot be made consecutive to a sentence being served at the time when the fine is imposed[6], but may be made consecutive to a sentence of imprisonment imposed on the same day[7].

Where an offender is allowed time to pay or to make payment by instalments, it is possible at the same time to impose the alternative of imprisonment in default of payment (to act no doubt as an incentive to payment), but only in limited circumstances[8]. These are that the gravity of the offence, the character of the offender or 'other special reason' render it expedient that he should be imprisoned without further inquiry in default of payment[9]. It is probably incompetent to impose an immediate alternative of imprisonment in respect of an offence which is not itself punishable by a sentence of imprisonment[10].

An offender may apply to the court for further time to pay[11]. The application may be made orally or in writing[12]. The application should be made to the court which imposed the fine or to any court to which the fine has been transferred for enforcement purposes[13]. The court must allow further time unless it is satisfied that the offender's failure to pay has been wilful or that the

---

1 1975 Act, s 396(1). There is no limit on the time which may be allowed for payment or over which instalments may be payable: *Johnston v Lockhart* 1987 SCCR 337.
2 1975 Act, s 396(2). A court of summary jurisdiction has power to have an offender searched and any money found on him applied to payment of the fine imposed (1975 Act, s 395(2)).
3 See below at p 197.
4 1975 Act, s 396(2), (3).
5 1980 Act, s 41(1). The court has power to grant legal aid in such circumstances: Legal Aid (Scotland) Act 1986, s 23(1)(b).
6 *Cairn v Carmichael* 1990 SCCR 369.
7 *Young v McGlennan* 1990 SCCR 373.
8 1975 Act, s 396(4).
9 1975 Act, s 396(4). The reason must be stated. 'Nature of the offence' is not a relevant reason for imposing the alternative under this section: *Buchanan v Hamilton* 1988 SCCR 378.
10 *Dunlop v Allan* 1984 SCCR 329. Strictly speaking all that was decided in this case was that a charge of careless driving (now a contravention of the Road Traffic Act 1988, s 3) was not an offence of 'gravity' within the meaning of the 1975 Act, s 396(4). There was, however, a strong suggestion by the court that no offence could be an offence of gravity unless it carries a sentence of imprisonment.
11 1975 Act, s 396(7).
12 1975 Act, s 397(3).
13 1975 Act, s 397(1).

offender has no reasonable prospect of being able to pay if further time is allowed[1]. A court has similar powers to vary instalments of a fine or to allow further time for payment of any instalment[2]. The offender need not attend court to have the instalments varied[3].

An offender who has been allowed time to pay a fine or to pay by instalments may be placed under the supervision of a social worker, either at the time of imposition of the fine or at a later time, 'for the purpose of assisting and advising the offender in regard to payment of the fine'[4]. This is commonly known as a fine supervision order (FSO). The supervision lasts until the fine is paid unless the fine is transferred or the order is discharged[5]. This form of supervision is used especially in the case of offenders under 21. The amount of supervision provided varies considerably according to where the offender lives and the resources available to the local social work department.

If an offender has been fined and no alternative has been imposed at the same time as the fine, imprisonment in default cannot be imposed unless the offender attends court on a subsequent occasion for the court to enquire 'into the reason why the fine has not been paid'[6]. Such enquiry is very often the subject of a separate sitting of the court known as a 'means enquiry court'. The offender may be cited to attend for enquiry, or he may be arrested and brought before the court[7]. In practice an arrest warrant is issued only if the offender's whereabouts are unknown. If an offender, having been cited, fails to attend for enquiry into his means, a warrant to apprehend him may be issued[8] (and almost invariably is).

If an offender is under a fine supervision order, a report from his supervising social worker on the offender's conduct and means should be available to the court when he attends for means enquiry[9]. The alternative of imprisonment should not be imposed unless the court has taken 'such steps as may be reasonably practicable' to obtain such a report (which may be oral)[9].

In the case of an offender under 21 the court must not impose the alternative for non-payment of a fine (which is not imprisonment but detention in a young offenders institution)[10] unless either the offender has been placed on a fine supervision order or the court is satisfied that it is impracticable to place him under such supervision[11]. In practice this means that it is virtually impossible to impose the alternative of detention on a young offender without having first made a fine supervision order.

At a means enquiry court (or any other court where enquiry is being made into the reason for non-payment of a fine) the offender is usually asked why he has not paid his fine, and what his income and expenditure are. The court will of course also have regard to the terms of any report which may be before it. Depending on the information which is given to the court from these

---

1 1975 Act, s 397(2).
2 1975 Act, s 399(2).
3 1975 Act, s 399(3).
4 1975 Act, s 400(1).
5 1975 Act, s 400(2), (3).
6 1975 Act, s 398(1) 'but this subsection shall not apply when the offender is in prison'.
7 1975 Act, s 398(2).
8 1975 Act, s 398(3). AA(C) 1988, r 124 provides the forms etc.
9 1975 Act, s 400(6).
10 1975 Act, s 401(2).
11 1975 Act, s 400(4).

sources, the offender may be allowed further time to pay, or the alternative may be imposed with immediate effect. It is not competent, as the law stands at the time of writing, to allow further time to pay and to impose the alternative of imprisonment in the event of future default in payment[1].

Custody for non-payment

The maximum alternative period of custody which may be imposed by a court for default in payment of a fine, whether at the time of imposition of the fine or at a later stage, varies according to the amount of the fine, and ranges from seven days for a fine of less than £50 to ten years for a fine of over £1,000,000[2]. If part of the fine has been paid, only a proportion of the alternative is served[3].

In the event of default by an offender on whom the alternative has been imposed the court grants a warrant for his arrest and imprisonment or detention. The warrant must specify the period during which he is to be detained[4]. If such a warrant has been issued, the offender may pay the full balance of the fine to the arresting officer, in which case the warrant will not be enforced[5]. The officer remits the fine to the clerk of the court which issued the warrant[5].

Transfer of fine orders

A fine may be transferred for the purposes of enforcement to a court other than that which imposed it, if the offender lives within the jurisdiction of the other court[6]. That court may be elsewhere in Scotland, or in England, Wales or Northern Ireland[6]. The order transferring the fine is known as a transfer of fine order[7]. The effect of the order is to transfer all functions of enforcement to the receiving court[8]. That court is responsible for remitting the fine, once paid, to the transferring court[9].

Fines imposed by the High Court

A fine imposed by the High Court is remitted for enforcement to the sheriff court of the district where the offender resides[10], or, if the offender resides outwith Scotland, the sheriff court before which he was brought for examination in relation to the offence for which the fine was imposed[11]. In the latter case the fine may then be transferred to another court within the United Kingdom as described in the preceding paragraph.

1 *Craig v Smith* 1990 SCCR 328. The effect of this decision (which is contrary to what was generally assumed to be the law) may be negatived by a provision in the Law Reform (Miscellaneous Provisions) (Scotland) Bill 1990, which is before Parliament at the time of writing.
2 1975 Act, s 407, which contains a full table of alternatives in sub-s 1A. This table may be amended by order of the Secretary of State (1975 Act, s 289D(1A)).
3 1975 Act, s 407(1C), (1D), and s 409.
4 1975 Act, s 408.
5 1975 Act, s 401(3).
6 1975 Act, s 403(1).
7 1975 Act, s 403(2). Forms are specified in AA(C) 1988, Forms 62, 63.
8 1975 Act, s 403(3), (4).
9 1975 Act, s 404(4).
10 1975 Act, s 196(2)(a).
11 1975 Act, s 196(2)(b).

Recovery of fines by civil diligence

A court always has the power to order that a fine shall be recoverable by civil diligence[1], although in practice this power is rarely used except in the case of partnerships, limited companies and other corporate bodies. In such a case the finding of the court imposing the fine includes a warrant for civil diligence[2]. Diligence (arrestment or poinding) may then be executed in the same manner as on an extract decree in a civil summary cause[3]. Civil diligence is not competent after the offender has been imprisoned or detained for default in payment of his fine[4].

CAUTION

A court may order an offender to find caution (ie a sum of money as a guarantee) for his good behaviour over a period of time. There is no statutory provision for the maximum amount of caution or length of the period of good behaviour in common law cases brought on indictment. In solemn statutory cases the court has power to order the finding of caution in a sum not exceeding the prescribed sum, for good behaviour for a period not exceeding twelve months[5]. The district court has power to order an offender to find caution in a sum not exceeding level 4 on the standard scale, for his good behaviour for a period not exceeding six months[6]. In the case of the sheriff sitting summarily the maximum sum is the prescribed sum, and the maximum period is twelve months[7].

Apart from the fact that there is no provision for the payment of caution by instalments, virtually all the provisions for payment and for enforcement are the same as those for fines[8].

There are certain additional provisions which apply to summary proceedings only. These are as follows: caution may be found by consignation of the amount with the clerk of court or by bond of caution. (ie a written undertaking to pay the money)[9]; forfeiture of the caution (because of failure to be of good behaviour) may be granted on the motion of the prosecutor and, where necessary, a warrant granted for the recovery thereof[10]; the court may, instead of ordering imprisonment in default of payment, order recovery by civil diligence[11].

If the offender remains of good behaviour throughout the period for which

---

1 1975 Act, s 396(6).
2 1975 Act, s 411(1). This section provides that the form of warrant is as specified in an Act of Adjournal, but the 1988 Act of Adjournal contains no such form.
3 1975 Act, s 411(1). For execution of diligence see the Debtors (Scotland) Act 1987 Pts II, and III.
4 1975 Act, s 411(3).
5 1975 Act, s 193(3).
6 1975 Act, s 284(c). Section 394(c) confirms the power to order caution in the case of statutory offences.
7 1975 Act, s 289(b). Section 394(c) confirms the power to order caution in the case of statutory offences.
8 Ie 1975 Act, ss 396, 397 (by reference from s 396), 398, 407 (although, no doubt owing to careless drafting, caution is not referred to in s 407(1) but is referred to in s 407(1A) and (2)).
9 1975 Act, s 303(1)(a).
10 1975 Act, s 303(1)(b).
11 1975 Act, s 303(1)(c).

he has found caution, he is entitled to recover the sum paid together with any interest which may have accrued thereon.

In practice an order for caution is a relatively rare disposal of a case. It appears to be most popular in some district courts.

COMPENSATION ORDER

Scope

Compensation orders were introduced into Scotland by the 1980 Act[1]. A compensation order is 'an order requiring (a person convicted of an offence) to pay compensation for any personal injury, loss or damage caused (whether directly or indirectly) by the acts which constituted the offence'[2]. A compensation order may not be made in respect of loss suffered in consequence of the death of any person[3]. Nor may it be made in respect of injury, loss or damage due to an accident arising out of the presence of a motor vehicle on a road except when a motor vehicle has been stolen or taken without authority and is recovered damaged, in which case the owner may be the beneficiary of a compensation order in respect of the damage[4].

When any property is dishonestly appropriated or unlawfully taken and used, or if a motor vehicle is taken without authority (in contravention of the Road Traffic Act 1988, s 178), and the property is recovered damaged, it is presumed that the damage was caused by the acts which constituted the offence[5].

A court may normally make a compensation order instead of or in addition to imposing any other sentence, but not where it gives an absolute discharge or defers sentence for good behaviour or on some other condition[6].

Amount

A compensation order may be made by all criminal courts. In the case of a court of solemn jurisdiction the amount which may be ordered to be paid as compensation is unlimited[7]. The maximum amount which may be ordered by a sheriff sitting summarily or a stipendiary magistrate is the prescribed sum[8]. In the case of a district court consisting of one or more lay justices, the

1 1980 Act, Pt IV.
2 1980 Act, s 58(1).
3 1980 Act, s 58(3)(a).
4 1980 Act, s 58(3)(b).
5 1980 Act, s 58(2).
6 1980 Act, s 58(1). This subsection also provides that a compensation order is not competent when the accused is put on probation. However, compensation may be a condition of probation, which amounts to virtually the same as making an order along with probation. Most of the compensation order provisions of the 1980 Act are applied to compensation as a condition of probation (1975 Act, ss 183(5B), 384(5B)) – see below at p 204. For absolute discharge see below at p 211. For deferred sentence see below at pp 212, 213. Note that sentence may be deferred with a condition of making restitution, which may have the same practical effect as a compensation order.
7 1980 Act, s 59(2).
8 1980 Act, s 59(3)(a).

maximum amount is level 4 on the standard scale[1]. In other words, the maximum amount in each case is the same as the maximum fine which may be imposed for a common law offence.

A court must take into consideration an offender's means so far as known to it when determining whether to make a compensation order and the amount thereof[2]. If the offender is serving a custodial sentence, or is just about to serve one, no account should be taken, when assessing his means, of what he may earn if he obtains a job on his release[3].

Assessment of the amount of a compensation order from the point of view of the victim is not covered by the 1980 Act. In practice the procurator fiscal usually obtains information from the police about the loss suffered by a victim, or details of the injuries in personal injury cases. If the case proceeds to trial, the witness is able to give evidence about his loss. If there is a plea of guilty, there is usually no evidence led, although it would no doubt be possible for there to be a proof on the matter if the value of the loss stated by the prosecutor were challenged by the accused. It is probably the law that corroboration of the amount of a loss is not required[4].

A court may take a fairly broad approach to the amount of compensation[5], and precision such as has been required by the courts in England[6] is not necessary in Scotland.

The conduct of the victim is a relevant factor. If he has contributed to his loss, the amount of compensation may be reduced, and, if his behaviour has been such that he would not obtain an award from the Criminal Injuries Compensation Board, he should not benefit at all from a compensation order[7].

Payment of compensation order

Payment is made to the clerk of court who must account for it to the victim[8]. The provisions relating to transfer of fines and payment of fines imposed by the High Court apply to compensation orders as if they were fines[9]. There are special rules governing compensation in favour of a person, eg a child, who is under a legal disability. The compensation is administered in the same way as an award made in favour of such a person in a civil case[10].

---

1 1980 Act, s 59(3)(b).
2 1980 Act, s 59(1).
3 1980 Act, s 59(1), proviso. See also *Clark v Cardle* 1989 SCCR 92, where a compensation order of £500 payable at £3 per week on release from a six months prison sentence was quashed on appeal as unreasonable, the accused having been given the maximum sentence of imprisonment.
4 *Goodhall v Carmichael* 1984 SCCR 247. The uncertainty springs from the fact that the court issued no opinions. See also Docherty and Maher, 'Corroboration and Compensation Orders', 1984 SLT (News) 125. Even if corroboration of loss were ever necessary, it is strongly arguable that it is no longer so since the coming into force of the Civil Evidence (Scotland) Act 1988, s 1, which abolished the need for corroboration in all civil proceedings.
5 Eg see *Stewart v HMA* 1982 SCCR 203.
6 Eg see *R v Vivian* [1979] 1 All ER 48, [1979] 1 WLR 291, [1978] RTR 106, (1978) 68 Cr App R 53; *R v Donovan* [1981] Crim LR 723.
7 *Brown v Normand* 1988 SCCR 229.
8 1980 Act, s 60(1).
9 1980 Act, s 66(2), applying 1975 Act, ss 196, 403 to compensation orders.
10 AA(C) 1988, rr 79, 82 (solemn) and r 125(3), (10) (summary).

Payment by the offender may be made in exactly the same way as in the case of a fine, ie as a lump sum, or by instalments, or after a period of time[1].

Priority of compensation order over fine

If an offender's means are such that he cannot afford to pay both a compensation order and a fine, then, even although both penalties might have been appropriate, the court should make a compensation order rather than impose a fine[2].

If both a compensation order and a fine have been imposed in respect of the same offence or on different offences in the same proceedings, payments by the offender are appropriated first to the compensation order and to the fine only after the compensation order has been paid off[3].

Review of compensation order

A court may review a compensation order and remit it in whole or in part in the same way as it may review a fine[4].

The amount of a compensation order may also be reviewed in the light of the victim's loss turning out to be less than it was thought to be at the time when the order was made[5]. An application for such a review is made in writing to the clerk of the appropriate court who causes intimation to be made to the prosecutor, and the court may then dispose of the application after making such inquiry as it thinks fit[6]. The court to which application should be made is either the court which made the order or the court to which it has been transferred (provided that that is a court of summary jurisdiction in Scotland), or, in the case of a compensation order made by the High Court, the court by which the order was first enforceable[7].

Enforcement of compensation order

The victim has no power to enforce a compensation order. Only the court may do so[8].

A compensation order is enforced in exactly the same way as a fine, and virtually all the provisions of the 1975 Act for enforcement of fines are applied to compensation orders[9]. There is only one notable exception. It is not competent to impose a period of imprisonment or detention in default of payment at the same time as actually making the compensation order[10]. A

---

1 1980 Act, s 66(2), applying 1975 Act, ss 396, 399 to compensation orders.
2 1980 Act, s 61.
3 1980 Act, s 62.
4 1980 Act, s 66(2), applying 1975 Act, s 395A to compensation orders. Any variation of the order may be made in chambers without attendance of the parties: AA(C) 1988, r 80(2) (solemn) and r 125(6) (summary).
5 1980 Act, s 64.
6 AA(C) 1988, r 81 (solemn) and r 125(7), (8), (9) (summary).
7 1980 Act, s 64.
8 1980 Act, s 60(2).
9 1980 Act, s 66.
10 1980 Act, s 66(2), restricting the application of 1975 Act, ss 395A, 396.

defaulter must therefore be summoned to a means enquiry court before the alternative may be imposed.

Where an offender is subject to both a fine and a compensation order, the court may impose imprisonment or detention in respect of the fine and decline to do so in respect of the compensation order, but not vice versa[1]. Where imprisonment in default is imposed in respect of both a fine and a compensation order, the two sums are aggregated for the purpose of calculating the maximum period of custody which may be imposed[1].

Effect of compensation order on damages in civil proceedings

The 1980 Act contains provisions[2] which are, in broad terms, to the effect that a person who receives an award of damages in a civil case and who has been the beneficiary under a compensation order in respect of the same incident, should not gain thereby. The amount of any payment made or to be made under a compensation order is set off against the amount of the damages payable. A similar principle is applied by the Criminal Injuries Compensation Board in respect of victims who make a claim and who have received compensation under a compensation order.

PROBATION

General

When any criminal court is satisfied that a person appearing before it has committed the offence with which he is charged, it may, instead of dealing with him in any other way, make him subject to a probation order. Although the statutory provisions governing probation are virtually identical for both solemn and summary cases, there is the distinction that in solemn cases probation follows conviction[3], whereas in summary cases the court makes a probation order without proceeding to conviction[4]. Even where an offender has been placed on probation after conviction, the conviction does not count as a conviction for most purposes[5], although it may appear in a notice of previous convictions if he subsequently offends[6].

A probation order is an order 'requiring the offender to be under supervision for a period to be specified in the order of not less than six months nor more than three years'[7]. The court may make an order 'if it is of opinion having regard to the circumstances, including the nature of the offence and the character of the offender and having obtained a report as to the circumstances and character of the offender, that it is expedient to do so'[7].

1   1980 Act, s 66(2), proviso to application of 1975 Act, s 407.
2   1980 Act, s 67.
3   1975 Act, s 183(1).
4   1975 Act, s 384(1). If the accused has been convicted and had sentence deferred under s 432, probation is nonetheless still competent.
5   1975 Act, ss 191, 392.
6   1975 Act, ss 191(1), 392(1).
7   1975 Act, ss 183(1), 384(1).

A probation order is usually made because the court considers that the offender is in need of some advice and guidance. It is used particularly in the case of young offenders and offenders with domestic difficulties such as single parents. The person under whose supervision the offender will be is a social worker employed by the social work department of the regional or islands authority in whose area the offender lives (or a probation officer attached to a magistrates' court if the offender lives in England or Wales). The nature and degree of the supervision will vary according to the circumstances of the offender and the resources of the social work department concerned.

Social enquiry report

The social enquiry report (SER), which the court must obtain before making a probation order, is prepared by a social worker for the area where the offender lives (or by a probation officer if he lives in England or Wales).

The period for which a case may be adjourned in order to obtain such a report must not exceed three weeks[1]. This restriction was almost certainly intended to prevent offenders being kept in custody for more than three weeks, but it also applies where the accused remains at liberty pending the preparation of the report. It forces courts on occasion to resort to the expedient of adjourning a case for three weeks and then calling it simply to adjourn it again for a further period, as it was known that the report would not be available within the three weeks. In many courts if an accused *is* remanded in custody for a report, the case is adjourned for only two weeks.

A copy of the social enquiry report must be given by the clerk of court to the offender or his solicitor except where the court is a summary court specially constituted for dealing with a child[2]. If the offender is under sixteen and unrepresented, the copy of the report may be given to his parent or guardian rather than to the offender himself[2].

Although a written report is normal, it is possible for the court to receive an oral report if the circumstances make this appropriate.

A judge should not interview a social worker in private about the contents of a social enquiry report. If he requires further information, the proper course is either to speak to the social worker in open court in the presence of the accused or to ask for a supplementary report[3].

Making the probation order

When a probation order is made the judge must explain to the offender in ordinary language what it means and what the consequences may be if he fails to comply with the order or commits a further offence[4]. The offender must agree to being placed on probation[4].

1 1975 Act, ss 179(1), 380(1). *HMA v Clegg* 1990 SCCR 293.
2 1975 Act, ss 192, 393.
3 *W v HMA* 1989 SCCR 461.
4 1975 Act, ss 183(6), 384(6).

Form and contents of the probation order

A probation order should be in the prescribed form[1]. It must name the local authority (regional or islands council) area in which the offender will be living and make provision for the offender to be under the supervision of a local social worker[1]. If the offender is to live outwith the jurisdiction of the court making the order, a court having jurisdiction in that area must be named (the 'appropriate court')[1]. The appropriate court will then require its local authority to arrange for supervision of the offender[1].

The order requires that the offender is '(1) to be of good behaviour; (2) to conform to the directions of the supervising officer; (3) to inform the supervising officer at once if he changes his residence or place of employment'[2]. Other requirements may be added according to the circumstances of the individual case[3]. The 1975 Act provides for certain specific additional requirements which will now be examined, but these are by no means exhaustive.

After considering the offender's home surroundings, the court may require him to live at a particular place for a given period of time not exceeding twelve months[4].

If the offender is sixteen or more and has committed an offence punishable by imprisonment, he may be required, as a condition of probation, to perform a number of hours (between 40 and 240) of unpaid work, in the same way as under a community service order[5].

As has already been mentioned[6], an offender may be required to pay compensation as a condition of probation[7]. The date by which payment of compensation must be completed should be no later than either eighteen months from the making of the order or two months before the end of the period of probation, whichever is the earlier[8]. Either the offender or his supervising social worker may apply to the court to have the condition of compensation varied on a change of circumstances[9], for example, if the offender lost his job.

An offender may be required to give security for his good behaviour during the period of probation[10]. The sum concerned may be consigned with the clerk of court or the offender may give an undertaking to pay it, and it may be forfeited and recovered in the same way as caution[11]. The sheriff in the case of *David Balfour*, it may be recalled, made use of this power.

In the case of a person suffering from a mental disorder the court may make it a condition of a probation order that he receives medical treatment for a period not exceeding twelve months[12]. This condition will be discussed in chapter 9.

---

1 1975 Act, ss 183(2), 384(2), AA(C) 1988, Form 35.
2 AA(C) 1988, Form 35.
3 1975 Act, ss 183(4), 384(4).
4 1975 Act, ss 183(5), 384(5).
5 1975 Act, ss 183(5A), 384(5A). For community service order see below at pp 207–210.
6 See above at p 119, note 6.
7 1975 Act, ss 183(5B), 384(5B).
8 1975 Act, ss 183(5C)(a), 384(5C)(a).
9 1975 Act, ss 183(5C)(b), 384(5C)(b).
10 1975 Act, ss 190(1), 391(1).
11 1975 Act, ss 190(2), 391(2). For caution see above at pp 198, 199.
12 1975 Act, ss 184, 385.

Amendment of probation order

If a probationer changes his residence, either he or his supervising social worker may apply to the court to have the probation order amended by substituting a different local authority area and a different court as the appropriate court[1]. The court has a discretion whether to grant such an application if made by the probationer, but must grant it if it is made by the social worker[1].

A probation order may also be amended by cancelling or by adding a requirement[2]. Again an application may be made to the court by either the probationer or his social worker[2]. There are three restrictions on the court's power of amendment: (1) the length of the order may not be reduced or extended beyond three years; (2) the twelve months limit on a condition of residence or medical treatment for a mental condition may not be extended; (3) a condition of medical treatment for a mental condition may be added only within the first three months of the order[2].

Discharge of probation order

Both the probationer and his social worker have the right to apply to the court for the order to be discharged[3]. Applications by probationers themselves are rare. A discharge might be sought if the social worker considered that the objectives of probation had been achieved, for example if the main purpose of probation had been to enable the offender to sort out his financial situation, and this was done. On the other hand, discharge might be sought because the probationer had received a long prison sentence. The court is under no obligation to discharge an order, but it is relatively unusual for an application by a social worker to be refused.

Failure to comply with a requirement of a probation order

If a probationer fails to comply with any requirement of an order, his social worker may apply to the court for what is commonly known as 'breach proceedings' to be taken. The usual procedure is for the social worker to submit a brief report to the court, describing the alleged breach and recommending whether or not proceedings should be taken. If the court decides to take the matter further, the social worker appears before the judge, is put on oath and gives evidence confirming the terms of his report. The judge may take the opportunity to discuss with the social worker how probation has progressed and his views on whether it should continue. The court may then either have the offender cited to attend or grant a warrant to apprehend[4].

When the offender appears before the court to answer the alleged failure to comply he may either admit it or deny it. If it is denied, evidence must be led

1 1975 Act, Sch 5, para 2(1).
2 1975 Act, Sch 5, para 3.
3 1975 Act, Sch 5, para 1.
4 1975 Act, ss 186(1), 387(1).

to prove it to the satisfaction of the court. Such evidence is presented by the procurator fiscal, and the offender may of course himself give and lead evidence.

If the failure to comply is proved or admitted, the court has a number of options. It may allow the probation order to continue and may express its displeasure at the breach by imposing a fine not exceeding level 3 on the standard scale (except where the breach consists of a failure to pay compensation)[1]. Next, it may convict the offender of the original offence (if that has not already been done) and sentence him for it[2]. This has the effect of terminating the probation order[3]. Or the court may vary the requirements of the probation order, but may not extend it beyond three years[4]. Finally, the court may, while allowing probation to continue, make a community service order[5]. This last disposal is not the same as making unpaid work a condition of probation[6] as here there is a separate community service order, which runs in tandem with the probation order.

Commission of further offence

Although the commission of a further offence while on probation is clearly a failure to comply with the requirement to be of good behaviour, it is not treated in the same way as other breaches[7]. The normal practice is, again, for the supervising social worker to submit a report describing the further offence, but there is no need for him to attend to 'swear the breach'. The probationer who has been convicted by a court in any part of Great Britain of an offence committed while on probation may be cited to attend the court which placed him on probation (or the appropriate court), or a warrant for his arrest may be granted[8]. When he appears before the court, either it may allow probation to continue, or it may convict him (if appropriate) and sentence him for the original offence[8]. There are no other options open to the court.

If, as often happens, a probationer is found guilty of a subsequent offence by the court which made the probation order (or by the appropriate court to which the order has been transferred), that court may take immediate cognisance of the breach of probation by commission of another offence and deal with the offender for both the new offence and the original offence[9]. In some courts with more than one sheriff this power is not widely used as it is felt that it should be the sheriff who made the probation order (rather than one of his colleagues) who decides whether to allow it to continue or to bring it to an end in respect of a new offence. Even if a judge is considering dealing with both offences, it would be normal for him to obtain the views of the supervising social worker on the possibility of probation being allowed to continue.

1 1975 Act, ss 186(2)(a), 387(2)(a).
2 1975 Act, ss 186(2)(b), 387(2)(b).
3 1975 Act, ss 185(2), 386(2).
4 1975 Act, ss 186(2)(c), 387(2)(c).
5 1975 Act, ss 186(2)(d), 387(2)(d).
6 See above at p 204.
7 1975 Act, ss 186(5), 387(5).
8 1975 Act, ss 187(1), 388(1).
9 1975 Act, ss 187(2), 388(2).

Probation orders for offenders resident in England or Wales

A Scottish court has power to make a probation order in respect of someone who lives in England or Wales[1]. There is no power to make an order in respect of a person living in Northern Ireland.

The provisions governing probation orders for those in England and Wales are complex, and it is not intended to examine them in detail here. An offender will be under the supervision of a probation officer for the petty sessions area where he lives[2]. Breach of a requirement of probation may be dealt with by the English or Welsh magistrates' court[3], or the offender may be brought back to the Scottish court which made or amended the order for it to deal with the breach[4]. If the probationer commits a further offence while on probation, he may be brought back to the Scottish court which made the order for it to dispose of the case[5].

COMMUNITY SERVICE ORDER

General

After an experimental period during which sheriff courts in certain areas of Scotland were empowered to make unpaid work a condition of probation, community service orders were introduced by the Community Service by Offenders (Scotland) Act 1978.

When an offender aged sixteen or over is convicted of an offence punishable, in the case of someone over 21, by imprisonment (except murder), the court may make a community service order, ie an order requiring him to perform unpaid work for a specified number of hours which must be not less than 40 nor more than 240[6]. Although the court has such a power in respect of any offender and any offence punishable by imprisonment, it is generally accepted that community service is appropriate only in cases where the court would otherwise almost certainly impose a custodial sentence. In other words a community service order is the last resort before custody.

A court may make a community service order only where certain conditions are satisfied[7]. These are: (a) the offender consents; (b) community service is available in the area where the offender lives or is going to live; (c) the court is satisfied, as a result of a report from a social worker[8] (and if necessary hearing the social worker), that the offender is a suitable person for a community service order; and (d) that suitable work will be available for the offender.

---

1 1975 Act, ss 188, 189, 389, 390. These sections refer only to 'England', but in s 462(1) 'England' is defined as including Wales!
2 1975 Act, ss 188(1), 389(1).
3 Powers of Criminal Courts Act 1973, s 6(3), applied by 1975 Act, ss 188(4), 389(4).
4 Powers of Criminal Courts Act 1973, s 6(4), applied by 1975 Act, ss 188(4), 389(4).
5 1975 Act, ss 188(5), 389(5).
6 Community Service by Offenders (Scotland) Act 1978, s 1(1).
7 Ibid, s 1(2).
8 The offender or his solicitor must receive a copy of the report (ibid, s 1(3)).

The making of the order

As in the case of probation the court must explain certain things about the order to the offender in ordinary language[1]. These are: (a) the purpose and effect of the order, especially the offender's obligations to report to his supervising social worker and notify him without delay of any change of address or change in the times at which he usually works[2], and the obligation to perform the specified number of hours work as directed by the supervising social worker[3]; (b) what may happen if the offender fails to comply with any of the requirements of the order; (c) that the court has power to review the order at the request of either the offender or his supervising social worker.

A community service order is normally the only sentence which a court may impose for the offence concerned[4], but a court may also disqualify an offender[5], make an order for forfeiture[6], order the offender to find caution for his good behaviour[7], or make a compensation order[8]. If an accused appears on several charges, some of which could not be the subject of a community service order because they are not punishable by imprisonment, the court may impose other sentences such as an admonition or a fine for these other offences while at the same time making a community service order in respect of the offences for which it is competent.

The order must: (a) specify the locality in which the offender resides or will reside when the order comes into force; (b) require the local authority for that locality (regional or island council) to appoint or assign an officer (who will be a social worker) to supervise the order; and (c) state the number of hours of work which the offender must perform[9].

One community service order may be made to run concurrently with or consecutive to another community service order or a period of unpaid work as a condition of probation[10], provided that, at no time, the offender has an outstanding number of hours of work to complete which exceeds 240[11].

The offender must be provided with a copy of the order[12].

Performance of community service order

The hours of work must be performed within twelve months from the date of the order[13] unless it is extended[14]. The times of work must, so far as practicable, avoid any conflict with the offender's religious beliefs and any interference with the times, if any, at which he normally works or attends any educational establishment[15].

1 Community Service by Offenders (Scotland) Act 1978, s 1(4).
2 Ibid, s 3(1)(a).
3 Ibid, s 3(1)(b).
4 Ibid, s 1(1).
5 Ibid, s 1(7)(a). For disqualification see below at pp 214, 215.
6 Ibid, s 1(7)(b). For forfeiture see below at p 213.
7 Ibid, s 1(7)(c). For caution see above at pp 198, 199.
8 1980 Act, s 58(1). For compensation order see above at pp 199–202.
9 Community Service by Offenders (Scotland) Act 1978, s 2(1).
10 See above at p 204.
11 Community Service by Offenders (Scotland) Act 1978, s 2(2).
12 Ibid, s 2(3)(a).
13 Ibid, s 3(2).
14 See below at p 209.
15 Community Service by Offenders (Scotland) Act 1978, s 3(3).

Failure to comply with requirements of order

The procedures for breach of a community service order are very similar to those for failure to comply with the requirements of a probation order[1]. The normal practice is that the supervising social worker submits a 'breach report' to the 'appropriate court'[2], describing the failure to comply and recommending whether further action should or should not be taken. If the court decides to proceed, the supervising social worker attends court to give evidence on oath of the failure to comply, and the court may then cite the offender to attend or grant a warrant for his arrest[3].

When the offender appears in court he may either admit the failure to comply or deny it. In the latter case evidence must be led to prove the failure to the satisfaction of the court[4]. If the breach is admitted or proved, the court may allow the order to continue with or without the imposition of a fine not exceeding level 3 on the standard scale[5], or it may revoke the order and deal with the offender for the original offence as if the order had not been made[6], or it may vary the number of hours, provided that the total does not exceed 240[7].

It should be noted that, in this respect differing from a probation order, there are no specific provisions for having an offender brought before the court because he has committed a further offence while being the subject of a community service order.

An offender may still be dealt with for a failure to comply, even although more than twelve months have elapsed since the order was made and it has not been extended[8], but he may not be required to work after that period without an extension.

Amendment of community service order

Either the offender or his supervising social worker may apply to the appropriate court to have the community service order amended by (a) extending the period of twelve months during which the hours of work are to be completed; or (b) varying the number of hours, subject to the upper and lower limits of 240 and 40 hours[9]. The court may grant the application if it appears 'that it would be in the interests of justice to do so having regard to the circumstances which have arisen since the order was made'[9]. Unless the application for amendment is by the offender himself he must be cited to attend court, and, if he fails to respond to the citation, the court may grant a warrant for his arrest[10].

---

1 See above at pp 205, 206.
2 The High Court, if it has made the order, otherwise the sheriff or district court which has jurisdiction over the locality where the offender resides (Community Service by Offenders (Scotland) Act 1978, s 12(1)).
3 Ibid, s 4(1).
4 Ibid, s 4(2).
5 Ibid, s 4(2)(a).
6 Ibid, s 4(2)(b).
7 Ibid, s 4(2)(c).
8 *HMA v Hood* 1987 SCCR 63.
9 Community Service by Offenders (Scotland) Act 1978, s 5(1).
10 Ibid, s 5(3).

If the offender has changed, or is going to change his residence, and community service for him is available in the new area, the court may (on the application of the offender) and must (on the application of the supervising social worker) amend the order to transfer it to the new locality[1].

Revocation of community service order

A community service order may be revoked on the application of either the offender or his supervising social worker[2]. The order may be revoked without any further action being taken[3], or it may be revoked and the offender dealt with as if no order had been made[4]. As with amendment of the order, the court may revoke if it appears 'that it would be in the interests of justice to do so having regard to the circumstances which have arisen since the order was made'[5].

Circumstances in which an order might simply be revoked could be if the offender became seriously ill or received a very long prison sentence. Circumstances in which an order might be revoked and another sentence substituted could be that the offender had committed a further offence during the currency of the order or that, although he was not actually in breach of the order, it became clear that he was not a suitable candidate for community service.

If a court is contemplating revoking an order and substituting an alternative sentence, the offender must be cited to attend, and, if he fails to answer the citation, a warrant may be granted for his arrest[6].

Community service orders on offenders living in England, Wales and Northern Ireland

A Scottish court may make a community service order in respect of an offender living in England, Wales or Northern Ireland[7]. The statutory provisions are complex, and it is not intended to examine them in detail here. Enforcement of the order is a matter for the 'home court' (the petty sessions court in the area of the offender's residence)[8]. In the event of a failure to comply with a requirement of the order, the home court may deal with the matter to a limited extent[9]. However, it may not revoke the order, whether with or without the substitution of an alternative sentence[9]. An order may be revoked (whether in respect of a breach or for any other reason) only by the court which made it, and the home court may require the offender's attendance at the sentencing court for that purpose[10]. The Scottish court has power to issue a warrant for the offender's arrest to ensure his attendance before it[11].

---

1 Community Service by Offenders (Scotland) Act 1978, s 5(2).
2 Ibid, s 5(1).
3 Ibid, s 5(1)(c).
4 Ibid, s 5(1)(d).
5 Ibid, s 5(1).
6 Ibid, s 5(3).
7 Ibid, ss 6, 6A, 6B.
8 Ibid, s 6B(2).
9 Ibid, s 6B(5).
10 Ibid, s 6B(6).
11 Ibid, s 6B(7).

ADMONITION

Both solemn and summary courts have the power to dismiss with an admonition a person convicted of an offence, 'if it appears to meet the justice of the case'[1]. An admonition is usually appropriate only if the offence is very minor or there are substantial mitigating circumstances. It is a disposal which is quite frequently used after sentence has been deferred for the accused to be of good behaviour and he has complied with that condition.

The offender is usually simply told: 'You are admonished'. What the court is, in effect, saying is: 'Go away. You are just being told off this time. Don't do it again'.

An offence for which an accused is admonished counts as a conviction for all purposes.

ABSOLUTE DISCHARGE

Nature of absolute discharge

An absolute discharge (which is an even more lenient disposal than an admonition) may be given by a court 'if it is of opinion, having regard to the circumstances, including the nature of the offence and the character of the offender, that it is inexpedient to inflict punishment and that a probation order is not appropriate'[2]. In a solemn case an absolute discharge follows conviction[3], while in a summary case the court gives an absolute discharge 'without proceeding to conviction'[4]. It is apparently not competent to give an absolute discharge in a summary case where a person has been convicted and had sentence deferred for good behaviour or the like[5].

Absolute discharge is a relatively rare form of disposal. The type of situation where a court might consider it appropriate could be where it felt that the prosecution should never really have been brought because of the triviality of the offence or for some reason peculiar to the offender.

Effect of absolute discharge

An absolute discharge counts as a conviction only for the purpose of the proceedings where it is made and of founding on it as a previous conviction in subsequent proceedings for another offence[6]. The offender's right to appeal against conviction or a finding of guilt is preserved[7]. A person who has

1 1975 Act, ss 181, 382.
2 1975 Act, ss 182, 383.
3 1975 Act, s 182.
4 1975 Act, s 383.
5 1975 Act, s 432(1), which provides specifically for a probation order being made after a period of deferred sentence, but does not mention absolute discharge.
6 1975 Act, ss 191(1), 392(1).
7 1975 Act, ss 191(3), 392(3), (4).

received an absolute discharge may also have his licence endorsed or be disqualified under the Road Traffic Acts 1988[1]. An exclusion order may be made against him[2]. He may not be made subject to a compensation order[3].

DEFERRED SENTENCE

General

All courts have the power to defer sentence following conviction[4]. Sentence may be deferred for any period and on any condition[4]. In the case of a summary court the fact that sentence has been deferred following conviction is not a bar to a probation order being made at the expiry of the period of deferment[5].

The most common condition on which sentence is deferred is that the accused should be of good behaviour. Another relatively common condition is that he should make restitution, although this is probably rarer now that the court has power to make a compensation order.

If an accused has been of good behaviour during the period of deferment, that should normally be reflected by the court's imposing a more lenient sentence than it might otherwise have done[6]. An admonition may be appropriate[7], but the court always has a discretion[8]. A judge should not tie his hands by promising a particular disposal in the event of an accused not behaving[9]. However, there is no reason why the likely consequences of offending should not be spelt out to the accused.

It is not appropriate to defer sentence on one charge while at the same time imposing a custodial sentence on another[10].

The High Court has stated that a sheriff who defers sentence should himself deal with the case at the end of the period of deferment if at all possible[11]. This may present a problem in the busier courts, especially with the increasing use of temporary sheriffs.

Conviction of other offences during deferred sentence

If an accused, who is on deferred sentence, is convicted of and dealt with for an offence by a court in any part of Great Britain during the period of deferment, the court which deferred sentence may have him brought before

---

1 Road Traffic Offenders Act 1988, s 46(3).
2 Licensed Premises (Exclusion of Certain Persons) Act 1980, s 1(2)(c). For exclusion order, see below at p 214.
3 1980 Act, s 58(1).
4 1975 Act, ss 219(1), 432(1).
5 1975 Act, s 432(1).
6 See eg *McPherson v HMA* 1986 SCCR 278; *Main v Jessop* 1989 SCCR 437.
7 *Main v Jessop* 1989 SCCR 437.
8 *Linton v Ingram* 1989 SCCR 487.
9 *Cassidy v Wilson* 1989 SCCR 6.
10 *Lennon v Copeland* 1972 SLT (Notes) 68.
11 *Islam v HMA* 1989 SCCR 109; *Main v Jessop* 1989 SCCR 437.

it immediately without waiting until the date to which sentence has been deferred, and it may cite the accused to attend or grant a warrant for his arrest for that purpose[1]. He may then be dealt with in any way which would have been competent at the end of the period of deferment[1].

If an accused, who is on deferred sentence, is convicted during the period of deferment by the court which deferred sentence, the case in which sentence was deferred may be accelerated from the deferment date, and both it and the new offence may be disposed of at the same time[2].

It may be noted that these provisions do not refer specifically to offences *committed* during the period of deferment, but to an accused being *convicted* during such a period. It is, however, suggested that the spirit, if not the letter, of the legislation is intended to cover offences actually committed while an accused is on deferred sentence and not offences committed earlier which happen not to come to court until after sentence has been deferred.

FORFEITURE

Several statutes make provision for forfeiture of specific items in the event of conviction of an offence committed under them[3]. There is also a general power given to the court under the 1975 Act to forfeit any property in the accused's possession or under his control at the time of his arrest which the court is satisfied '(a) has been used for the purpose of committing, or facilitating the commission of, any offence; or (b) was intended by him to be used for that purpose'[4]. The property is to be disposed of as the court directs[4]. 'Facilitating the commission is an offence' includes 'the taking of any steps after it has been committed for the purpose of disposing of any property to which it relates or of avoiding apprehension or detention'[5].

If a statute prohibits forfeiture in certain circumstances, a court should not order forfeiture under the general provisions of the 1975 Act in order to get round the prohibition[6].

The forfeited articles need not be the property of the offender[7], unless the statute under which forfeiture is ordered specifies that forfeiture is to be 'in addition to any other penalty'. In that case the article must be the property of the offender[8].

After hearing evidence on oath to the effect that an article ordered to be forfeited is likely to be in a particular place and that admission thereto has been or is likely to be refused, a court (or any justice of the peace) may issue a search warrant[9].

---

1 1975 Act, ss 219(2), 432(2).
2 1975 Act, ss 219(3), 432(3).
3 Eg Misuse of Drugs Act 1971; Salmon and Freshwater Fisheries (Protection) (Scotland) Act 1951.
4 1975 Act, ss 223(1), 436(1).
5 1975 Act, ss 223(2), 436(2).
6 *Aitken v Lockhart* 1989 SCCR 368.
7 See eg *Bain v Wilson* 1987 SCCR 270.
8 *JW Semple & Sons v Macdonald* 1963 JC 90, 1963 SLT 295.
9 1975 Act, ss 224, 437.

EXCLUSION ORDER

If a person is found guilty of an offence committed on licensed premises and the court is satisfied that, in committing the offence, he resorted to violence or offered or threatened to resort to violence, it may make an exclusion order[1]. This is an order prohibiting the offender from entering 'these premises or any other specified premises, without the express consent of the licensee of the premises or his servant or agent'[1]. The order may be for any period not less than three months or more than two years[2].

An exclusion order may be imposed in addition to any other sentence, and is competent even if the offender is placed on probation or given an absolute discharge[3].

A person who enters premises in breach of an exclusion order is guilty of an offence and is liable to a fine not exceeding £200 and/or imprisonment for a term not exceeding one month[4]. The court convicting a person of such an offence may terminate the exclusion order or may vary it by deleting the name of any specified premises[5].

The licensee of premises may expel any person entering them in breach of an exclusion order and may call on the assistance of a police officer for that purpose[6].

DISQUALIFICATION

General

Under various statutes an offender may be disqualified from doing something which he could otherwise legally do. The most obvious example is disqualification for holding or obtaining a driving licence in terms of the Road Traffic Act 1988, but an offender may also, for example, be disqualified from holding public office[7], or from keeping an animal[8]. If sentence is deferred in a case where disqualification is competent, the order for disqualification must be made at the date of sentencing and not at the date when sentence is deferred.

Disqualification under the Road Traffic Acts

It is not intended to examine disqualification from driving (as it is commonly called) in any detail here. Reference should be made to one of the specialist

---

1 Licensed Premises (Exclusion of Certain Persons) Act 1980, s 1(1).
2 Ibid, s 1(3).
3 Ibid, s 1(2).
4 Ibid, s 2(1).
5 Ibid, s 2(2).
6 Ibid, s 3.
7 Public Bodies Corrupt Practices Act 1889, s 2.
8 Protection of Animals (Amendment) Act 1954, s 1(1).

works on road traffic law[1]. However, the following points should be noted.

A court should not normally disqualify an offender without giving him an opportunity to make representations about disqualification, if disqualification is to any extent discretionary[2]. It happens quite often that an accused pleads guilty by letter to an offence for which disqualification is competent but not obligatory, and says nothing in mitigation in his letter. If the court is contemplating disqualification in such a case, the accused should be informed of this and given the opportunity of either appearing personally or stating mitigating circumstances in writing. He should also be told that, if he is not to appear personally, he must not drive between the date of the next calling of the case in court and his being informed what its outcome is. This is to avoid the possibility of his inadvertently driving while disqualified.

Where a court disqualifies an offender in respect of a number of offences committed at the same time, each offence has to be considered separately and the appropriate disqualification for *that* offence only imposed on each[3]. Some doubts were expressed as to whether this was still the law, given the provisions of a subsection of the Road Traffic Offenders Act 1988[4]. This appears to say that, when an offender is convicted on the same occasion of more than one offence involving obligatory or discretionary disqualification, not more than one disqualification must be imposed, and in deciding the period of disqualification the court must take into account all the offences. The problem is that this subsection is in the section dealing with the so-called 'totting up' provisions, where it makes little if any sense, and not in the preceding section where it would make perfect sense. Is it possible that an error has been made?

In addition to disqualification for an offence under the Road Traffic Act 1988, the court also has power in certain circumstances to disqualify from driving in respect of common law offences. Firstly, disqualification is competent but not obligatory in the case of theft of a motor vehicle[5]. Secondly, if a person is convicted on indictment of an offence, and the court is satisfied that a motor vehicle was used for the purpose of committing or facilitating the commission of that offence, the court may disqualify the offender from driving[6]. In this context 'facilitating' has the same extended meaning as it has for the purposes of forfeiture[7].

DEPORTATION

When a person over seventeen, who is not a British subject, is found guilty of an offence punishable with imprisonment in the case of someone over 21, the court may recommend that he be deported[8]. The power to recommend

---

1 Eg J Wheatley *Road Traffic Law in Scotland* (Law Society of Scotland/Butterworth 1989); Road Traffic Encyclopaedia (Sweet and Maxwell, looseleaf, regularly updated); Wilkinson's Road Traffic Offences (Longman Professional – new editions appear regularly).
2 *Stephens v Gibb* 1984 SCCR 195.
3 *McMurrich v Cardle* 1988 SCCR 20 which was decided under the former road traffic legislation. In *Patterson v Whitelaw* 1990 GWD 23–1308 (a case under the new legislation) *McMurrich* was affirmed and followed.
4 Road Traffic Offenders Act 1988, s 35(3).
5 Ibid, s 97(2), Sch 2, Pt II.
6 Criminal Justice Act 1972, s 24(2).
7 Ibid, s 24(4). See above at p 213.
8 Immigration Act 1971, s 3(6), read in conjunction with s 6(3).

deportation may be exercised only by the High Court and the sheriff court[1]. The court may not recommend deportation unless the offender has received at least seven days' notice in writing stating that a person is not liable to deportation if he is a British subject[2]. After an accused has been found guilty the court may adjourn to enable such a notice to be served[3]. A recommendation for deportation may be made in the case of a person sentenced to life imprisonment[4]. An appeal against a recommendation for deportation is competent as an appeal against sentence[5].

There are restrictions on the making of a deportation order in respect of certain Commonwealth citizens and citizens of the Republic of Ireland[6].

Deportation may be recommended only in relation to a serious charge or series of charges, the test being whether to allow the offender to remain in this country would be contrary to the national interest[7]. In the case of a national of a country of the European Community, in terms of the provisions of the EEC Treaty, a recommendation for deportation is justified only if the continued presence of the offender in the United Kingdom would be 'in addition to the perturbation of the social order which any infringement of the law involves, a genuine and sufficiently serious threat to the requirements of public policy affecting one of the fundamental interests of society'[8].

It should be remembered that it is not the court which makes the actual deportation order. The court merely recommends. The ultimate decision whether or not to deport is taken by the Home Secretary, and any order is made by him[9].

---

1 Immigration Act 1971, s 6(1).
2 Ibid, s 6(2).
3 Ibid. The adjournment may be under the 1975 Act, s 179 or s 380.
4 Immigration Act 1971, s 6(4).
5 Ibid, s 6(5).
6 Ibid, s 7.
7 *Willms v Smith* 1982 JC 9, 1981 SCCR 257, 1982 SLT 163. See also *Faboro v HMA* 1982 SCCR 22 and *Salehi v Smith* 1982 SCCR 552.
8 *R v Bouchereau* [1978] QB 146, [1981] 2 All ER 924, [1978] 2 WLR 250, (1977) Cr App R 202. This was a decision of the Court of Justice of the European Communities.
9 Immigration Act 1971, s 5(1).

Chapter 8

Appeals

INTRODUCTION

Mention has been made in various parts of the text of appeals to the High Court of Justiciary in matters before final disposal of a case, such as bail[1] or decisions on competency and relevancy in summary cases[2]. This chapter is concerned primarily with appeals following final disposal, but other matters will be touched upon.

We shall first of all examine appeals in cases under solemn procedure, then appeals in cases under summary procedure. We shall then look briefly at appeal by advocation and appeal to the *nobile officium* of the High Court, both of which may apply to solemn and summary cases.

The High Court when acting as an appellate court is often called the Court of Criminal Appeal or the Justiciary Appeal Court, although these nomenclatures are not used in the current legislation.

APPEALS UNDER SOLEMN PROCEDURE

Scope of appeal

A person who has been convicted on indictment, whether in the High Court or the sheriff court, may appeal against conviction, conviction and sentence, or sentence alone[3]. 'By an appeal . . . a person may bring under review of the High Court any alleged miscarriage of justice in the proceedings in which he was convicted, including any alleged miscarriage of justice on the basis of the existence and significance of additional evidence which was not heard at the trial and which was not available and could not reasonably have been made available at the trial'[4].

Legal aid

An appellant may apply for legal aid to the Scottish Legal Aid Board. Legal aid will be granted if the Board is satisfied that the appellant 'has substantial

1 See above at pp 95, 97.
2 See above at p 166.
3 1975 Act, s 228(1).
4 1975 Act, s 228(2).

grounds for making the appeal and that it is reasonable, in the particular circumstances of the case, that legal aid should be made available to him'[1]. If he has had legal aid in the trial court, he does not require to qualify financially for the appeal[2], but otherwise he will receive legal aid only if he is unable to meet the expenses of the appeal without undue hardship to himself or his dependents[3].

The application for legal aid is signed by the appellant and must include a statement signed by or on behalf of the appellant's solicitor as to his willingness to act for the appellant[4]. It must also include a statement by the solicitor of the nature of the grounds of appeal where the solicitor is of the opinion that in all the circumstances they are substantial[5].

Appeals against conviction

Intimation of intention to appeal

A person who wishes to appeal against conviction (whether or not appealing also against sentence) must lodge with the Clerk of Justiciary written intimation of his intention to appeal within two weeks of the final determination of the proceedings in the trial court[6]. 'Final determination' means the date when sentence is passed, except when sentence has been deferred for a period, in which case it is the date when sentence is first deferred[7]. The two-week period may be extended by a single judge of the High Court on application by the appellant[8].

Note of appeal

Within six weeks of lodging his intimation of intention to appeal the appellant must lodge a note of appeal with the Clerk of Justiciary[9]. This must contain a full statement of all the grounds of appeal[10]. An appellant will not be allowed to found on a ground of appeal not stated in the note except by leave of the High Court on cause shown[11]. The period of six weeks may be extended by the Clerk of Justiciary[12]. This is to ensure that the appellant is able to see the transcript of the judge's charge to the jury before he lodges his note of appeal. The six-week period (or the longer period prescribed by the

1 Legal Aid (Scotland) Act 1986, s 25(2)(b).
2 Ibid, s 25(4).
3 Ibid, s 25(2)(a).
4 Criminal Legal Aid (Scotland) Regulations 1987, SI 1987/307, reg 13(1)(a), (b).
5 Ibid, SI 1987/307, reg 13(1)(c).
6 1975 Act, s 231(1). The form of intimation is AA(C) 1988, Form 37. Forms are available from the Clerk of Justiciary who should also provide all other forms in connection with appeals to courts and prisons (1975 Act, s 271).
7 1975 Act, s 231(4).
8 1975 Act, s 236B(2). The form of application is AA(C) 1988, Form 39. There is a right of appeal to a bench of three judges from a refusal by the single judge (s 247).
9 1975 Act, s 233(1). The form of note is AA(C) 1988, Form 38.
10 1975 Act, s 233(2). It is essential that the grounds of appeal are fully stated. Otherwise the court may not entertain the appeal: *Smith v HMA* 1983 SCCR 30.
11 1975 Act, s 233(3).
12 1975 Act, s 233(1).

Clerk of Justiciary) may be extended by a single judge of the High Court on application by the appellant[1].

Judge's report

On receipt of the note of appeal the Clerk of Justiciary sends a copy of it to the trial judge[2]. As soon as reasonably practicable thereafter the judge should provide the Clerk of Justiciary with a report giving his opinion on the case generally and on the grounds contained in the note of appeal[3]. Such a report used to be confidential to the High Court and was not seen by either the appellant or the respondent. Now, however, a copy of the report must be sent to the appellant or his solicitor and to the Crown Agent[3]. If the case is not a normal appeal, but has been referred to the court by the Secretary of State under s 263(1) of the 1975 Act[4], a copy of the judge's report is also sent to the Secretary of State[5]. The High Court may hear and determine an appeal without a report[6].

The trial judge may be required by the High Court to produce any notes taken by him at the trial[7]. This requirement is very seldom made, which is perhaps just as well, considering the illegibility in some cases of such notes, including those of the present writer!

Bail

At any time after lodging an intimation of intention to appeal an appellant may apply to the High Court for bail pending his appeal[8]. The bail application is considered by a single judge[9], but the appellant may appeal against a refusal of bail to a bench of three judges[9]. If bail is granted and the appellant then fails to attend the High Court for the hearing of his appeal, the court may dismiss it[10].

Intimation of hearing

The Clerk of Justiciary gives notice of the date of the appeal hearing to the appellant or his solicitor, who must then lodge three copies of the appeal for the use of the court[11]. The appellant is entitled to be present at the hearing if he wishes, except where the appeal involves only a question of law[12]. In that case the appellant may be given leave to be present by a single judge of the High Court[13].

1 1975 Act, ss 236B(2), 247. The form of application is AA(C) 1988, Form 39. There is a right of appeal to a bench of three judges from a refusal by the single judge (s 247).
2 1975 Act, s 233(1).
3 1975 Act, s 236A(1).
4 See below at p 223.
5 1975 Act, s 236A(1).
6 1975 Act, s 236A(2).
7 1975 Act, s 237.
8 1975 Act, s 238(1), (3). The form is AA(C) 1988, Form 40.
9 1975 Act, s 247.
10 1975 Act, s 238(2).
11 1975 Act, s 239(1).
12 1975 Act, s 240.
13 1975 Act, ss 240, 247. A refusal by the single judge may be appealed to a bench of three judges.

Frivolous or vexatious appeal

The court may, without fixing a hearing, summarily dismiss an appeal involving only a question of law if it considers that it is frivolous or vexatious[1].

Failure of appellant to attend

If an appellant fails to attend an appeal hearing where no written case or argument has been lodged, the appeal will be disposed of as if it had been abandoned[2], ie it will be dismissed.

Abandonment of appeal

An appellant may abandon his appeal against conviction by lodging a notice of abandonment with the Clerk of Justiciary, and the appeal is then deemed to have been dismissed[3]. A person who has appealed against both conviction and sentence may abandon his appeal against conviction and proceed with the appeal against sentence[4].

Hearing of appeal

The hearing of the appeal usually takes place before a bench of three judges[5], but a bench of five or seven judges may be convened when it is desired to reconsider an earlier decision of the court[6].

The appeal is almost invariably conducted by means of oral debate, but there is a rarely used provision for an appellant to present his argument in writing[7]. Notice of his intention to do so must be made at least four days prior to the hearing of the appeal, and three copies of the written argument must be lodged with the Clerk of Justiciary at the same time[7]. The respondent does not make a written reply, but responds orally[8]. If the appellant presents a written argument, he is not entitled also to make oral submissions except with the leave of the court[9].

Powers of the High Court

The court is given various powers for the purposes of an appeal under s 228(1) of the 1975 Act[10]. These powers (which apply to appeals against both conviction and sentence) are:

(a) to order the production of any document or other thing connected with the proceedings[11];

(b) to hear any additional evidence relevant to any alleged miscarriage of

---

1 1975 Act, s 256.
2 1975 Act, s 257.
3 1975 Act, s 244(1). The form is AA(C) 1988, Form 41.
4 1975 Act, s 244(2).
5 1975 Act, s 245(1).
6 Eg *Templeton v McLeod* 1985 SCCR 357, 1986 SLT 149 (five judges): overruled by *Leggate v HMA* 1988 SCCR 391, 1988 SLT 665 (seven judges).
7 1975 Act, s 234(1).
8 1975 Act, s 234(2).
9 1975 Act, s 234(3).
10 1975 Act, s 252.
11 There is separate provision (1975 Act, ss 274, 275) for production of the transcript of shorthand notes taken at a trial.

justice or order such evidence to be heard by a judge of the High Court or by such other person as it may appoint for that purpose;

(c) to take account of any circumstances relevant to the case which were not before the trial judge[1];

(d) to remit to any fit person to enquire and report in regard to any matter or circumstance affecting the appeal[2];

(e) to appoint a person with expert knowledge to act as assessor to the High Court in any case where it appears to the court that such expert knowledge is required for the proper determination of the case.

Additional evidence

The law on the subject of additional evidence before the High Court on appeal and its effect has been clarified recently by the case of *Cameron v Her Majesty's Advocate*[3]. Where the appeal court is satisfied that, if the original jury had heard the new evidence, they would have been bound to acquit, the court will quash the conviction. Where the appeal court is satisfied that the additional evidence is at least capable of being described as important and reliable evidence which would have been at least likely to have had material bearing on, or a major part to play in, the jury's determination of a critical issue at the trial, it will be open to the court to hold that a conviction returned in ignorance of that evidence represents a miscarriage of justice, and to set aside the verdict and authorise a new prosecution[4]. The court will never entertain an appeal based on the proposition that a witness who has given evidence at a trial merely wishes to change his story; that is not additional evidence within the meaning of s 228(1)(b)[5].

An application to the court to hear fresh evidence should be supported by a precognition from the witness concerned. That precognition should be taken by a qualified solicitor[6].

Additional evidence may be led before the appeal court itself (although this rarely if ever occurs) or before a single judge[7]. The evidence is taken by examination and cross-examination in the normal way[7].

Disposal of appeals against conviction

There are three ways in which the appeal court may dispose of an appeal against conviction[8]. It may affirm the verdict of the trial court; or it may set aside the verdict and either quash the conviction or substitute an amended verdict of guilty (provided that such a verdict would have been competent before the trial court); or it may set aside the verdict and grant authority to bring a new prosecution. If the court sets aside a verdict it may quash the

1 The opinion has been expressed that this provision is designed only for appeals against sentence: *Rubin v HMA* 1984 SCCR 96 at 107, 1984 SLT 369 at 371, per Lord Justice-General Emslie.

2 It would be competent under this provision to order an enquiry into allegations of prejudice on the part of a juror notwithstanding the terms of the Contempt of Court Act 1981, s 8: *McCadden v HMA* 1985 SCCR 282, 1986 SLT 138.

3 *Cameron v HMA* 1987 SCCR 608, 1988 SLT 169.

4 See below at p 222.

5 *Mitchell v HMA* 1989 SCCR 502.

6 *Allison v HMA* 1985 SCCR 408.

7 1975 Act, s 253(1).

8 1975 Act, s 254(1).

sentence imposed on the indictment and substitute another (but not more severe) sentence[1].

The only ground of appeal is now that there has been a miscarriage of justice[2]. It has been held that, even if a miscarriage of justice has occurred, the verdict will not necessarily be set aside if the miscarriage of justice is not such as to warrant quashing the conviction[3].

Authorisation of new prosecution

If a new prosecution is authorised by the appeal court, proceedings therein must be commenced within two months of the date on which authority was granted[4]. Proceedings are commenced on the date when a warrant to apprehend or to cite the accused is granted 'where such warrant is executed without unreasonable delay', and otherwise on the date when the warrant is executed[5]. If proceedings are not commenced within the two months, the setting aside of the verdict by the appeal court has the effect of an acquittal[6]. The other time limits applying to proceedings on indictment do not, however, apply here[7].

The new prosecution may be for the same offence as was originally charged or for any similar offence arising out of the same facts[8], but no sentence may be pronounced which could not have been pronounced on conviction under the earlier proceedings[8].

A new trial has most frequently been authorised where the miscarriage of justice has been procedural rather than going to the merits of the case[9]. However, even though a conviction is quashed on a procedural matter it does not necessarily mean that a new prosecution will be authorised[10].

Appeals against sentence

The procedure for appealing against sentence only in solemn proceedings is very similar to that for appealing against conviction, except that there is no intimation of intention to appeal. The first document lodged is a note of appeal, and that must be lodged with the Clerk of Justiciary within two weeks of the imposition of the sentence appealed against[11]. Thereafter the procedure regarding bail, application for extension of time, judge's report, form of hearing etc is exactly the same as in the case of appeals against conviction.

The provision about abandonment of an appeal[12] applies equally to an appeal against sentence. However, it is particularly important in the case of an

---

1 1975 Act, s 254(2). See *Caringi v HMA* 1989 SCCR 223, 1989 SLT 714.
2 1975 Act, s 228(2).
3 *McCuaig v HMA* 1982 JC 59, 1982 SCCR 125, 1982 SLT 383.
4 1975 Act, s 255(3).
5 1975 Act, s 255(3). For execution of warrants without unreasonable delay see above at pp 164, 165.
6 1975 Act, s 255(4).
7 1975 Act, s 255(2).
8 1975 Act, s 255(1).
9 Eg *Mackenzie v HMA* 1982 SCCR 499, 1983 SLT 220; *Cunningham v HMA* 1984 JC 37, 1984 SCCR 40, 1984 SLT 249.
10 *McColl v HMA* 1989 SCCR 229, 1989 SLT 691.
11 1975 Act, s 233(1).
12 1975 Act, s 244.

appeal against sentence to lodge a proper notice of abandonment. The court may well not permit the appeal to be abandoned at the bar without proper notice having been given, as it is may be considering increasing the sentence[1].

After hearing the appeal the court may affirm the sentence or it may quash it and pass another sentence which may be more or less severe[2]. Cases of a sentence being increased are not common, but they do occur[3]. In the case of an appeal from a sentence imposed in the sheriff court the appeal court may even impose a sentence which would have been beyond the powers of the sheriff[4].

Time spent pending appeal

If an appellant is released on bail pending appeal, then time spent on bail does not count towards any custodial sentence which may still exist following the determination of the appeal[5]. If an appellent is not released on bail, or if bail is recalled at any stage, the period spent in custody pending appeal will count as part of a custodial sentence unless the court directs otherwise[6]. If an appellant is in custody on another matter pending his appeal, his sentence in the appeal case will run from the date when his appeal is determined or abandoned[7].

Reference by the Secretary of State

The Secretary of State for Scotland may refer a case to the High Court at any time, whether or not there has already been an appeal in the case[8]. The reference is to be heard and determined as if it were an appeal[8]. This power is rarely used but would obviously be beneficial, for example, in a case where there has been an unsuccessful appeal and new evidence emerges.

Reference by the Lord Advocate

Although there is no right of appeal by the Crown against the verdict of a jury, provision is now made for the Lord Advocate, in effect, to have it declared that the trial court has gone wrong in law. The actual provision[9] is to the effect that, when a person tried on indictment is acquitted of a charge, the Lord Advocate may refer a point of law which has arisen in relation to that charge to the High Court for their opinion.

A copy of the reference and intimation of the date of the hearing must be given to the former accused[9]. The latter is entitled to appear personally or by counsel at the hearing. If he elects to do so, he must intimate that fact to the

---

1 *Ferguson v HMA* 1980 JC 27, 1980 SLT 21.
2 1975 Act, s 254(3).
3 Eg *Ferguson v HMA* 1980 JC 27, 1980 SLT 21.
4 *Connelly v HMA* 1954 JC 90, 1954 SLT 259.
5 1975 Act, s 268(1).
6 1975 Act, s 268(2).
7 1975 Act, s 268(3)(b).
8 1975 Act, s 263(1).
9 1975 Act, s 263A(1).

Clerk of Justiciary no later than seven days before the date of the hearing[1]. If he does not so intimate, he is not entitled to appear or to be represented at the hearing except by leave of the court on cause shown[1]. Representation by counsel is paid for by the Crown[2]. If the former accused does not appear and is not represented, the court appoints counsel to act as *amicus curiae*[3].

Whatever the court may decide in the reference, the acquittal of the former accused is not affected[4].

At the date of writing there have been only two references by the Lord Advocate[5].

APPEALS UNDER SUMMARY PROCEDURE

Legal aid

The provisions for Legal Aid in summary appeals are the same as those for Legal Aid in solemn appeals[6].

Scope of appeal

An accused who has been convicted in summary proceedings may appeal against conviction, conviction and sentence, or sentence alone[7]. The prosecutor may appeal on a point of law only against an acquittal or against a sentence[8]. An appeal by an accused or by the prosecutor against an acquittal may 'bring under review of the High Court any alleged miscarriage of justice in the proceedings, including, in the case of an appeal (by an accused) any alleged miscarriage of justice on the basis of the existence and significance of additional evidence which was not heard at the trial and which was not available and could not reasonably have been made available at the trial'[9].

An appeal against conviction (whether with or without an appeal against sentence) by an accused and all appeals by a prosecutor are normally by way of stated case[10]. An accused may also, in certain limited circumstances, appeal against conviction and/or sentence by bill of suspension. A prosecutor may also, again in certain limited circumstances, appeal by bill of advocation. Both of these methods of appeal will be discussed below[11]. It must be stressed that stated case is the normal appeal procedure. Bills of suspension and advocation are the exception.

---

1 1975 Act, s 263A(2).
2 1975 Act, s 263A(4).
3 1975 Act, s 263A(3).
4 1975 Act, s 263A(5).
5 *Lord Advocate's Reference (No 1 of 1983)* 1984 JC 52, 1984 SCCR 62, 1984 SLT 337: *Lord Advocate's Reference (No 1 of 1985)* 1986 SCCR 329, 1987 SLT 187.
6 See above at pp 217, 218.
7 1975 Act, s 442(1)(a).
8 1975 Act, s 442(1)(b).
9 1975 Act, s 442(2).
10 1975 Act, ss 442A(1), 444(1).
11 See below at pp 232–234, 236.

Appeal by stated case

Time of application

The appellant must apply for a stated case by lodging an application with the clerk of the summary court within one week of final determination of the proceedings in that court[1]. At the same time a copy of the application should be sent to the respondent or his solicitor[2].

'Final determination' normally means the date when sentence is passed in open court[3]. However, if sentence has been deferred, and the appeal is against conviction only, or by the prosecutor against an acquittal of an accused who has been convicted (and had sentence deferred) on another charge, 'final determination' means the date when sentence is first deferred[3].

The application must actually be received by the clerk of the summary court within the week; it is not enough that it is posted within that time[4].

If an application is refused as not being in proper form, a second application may competently be lodged provided that this is done within the week[5].

On application by an appellant the High Court may allow a further period of time for lodging an application for a stated case[6]. Such an application falls to be treated in the same way as a bail appeal[7], ie it is normally heard by a single judge, although he may remit it to a bench of three[8]. The High Court may dispense with a hearing or order such enquiry as it thinks fit[9].

Contents of application

The application for a stated case must contain a full statement of all the matters which the appellant wishes to bring under review and should state whether it includes an appeal against sentence[10]. It is absolutely essential that this requirement for a full statement is complied with. If it is not, the trial court may be entitled to refuse to state a case[11]. The reason for the requirement is so that the trial judge may be in no doubt as to what the issues are and should thus be able to make appropriate findings in fact[12].

If the application does contain a full statement of what it is desired to bring under review, a case must be stated, notwithstanding that the trial judge may consider what is said to be irrelevant[13].

1 1975 Act, s 444(1)(a), (c). The form of application is AA(C) 1988, Form 71.
2 1975 Act, s 444(1).
3 1975 Act, s 451(3).
4 *Elliot, Applicant* 1984 JC 37, 1984 SCCR 125, 1984 SLT 294.
5 *Singh, Petr* 1986 SCCR 215, 1987 SLT 63.
6 1975 Act, s 444(3). There is no prescribed form, but the application must be made in writing to the Clerk of Justiciary (s 444(4)).
7 1975 Act, s 444(5).
8 See *Elliot, Applicant* 1984 JC 37, 1984 SCCR 125, 1984 SLT 294.
9 1975 Act, s 444(5)(a), (b).
10 1975 Act, s 444(1)(b).
11 *Dickson v Valentine* 1988 SCCR 325, 1989 SLT 19 (the only ground stated was 'The sheriff erred in law' without further specification): *McQuarrie v Carmichael* 1989 SCCR 371 (the ground was 'Police evidence at the time of the trial which was untrue, namely the evidence of senior officer').
12 *Durant v Lockhart* 1986 SCCR 23, 1986 SLT 312.
13 *McDougall, Petr* 1986 SCCR 128; *McTaggart, Petr* 1987 SCCR 638.

What is contained in the application may be amended or added to during the period of adjustment of the draft stated case[1].

Bail

If the appellant is in custody, the trial court may grant him bail pending the appeal[2]. An application for bail must be disposed of within 24 hours after the making of the application[3]. It has been suggested that the 24-hour period commences when the application is actually presented to the court and not when it is lodged with the clerk of court[4], and this is surely correct. The Act is silent on what should happen if the application is not disposed of within 24 hours.

The appellant may appeal to the High Court against the decision on bail of the trial court within 24 hours of the decision being given[5]. The appeal may be heard by a single judge of the High Court[5].

If an appellant, having been granted bail and having been subsequently imprisoned for another offence, abandons his appeal, the trial court may order that his sentence for the original offence should run from a particular date, which must not be later than the expiry of the sentence subsequently imposed[6].

An appellant, who has been granted bail should appear at the hearing of his appeal. If he fails to do so, the appeal court may dispose of the appeal as if it had been abandoned[7]. Alternatively, on cause shown, it may permit the appeal to be heard in the absence of the appellant[8].

Suspension of disqualification

If an appellant has been disqualified from driving and the appeal includes an appeal against the disqualification, he may apply to the trial court for the disqualification to be suspended pending the appeal. This application should be made together with the application for a stated case[9]. The trial court may grant or refuse the application[10].

If the application is refused, the appellant may apply to the High Court for suspension of the disqualification[11]. The application may be heard by a single judge, whose decision is not open to review[12].

Suspension of forfeiture etc

If an appellant was, on conviction, disqualified (other than from driving) or had property ordered to be forfeited, the disqualification or forfeiture may be

1 1975 Act, s 444(1B). For adjustment of the draft case see below at p 228.
2 1975 Act, s 446(1).
3 1975 Act, s 446(2).
4 RW Renton and HH Brown *Criminal Procedure according to the Law of Scotland* (5th edn, 1983) para 16–67.
5 1975 Act, s 446(2).
6 1975 Act, s 446(5). If the trial court is contemplating making the sentence run from a date later then that of abandonment of the appeal, it should give the appellant the opportunity of making representations: *Proudfoot v Wither* 1990 SCCR 96.
7 1975 Act, s 453E(a).
8 1975 Act, s 453E(b).
9 AA(C) 1988, r 132(1). There is no prescribed form of application.
10 AA(C) 1988, r 132(2).
11 AA(C) 1988, r 132(3). The application is by note: AA(C) 1988, Form 80.
12 AA(C) 1988, r 132(10).

suspended at the discretion of the trial court, pending the appeal[1]. This provision does not apply in the case of disqualification or forfeiture under any statute which makes specific provision for suspension pending appeal[2].

Draft stated case

A draft stated case must be prepared within three weeks of the final determination of the proceedings which are the subject of the appeal[3]. This time limit may be extended by the sheriff principal of the sheriffdom where the trial court is situated, if the trial judge is temporarily absent from duty[4]. In the case of an appeal from a sheriff court the draft case is prepared by the sheriff[5]. In the case of an appeal from a district court the draft case is prepared by the clerk of court, except where the judge is a stipendiary magistrate, in which case he prepares the draft himself[6].

The form prescribed for a stated case[7] provides only a bare outline. The case must 'set forth the particulars of any matters competent for review which the appellant desires to bring under the review of the High Court and of the facts, if any, proved in the case, and any point of law decided, and the grounds of the decision'[8].

The usual form of case starts with a statement of the charge(s) in the case and a summary of the procedure up to and including the trial. It then has a statement of the facts found to be proved or admitted. There is then usually a note giving the court's reasons for reaching the conclusion which it did, with particular reference to the points raised in the application for the stated case. Finally it poses a question or questions of law for the opinion of the High Court. The questions asked will depend on the issues raised by the appeal. They might, eg, be concerned with the sufficiency of evidence, with the admissibility of evidence, or whether the court was entitled to draw an inference of guilt from the stated facts.

If the appeal is against a decision of the court finding no case to answer in terms of s 354A of the 1975 Act[9], there should be no findings in fact, but the evidence led should be set out together with any inference drawn therefrom[10]. However, if a submission of no case to answer was rejected, defence evidence was led, the accused was convicted and then appeals against his conviction on the basis that the submission was wrongly rejected, the stated case must contain findings in fact based on the whole evidence and not just on that of the Crown[11].

The draft case and a duplicate thereof are issued to the appellant and the respondent respectively, or to their solicitors[12].

1 1975 Act, s 443A(1).
2 1975 Act, s 443A(2).
3 1975 Act, s 447(1).
4 1975 Act, s 451(2).
5 1975 Act, s 447(1).
6 1975 Act, s 447(1). The sheriff principal has no power under s 451(2) to extend the three-week time limit in respect of the temporary absence of the clerk of the district court: *Renfrew District Council, Applicants* 1987 SCCR 522 (Sh Ct), 1988 SLT (Sh Ct) 15 sub nom *Mackinnon v McGarry*.
7 AA(C) 1988, Form 72.
8 1975 Act, s 447(2). The grounds should be fully set forth on any important issue: *Petrovich v Jessop* 1990 SCCR 1, 1990 SLT 594.
9 See above at pp 181, 182.
10 *Keane v Bathgate* 1983 SCCR 251, 1983 SLT 651.
11 *Bowman v Jessop* 1989 SCCR 597.
12 1975 Act, s 447(1).

Adjustment of draft case

Within three weeks from the issue of the draft case each party must send to the clerk of court and to the other parties or their solicitors a note of any adjustment which he wishes to be made[1]. Adjustments may be proposed to the findings in fact and, in certain circumstances, to the judge's note[2]. The questions in law may also be adjusted. If an issue is not raised in the course of adjustment, the High Court may not allow it to be argued in the appeal[3]. If he has no adjustments to propose, the appellant *must* intimate that fact to the clerk of court within the period for adjustment[4]. The reason for emphasising this point is that, if the appellant does not send any proposed adjustments or intimate that he has none, he is deemed to have abandoned his appeal[5].

On application by either party to the High Court the time limit of three weeks may be extended[6]. The provisions for disposing of such an application are the same as those for an application to extend the period for lodging an application for a stated case[7].

During the three-week period (or any extension thereof granted by the High Court) the appellant may also make amendments or additions to his application for a stated case[8]. Any such amendments or adjustments must be intimated to the respondent or his solicitor[8].

Hearing on adjustments

If adjustments have been proposed, or if the trial judge wishes to make any alteration to the draft stated case (eg to take account of an amendment or addition to the application for a stated case by the appellant), a hearing must be fixed within one week of the expiry of the period for adjustment (either original or extended as the case may be)[9]. The hearing must take place even if one or more of the parties is neither present nor represented[10].

At the hearing the judge must consider representations made to him about the adjustments or his own proposed alterations. If he rejects any adjustment, that fact must be recorded in the minute of proceedings[11]. The final version of the stated case must have appended to it the terms of any rejected adjustment together with a note of any evidence rejected by the judge which is alleged to support that adjustment, and the reasons for his rejection of the adjustment and evidence[12].

The High Court may take account of a rejected adjustment[13]. If a judge wrongly rejects a question proposed at adjustment, the High Court may allow the question to be argued at the appeal[14].

1 1975 Act, s 448(1).
2 *Ballantyne v Mackinnon* 1983 SCCR 97.
3 *McLeod v Campbell* 1986 SCCR 132.
4 1975 Act, s 448(1).
5 1975 Act, s 448(2).
6 1975 Act, s 448(6), (7), (8).
7 See above at p 225.
8 1975 Act, s 444(1B).
9 1975 Act, s 448(2A).
10 1975 Act, s 448(2B).
11 1975 Act, s 448(2C)(a).
12 1975 Act, s 448(2D)(a).
13 1975 Act, s 452(4)(f). See *Wilson v Carmichael* 1982 SCCR 528.
14 *O'Hara v Tudhope* 1986 SCCR 283, 1987 SLT 67.

At the hearing on adjustments, if an alteration proposed by the judge is not accepted by all parties, that must be recorded in the minute of proceedings[1].

If, at the conclusion of the hearing, there is any finding in fact which any party maintains is not supported by evidence, the judge must append to the case a note of the evidence upon which he bases that finding[2].

Signing and lodging of stated case

Within two weeks of the date of the hearing on adjustments the judge must finalise and sign the case, which must have appended to it the items referred to in the preceding section[3]. The clerk of court sends a copy of the case to the parties or their solicitors and transmits the trial court process to the Clerk of Justiciary[4]. Within one week of receiving the case the appellant or his solicitor must have it lodged with the Clerk of Justiciary[5]. If this is not done, the appeal is deemed to have been abandoned[6], subject to the appellant's right to apply to the High Court to have the time extended[7]. The provisions for disposing of such an application are the same as those for an application to extend the time for lodging an application for a stated case[8].

If the appellant's solicitor does not practise in Edinburgh, he must appoint an Edinburgh solicitor 'to carry out the duties of solicitor to the appellant in relation to' the appeal[9]. The appellant will continue to deal with his local solicitor. The Edinburgh solicitor is concerned only with what requires to be done in Edinburgh.

Abandonment of appeal

An appellant may abandon his appeal at any time. Before the stated case is lodged with the Clerk of Justiciary, abandonment is effected by lodging with the clerk of the trial court a minute signed by the appellant or his solicitor. The minute may either be written on the complaint or lodged as a separate document[10]. Such abandonment is without prejudice to any other competent mode of appeal, review, advocation or suspension which may be open to the appellant[10]. After the case has been lodged with the Clerk of Justiciary the statute does not make it clear how the appeal should be abandoned, but it is suggested, by analogy with the procedure described in the next paragraph, that a minute of abandonment should be lodged with the Clerk of Justiciary. The lodging of the case with the Clerk of Justiciary means that the appellant is deemed to have abandoned any other form of appeal, except for suspension or advocation under s 453A of the 1975 Act[11].

An appellant who has appealed against both conviction and sentence may abandon his appeal against conviction and proceed with an appeal against

---

1 1975 Act, s 448(2c)(b).
2 1975 Act, s 448(2D)(b).
3 1975 Act, s 448(2D).
4 1975 Act, s 448(3).
5 1975 Act, s 448(4).
6 1975 Act, s 448(5).
7 1975 Act, s 448(6), (7), (8).
8 See above at p 225.
9 AA(C) 1988, r 135(2).
10 1975 Act, s 449(1).
11 1975 Act, s 449(2).

sentence only[1]. The abandonment is effected by minute lodged either with the clerk of the trial court[2], or, if the case has already been lodged with the Clerk of Justiciary, the minute is to be lodged with him[3].

Hearing of the appeal

Usually three judges sit to hear an appeal by stated case, but, as under solemn procedure, a larger court may be convened if it is desired to reconsider an earlier decison. The hearing is conducted by oral debate. There is no provision for written argument being submitted to the court.

Limitations of the hearing

At the hearing of the appeal the appellant may, as a general rule, found only on what is contained in his original application for a stated case together with any duly made amendment or addition thereto[4]. However, the High Court may allow him to found on some other matter, if he shows cause why he should be allowed to do so[4]. If the appellant has referred in his applicaton for a stated case to an alleged miscarriage of justice which, for whatever reason, the trial court is unable to take into account when stating the case, the High Court may nevertheless have regard to that allegation at the hearing of the appeal[5].

Powers of the High Court

The High Court is given various powers for the purposes of an appeal by stated case[6]. These powers are:

(a) to order the production of any document or other thing connected with the proceedings;

(b) to hear any additional evidence relevant to any alleged miscarriage of justice, or to order such evidence to be heard by a judge of the High Court or by such other person as it may appoint for that purpose[7];

(c) to take account of any circumstances relevant to the case which were not before the trial judge[8];

(d) to remit to any fit person to enquire and report in regard to any matter or circumstance affecting the appeal[9];

(e) to appoint a person with expert knowledge to act as assessor to the High Court in any case where it appears to the court that such expert knowledge is required for the proper determination of the case;

(f) to take account of any matter proposed in any adjustment rejected by the trial judge and of the reasons for such rejection;

(g) to take account of any evidence contained in a note either of evidence

---

1 1975 Act, s 442A(2).

2 AA(C) 1988, r 129(3). There is no prescribed form.

3 AA(C) 1988, r 129(4). There is no prescribed form.

4 1975 Act, s 452(3).

5 1975 Act, s 452(2).

6 1975 Act, s 452(4).

7 In *Marshall v MacDougall* 1986 SCCR 376, 1987 SLT 123, the High Court remitted the case to the sheriff principal to hear evidence. The court may take account of additional evidence without having it actually led, if the Crown agrees that it is correct: *Marshall v Smith* 1983 SCCR 156.

8 See eg *Marshall v Smith* 1983 SCCR 156.

9 See eg *Marshall v MacDougall* 1986 SCCR, 1987 SLT 123. The High Court remitted the case to the sheriff principal to hear evidence and to make further enquires.

rejected by the trial judge or of evidence upon which the trial judge based a finding in fact which has been challenged by any party[1].

The High Court may also remit the stated case back to the trial court so that it may be amended and returned to the High Court[2]. Alternatively, the High Court may itself make the amendment and proceed to hear the case as amended[3].

Disposal of appeal by stated case

There are four ways in which the High Court may dispose of an appeal by stated case[4]. Firstly, it may remit the case to the trial court with its opinion and a direction as to what the trial court should do[5]. Secondly, the High Court may affirm the verdict of the trial court. Thirdly, it may set aside the verdict and either quash the conviction or substitute an amended verdict of guilty (which must be one which was competent to the trial court on the complaint). Finally, the High Court may set aside the verdict of the trial court and grant authority to bring a new prosecution. The provisions in connection with a new prosecution[6] are identical with the equivalent provisions under solemn procedure[7].

If the court sets aside a verdict of guilty, it may quash the sentence imposed on the complaint and substitute another (but not more severe) sentence[8].

If an appeal by the Crown against an acquittal is successful, the High Court has three available options[9]. Firstly, it may itself convict and sentence the respondent, but may not impose any sentence which would have been beyond the powers of the trial court. Secondly, it may remit the case to the trial court with a direction to convict and sentence the respondent. The respondent must attend any diet in the trial court which is fixed for that purpose. Thirdly, the High Court may simply remit the case to the trial court with its opinion.

If an appellant, who received a custodial sentence but was released on bail pending his appeal, loses his appeal, the High Court may grant a warrant for his arrest and imprisonment or detention[10]. The warrant specifies the term of custody which must not, of course, exceed the unexpired part of the sentence originally imposed[10]. If such an appellant, having been released on bail, subsequently receives another custodial sentence for another offence and is actually serving that sentence when his appeal against conviction is refused, the High Court has the same power as the trial court would have had on abandonment of the appeal[11]. This means that the High Court may direct that the unexpired part of the original sentence is to begin from a given date not later than the end of the sentence actually being served.

1 See eg *Wilson v Carmichael* 1982 SCCR 528.
2 1975 Act, s 452(5).
3 *O'Hara v Tudhope* 1986 SCCR 283, 1987 SLT 67, where the sheriff had rejected a question in law, and the High Court allowed it to be added and then argued.
4 1975 Act, s 452A.
5 In *Aitchison v Rizza* 1985 SCCR 297, the court remitted the case to the sheriff so that he could hear evidence which he had wrongly excluded.
6 1975 Act, s 452B.
7 1975 Act, s 255. See above at p 222.
8 1975 Act, s 452A(3).
9 1975 Act, s 452A(4).
10 1975 Act, s 452A(6)(a).
11 1975 Act, s 452A(6)(b). The power of the trial court on abandonment is set forth in s 446(5). See above at p 226.

Expenses

The High Court has power to award such expenses in respect of the proceedings before it and before the trial court as it thinks fit[1]. Full expenses may be awarded[2], but in practice expenses are almost invariably modified. If (which is very unlikely) the expenses were not modified or the exact amount thereof determined by the High Court, the account of expenses would be taxed by the Auditor of the Court of Session as if it were a Court of Session account[3].

Appeal by bill of suspension

When appropriate

An accused may, in certain circumstances, appeal against his conviction by bill of suspension. He may do so 'when an appeal (by stated case) would be incompetent or would in the circumstances be inappropriate'[4]. The ground of appeal under a bill of suspension is 'an alleged miscarriage of justice in the proceedings'[5]. If an appellant has already taken an appeal by stated case, he may not proceed with an appeal on the same ground by bill of suspension until the appeal by stated case has been fully disposed of or abandoned, unless he has obtained leave of the High Court[6].

Appeal by bill of suspension is appropriate 'when some step in the procedure has gone wrong or some factor has emerged which satisfies the court that a miscarriage of justice has taken place resulting in a failure to do justice to an accused'[7]. It is, for example, appropriate if the appeal is based on alleged oppression or irregular conduct on the part of the trial court[8]. A bill of suspension is also appropriate, and indeed the only competent method of appeal against conviction, if the trial judge dies before signing a stated case or is precluded by illness or some other cause from doing so[9].

Time

There is no time limit for appealing by way of bill of suspension, although it is obviously desirable to do so as soon as possible after conviction[10].

Bail

An appellant who has received a custodial sentence and who is taking an appeal by bill of suspension may apply for bail. He does so by craving interim

---

1 1975 Act, s 452A(5).
2 As in *Walker v Linton* (1892) 3 White 329, 20R(J) 1.
3 Courts of Law Fees (Scotland) Act 1895, s 3.
4 1975 Act, s 453A(1). For a full discussion of the circumstances where a bill of suspension is competent and appropriate see *Renton and Brown* paras 16–135 to 16–151.
5 1975 Act, s 453A(1).
6 1975 Act, s 453A(1) (proviso).
7 *MacGregor v McNeill* 1975 JC 57 at 60, 1975 SLT (Notes) 54 at 55, per Lord Justice-Clerk Wheatley.
8 Eg *Fraser v MacKinnon* 1981 SCCR 91; *Hawthorn v MacLeod* 1986 SCCR 150, 1986 SLT 657.
9 1975 Act, s 444(2).
10 In *McPherson v Henderson* 1984 SCCR 294 it was sought to suspend a conviction and sentence imposed nearly twenty years previously. Although the bill was refused, it was not suggested that it was incompetent because of the delay.

liberation in the bill, which is then, strictly speaking, a bill of suspension and liberation.

Form

The bill of suspension is in form rather similar to a writ or petition in civil proceedings. It begins by narrating the fact of the appellant's conviction and sentence. Then come the craves, which would usually be for (1) warrant to serve a copy of the bill on the respondent; (2) warrant ordaining the clerk of the trial court to transmit the process to the Clerk of Justiciary; (3) suspension of the conviction and sentence; (4) liberation and interim liberation; and (5) expenses. Next there is a statement of facts which should be in separate numbered articles, as in the condescence of an initial writ or summons. Finally there are pleas in law[1]. The bill is signed by the appellant or by his counsel or solicitor.

Further procedure

The bill is lodged with the Clerk of Justiciary who places it before a single judge of the High Court in order to obtain the warrant to serve. The bill may be served by any officer of law[2]. If the bill craves interim liberation or interim suspension of any order (for example disqualification), the judge before whom it is placed assigns a diet at which counsel for both the appellant and the respondent may be heard[3]. Interim suspension of disqualification from driving is subject to special rules. It does not take effect until the bill has been served on the respondent, and the principal bill has been exhibited to the clerk of the trial court and been returned to the Clerk of Justiciary[4].

Answers

After the bill has been served on the respondent he may, and usually does, lodge answers to it. The answers are in similar form to defences in a civil action. Each statement of fact is answered, and the respondent appends appropriate pleas in law.

Edinburgh solicitor

The same provisions about appointing an Edinburgh solicitor and his duties apply to bill of suspension procedure as to stated case procedure[5].

Hearing

The hearing takes the same form as in an appeal by stated case. The High Court has virtually the same powers as in such an appeal[6]. These powers include the hearing or ordering to be heard of additional evidence[7], and the power to remit to a fit person (such as the sheriff principal) to make enquiry into any matter[8]. In disposing of the appeal the High Court may, as well as

1 A form of bill of suspension is given in *Renton and Brown* App C, Form 5.
2 1975 Act, s 455(2).
3 AA(C) 1988, r 139.
4 AA(C) 1988, r 133(2).
5 AA(C) 1988, r 135(2).
6 1975 Act, s 453A(3).
7 1975 Act, s 452(4)(b), applied by s 453A(2) to bills of suspension.
8 1975 Act, s 452(4)(d), applied by s 453A(2) to bills of suspension.

simply quashing the conviction, grant authority to the prosecutor to bring a new prosecution[1]. It may also, when quashing a conviction, quash a sentence and substitute another sentence[2]. The High Court has power to award expenses in the same way as in an appeal by stated case.

Consent by prosecutor to set aside conviction

In an appeal against conviction, whether by stated case or bill of suspension, the prosecutor may indicate his consent to the conviction being set aside as soon as the appeal is intimated to him[3]. The decision whether to set aside the conviction remains with the High Court, but is taken by a single judge[4]. If the conviction is set aside, the appellant is entitled to expenses not exceeding £40[4]. If the High Court refuses to set the conviction aside, the appeal proceeds along the usual course[4].

Appeals against sentence

Bill of suspension

Appeal against sentence by bill of suspension is competent if the appeal is based on an alleged fundamental irregularity relating to the imposition of the sentence[5]. However, such an appeal is not common. The procedure is the same as in a bill of suspension appealing against conviction[6].

Note of appeal

The usual method of appealing against sentence in a summary case is by means of a note of appeal[7], which must state the ground of appeal[8].

Time limits and procedure

The note of appeal must be lodged with the clerk of the trial court within one week of the date of imposition of the sentence which is appealed against[9]. When he receives the note the clerk of court must send a copy of it to the respondent and obtain a report from the judge who imposed the sentence appealed against[10].

The judge *must* submit a report, even if the grounds of appeal are inadequate[11].

Within two weeks of the date of the sentence the clerk of court must send

---

1 1975 Act, s 453A(2), applying s 452A(1)(d) to bills of suspension.
2 1975 Act, s 453A(2), applying s 452A(3) to bills of suspension.
3 1975 Act, s 453.
4 1975 Act, s 453(3).
5 1975 Act, s 442B.
6 See above at pp 232–234.
7 1975 Act, ss 442B, 453B(1). The form is AA(C) 1988, Form 76.
8 1975 Act, s 453B(1). The ground of appeal must be specific and not something vague such as 'severity of sentence': High Court Practice Note of 29 March 1985.
9 1975 Act, s 453B(2).
10 1975 Act, s 453B(3).
11 *Henry v Docherty* 1989 SCCR 426, 1990 SLT 301.

the process in the case, including the note of appeal and the judge's report, to the Clerk of Justiciary[1]. A copy of the judge's report must, at the same time, be sent to the respondent[2].

This period of two weeks may be extended by the sheriff principal of the sheriffdom where the trial court is situated if the sentencing judge is temporarily absent from duty[3]. If the judge does not provide a report within the appropriate time, the High Court may extend the time for furnishing it, or it may proceed to deal with the appeal without a report[4].

As in the case of an appeal against conviction, the appellant may apply to the High Court for an extension of the time for lodging a note of appeal against sentence[5].

Abandonment of appeal

An appeal against sentence may be abandoned at any time prior to the hearing of the appeal. This is done by way of a minute signed by the appellant or his solicitor[6]. The minute should be lodged with the Clerk of Justiciary, unless the process has not yet been sent to him, in which case it should be lodged with the clerk of the trial court[6].

Bail

The appellant may apply for bail pending the hearing of his appeal in the same way as if he were appealing against conviction[7].

Hearing and disposal of appeal

The High Court, when hearing the appeal, has the same powers to order production of documents, hear evidence and cause enquiry to be made as it has in the case of an appeal against conviction[8].

The Court will not usually entertain any submission in mitigation which could have been stated before the sentencing court but was not[9].

The High Court may affirm the sentence appealed against. Or it may quash it and pass a different sentence, whether more or less severe, provided that it may not impose a sentence which would have been outwith the competency of the sentencing court[10]. If the appellant remains liable to a custodial sentence following the appeal, identical provisions apply as in the case of an unsuccessful appeal against conviction[11].

The High Court has power to award expenses in an appeal against sentence[12].

---

1 1975 Act, s 453B(4)(a).
2 1975 Act, s 453B(4)(b).
3 1975 Act, s 453B(4) (proviso).
4 1975 Act, s 453B(5).
5 1975 Act, s 444(3), (4), (5), applied to appeals against sentence by s 453B(6). See also AA(C) 1988, r 130.
6 1975 Act, s 453B(7).
7 1975 Act, s 453B(8), applying s 446 to appeals against sentence.
8 1975 Act, s 445B(8), applying s 452(4)(a)–(e) to appeals against sentence.
9 Eg *Stewart v Carnegie* 1988 SCCR 431.
10 1975 Act, s 453C(1).
11 1975 Act, s 453C(3). See above at p 231.
12 1975 Act, s 453C(2).

ADVOCATION

General

The right of appeal by way of bill of advocation is preserved by the 1975 Act for both solemn and summary proceedings[1].

Advocation in solemn proceedings

Under solemn procedure advocation is a method of appeal open only to the prosecutor. It is available to bring to the High Court for review the decision of any solemn court of first instance, including the High Court sitting as a trial court[2]. It cannot be used to review a verdict of acquittal by a jury, but may be appropriate for appealing against an alleged irregularity in the court of first instance[3].

Advocation as a method of appeal in solemn proceedings is relatively rare and is unlikely to become more common, given the introduction of preliminary diets and the provisions for appeals therefrom[4].

Advocation in summary proceedings

In summary proceedings a bill of advocation is considered primarily to be the prosecution counterpart of a bill of suspension for the defence[5]. Like suspension advocation may be brought where an appeal by stated case would be incompetent or inappropriate, and the ground for bringing it is an alleged miscarriage of justice[5].

However, advocation in summary proceedings is also a remedy open to an accused, if he wishes to appeal on the ground of an irregularity allegedly occurring during the currency of a case[6]. Suspension is not competent prior to conviction[7].

A bill of advocation is in similar form to that of a bill of suspension, and the respondent may lodge answers to it. The powers of the High Court in hearing a bill of advocation in summary proceedings are identical with those in hearing a bill of suspension[8]. The Court may, if it quashes an acquittal, grant authority to the prosecutor to bring a new prosecution[9].

---

1 Section 280A (solemn procedure); s 453A(1), (3) (summary procedure).
2 1975 Act, s 290A(1).
3 Eg *HMA v Walker* 1981 JC 102, 1981 SCCR 154, 1981 SLT (Notes) 3 (a case dealing with the application of the 80-day rule). See also *HMA v McKenzie* 1989 SCCR 587, 1990 SLT 28, a very unusual case where the Crown brought a bill of advocation between a plea of guilty and sentence.
4 1975 Act, s 76A. See above at pp 119, 120.
5 1975 Act, s 453A(1).
6 As in *Platt v Lockhart* 1988 SCCR 308, 1988 SLT 845.
7 *Durant v Lockhart* 1985 SCCR 72, 1985 SLT 394.
8 1975 Act, s 453A(2). See above at pp 233, 234.
9 1975 Act, s 452A(1)(d) applied to advocation by s 453A(2).

APPEAL TO THE *NOBILE OFFICIUM* OF THE HIGH COURT

There is at common law a 'long stop' right of appeal to the *nobile officium* of the High Court of Justiciary. This has been commented on in two recent cases. 'It is neither necessary nor desirable to attempt to lay down comprehensively the circumstances in which application may appropriately be made to the *nobile officium*. . . . Suffice it to say that it is well recognised that this court has a power to provide a remedy for all extraordinary or unforeseen occurrences in the course of criminal business'[1]. 'The jurisdiction which this court is empowered to exercise under the *nobile officium* exists for the purpose of preventing injustice or oppression. Its scope is limited by the principle which is now well settled that the power will only be exercised where the circumstances are extraordinary or unforeseen, and where no other remedy or procedure is prescribed by the law'[2].

This form of appeal is not appropriate or competent if there is statutory provision for the eventuality concerned. Thus, where an appellant had applied under the 1975 Act for an extension of time to lodge a stated case, and his application had been refused, it was held incompetent for him to apply to the *nobile officium* for an extension of time[3].

In recent years the High Court has held an application to the *nobile officium* to be competent in the following circumstances: to seek the release of a witness who had been arrested for non-attendance at a trial[4]; where a sheriff refused to state a case in an appeal by the Crown, to direct him to do so[5]; to authorise a medical examination of a child in local authority care on behalf of a person accused of assaulting it[6]; to recall a pretended desertion of the diet in a High Court trial and allow the jury to be excused and a new jury to be empanelled[7].

An application to the *nobile officium* is made by petition[8], and the respondent may lodge answers[9]. The application is heard by a bench of at least three judges.

---

1 *Hughes, Petr* 1989 SCCR 490 at 497, 1990 SLT 142 at 145, per Lord Justice-Clerk Ross.
2 *Macpherson, Petr* 1989 SCCR 518 at 522 per Lord Justice-General Hope.
3 *Berry, Petr* 1985 SCCR 106.
4 *Gerrard, Petr* 1984 SCCR 1, 1984 SLT 108.
5 *MacDougall, Petr* 1986 SCCR 128.
6 *K, Petr* 1986 SCCR 709.
7 *Hughes, Petr* 1989 SCCR 490, 1990 SLT 142.
8 See the cases cited in this section (ie Appeal to the *Nobile Officium* of the High Court) for the form which the petition may take.
9 As in *Hughes, Petr* 1989 SCCR 490, 1990 SLT 142.

Chapter 9

Mentally Disordered Persons in the Criminal Courts

INTRODUCTION

Sadly it is not uncommon for the criminal courts to have before them persons suffering from some form of mental disorder, a term which is used as meaning 'mental illness or mental handicap however caused or manifested'[1]. In some contexts the more old fashioned terms 'insane' and 'insanity' are used.

In this chapter we shall examine briefly the procedures for dealing with those suffering from mental disorder at various stages of the proceedings. As the statutory provisions for both solemn and summary procedure are substantially the same, both forms of procedure will be examined together.

AT FIRST APPEARANCE IN COURT

If the procurator fiscal has reason to believe that an accused person is suffering from mental disorder, he must bring before the court any evidence which he may have of that person's mental condition[2].

If a person is charged in the district court with an offence punishable with imprisonment, and he appears to the court to be suffering from mental disorder, he must be remitted to the sheriff court[3]. The reason for this is that the sheriff court has powers of disposal for such persons which are not available to the district court[4].

A court may remand an accused in hospital rather than in prison if he appears to be suffering from mental disorder[5]. The court must have medical evidence (either written or oral) before it can make such a remand[6]. The accused will be detained in the hospital if he appears to be suffering from a mental disorder such as would justify his admission to hospital under Part V of the Mental Health (Scotland) Act 1984[7] (which is the part of the Act dealing with compulsory admission to hospital). If the hospital reports to the court

1 Mental Health (Scotland) Act 1984, s 1(2). This definition is effectively incorporated into the 1975 Act by references to the 1984 Act in various sections.
2 1975 Act, ss 175(2), 376(5).
3 1975 Act, s 376(4).
4 Hospital order and guardianship order under the 1975 Act, s 376(1). See below at pp 241–243.
5 1975 Act, ss 25(1), 330(1).
6 1975 Act, ss 25(4), 330(4).
7 1975 Act, ss 25(2), 330(2).

that the accused is not suffering from such a mental disorder, the court may then remand him in prison or deal with him in some other way[1]. A remand in hospital is usually used prior to trial, but there is no reason why it should not also be used after conviction if it is desired to obtain reports about the accused.

INSANITY IN BAR OF TRIAL

If a person is unable, because of mental disorder, to plead or to give instructions for his defence, he cannot go to trial. If the prosecutor does not accept the position , a plea in bar of trial must be taken. The statutory provisions for both solemn and summary procedure use the terms 'insane' and 'insanity' in this connection[2].

Under solemn procedure the normal provisions for a plea in bar of trial apply, and notice of the plea must be given at least ten days prior to the trial date[3], except with leave of the court on cause shown[4]. Although it is competent to have the question of the accused's fitness to plead decided by a jury[5], the matter would today almost certainly be resolved by some form of enquiry at a preliminary diet.

In a summary case, notice of the plea in bar of trial must be given before the first prosecution witness is called[6].

Under both solemn and summary procedure, evidence of the accused's fitness to plead may be led in his absence if it appears to the court that it is not practicable or appropriate for him to be in court and if no objection is taken by him or on his behalf[7].

If a plea in bar of trial on the ground of insanity is sustained under solemn procedure, the court must order that the accused be detained 'in a State hospital or such other hospital as for special reason the court may specify'[8]. If the plea is sustained under summary procedure, the court must order that the accused by detained in hospital[9], but the hospital should not be a State hospital unless the court is satisfied that the accused requires treatment under conditions of special security[10].

INSANITY AS A DEFENCE

If an accused is insane at the time of doing something which would be criminal if he were sane, he is entitled to be acquitted.

---

1 1975 Act, ss 25(3), 330(3).
2 1975 Act, ss 174(1), 375(1).
3 1975 Act, ss 75(1)(b), (7)(b), providing for the holding of a preliminary diet. See above at pp 118, 119.
4 1975 Act, s 108(2)(b).
5 1975 Act, s 174(1). See also *HMA v Brown* (1907) 5 Adam 312, 1907 SC(J) 67, 14 SLT 952.
6 1975 Act, s 375(3).
7 1975 Act, ss 174(5), 375(4).
8 1975 Act, s 174(3). Detention in a State hospital means detention without limitation of time: s 174(4). See below at p 242.
9 1975 Act, ss 375(2), 376(2).
10 1975 Act, s 376(7).

Solemn procedure

Under solemn procedure insanity at the time is a special defence, notice of which must normally be given not less than ten clear days before the trial diet[1]. The jury should be directed that, if they acquit the accused, they must declare whether he was acquitted on account of his insanity at the time[2]. An accused acquitted on the ground of insanity is dealt with in the same way as a person who is found insane in bar of trial, ie he is ordered to be detained 'in a State hospital or such other hospital as for special reason the court may specify'[3]. Such an order for detention has the effect of a hospital order[4] together with a restriction order[5] made without limit of time[6]. This means, for practical purposes, that the accused may not be released from hospital until the Secretary of State directs[7].

Summary procedure

Under summary procedure the position of an accused who is acquitted on the ground of insanity is not entirely clear. The view has been expressed that the court has power to do nothing other than to discharge the accused[8]. This view has been accepted in at least one sheriff court case[9]. The contrary view[10] is that, under s 376(3) of the 1975 Act, the sheriff has power to make a hospital order[11]. Section 376(3) provides: 'Where in the case of a person charged . . . the court would have power, on convicting him, to make (a hospital order), then if it is satisfied that the person did the act or made the omission charged, the court may, if it thinks fit, make such an order without convicting him'. This is not the easiest of statutory provisions to understand, and it is unfortunate that Parliament has not yet taken the opportunity to clarify the situation. The matter is further confused by the terms of s 453D of the 1975 Act[12]. It is submitted, very tentatively, that the view that a hospital order may be made is the correct one.

DISPOSAL AFTER FINDING OF GUILT

If a mentally disordered person is found guilty of committing an offence or pleads guilty, there are certain disposals open to the court as well as the various forms of sentence discussed in chapter 7. These disposals are: hospital order; guardianship order; probation with a condition of treatment.

 1 1975 Act, s 82(1). See above at pp 116, 117.
 2 1975 Act, s 174(2).
 3 1975 Act, s 174(3).
 4 See below at p 241.
 5 See below at p 242.
 6 1975 Act, s 174(4).
 7 Mental Health (Scotland) Act 1984, Part VI (ss 60–76) especially ss 62–68.
 8 CGB Nicholson *The Law and Practice of Sentencing in Scotland* (1981, with Supp 1985) para 4–10.
 9 *Smith v M* 1983 SCCR 67 (Sh Ct), 1984 SLT (Sh Ct) 28.
10 Expressed by Sheriff G H Gordon (editor of *Renton and Brown* (5th edn), and editor of SCCR) in *Renton and Brown* para 20–17, and in 1983 SCCR 70 (commenting on *Smith v M*).
11 See below at pp 116, 117.
12 See below at p 244.

Hospital order

A hospital order is an order for the admission of a person to a specified hospital and his detention there[1]. The practical effect of the order is that the accused is in the same position as a person admitted to hospital as a compulsory patient under Part V of the 1984 Act, except that the accused's nearest relative may not order his discharge[2].

A hospital order may be made by both the High Court and the sheriff court in the case of an accused convicted of an offence punishable by imprisonment[3]. The court must be satisfied that the accused is suffering from mental disorder of a nature or degree which makes it appropriate for him to receive medical treatment in hospital, that it is necessary for the health or safety of the accused or for the protection of other persons that he should receive such treatment, and that treatment cannot be provided unless he is detained in hospital[4].

The court must have evidence from two doctors, which may be either written or oral[5]. One of the doctors must be approved by a Health Board as having special experience in the diagnosis or treatment of mental disorder[6]. Detailed provisions about the medical evidence are made in the 1975 Act[7].

The accused's legal representative is entitled to see a copy of any written medical report[8]. If the accused is unrepresented, the substance of the report must be disclosed to him (or to his parent or guardian if he is under sixteen)[9]. The accused may insist on oral evidence being given by a doctor who has submitted a written report, and he may lead evidence in rebuttal[10].

Both doctors must agree that the accused is suffering from the same form of mental disorder (either mental illness or mental handicap)[11].

If the court has satisfactory medical evidence, then it may make a hospital order if it 'is of opinion, having regard to all the circumstances including the nature of the offence and the character and antecedents of the offender, and to the other available methods of dealing with him, that the most suitable method of disposing of the case' is by making the order[12]. The court must also be satisfied that there will be accommodation for the accused in the specified hospital within 28 days of the date of the order being made[13].

The hospital specified in the hospital order should not be a State hospital unless the court is satisfied from the medical evidence that 'the offender, on account of his dangerous, violent or criminal propensities, requires treatment under conditions of special security, and cannot suitably be cared for in a hospital other than a State hospital'[14].

---

1 1975 Act, ss 175(1), (3), 376(1), (6).
2 Mental Health (Scotland) Act 1984, s 60(2).
3 1975 Act, ss 175(1), 376(1).
4 Mental Health (Scotland) Act 1984, s 17(1), applied by 1975 Act, ss 175(1)(a), 376(1)(a). Section 17(1) contains further provisions and its exact terms should be studied.
5 1975 Act, ss 175(1)(a), 376(1)(a).
6 1975 Act, ss 176(1), 377(1).
7 1975 Act, ss 176(2)–(4), 377(2)–(4).
8 1975 Act, ss 176(3)(a), 377(3)(a).
9 1975 Act, ss 176(3)(b), 377(3)(b).
10 1975 Act, ss 176(3)(c), 377(3)(c).
11 1975 Act, ss 175(6), 376(9).
12 1975 Act, ss 175(1)(b), 376(1)(b).
13 1975 Act, ss 175(3), 376(6).
14 1975 Act, ss 175(4), 376(7).

Restriction order

A hospital order is usually not subject to any restriction. This means in effect that an accused may be discharged from hospital when the hospital doctors consider that he no longer requires compulsory treatment. However, a court may direct that an accused be subject to a restriction order, in which case his discharge from hospital is strictly controlled[1].

A restriction order may be made only if 'it appears to the court, having regard to the nature of the offence with which (the accused) is charged, the antecedents of the (accused) and the risk that as a result of his mental disorder he would commit offences if set at large, that it is necessary for the protection of the public from serious harm so to do'[2]. The restriction order may be without limit of time or for a specific period[2].

A restriction order may not be made unless the doctor approved by the Health Board has given evidence orally in court[3].

Other orders with hospital order

A court which makes a hospital order may not impose a sentence of imprisonment or a fine, or make a probation order or a community service order in respect of the offence concerned, but it may make any other competent order[4]. For example, the court may disqualify from driving.

Interim hospital order

The courts have a limited power to have an offender detained in hospital for a reasonably lengthy period in order that it may be established whether a hospital order would, at the end of the day, be appropriate. This is called an interim hospital order. Such an order is competent only where there is reason to suppose that any hospital order ultimately made would specify a State hospital[5], and therefore applies only to those of dangerous, violent or criminal propensities. An interim hospital order authorises the offender's admission to a State hospital, or such other hospital as for special reasons the court may specify[5], and his detention there for a specific period not exceeding twelve weeks[6].

The order may be renewed for further periods of not more than 28 days at a time if it appears to the court on the written or oral evidence of the responsible medical officer that the continuation of the order is warranted[7]. It may not, however, continue in force for more than six months in all[8]. An interim hospital order may be renewed without the offender being in court provided

---

1 For the restrictions on discharge see the Mental Health (Scotland) Act 1984, ss 62–68.
2 1975 Act, ss 178(1), 379(1).
3 1975 Act, ss 178(2), 379(2).
4 1975 Act, ss 175(7), 376(10).
5 1975 Act, ss 174A(1), 375A(1).
6 1975 Act, ss 174A(6), 375A(7).
7 1975 Act, ss 176A(6), 375A(7). See also AA(C) 1988, rr 62, 112, Forms 29, 30.
8 1975 Act, ss 174A(6), 375A(7).

that he is legally represented and that his representative has an opportunity to be heard[1].

As in the case of a hospital order evidence from two doctors is required[2], but one of the doctors must be employed by the hospital which is to be specified in the order[3].

The court must be satisfied that there will be accommodation available for the offender in the specified hospital within 28 days of the making of the order[4].

When making an interim hospital order the court may not impose a custodial sentence or a fine or make a probation order or community service order, but it may make any other order which it has the power to make[5].

Interim hospital orders are made relatively infrequently, but are useful in cases where it is desired to carry out an assessment of an offender over a period of time longer than the three weeks usually allowed for obtaining a medical report[6].

Guardianship order

If a person is convicted of an offence punishable by imprisonment, and the court is satisfied that he is 'suffering from mental disorder of a nature or degree which warrants his reception into guardianship'[7], it may make a guardianship order. This is an order placing the offender under the guardianship of a specified local authority (island or regional council) or of a specified person approved by a local authority[8]. The provisions for guardianship orders are, *mutatis mutandis*, the same as those for hospital orders[9].

Guardianship orders are made less frequently than are hospital orders, but provide a useful way of disposing of a case where it is possible for the offender to remain at liberty rather than being confined in hospital. A guardianship order is probably more likely to be used in the case of a person suffering from mental handicap than in the case of someone suffering from mental illness.

Probation with a condition of treatment

There is specific provision in the 1975 Act for an offender to be placed on probation with a condition that he must submit to treatment for his mental condition[10].

The court must have evidence from one doctor that the mental condition of the offender is such as requires and may be susceptible to treatment but is not such as to warrant his detention under a hospital order[11]. The doctor who

---

1 1975 Act, ss 174A(7), 375A(8).
2 1975 Act, ss 174A(1), 375A(1).
3 1975 Act, ss 174A(2), 375A(3).
4 1975 Act, ss 174A(3), 375A(4).
5 1975 Act, ss 174A(4), 375A(5).
6 1975 Act, ss 180(1), 381(1).
7 Mental Health (Scotland) Act 1984, s 36(a), applied by 1975 Act, ss 175(1)(a), 376(1)(a).
8 1975 Act, ss 175(1), 376(1).
9 1975 Act, ss 175, 376 apply to both forms of order.
10 1975 Act, ss 184, 385.
11 1975 Act, ss 184(1), 385(1).

provides the evidence must be approved by a Health Board as having special experience in the diagnosis or treatment of mental disorder[1]. The offender may insist on oral evidence being given and may lead evidence in rebuttal[2].

The probation order must specify whether the treatment is to be as an in-patient or out-patient at a named hospital, or by or under the direction of a named doctor[3]. Before making the order the court must be satisfied that arrangements for the treatment have been made[4].

Provision is made for variation of the conditions of treatment subject to agreement by the probationer and his supervising social worker without the necessity of returning to court[5].

All the provisions relating to probation orders in general[6] apply to an order with a condition of treatment. The order may be varied and discharged in the same way as any other probation order, but may not be varied so as to extend the period of treatment beyond twelve months[7].

APPEALS

An accused has the right to appeal against a hospital order, interim hospital order (but not a renewal thereof), guardianship order or an order restricting discharge, in the same way as against any sentence[8]. This right of appeal applies also to an order committing an accused to a State hospital under s 174 of the 1975 Act[9].

In an appeal against conviction (whether under solemn or summary procedure), if the High Court finds that the accused committed the act charged but was insane at the time, it may substitute a verdict of acquittal on the ground of insanity and deal with the accused by committing him to a State hospital[10]. It seems paradoxical tht the High Court's powers are the same in an appeal from a summary court as in an appeal from a court of solemn jurisdiction. This exacerbates the uncertain situation which exists as to the sheriff's power on acquitting an accused on the ground of insanity under summary procedure[11].

It has been stated that, in an appeal against sentence under solemn procedure, the High Court has power to substitute a hospital order for another sentence[12]. If this is correct (as it is submitted it is), there seems to be no reason in principle why the power should not also apply in the case of an appeal against sentence under summary procedure.

---

1 1975 Act, ss 184(1), 385(1).
2 1975 Act, ss 176(3), 377(3), applied by ss 184(7), 385(7).
3 1975 Act, ss 184(2), 385(2).
4 1975 Act, ss 184(3), 385(3).
5 1975 Act, ss 184(5), (5A), (5B), (6), 385(5), (5A), (5B), (6).
6 See above at pp 202–207.
7 1975 Act, Sch 5, para 3(b).
8 1975 Act, ss 280, 443.
9 *Smith v HMA* 1980 SLT (Notes) 56.
10 1975 Act, ss 254(4), 453D.
11 See above at p 240.
12 *Renton and Brown* para 20–31.

Chapter 10

Children in the Criminal Courts

INTRODUCTION

The great majority of children, under sixteen who commit offences in Scotland do not appear in court at all. They are dealt with under the children's hearing system, which was established by Part III of the Social Work (Scotland) Act 1968[1]. The sheriff court has a limited involvement in the hearing system in respect that proof may be led before a sheriff if the ground of referral to the hearing is not accepted[2], and there is an appeal to the sheriff against the decision of a hearing[3]. The hearing system is outwith the scope of this book[4]. This chapter will deal briefly with the relatively rare situation when a child does appear in court accused of having committed an offence.

DETENTION AND ARREST

The general law of detention and arrest applies to children. In addition there are certain special rules applying to children, which will now be examined.

If a child is arrested or detained under s 2 of the Criminal Justice (Scotland) Act 1980[5], his parent should be informed of the fact without delay[6]. The parent must then be allowed access to the child, unless he too is suspected of being involved in the crime, in which case access may be refused[7]. Access may be restricted in the interests of furthering the investigation of the case or the well-being of the child[8].

There are special provisions covering the case of a child detained in

---

1 A child is defined as a person under sixteen years of age, subject to an extension to the age of eighteen if the child is under supervision by direction of a children's hearing (Social Work (Scotland) Act 1968, s 30(1)).
2 Ibid, s 42(2)(c).
3 Ibid, s 49(1). There is also a limited right of appeal from the sheriff to the Court of Session (s 50).
4 For a detailed examination of the hearing system and its relationship with the court see B Kearney *Children's Hearings and the Sheriff Court* (1987). See also Martin and Murray *Children's Hearings* (Scottish Academic Press, 1976 and RW Renton and HH Brown *Criminal Procedure according to the Law of Scotland* (5th edn, 1983) paras 19–28 to 19–107.
5 See above at pp 78–80.
6 1980 Act, s 3(3). 'Parent' includes a guardian or a person having custody of the child (s 3(5)).
7 1980 Act, s 3(3).
8 1980 Act, s 3(4).

connection with terrorism, allowing for intimation to be sent to his parent and for the parent to have access to the child[1].

A child who has been arrested should normally be released on an undertaking being given by him or his parent or guardian that he will attend court for his case to be heard[2]. The decision whether or not to release the child must be taken by an officer of the rank of inspector or above, or by the officer in charge of the police station to which the child has been brought[3]. The child will not be released if '(a) the charge is one of homicide or other grave crime; or (b) it is necessary in his interest to remove him from association with any reputed criminal or prostitute; or (c) the officer has reason to believe that his liberation would defeat the ends of justice'[3].

If the child is not liberated, he should be detained in a place of safety other than a police station[4] unless the senior police officer certifies '(a) that it is impracticable to do so; or (b) that he is of so unruly a character that he cannot safely be so detained; or (c) that by reason of his state of health or of his mental or bodily condition it is inadvisable so to detain him'[5]. The certificate must be produced to the court before which the child is brought[5]. If the child continues to be detained, but it is decided not to proceed with the charge against him, the reporter[6] must be informed, and the child may then be dealt with under the hearing system[7].

PROSECUTION

No child under the age of eight may be prosecuted as it is conclusively presumed that such a child cannot be guilty of any offence[8].

No child under sixteen may be prosecuted except on the authority of the Lord Advocate or at his instance[9]. Summary proceedings against a child may be commenced only on the instructions of the Lord Advocate by complaint at the instance of the procurator fiscal[10]. Thus a summary private prosecution[11] against a child would not be competent. The Lord Advocate from time to time issues general directions to fiscals about the prosecution of children. Such general directions are sufficient to comply with the statutory requirement[12]. If it is wished to challenge the competency of proceedings against a

---

1 1980 Act, s 3B.
2 1975 Act, s 296(1). If the child fails without reasonable excuse to attend court, the person giving the undertaking is guilty of an offence punishable by a maximum fine of £200 (s 296(5)).
3 1975 Act, s 296(1).
4 1975 Act, s 296(2). A place of safety is 'any residential or other establishment provided by a local authority, a police station, or any hospital, surgery or other suitable place, the occupier of which is willing temporarily to receive a child' (Social Work (Scotland) Act 1968, s 94(1), applied by 1975 Act, s 462(1)).
5 1975 Act, s 296(2).
6 The reporter is the officer of the local authority charged with the administration of the hearing system (1968 Act, s 36).
7 1975 Act, s 296(3).
8 1975 Act, ss 170, 369.
9 Social Work (Scotland) Act 1968, s 31(1).
10 AA(C) 1988, r 142.
11 See below at pp 252, 253.
12 *McGuire v Dean* 1973 JC 20, 1974 SLT 229 sub nom *M v Dean*.

child on the ground of lack of authority from the Lord Advocate, this must be done at the appropriate time for pleas to the competency[1].

A child may be prosecuted only in the High Court and the sheriff court[2].

APPEARANCE IN COURT

A child must be prevented from associating with any adult charged with an offence other than that with which the child himself is charged, while at a police station, while being conveyed to or from court and while waiting before or after attendance at court[3]. A female child must at all these times be under the care of a woman[3].

A child's parent or guardian is under an obligation to attend the court, unless the court is satisfied that it would be unreasonable to require his attendance[4]. To this end the police officer arresting a child or the officer in charge of the police station where the child is brought must cause the parent or guardian to be warned to attend court[5]. The attendance of a child's parent is not required if the child has been removed from the parent's custody or charge by a court order[6].

When a child is to be brought before a court, the chief constable for the area where the offence is alleged to have been committed must notify the local authority (in practice the social work department) for the area in which the court will sit of the time and place of the child's appearance and of the nature of the charge against him[7]. The local authority must then carry out investigations and furnish the court with a report on the child's background[8].

PROCEDURE IN COURT

Restrictions on reporting

In both solemn and summary proceedings there is a restriction on the reporting by the press and other media of proceedings in court involving any child under sixteen[9]. The restriction is against publication of the name, address or school or of any particulars calculated to lead to the identification of any such child concerned in the proceedings, whether he be the accused, the complainer or a witness[10]. The restriction extends to publication of any

---

1 *McGuire v Dean* 1973 JC 20, 1974 SLT 229, sub nom *M v Dean*. For the time when pleas to the competency should be made see the 1975 Act, ss 76(1), 334(1).
2 Social Work (Scotland) Act 1968, s 31(1).
3 1975 Act, ss 38, 306.
4 1975 Act, ss 39(1), 307(1). The parent or guardian concerned is the one having actual possession and control of the child, and, if that is not the father, the father's attendance may also be required (ss 39(4), 307(4)).
5 1975 Act, ss 39(2), 307(2).
6 1975 Act, ss 39(5), 307(5).
7 1975 Act, ss 40(1), 308(1).
8 1975 Act, ss 40(2), 308(2).
9 1975 Act, ss 169, 374.
10 1975 Act, ss 169(1), (2), 374(1), (2).

picture including the child[1]. If the only involvement of a child under sixteen is as a witness (other than a complainer), and no one accused is under sixteen, the restriction applies only if the court so directs[1]. At any stage of the proceedings the court may direct that the statutory requirement should be dispensed with if it is satisfied that it is in the public interest to do so[1]. This dispensing power has on occasion been used to permit the media to identify a child accused in a particularly bad case.

Any person who contravenes this statutory requirement is guilty of an offence punishable by a fine not exceeding level 4 on the standard scale[2].

Summary proceedings

When a child appears as an accused on a summary complaint the sheriff should either sit in a different court room or building from that in which he normally sits to conduct criminal business, or on a day when other courts in the building are not engaged in criminal proceedings[3]. The only persons entitled to be in court during the hearing of such a case are (a) members and officers of the court; (b) parties to the case, their legal representatives, and witnesses and other persons directly concerned in the case (this would, of course, include the parents of the child); (c) bona fide reporters of the press or news agencies; (d) such other persons as the court may specially authorise[3]. These restrictions do not apply where a child appears charged jointly with a person who is not a child[4].

The court must take steps as far as possible to prevent children attending sittings of the court from mixing with one another[5].

There are detailed provisions in the 1988 Act of Adjournal governing the appearance of a child who is without legal representation[6]. These are not examined here as it must be very seldom nowadays that a child would appear in court unrepresented. It is to be hoped that, if he did so, the sheriff could use his powers under the legal aid legislation to allow the child to apply for legal aid[7].

DISPOSAL OF CASE AGAINST A CHILD

Summary proceedings

In a summary case the terms 'conviction' and 'sentence' should not be used in relation to a child. Instead the terms 'finding of guilt' and 'order' are appropriate[8].

---

1 1975 Act, ss 169(1), 374(1).
2 1975 Act, ss 169(3), 374(3).
3 1975 Act, s 366(1).
4 1975 Act, s 370.
5 AA(C) 1988, r 147(1).
6 AA(C) 1988, rr 143, 144.
7 Legal Aid (Scotland) Act 1986, s 24(6) – see above at p 172.
8 1975 Act, s 429.

Reference to 'the panel'

If a child is found guilty or pleads guilty under either solemn or summary procedure, the court may, instead of dealing with the case itself, remit the case to the reporter to arrange for the disposal of the case by a children's hearing[1]. This is popularly known as remitting the case to 'the panel'. Alternatively, the court may request the reporter to arrange a hearing to provide the court with advice as to the treatment of the child[2]. Once the advice has been obtained the court may dispose of the case itself or remit to the hearing itself for disposal[3].

If a child who is subject to a supervision requirement from a children's hearing[4] pleads or is found guilty in the sheriff court, the court must, before dealing with the child, obtain the advice of a children's hearing. It may then dispose of the case itself or remit to the hearing for disposal[5]. The High Court has the option whether or not to obtain such advice[6].

Non-custodial disposals

A child may be given an absolute discharge or admonition, may be placed on probation[7], and may be fined in the same way as an adult offender. A child may not be imprisoned in default of payment of a fine, but may be detained for a period not exceeding one month in a place chosen by the local authority in whose area the court is situated[8]. As with any other offender under 21, the alternative of detention may not be imposed in the case of a child unless he has been under supervision in respect of the fine or the court is satisfied that it is impracticable to place him under supervision[9].

A court may order the parent or guardian of a child to find caution for the child's good behaviour[10]. The parent or guardian must be given the opportunity to be heard, unless he or she has been required to attend court and has failed to do so[11].

Custodial disposal – solemn procedure

If a court of solemn jurisdiction convicts a child of a crime other than murder[12] and is of opinion that no other method of dealing with him is

---

1 1975 Act, ss 173(1)(a), 372(1)(a).
2 1975 Act, ss 173(1)(b), 372(1)(b).
3 1975 Act, ss 173(2), 372(2).
4 1968 Act, s 44(1).
5 1975 Act, ss 173(3), 372(3).
6 1975 Act, s 173(3).
7 Procedure for breach of probation in the case of a child who is unrepresented is governed by AA(C) 1988, r 145.
8 1975 Act, s 406 (applied also to solemn procedure by s 194(1)).
9 1975 Act, s 400(4) (applied also to solemn procedure by s 194(1)).
10 1975 Act, ss 37(1), 304(1).
11 1975 Act, ss 37(2), 304(2).
12 For murder, see the 1975 Act s 205(2), commented on above at p 192.

appropriate, it may sentence him to be detained for a specified period[1]. The place and conditions of detention will be as directed by the Secretary of State[2].

The Secretary of State may release the child from detention on licence prior to the expiry of the period specified by the court[3], but, if the period of detention is more than eighteen months, release may be only on the recommendation of the Parole Board[4]. There are detailed provisions covering the duration and recovation of the licence[5]. A child who is not released on licence may be required to be under supervision on his eventual release[6].

Custodial disposal – summary procedure

A child who has pleaded guilty or been found guilty under summary procedure in the sheriff court may be ordered to be detained in residential care by the appropriate local authority[7] for a specified period not exceeding one year[8]. The child's case must be reviewed at least every six months by the local authority, and the child may be released conditionally or unconditionally following a review[9]. A condition of release could be that the child would be under supervision.

---

1 1975 Act, s 206. This section does not restrict a sheriff's power to three years' detention. The limitation on a sheriff's power of sentencing contained in ss 2(2) and 221(1) refers only to imprisonment, and there is no equiperation of detention of a child under s 206 to imprisonment, as there is in the case of detention of a young offender under s 207(2). A sheriff could therefore, in theory, sentence a child to detention for more than three years.
2 1975 Act, s 206.
3 Prisons (Scotland) Act 1989, s 25(1).
4 Ibid, s 25(2).
5 Ibid, s 25(3)–(6).
6 Ibid, s 31(1).
7 The appropriate local authority is the islands or regional council for the area where the child usually resides, or, if he does not reside in Scotland, the area where the offence was committed (1975 Act, s 413(3)).
8 1975 Act, s 413(1), (2).
9 1975 Act, s 413(6).

Chapter 11

Private Prosecution

In Scotland private prosecution is rare, and therefore the topic will be dealt with here relatively briefly.

SOLEMN PROCEDURE

This century there have been only two occasions when a private prosecution has been allowed under solemn procedure[1].

Competency

In order to bring a private prosecution a person must be able to maintain that the alleged crime amounts to a wrong towards him personally[2]. Not entirely convincingly the High Court has held that perjury, even although it may have resulted in a person being wrongly convicted or suffering some other form of injury, can never be the subject of a private prosecution as it is essentially a crime against public justice[3]. Even although a person holds office in an organisation whose members may be harmed by the alleged crime, he is not entitled to bring a private prosecution to protect the members. Thus the vice-president of a union of boys' clubs was not allowed to prosecute a bookseller for selling an allegedly obscene book, which he feared could corrupt members of the clubs[4].

The potential private prosecutor must also have applied to the Lord Advocate for his concurrence in the prosecution[5]. If the Lord Advocate refuses his concurrence, the High Court may authorise the private prosecution to proceed without it[6]. The fact that the Crown has abandoned its right to prosecute is no bar to a private prosecution[7].

1 *J & P Coats Ltd v Brown* (1909) 6 Adam 19, 1909 SC(J) 29, 1909 1 SLT 432; *X v Sweeney* 1982 JC 70, 1982 SCCR 161, 1983 SLT 48, sub nom *H v Sweeney* (popularly known as 'the Glasgow rape case').
2 *J & P Coats Ltd v Brown* (1909) 6 Adam 19 at 37, 1909 SC(J) 29 at 33, 1909 1 SLT 432 at 437, per Lord Justice Clerk Macdonald.
3 *Trapp v M; Trapp v Y* 1971 SLT (Notes) 30; *Meehan v Inglis* 1975 JC 9, 1974 SLT (Notes) 61
4 *McBain v Crichton* 1961 JC 25, 1961 SLT 209.
5 *J & P Coates Ltd v Brown* (1909) 6 Adam 19 at 37, 1909 SC(J) 29 at 33, 1909 1 SLT 432 at 437, per Lord Justice-Clerk Macdonald.
6 As in both the cases which have gone ahead this century (see note 1 above).
7 *X v Sweeney* 1982 JC 70, 1982 SCCR 161, 1983 SLT 48, sub nom *H v Sweeney*.

A private prosecution under solemn procedure is probably competent only in the High Court[1].

Procedure

An application for a private prosecution is made to the High Court by a bill for criminal letters. This should be supported by productions and precognitions. If the bill is passed (ie the application is granted), criminal letters are issued[2]. The case then proceeds to trial before a jury like any other High Court case.

Expenses

An unsuccessful private prosecutor may be found liable in expenses[3].

SUMMARY PROCEDURE

Prosecutors in the public interest

Under summary procedure there is a category of cases which are often referred to as 'private prosecutions', although, strictly speaking, they are not. These are where a statute gives a person or body the right to prosecute in respect of a contravention which affects the public or part of it rather than an individual. Thus, for example, a customs officer is empowered to prosecute in respect of various offences under the Customs and Excise Acts[4], and an officer of an education authority may bring a prosecution on behalf of the authority against the parent of a child who has failed to attend school[5]. Such prosecutors are really prosecuting in the public interest and are therefore not considered to be private prosecutors[6].

Individual private prosecutors

Private prosecution in the strict sense is rare but does exist in respect of certain statutory offences[7]. A private prosecutor must have the concurrence of the public prosecutor (ie the procurator fiscal) for a statutory offence where a competent sentence is imprisonment without the option of a fine[8]. It is

---

1 *Dunbar v Johnston* (1904) 4 Adam 505, 7F(J) 40.
2 See *X v Sweeney* 1982 SCCR 161 at 178–80, for the form of criminal letters.
3 *Hume* II, 127; Alison *Principles* p 113.
4 Customs and Excise Management Act 1979, s 145(2) (applied to Scotland by s 175(1)(c)).
5 Education (Scotland) Act 1962, s 43(2).
6 *Templeton v King* 1933 JC 58, 1933 SLT 443. See the definition of prosecutor in the 1975 Act, s 462(1).
7 Eg Salmon Fisheries (Scotland) Act 1868 – see *Fairly v Fishmongers of London* 1951 JC 14, 1951 SLT 54.
8 1975 Act, s 311(4).

provided that similar concurrence is required in the case of private prosecution for a common law offence[1], but such a prosecution is unheard of.

Procedure

A private prosecution under summary procedure is commenced by complaint at the instance of the prosecutor and proceeds exactly like a case brought by the fiscal.

Expenses

An award of expenses may be made in favour of or against a private prosecutor[2], and a person (other than the procurator fiscal) who prosecutes in the public interest may be entitled to an award of expenses against an accused. However, no award or expenses against a person prosecuting in the public interest may be made unless the statute under which the prosecution is brought expressly or implied authorises such an award[2].

The court may direct that expenses be met out of any fine[3], and this is the normal practice.

Expenses, other than those payable out of a fine, are recoverable by civil diligence[4].

---

1 1975 Act, s 311(4).
2 1975 Act, s 435(a).
3 1975 Act, s 435(d).
4 1975 Act, s 435(g). For recovery by civil diligence, see s 411 discussed above at p 198.

Chapter 12

References to the European Court

THE TREATIES AND THE COURT

As the United Kingdom is a member of the European Community it is bound by the three Community Treaties[1]. The Court of Justice of the European Communities (usually referred to as 'the European Court') which sits in Luxembourg, is vested with the duty of ensuring that the law is observed in the interpretation and application of the Treaties[2]. The Court has authority to give preliminary rulings on the interpretation of Community law[3]. A question of law may be referred to the European Court for such a ruling by a Scottish court[4].

This chapter will examine the procedure for such references from courts of both solemn and summary jurisdiction and from the High Court sitting in its appellate capacity.

SOLEMN PROCEDURE

The procedure for referring a question to the European Court is laid down in the 1988 Act of Adjournal[5].

Notice of intention to raise the question must be given to the trial court and to the other parties no later than fifteen days after service of the indictment[6]. Consideration of the matter is then reserved to the trial diet[7], and the court may order that no jurors or witnesses should be cited to that diet[8]. At the trial diet the court may determine the question itself or may decide that a preli-

---

1 The treaties are those setting up the European Coal and Steel Community (ECSC), the European Economic Community (EEC) and the European Atomic Energy Community (Euratom). The relevant United Kingdom legislation is the European Communities Act 1972.
2 ECSC Treaty, art 31; EEC Treaty, art 164; Euratom Treaty, art 136.
3 ECSC Treaty, art 41; EEC Treaty, art 177; Euratom Treaty, art 150.
4 In the case of a question arising under the ECSC Treaty, art 41, a reference to the European Court is obligatory. A reference is also obligatory if the question arises before a court from which there is no appeal (EEC Treaty, art 177, and Euratom Treaty, art 150). Thus, in the present context, a reference is obligatory from the High Court in its appellate capacity.
5 AA(C) 1988, rr 63–67.
6 AA(C) 1988, r 64(1).
7 AA(C) 1988, r 64(2).
8 AA(C) 1988, r 64(3).

minary ruling should be sought from the European Court[1]. If the court determines the question itself, the accused is called on to plead (if appropriate) and the trial may thereafter proceed, provision being made for extension of time limits and the like[2].

If the court decides that a preliminary ruling should be sought, it must give its reasons for doing so[3]. The proceedings are thereafter continued from time to time as necessary[4]. The reference is in a form similar to a stated case and includes the question or questions on which the preliminary ruling is sought[5]. The court may give directions to the parties about the drafting and adjustment of the reference[6]. When it is in its final form the reference is transmitted to the Registrar of the European Court with other parts of the process[7].

When the ruling has been made by the European Court and been received by the clerk of the trial court, that court gives directions as to further procedure in the light of the ruling, and these directions are intimated to the parties together with a copy of the ruling[8].

There is a right of appeal to the High Court in its appellate capacity against an order making a reference to the European Court. The appeal must be taken within fourteen days of the order being made[9].

SUMMARY PROCEDURE

The procedure for referring a question to the European Court from a court of summary jurisdiction is also laid down by the 1988 Act of Adjournal[10].

Notice of intention to raise a question must be given before the accused is called on to plead to the complaint[11]. The court may then hear parties immediately or it may adjourn to a later date in order to do so[12]. After hearing submissions the court may determine the question itself or may decide that a preliminary ruling should be sought[13]. If the court decides to determine the question itself, the accused is called on to plead (where appropriate) and the case thereafter proceeds in the usual way[14]. If the court decides to seek a preliminary ruling, the procedure is identical with that under solemn procedure[15].

---

1 AA(C) 1988, r 64(4).
2 AA(C) 1988, r 64(5), (6), (7).
3 AA(C) 1988, r 65(1)(a).
4 AA(C) 1988, r 65(1)(b).
5 AA(C) 198, Form 31. For an example of the form of reference, see *Gewiese v Mackenzie; Mehlich v Mackenzie* 1984 SCCR 130, 1984 SLT 449.
6 AA(C) 1988, r 65(2)(a), (b).
7 AA(C) 1988, r 65(2)(c).
8 AA(C) 1988, r 66.
9 AA(C) 1988, r 67(1). The procedure in such an appeal is governed by the remaining paragraphs of r 67.
10 AA(C) 1988, rr 113–118.
11 AA(C) 1988, r 114(1).
12 AA(C) 1988, r 114(3).
13 AA(C) 1988, r 114(4).
14 AA(C) 1988, r 114(5).
15 AA(C) 1988, rr 116, 177 which are in terms identical with those of rr 65, 66.

There is a right of appeal to the High Court against an order making a reference to the European Court. The appeal must be taken within fourteen days of the order being made[1].

REFERENCES BY THE HIGH COURT IN APPEALS

If in the course of an appeal to the High Court, whether under the 1975 Act, or by bill of suspension or advocation, or by petition to the *nobile officium*, a question of Community law arises, the High Court *must* make a reference to the European Court for a preliminary ruling[2]. This may take some time[3].

---

1 AA(C) 1988, r 118(1). The procedure in such an appeal is governed by the remaining paragraphs of r 118.
2 AA(C) 1988, rr 64A, 115.
3 In *Gewiese v Mackenzie; Mehlich v Mackenzie* 1984 SCCR 130, 1984 SLT 449, the appeals first came before the High Court on 8 July 1982 and were finally disposed of on 20 March 1984. The reference to the European Court was made on 1 February 1983, and that court gave its judgment on 14 February 1984.

Index